The Wordsworth
Golden Treasury of Verse

The Wordsworth

Golden Treasury of Verse

with a Foreword and Notes by Antonia Till

Wordsworth Poetry Library

This edition published 1997 by Wordsworth Editions Ltd,
Cumberland House, Crib Street, Ware, Hertfordshire SG12 9ET

ISBN 1 85326 451 2

Typeset by Antony Gray
Printed and bound in Great Britain by
Mackays of Chatham plc, Chatham, Kent

*This anthology is dedicated
to all students of the Open University,
past and present*

ACKNOWLEDGEMENTS

We gratefully acknowledge permission to reprint the following copyright poems.

Lascelles Abercrombie: 'The Nightingale' reprinted from *The Poems of Lascelles Abercrombie* (Oxford University Press, 1930) by permission of Jeff Cooper.

Hilaire Belloc: 'Tarantella', 'The Python', 'On His Book' and 'On a General Election' reprinted from *Complete Verse* (Random House UK Ltd) by permission of The Peters Fraser & Dunlop Group Limited on behalf of The Estate of Hilaire Belloc.

John Peale Bishop: 'Speaking of Poetry' reprinted from *The Collected Poems of John Peale Bishop*, edited by Allen Tate, copyright 1948 by Charles Scribner's Sons; copyright renewed ©1976, by permission of Scribner, a division of Simon & Schuster.

Edmund Blunden: 'The Midnight Skaters' reprinted from *Selected Poems* (1982) by permission of Carcanet Press Limited.

Robert Bridges: 'A Passer-by', 'Awake My Heart' and 'I Love All Beauteous Things' reprinted from *Poetic Works of Robert Bridges* (Oxford University Press, 1936) by permission of Oxford University Press.

Frances Cornford: 'To a Fat Lady Seen from a Train' reprinted from *Collected Poems* (Hutchinson) by permission of the Estate of Frances Cornford and Random House UK Ltd.

Kevin Crossley Holland: Translation of two Early English riddles, copyright © 1982 by Kevin Crossley Holland, reprinted by permission of the author, c/o Rogers, Coleridge & White, 20 Powis Mews, London W11 1JN.

e e cummings: 'next to of course god america i' reprinted from *Complete Poems 1904–1962* by e e cummings, edited by George J. Firmage,

'Poetry makes nothing happen,' wrote W. H. Auden in 1939. This was from the poem *In Memory of W. B. Yeats*, the poet whose high passions included a fervent Irish nationalism and desire for Home Rule. Auden himself, at least during the 1930s, felt that all artists should be committed to a political position, that 'art for art's sake' led to sterile, self-regarding and ultimately decadent art. Shakespeare, especially in *Macbeth* and *Henry VIII*, wrote to please his monarch, and in other plays meditated on the nature of the good ruler. John Dryden (1631–1700) wrote a powerful satire on political and courtly conspiracy in *Absalom and Achitophel*. Alexander Pope (1688–1744), more indirectly, satirised those people in high office whom he disliked or despised. William Blake (1757–1827) wrote against a society and government which he believed stunted humanity's soul. Wordsworth (1780–1850), though he ended his days in a very conservative frame of mind, had hailed the French Revolution ecstatically – 'Bliss was it in that dawn to be alive' – while Byron (1788–1824), though maintaining an aloofly patrician stance, could inveigh savagely against the wily statesman, Castlereagh. Shelley (1792–1822) was throughout his life passionately committed to a radical utopian kind of communism. But Wilfred Owen, witnessing the cruel massacre and devastation of the 1914–18 war, knew that 'All a poet can do is warn.' And today, Seamus Heaney tells us, 'In a sense the efficacy of poetry is nil – no lyric has ever stopped a tank.'

So what is poetry for? Well, many read it simply for its beauty – though that raises aesthetic questions too complex to go into here, and many great poems are not particularly melodious or elegant. It isn't ignoble to admit that we sometimes go to poetry for comfort or even escape. It offers something complete and assured, something different from and grander than our boring or tiring lives. Or – and this goes especially for love poetry – it may express, validate, even aggrandise, the emotions we feel. And this may be the clue to what we might call the purpose of poetry. Poets themselves often had very elevated notions of what that was. For Philip Sidney in his *Apologie for Poetry* (published posthumously in 1597) the purpose is a moral one: 'The poet is the right popular philosopher . . . for he doth not only show the way, but giveth so sweet a prospect into the way as will entice any man to enter into it.' Coleridge remarked briskly that while prose was 'words in their best order', poetry was 'the *best* words in the best order' but his friend and colleague, Wordsworth, stresses the Romantic emphasis on feelings. The famous remark (in the *Preface to Lyrical Ballads*, 1800) that 'poetry is the spontaneous overflow of powerful feeling: it takes its origin from emotion recollected in tranquillity' is given intellectual weight by his statement that 'poems to which any value can be attached were never produced on any variety of subjects but by a man who, being possessed of more than organic sensibility, had also thought long and deeply'. Shelley's equally famous statement – 'Poetry is the record of the best and happiest moments of the happiest and best minds' – comes from his *Defence of Poetry* (1821). This lyrical and passionate defence of poetry seems – like Keats – to equate the beautiful with the good: 'to be a poet is to apprehend the true and the beautiful, in a word, the good which exists in the relation subsisting first, between existence and perception and, second, between perception and expression'. Shelley gives us a ringing conclusion: 'Poets are . . . the mirrors of the gigantic shadows which futurity casts upon the present . . . Poets are the unacknowledged legislators of the world!'

This last statement has to be called into question, even though one of the world's present legislators is the poet and playwright Vaclav Havel, and the great and courageous *samizdat* poets of the Soviet Union may have made a perceptible contribution to the change of opinion which brought about the downfall of the Soviet monolith. Poetry *doesn't* stop tanks; it makes very little happen. Indeed, George Steiner, in his troubled and searching *In Bluebeard's Castle* (1971), calls into question the assumption of most of the poets quoted above, and of Dr Johnson, Matthew Arnold and F. R. Leavis (among many, many others), that literature can have moral or humanising weight. The events of the twentieth century, especially the Holocaust, provide proof for him: many Nazis, perpetrators of inexpressible evil, were highly cultivated people.

That is difficult to argue with. But – if you have bought this anthology for yourself, rather than using it as a school textbook – you do believe that there is something important about poetry, that it is and says and does different things from a novel or short story or play. Shelley touches on this in his remark on the relation between existence, perception and expression. Seamus Heaney (in *The Government of the Tongue: The 1986 T. S. Eliot Memorial Lectures and Other Critical Writings*, 1988) says: 'The poet is credited with a power to open unexpected and unedited communications between our nature and the nature of the reality we inhabit.' A poem can short-circuit the relationship between emotion and external reality, confusing and perplexing as it is. It should be an abiding epiphany or revelation – whether it is as long as Wordsworth's *The Prelude* or a sonnet by Gerard Manley Hopkins, or even a two-line epigram by Pope. And this epiphany is enlarging – it makes a palpable addition to our lives.

However, reading and enjoying poetry is an acquired skill. It requires a sort of relaxed alertness, a state of mind difficult to arrive at or sustain these days. If you are not a regular reader of poetry, take it in small doses to begin with. And don't worry if it doesn't 'take' at first. Often you will find that a poem you thought you had read only superficially clings to your mind. It's worth going back to it a week or two later if that's the case. And a poem can 'work' even if you don't understand it completely. Poetry, as both A. E. Housman and T. S. Eliot have noted, operates through the senses as well as the intellect – indeed many poems evoke a strong sensuous response well before complete understanding is arrived at: the poems of John Donne, Gerard Manley Hopkins and W. B. Yeats spring to mind here. Page through until you find something that appeals to you, and if everything here by that poet interests you, get yourself the Wordsworth Editions collected works and explore further . . .

. . . Because, in some ways, an anthology is a very odd and unsatisfactory way of reading poetry. Here someone has picked out a number of poems, isolating them from their context and presenting them in a kind of bouquet. (Field Marshal Wavell brazenly called his anthology *Other Men's Flowers*, while the Victorian, Palgrave, evoked a jewel box in calling his *The Golden Treasury*.) Every reader would make a selection different from anyone else's, in some details at least, and every anthologist will enrage someone with what has been omitted or included.

The choices here have been dictated by various considerations. All the poets represented were born before the beginning of the twentieth century since problems of selection and copyright would have been almost insuperable otherwise. The publishers felt that we should include as many of the old favourites as possible, and here we were helped by the BBC's ballot to find the nation's hundred best-loved poems. We also thought it would be helpful to include substantial representation from the poets recommended for the National Curriculum. There are also poems here which, though not necessarily 'great', have historical or social interest, like the poems by Henry VIII and Elizabeth I, some early hymns, eighteenth-century poems of social life and nineteenth-century broadsheet ballads. Today's readers may be surprised by the number of religious poems included. It is difficult, in the twentieth century, to realise that – until the eighteenth century at least – religion was as much a part of people's lives as, say, the family, and that it could, in the fourteenth and fifteenth centuries, in Donne or Crashaw, in Herbert or the Victorian Hopkins, inspire emotions as strong as those of romantic love. The most difficult decision of all was to exclude extracts from longer poems, This was partly on practical grounds – which bits of the *Canterbury Tales* would be the 'best' ones? – and partly on aesthetic ones – is a 'bleeding chunk' a representative poem? But it means that some of the greatest English poems have been excluded. Chaucer and Spenser (whose *The Faerie Queene* is a daunting read, but has ravishing episodes) are wickedly under-represented, as are Dryden and Pope. Much of Shakespeare's greatest poetry is in his plays, and Wordsworth is at his most characteristic in *The Prelude*. Many people think that Tennyson's finest poem is *In Memoriam*, again missing from this collection. Perhaps it would have been permissible to include sections from it, since sonnets have been extracted from sonnet sequences, but the line had to be drawn somewhere. If you are at all interested, get hold of Pope's *The Rape of the Lock* or dip into Neville Coghill's racy modern version of the *Canterbury Tales*.

Above all, use this anthology to discover your own taste and what answers your needs, to compare century with century, poet with poet, and, we hope, to find pleasure, enlightenment and perhaps that rare but telling epiphany.

A NOTE ON THE MECHANICS OF POETRY

This may seem too obvious to be worth saying, but among the (many) things that distinguish poetry from prose are that a poem has an evident shape and, until the twentieth century, an evident rhythm. Again, before the twentieth century, it usually has rhymes. (There is an exception, of course, in so-called 'blank verse' – the unrhymed, but rhythmically regular verse of, say, Shakespeare's plays or Milton's *Paradise Lost*. The technical word for the mechanics of poetry is 'prosody' – the study of how versification works, with metre, rhyme, rhythm, line-length, sound and the shape of what are generally called 'verses' but which prosodists call 'stanzas'. A knowledge of prosody is not essential to the appreciation and understanding of a poem, but alertness to the way a poet shapes his or her verse undoubtedly deepens appreciation and understanding. It's worth adding that, for a good poet, so-called 'free verse' – apparently shapeless, unrhyming verse – is far from free: the poet will have a powerful sense of underlying form and will feel unable to distort or cheat on this. Just as an abstract artist will have had a long apprenticeship of draughtsmanship, measuring, looking, and painting or drawing from life, all (good) poets have a profound awareness of prosody, even if they avoid the earlier, stricter forms.

One of the strictest forms, and one with which everyone is familiar, is the limerick. It seems ridiculously pompous to subject a limerick to prosodic analysis, but a quick explanation of some technical terms should make it easier to talk about other verse forms. A limerick could be described as a single-stanza form of five predominantly anapaestic lines of which the first two and the last are trimeters and the third and fourth dimeters, and with a rhyme scheme *a a b b a*.

'Trimeter' means that there are three stresses to the line –

> There **was** a young **la**dy of **Riga***
> Who **went** for a **ride** on a **tiger** –

*the rhyme requires the old-fashioned pronunciation – 'Ryega' and 'anapaestic' indicates the lolloping rhythm, with two unstressed syllables followed by a stressed one. The prosodist's way of indicating long and short beats is thus − ⌣, so an anapaest is ⌣ ⌣ − . (An example of a true anapaest is helpfully provided by Coleridge: 'With a leap and a bound the swift anapaests throng'.) As you will have noted, the limerick here has only one unstressed beat before the first stress, which is why we call it 'predominantly anapaestic'; most limericks have this unstressed first syllable in their trimeters. (Incidentally, the mirror image of the anapaest, and one rarely used in English verse, is the dactyl − ⌣ ⌣ . You find it in 'Myfanwy' by John Betjeman: '**Kind** o'er the **Kind**erbank **leans** my Myfanwy'.)

'Dimeter', you will have gathered, indicates two stresses to the line −

> They re**turned** from the **ride**
> With the **lady** in**side**.

As for the rhyme scheme − *a a b b a* − it should explain itself: the last line has the same rhyme as the first two −

> And a **smile** on the **face** of the **tiger**.

Apart from the limerick's most valued subject matter, witty ribaldry (see Wordsworth Editions' *The Wordsworth Book of Limericks*), it is also charmingly used for pithy philosophical statements, like this one on Free Will and Predestination:

> There was a young man who said, 'Damn!
> It is borne in upon me I am
>   A creature that moves
>   In predestinate grooves.
> I'm not even a bus, I'm a tram.'

Or there's Ronald Knox's famous parody of Bishop Berkeley's views on sense data:

> There once was a man who said, 'God
> Must think it exceedingly odd
>   If he finds that this tree
>   Still continues to be
> When there's no one about in the quad' −

along with the reply:

> 'Dear sir, your astonishment's odd:
> *I* am always about in the quad.
> And that's why the tree
> Will continue to be,
> Since observed by Yours Faithfully, God.'

Perhaps the best known verse form is the sonnet,* the fourteen-line single stanza which many of us studied at school. This form originated in Italy, and reached a high development in the sonnets of Petrarch (1304–74). The classic form uses the iambic pentameter, a line of five stresses with the light syllable preceding the stress – 'When **I** con**sid**er **how** my **light** is **spent**'. (The iambic pentameter seems to be the most natural line for English, and if you look through this collection you will find innumerable examples. Of course the confident poet will vary the stresses for differing effects – Shakespeare does it all the time – but the underlying rhythm continues to beat in the mind of the reader or speaker). Fourteen lines give scope for various rhyme-schemes, of which the earliest and perhaps most enduring is the so-called Petrarchan one – an octave (eight lines) rhyming *abbaabba*, followed by a sestet (six lines) rhyming either *cdecde* or *cdcdcd*. There are countless examples in this anthology, of which Wordsworth's sonnet 'Upon Westminster Bridge' is one of the most famous:

Earth has not anything to show more fair:	*a*
Dull would he be of soul who could pass by	*b*
A sight so touching in its majesty;	*b*
This city now doth like a garment wear	*a*
The beauty of the morning; silent, bare,	*a*
Ships, towers, domes, theatres, and temples lie	*b*
Open unto the fields, and to the sky,	*b*
All bright and glittering in the smokeless air.	*a*
Never did sun more beautifully steep	*c*
In his first splendour valley, rock, or hill;	*d*
Ne'er saw I, never felt, a calm so deep!	*c*
The river glideth at his own sweet will:	*d*
Dear God! the very houses seem asleep;	*c*
And all that mighty heart is lying still!	*d*

Or there's Milton's sonnet 'On his Blindness':

---

* 'Sonnet', coming from the Italian, means 'little sound'. Thus some sixteenth- and seventeenth-century poets called any love lyric a sonnet.

When I consider how my light is spent   *a*
   Eer half my days in this dark world and wide,   *b*
   And that one talent which is death to hide   *b*
   Lodged with me useless, though my soul more bent *a*
To serve therewith my Maker, and present   *a*
   My true account, lest He returning chide;   *b*
   'Doth God exact day-labour, light denied?'   *b*
   I fondly ask; but Patience, to prevent   *a*
That murmur, soon replies, 'God doth not need   *c*
   Either man's work or his own gifts. Who best   *d*
   Bear his mild yoke, they serve him best; his state *e*
   Is kingly: thousands at his bidding speed,   *c*
And post o'er land and ocean without rest;   *d*
They also serve who only stand and wait.'   *e*

There is the Spenserian sonnet, of three quatrains (groups of four lines) and a couplet (two lines):

One day I wrote her name upon the strand.   *a*
But came the waves and washèd it away.   *b*
Again I wrote it with a second hand,   *a*
But came the tide, and made my pains his prey. *b*
'Vain man,' said she, 'that dost in vain essay *b*
A mortal thing so to immortalise;   *c*
For I myself shall like to this decay,   *b*
And eke my name be wipèd out likewise.'   *c*
'Not so,' quoth I; 'let baser things devise   *c*
To die in dust, but you shall live by fame: *d*
My verse your virtues rare shall eternise,   *c*
And in the heavens write your glorious name: *d*
Where, whenas Death shall all the world subdue, *e*
Our love shall live, and later life renew.'   *e*

The Shakespearean sonnet has a looser rhyme scheme but requires fierce control if it is to retain the power of its brief message:

Let me not to the marriage of true minds   *a*
   Admit impediments. Love is not love   *b*
Which alters when it alteration finds,   *a*
   Or bends with the remover to remove: *b*
O no! It is an ever-fixèd mark,   *c*
   That looks on tempests and is never shaken;   *d*

It is the star to every wandering bark,   c
    Whose worth's unknown, although his height be taken. *d*
Love's not Time's fool, though rosy lips and cheeks   e
    Within his bending sickle's compass come;   *f*
Love alters not with his brief hours and weeks,   e
    But bears it out even to the edge of doom.   *f*
    If this be error and upon me proved,   g
    I never writ, nor no man ever loved.   g

This does not seem to have the octave (group of eight lines) followed by the sestet (group of six lines) but is in three groups of quatrains (four lines) followed by a couplet (two lines). So the Shakespearean sonnet is a kind of 'sport'. If you check on the (many) other sonnets in this anthology you will find that only Shakespeare really mastered the Shakespearean sonnet. The point of the classic sonnet form is that there is a statement of what is preoccupying the poet in the octave, while the sestet meditates or enlarges or philosophises on it. Milton, in the sonnet above, daringly crosses over the border between octave and sestet by giving the personified Patience her entrance in the last line of the octave; her reply, answering the poet's complaint, forms the matter of the sestet. Shakespeare uses the final couplet for his summing up.

There are two other major forms, and a variant, in English prosody. The first of these is the heroic couplet – decasyllables (lines of ten syllables) rhyming in pairs, usually in iambs (and thus, again, iambic pentameters). The word 'heroic' comes from the fact that this form is often used for long narrative poems – for instance, in Chaucer's *Canterbury Tales* – sometimes with epic aspirations, that is to say with very high themes, like Homer's *Iliad*, Virgil's *Aeneid* or Milton's *Paradise Lost*. Among the masters of the rhyming couplet in English poetry are Dryden and Pope, Dryden manifesting a muscular vigour –

Of these, the false *Achitophel* was first!
A name to all succeeding ages cursed.
For close designs and crooked counsels fit,
Sagacious, bold, and turbulent of wit . . .
. . . A daring pilot in extremity;
Pleased with the danger when the waves went high,
He sought the storms but, for a calm unfit,
Would steer too close the sands, to boast his wit.
Great wits are sure to madness near allied,
And thin partitions do their bounds divide –

while Pope brings the form to polished perfection:

> Know then thyself, presume not God to scan;
> The proper study of Mankind is Man.
> Placed on this isthmus of a middle state,
> A being darkly wise, and rudely great:
> With too much knowledge for the Sceptic side,
> With too much weakness for the Stoic's pride . . .
> . . . Created half to rise, and half to fall;
> Great Lord of all things, yet a prey to all;
> Sole judge of truth, in endless error hurled,
> The glory, jest and riddle of the world.

And there's the Spenserian stanza. Edmund Spenser (1552–99) seems to have invented and developed this, as he did the sonnet form named after him. It is a ten-line stanza (verse), whose first nine lines are iambic pentameters and whose last line is a hexameter (line with six stresses – sometimes known as the alexandrine)* and rhyming *ababbcbcc*:

> In that same Garden all the goodly flowers,
> Wherewith Dame Nature doth her beautify,
> And decks the garlands of her paramours,
> Are fetched. There is the first seminary
> Of all things that are born to live or die,
> According to their kinds. Long work it were
> Here to account the endless progeny
> Of all the weeds that bud and blossom there;
> But so much as doth need, must needs be counted there.

Spenser used it for his long epic romance, *The Faerie Queene*, Shelley in *Adonais*, Keats in *The Eve of St Agnes*, and Byron found its style suited his semi-autobiographical romantic travelogue, *Childe Harold*:

> I stood in Venice, on the Bridge of Sighs,
> A palace and a prison on each hand:
> I saw from out the wave her structures rise

---

* The alexandrine seems to 'fit' French verse as the iambic pentameter does English verse. Although Pope uses it for special effect –

> A needless Alexandrine ends the song,
> That like a wounded snake drags its slow length along –

it has never played any great part in English poetry.

> As from the stroke of some enchanter's wand:
> A thousand years their cloudy wings expand
> Around me, and a dying glory smiles
> O'er the far times, when many a subject land
> Looked to the wingèd Lion's marble piles,
> Where Venice sate in state, throned on her hundred isles!

The Spenserian stanza is a close relation of the Italian verse form, *ottava rima*, used by Boccaccio (1313–75), Ariosto (1474–1535) in *Orlando Furioso* and Tasso (1544–95) for *Gerusalemme Liberata*. Spenser used it, and it was doubtless the main influence in his development of the Spenserian stanza; the Romantic poets Keats and Shelley experimented with it, and it found vigorous expression in Byron's unfinished mock-epic, *Don Juan*:

> 'Tis pity learnèd virgins ever wed
>   With persons of no sort of education,
> Or gentlemen, who, though well born and bred,
>   Grow tired of scientific conversation;
> I don't choose to say much upon this head,
>   I'm a plain man, and in a single station,
> But – Oh! ye lords of ladies intellectual,
>   Inform us truly, have they not hen-pecked you all? . . .

> . . . 'Tis a sad thing, I cannot choose but say,
>   And all the fault of that indecent sun,
> Who cannot leave alone our hapless clay,
>   But will keep baking, broiling, burning on,
> That howsoever people fast and pray,
>   The flesh is frail, and so the soul undone;
> What men call gallantry, and gods adultery,
>   Is much more common where the climate's sultry.

Byron uses this exacting rhyme scheme – three rhymes only for each stanza – to rollicking effect with, as these examples show, a delight in the outrageous or elaborate final rhyme.

There are, of course, many other verse-forms used by English poets: G. K. Chesterton employs the French *ballade* with jocular confidence; in this anthology you will find the *triolet* – French again – in Frances Cornford's 'To a Fat Lady Seen From the Train' on page 187; and there is the demanding French form of the *villanelle*, brilliantly and movingly displayed in Dylan Thomas's 'Do not go gentle into that good night'.

There are other metres and stresses, including Gerard Manley Hopkins's 'sprung rhythm'. Prosody can be pursued further in encyclopaedias or books on poetry and its forms, and for quick reference there is *A Dictionary of Literary Terms* by J. A. Cuddon (André Deutsch and Penguin). What I have tried to give here are the basics of technical prosody and a discussion of the forms most frequently – or readily – used in English verse, in the hope of increasing enjoyment and admiration of the richness and complexity of the formal challenges which poets meet and master, to underline, inform and clothe their message.

TECHNICAL TERMS

alexandrine a six-foot iambic line

anapaest a metrical foot consisting of two unstressed syllables followed by a stressed one

ballade an elaborate poem consisting of three eight- (or ten-) line stanzas and a four- (or five-) line envoy, all on three (or four) rhymes only in the same order in each stanza, and with the same line ending each stanza and the envoy

couplet two lines of verse, especially when of equal metre, rhyming and forming a whole

dactyl a foot consisting of a stressed syllable followed by two unstressed ones

dimeter two stresses to the line

envoy, envoi the parting words of a poem, especially the final stanza of a poem

foot a unit of length in verse with a varying number of syllables one of which bears a main stress

heroic verse, couplet, etc. used for long narrative poems; either rhymed or unrhymed iambic pentameters

hexameter a verse of six feet

iambic a foot consisting of an unstressed syllable followed by a stressed syllable

octave eight lines of verse

ottava rima eight five-foot iambic lines rhyming *abababcc*

pentameter a verse of five feet

Petrarchan sonnet an octave rhyming *abbaabba* followed by a sestet rhyming either *cdecde* or *cdcdcd*

quatrain a stanza of four lines, usually rhyming alternately

rhyme, rime royal a metre in stanzas of five-foot iambic lines rhyming *ababbcc*

sestet a group of six lines of verse, generally the last six lines of a sonnet

sprung rhythm developed by the English poet Gerard Manly Hopkins; it stresses only those words which carry emotional weight, letting the remaining syllables scramble in anyhow

stanza a group of lines of verse forming a definite pattern, usually consisting of a series of units in a poem

tercet a group of three lines that rhyme together or half a sestet

trimeter a verse of three feet

triolet eight-line poem in which the first line occurs three times (lines l, 4 and 7), the second line twice (2 and 8) and the other lines rhyme with these two

trochee a foot with the first syllable stressed and the second unstressed

verse technically this is a line of metre, but is frequently used as an alternative for *stanza*

villanelle a poem on two rhymes, in five tercets and a quatrain

CONTENTS

The Wordsworth
Golden Treasury of Verse

9th–10th Century

A Dream of the Cross
(Dream of the Rood)

Lo! I will tell the dearest of dreams
That I dreamed in the midnight when mortal men
Were sunk in slumber. Me-seemed I saw
A wondrous Tree towering in air,
Most shining of crosses compassed with light.
Brightly that beacon was gilded with gold;
Jewels adorned it fair at the foot,
Five on the shoulder-beam, blazing in splendour.
Through all creation the angels of God
Beheld it shining – no cross of shame!
Holy spirits gazed on its gleaming,
Men upon earth and all this great creation.
   Wondrous that Tree, that Token of triumph,
And I a transgressor, soiled with my sins!
I gazed on the Rood arrayed in glory,
Shining in beauty and gilded with gold,
The Cross of the Saviour beset with gems.
But through the gold-work outgleamed a token
Of the ancient evil of sinful men
Where the Rood on its right side once sweat blood.
Saddened and rueful, smitten with terror
At the wondrous Vision, I saw the Cross
Swiftly varying vesture and hue,
Now wet and stained with the Blood outwelling,
Now fairly jewelled with gold and gems.
   Then, as I lay there, long I gazed
In rue and sadness on my Saviour's Tree,
Till I heard in dream how the Cross addressed me,
Of all woods worthiest, speaking these words:
   'Long years ago (well yet I remember)
They hewed me down on the edge of the holt,

Severed my trunk; strong foemen took me,
For a spectacle wrought me, a gallows for rogues.
High on their shoulders they bore me to hilltop,
Fastened me firmly, an army of foes!
   'Then I saw the King of all mankind
In brave mood hasting to mount upon me.
Refuse I dared not, nor bow nor break,
Though I felt earth's confines shudder in fear;
All foes I might fell, yet still I stood fast.
   'Then the young Warrior, God, the All-Wielder,
Put off His raiment, steadfast and strong;
With lordly mood in the sight of many
He mounted the Cross to redeem mankind.
When the Hero clasped me I trembled in terror,
But I dared not bow me nor bend to earth;
I must needs stand fast. Upraised as the Rood
I held the High King, the Lord of heaven.
I dared not bow! With black nails driven
Those sinners pierced me; the prints are clear,
The open wounds. I dared injure none.
They mocked us both. I was wet with blood
From the Hero's side when He sent forth His spirit.
   'Many a bale I bore on that hillside
Seeing the Lord in agony outstretched.
Black darkness covered with clouds God's body,
That radiant splendour. Shadow went forth
Wan under heaven; all creation wept
Bewailing the King's death. Christ was on the Cross.
   'Then many came quickly, faring from far,
Hurrying to the Prince. I beheld it all.
Sorely smitten with sorrow, in meekness I bowed
To the hands of men. From His heavy and bitter pain
They lifted Almighty God. Those warriors left me
Standing bespattered with blood; I was wounded with
                              spears.
Limb-weary they laid Him down; they stood at His head,
Looked on the Lord of heaven as He lay there at rest
From His bitter ordeal all forspent. In sight of His slayers
They made Him a sepulchre carved from the shining stone;
Therein laid the Lord of triumph. At evening tide

Sadly they sang their dirges and wearily turned away
From their lordly Prince; there He lay all still and alone.
   'There at our station a long time we stood
Sorrowfully weeping after the wailing of men
Had died away. The corpse grew cold,
The fair life-dwelling. Down to earth
Men hacked and felled us, a grievous fate!
They dug a pit and buried us deep.
But there God's friends and followers found me
And graced me with treasure of silver and gold.
   'Now may you learn, O man beloved,
The bitter sorrows that I have borne,
The work of caitiffs. But the time is come
That men upon earth and through all creation
Show me honour and bow to this sign.
On me a while God's son once suffered;
Now I tower under heaven in glory attired
With healing for all that hold me in awe.
Of old I was once the most woeful of tortures,
Most hateful to all men, till I opened for them
The true Way of life. Lo! the Lord of glory,
The Warden of heaven, above all wood
Has glorified me as Almighty God,
Has honoured His Mother, even Mary herself,
Over all womankind in the eyes of men.
   'Now I give you bidding, O man beloved,
Reveal this Vision to the sons of men,
And clearly tell of the Tree of glory
Whereon God suffered for man's many sins
And the evil that Adam once wrought of old.
   'Death He suffered, but our Saviour rose
By virtue of His great might as a help to men.
He ascended to heaven. But hither again
He shall come unto earth to seek mankind,
The Lord Himself on the Day of Doom,
Almighty God with His angel hosts.
And then will He judge, Who has power of judgment,
To each man according as here on earth
In this fleeting life he shall win reward.
   'Nor there may any be free from fear

Hearing the words which the Wielder shall utter.
He shall ask before many: Where is the man
Who would taste bitter death as He did on the Tree?
And all shall be fearful and few shall know
What to say unto Christ. But none at His Coming
Shall need to fear if he bears in his breast
This best of symbols; and every soul
From the ways of earth through the Cross shall come
To heavenly glory, who would dwell with God.'
  Then with ardent spirit and earnest zeal,
Companionless, lonely, I prayed to the Cross.
My soul was fain of death. I had endured
Many an hour of longing. It is my life's hope
That I may turn to this Token of triumph,
I above all men, and revere it well.
  This is my heart's desire, and all my hope
Waits on the Cross. In this world now
I have few powerful friends; they have fared hence
Away from these earthly gauds seeking the King of glory,
Dwelling now with the High Father in heaven above,
Abiding in rapture. Each day I dream
Of the hour when the Cross of my Lord, whereof here on
                                                    earth
I once had vision, from this fleeting life may fetch me
And bring me where is great gladness and heavenly bliss,
Where the people of God are planted and stablished for ever
In joy everlasting. There may it lodge me
Where I may abide in glory, knowing bliss with the saints.
  May the Lord befriend me who on earth of old
Once suffered on the Cross for the sins of men.
He redeemed us, endowed us with life and a heavenly home.
Therein was hope renewed with blessing and bliss
For those who endured the burning. In that great deed
God's Son was triumphant, possessing power and strength!
Almighty, Sole-Ruling, He came to the kingdom of God
Bringing a host of souls to angelic bliss,
To join the saints who abode in the splendour of glory,
When the Lord, Almighty God, came again to His throne.

10th–11th Century

Two Riddles

On the way a miracle: water become bone.

The deep sea suckled me, the waves sounded over me;
rollers were my coverlet as I rested on my bed.
I have no feet and frequently open my mouth
to the flood. Sooner or later some man will
consume me, who cares nothing for my shell.
With the point of his knife he will pierce me through,
ripping the skin away from my side, and straight away
eat me uncooked as I am . . .

[*probable answers*: ice and oyster]

13th Century

Summer is i-comen in.
    Loud sing cuckoo!
Groweth seed and bloweth mead
And springeth the wood anew.
    Sing cuckoo!

Ewe bleateth after lamb,
Loweth after calf the cow,
Bullock starteth, buck farteth,
    Merry sing cuckoo!
      Cuckoo, cuckoo,
    Well singest thou cuckoo,
    And cease thou never now.

14th Century

A New Year Carol

Here we bring new water
   from the well so clear,
For to worship God with,
   this happy New Year.

Sing levy dew, sing levy dew,
   the water and the wine;
The seven bright gold wires
   and the bugles that do shine.

Sing reign of Fair Maid,
   with gold upon her toe –
Open you the West Door,
   and turn the Old Year go.

Sing reign of Fair Maid
   with gold upon her chin –
Open you the East Door,
   and let the New Year in.

Sing levy dew, sing levy dew,
   the water and the wine;
The seven bright gold wires
   and the bugles they do shine.

14th Century

Maiden in the moor lay,
In the moor lay.
Seven nights full,
Seven nights full,
Maiden in the moor lay,
In the moor lay,
Seven full nights and a day.

Well was her meat.
What was her meat?
The primrose and the –
The primrose and the –
Well was her meat.
What was her meat?
The primrose and the violet.

Well was her drink.
What was her drink?
The cold water of the –
The cold water of the –
Well was her drink.
What was her drink?
The cold water of the wellspring.

Well was her bower.
What was her bower?
The red rose and the –
The red rose and the –
Well was her bower.
What was her bower?
The red rose and the lily flower.

14th Century

I am of Ireland,
And of the holy land
　　Of Ireland.
Good sir, I pray thee,
For holy charity,
Come dance with me
　　In Ireland.

15th Century

Songs of the Months

January:	By this fire I warm my hands,
February;	And with this spade I delve my lands.
March:	Here I set my crops to spring,
April:	And here I hear the sweet birds sing.
May:	I am as light as bird on bough,
June:	And I weed my cornfields well enow.
July:	With my scythe my field I mow,
August:	And here I shear my corn full low.
September:	With my flail I earn my bread,
October:	And here I sow my wheat so red.
November:	At Martinmas I kill my kine,
December:	And at Christmas I drink red wine.

15th Century

The Corpus Christi Carol

Lully lullay, lully lullay,
The falcon hath borne my mate away.

He bore him up, he bore him down,
He bore him into an orchard brown.

An in that orchard there was a hall
That was hung over with purple and pall.

And in that hall there was a bed
That was hung over with gold so red.

And on that bed there was a knight,
His wounds a-bleeding both day and night.

By that bedside there kneels a maid,
And she weeps both night and day.

And by that bedside there stands a stone:
Corpus Christi is written thereon.

Lully lullay, lully lullay,
The falcon hath borne my mate away.

15th Century

I sing of a maid without a peer,
King of all kings she chose to bear.

He came all so still where his mother was,
As dew in April that falleth on the grass.

He came all so still to his mother's bower,
As dew in April that falleth on the flower.

He came all so still where his mother lay,
As dew in April that falleth on the spray.

Mother and maiden was never none but she.
Well may such a lady God's mother be.

15th Century

Western wind, when will thou blow,
    The small rain down can rain?
Christ, if my love were in my arms
    And I in my bed again!

15th Century (?)

The Seven Virgins

1

All under the leaves and the leaves of life
   I met with virgins seven,
And one of them was Mary mild.
   Our Lord's mother of Heaven.

2

'O what are you seeking, you seven fair maids,
   All under the leaves of life?
Come tell, come tell, what seek you
   All under the leaves of life?'

3

'We're seeking for no leaves, Thomas,
   But for a friend of thine;
We're seeking for sweet Jesus Christ,
   To be our guide and thine.'

4

'Go down, go down, to yonder town,
   And sit in the gallery,
And there you'll see sweet Jesus Christ
   Nail'd to a big yew-tree.'

5

So down they went to yonder town
   As fast as foot could fall,
And many a grievous bitter tear
   From the virgins' eyes did fall.

6

'O peace, Mother, O peace, Mother.
   Your weeping doth me grieve:
I must suffer this,' He said,
   'For Adam and for Eve.'

7

'O Mother, take you John Evangelist
　　All for to be your son,
And he will comfort you sometimes,
　　Mother, as I have done.'

8

'O come, thou John Evangelist.
　　Thou'rt welcome unto me;
But more welcome my own dear Son.
　　Whom I nursed on my knee.'

9

Then He laid his head on His right shoulder.
　　Seeing death it struck Him nigh –
'The Holy Ghost be with your soul,
　　I die, Mother dear, I die.'

10

O the rose, the gentle rose,
　　And the fennel that grows so green!
God give us grace in every place
　　To pray for our king and queen.

11

Furthermore for our enemies all
　　Our prayers they should be strong:
Amen, good Lord; your charity
　　Is the ending of my song.

15th Century (?)

The Cherry Tree Carol

PART ONE

1

Joseph was an old man,
    And an old man was he,
When he wedded Mary
    In the land of Galilee.

2

Joseph and Mary walk'd
    Through an orchard good.
Where was cherries and berries
    So red as any blood.

3

Joseph and Mary walk'd
    Through an orchard green.
Where was berries and cherries
    As thick as might be seen.

4

O then bespoke Mary,
    So meek and so mild,
'Pluck me one cherry, Joseph,
    For I am with child.'

5

O then bespoke Joseph,
    With words so unkind,
'Let him pluck thee a cherry
    That brought thee with child.'

6

O then bespoke the babe,
    Within his mother's womb,
'Bow down then the tallest tree
    For my mother to have some.'

7

Then bow'd down the highest tree
  Unto his mother's hand:
Then she cried. 'See, Joseph,
  I have cherries at command!'

8

O then bespake Joseph –
  'I have done Mary wrong;
But cheer up, my dearest,
  And be not cast down.

9

'O eat your cherries, Mary,
  O eat your cherries now;
O eat your cherries, Mary,
  That grow upon the bough.'

10

Then Mary pluck'd a cherry
  As red as the blood;
Then Mary went home
  With her heavy load.

PART TWO
11

As Joseph was a-walking,
  He heard an angel sing:
'This night shall be born
  Our heavenly King.

12

'He neither shall be born
  In housen nor in hall,
Nor in the place of Paradise,
  But in an ox's stall.

13

He neither shall be clothèd
  In purple nor in pall,

But all in fair linen.
  As were babies all.

14

He neither shall be rock'd
  In silver nor in gold.
But in a wooden cradle
  That rocks on the mould.

15

He neither shall be christen'd
  In white wine nor red,
But with fair spring water
  With which we were christenèd.

PART THREE

16

Then Mary took her young son
  And set him on her knee;
'I pray thee now, dear child,
  Tell how this world shall be.'–

17

'O I shall be as dead, mother,
  As the stones in the wall;
O the stones in the street, mother,
  Shall mourn for me all.

18

'And upon a Wednesday
  My vow I will make,
And upon Good Friday
  My death I will take.

19

'Upon Easter-day, mother,
  My uprising shall be;
O the sun and the moon, mother,
  Shall both rise with me!'

before 1500

Lord Randal

1

'O where hae ye been, Lord Randal, my son?
O where hae ye been, my handsome young man?'–
'I hae been to the wild wood; mother, make my bed soon,
For I'm weary wi' hunting, and fain wald lie down.'

2

'Where gat ye your dinner, Lord Randal, my son?
Where gat ye your dinner my handsome young man?' –
'I dined wi' my true-love; mother, make my bed soon'
For I'm weary wi' hunting, and fain wald lie down.

3

'What gat ye to your dinner, Lord Randal, my son?
What gat ye to your dinner, my handsome young man?' –
'I gat eels boil'd in broo'; mother, make my bed soon,
For I'm weary wi' hunting, and fain wald lie down.'

4

'What became of your bloodhounds, Lord Randal, my son?
What became of your bloodhounds, my handsome young
                                        man?' –
'O they swell'd and they died; mother, make my bed soon,
For I'm weary wi' hunting, and fain wald lie down.'

5

'O I fear ye are poison'd, Lord Randal, my son!
O I fear ye are poison'd, my handsome young man!' –
'O yes! I am poison'd; mother, make my bed soon,;
For I'm sick at the heart, and I fain wald lie down.'

before 1500

A Lyke-Wake Dirge

1

This ae nighte, this ae nighte
   — Every nighte and alle,
Fire and fleet and candle-lighte,
   And Christe receive thy saule.

2

When thou from hence away art past
   — Every nighte and alle,
To Whinny-muir thou com'st at last:
   And Christe receive thy saule.

3

If ever thou gavest hosen and shoon
   — Every nighte and alle,
Sit thee down and put them on:
   And Christe receive thy saule.

4

If hosen and shoon thou ne'er gav'st nane
   — Every nighte and alle,
The whinnes sall prick thee to the bare bane;
   And Christe receive thy saule.

5

From Whinny-muir when thou may'st pass
   — Every nighte and alle,
To Brig o' Dread thou com'st at last;
   And Christe receive thy saule.

6

From Brig o' Dread when thou may'st pass
   — Every nighte and alle,
To Purgatory fire thou com'st at last;
   And Christe receive thy saule.

7

If ever thou gavest meat or drink
  – *Every nighte and alle,*
The fire sall never make thee shrink;
  And Christe receive thy saule.

8

If meat or drink thou ne'er gav'st nane
  – *Every nighte and alle,*
The fire will burn thee to the bare bane;
  And Christe receive thy saule.

9

This ae nighte, this ae nighte
  – *Every nighte and alle,*
Fire and fleet and candle lighte.
  And Christe receive thy saule.

before 1500

The Wife of Usher's Well

1

There lived a wife at Usher's well,
  And a wealthy wife was she;
She had three stout and stalwart sons,
  And sent them o'er the sea.

2

They hadna been a week from her,
  A week but barely ane,
When word came to the carline wife
  That her three sons were gane.

3

They hadna been a week from her,
    A week but barely three,
When word came to the carline wife
    That her sons she'd never see.

4

'I wish the wind may never cease,
    Nor fashes in the flood,
Till my three sons come hame to me
    In earthly flesh and blood!'

5

It fell about the Martinmas.
    When nights are lang and mirk,
The carline wife's three sons came hame,
    And their hats were o' the birk.

6

It neither grew in syke nor ditch,
    Nor yet in ony sheugh;
But at the gates o' Paradise
    That birk grew fair eneugh.

7

'Blow up the fire, my maidens!
    Bring water from the well!
For a' my house shall feast this night,
    Since my three sons are well.'

8

And she has made to them a bed,
    She's made it large and wide;
And she's ta'en her mantle her about,
    Sat down at the bedside.

9

Up then crew the red, red cock,
    And up and crew the grey;
The eldest to the youngest said,
    ' 'Tis time we were away.'

10

The cock he hadna craw'd but once,
   And clapp'd his wings at a',
When the youngest to the eldest said,
   'Brother, we must awa'.

11

'The cock doth craw, the day doth daw,
   The channerin' worm doth chide;
Gin we be miss'd out o' our place,
   A sair pain we maun bide.' –

12

'Lie still, lie still but a little wee while,
   Lie still but if we may;
Gin my mother should miss us when she wakes,
   She'll go mad ere it be day.'

13

'Fare ye weel, my mother dear!
   Fareweel to barn and byre!
And fare ye weel, the bonny lass
   That kindles my mother's fire!'

before 1500

The Daemon Lover

1

'O where hae ye been, my long, long love,
   These seven long years and more?'
'O I'm come to seek my former vows,
   That ye promised me before.'

2

'Awa' wi' your former vows,' she says,
    'For they will breed but strife;
Awa' wi' your former vows,' she says
    'For I am become a wife.

3

'I am married to a ship-carpenter,
    A ship-carpenter he's bound;
I wadna he kenn'd my mind this nicht
    For twice five hundred pound.'

4

He turn'd him round and round about,
    And the tear blinded his e'e:
'I wad never hae trodden on Irish ground
    If it hadna been for thee.

5

'I might hae had a noble lady,
    Far, far beyond the sea;
I might hae had a noble lady,
    Were it no for the love o' thee.'

6

'If ye might hae had a noble lady,
    Yoursel' ye had to blame;
Ye might hae taken the noble lady,
    For ye kenn'd that I was nane.'

7

'O fause are the vows o' womankind,
    But fair is their fause bodie:
I wad never hae trodden on Irish ground,
    Were it no for the love o' thee.'

8

'If I was to leave my husband dear,
    And my wee young son alsua,
O what hae ye to tak' me to,
    If with you I should gae?'

9

'I hae seven ships upon the sea,
  The eighth brought me to land;
With mariners and merchandise,
  And music on every hand.

10

'The ship wherein my love sall sail
  Is glorious to behowd;
The sails sall be o' the finest silk,
  And the mast o' beaten gowd.'

11

She has taken up her wee young son,
  Kiss'd him baith cheek and chin;
'O fare ye weel, my wee young son,
  For I'll never see you again!'

12

She has put her foot on gude ship-board,
  And on ship-board she has gane.
And the veil that hangit ower her face
  Was a' wi' gowd begane.

13

She hadna sail'd a league, a league,
  A league but barely twa,
Till she minded on her husband she left
  And her wee young son alsua.

14

'O haud your tongue o' weeping,' he says,
  'Let a' your follies a-bee;
I'll show where the white lilies grow
  On the banks o' Italie.'

15

She hadna sail'd a league, a league,
  A league but barely three,
Till grim, grim his countenance
  And gurly grew the sea.

16

'What hills are yon, yon pleasant hills,
  The sun shines sweetly on?'
'O yon are the hills o' Heaven,' he said,
  'Where you will never won.'

17

'O whaten-a mountain is yon,' she said,
  'Sae dreary wi' frost and snae?'
'O yon is the mountain o' Hell,' he said,
  'Where you and I will gae.

18

'But haud your tongue, my dearest dear,
  Let a' your follies a-bee,
I'll show where the white lilies grow,
  In the bottom o' the sea.'

19

And aye as she turn'd her round about,
  Aye taller he seem'd to be;
Until that the tops o' that gallant ship
  Nae taller were than he.

20

He strack the top-mast wi' his hand,
  The fore-mast wi' his knee;
And he brake that gallant ship in twain,
  And sank her in the sea.

before 1500

The Seeds of Love

I sowed the seeds of love,
I sowed them in the Spring,
In April, May and June likewise,
While the small birds sweetly do sing.

My garden was planted full
With flowers everywhere,
But for myself I could not choose
The flower I held most dear.

My gardener was standing by,
I asked him to choose for me.
He chose me the violet, lily and pink
But these I refused all three.

The violet I forsook
Because it came too soon.
The lily and pink I did overlook
And found I would stay till June.

In June there's the rose so red,
That flower so dear to me,
But when I had plucked the rose so red
I found but the willow tree.

Green willow it will twist,
Green willow it will twine,
And I wish I was in that young man's arms
That now has the heart of mine.

My garden is all over-run,
No flowers in it grew,
For the beds that were once all covered
                                    with green thyme
Are all over-run with rue.

before 1500

Waly Waly

The water is wide, I cannot get o'er,
And neither have I wings to fly.
Give me a boat that will carry two,
And both shall row, my love and I.

Down in the meadow the other day,
A-gathering flowers both fine and gay,
A-gathering flowers both red and blue,
I little thought what love can do.

I put my hand into the bush,
Thinking the sweetest flower to find,
I pricked my finger to the bone
And left the sweetest flower alone.

I leaned my back against some oak,
Thinking it was a trusty tree,
But first it bended and then it broke
And so did my false love to me.

A ship there is and she sails the sea,
She's loaded deep as deep may be,
But not so deep as the love I'm in.
I know not if I sink or swim.

O love is handsome and love is fine
And love's a jewel when it is new,
But when it is old it groweth cold
And fades away like morning dew.

before 1500

The Twa Corbies
(Scottish Version)

1

As I was walking all alane,
I heard twa corbies making a mane;
The tane unto the tither did say,
'Whar sall we gang and dine the day?'

2

' – In behint yon auld fail dyke
I wot there lies a new-slain knight;
And naebody kens that he lies there
But his hawk, his hound, and his lady fair.

3

'His hound is to the hunting gane,
His hawk to fetch the wild-fowl hame,
His lady's ta'en anither mate,
So we may mak' our dinner sweet.

4

'Ye'll sit on his white hause-bane,
And I'll pike out his bonny blue e'en:
Wi' ae lock o' his gowden hair
We'll theek our nest when it grows bare.

5

'Mony a one for him maks mane,
But nane sall ken whar he is gane:
O'er his white banes, when they are bare,
The wind sall blaw for evermair.'

before 1500

The Trees So High

1

All the trees they are so high,
  The leaves they are so green,
The day is past and gone, sweetheart,
  That you and I have seen.
    It is cold winter's night,
    You and I must bide alone:
      Whilst my pretty lad is young
                And is growing.

2

In a garden as I walked,
  I heard them laugh and call;
There were four and twenty playing there,
  They played with bat and ball.
    O the rain on the roof,
    Here and I must make my moan:
      Whilst my pretty lad is young
                And is growing.

3

I listen'd in the garden,
  I looked o'er the wall;
'Midst five and twenty gallants there
  My love exceeded all.
    O the wind on the thatch,
    Here and I alone must weep:
      Whilst my pretty lad is young
                And is growing.

4

O father, father dear,
  Great wrong to me is done,
That I should married be this day,
  Before the set of sun.
    At the huffle of the gale,
      Here I toss and cannot sleep:
        Whilst my pretty lad is young
          And is growing.

5

My daughter, daughter dear,
  If better be, more fit,
I'll send him to the court awhile,
  To point his pretty wit.
    But the snow, snowflakes fall,
      O and I am chill and dead:
        Whilst my pretty lad is young
          And is growing.

6

To let the lovely ladies know
  They may not touch and taste,
I'll bind a bunch of ribbons red
  About his little waist.
    But the raven hoarsely croaks,
      And I shiver in my bed;
        Whilst my pretty lad is young
          And is growing.

7

I married was, alas,
  A lady high to be,
In court and stall and stately hall,
  And bower of tapestry.
    But the bell did only knell,
      And I shuddered as one cold:
        When I wed the pretty lad
          Not done growing.

8

As fourteen he wedded was,
    A father at fifteen,
At sixteen 's face was white as milk,
    And then his grave was green;
        And the daisies were outspread,
        And buttercups of gold,
            O'er my pretty lad so young
                        Now ceased growing.

15th–16th Century

The Two Magicians

O she looked out of the window,
    As white as any milk;
But he looked into the window,
    As black as any silk.

Hulloa, hulloa, hulloa, hulloa, you coal-black smith!
    O what is your silly song?
You never shall change my maiden name
    That I have kept so long;
I'd rather die a maid, yes, but then she said,
And be buried all in my grave,
Than I'd have such a nasty, husky, dusky, musty, fusky,
    Coal-black smith
                        A maiden I will die.

Then she became a duck,
    A duck all on the stream;
And he became a water dog,
    And fetched her back again.
        Hulloa, &c.

Then she became a hare,
  A hare all on the plain;
And he became a greyhound dog,
  And fetched her back again.
    Hulloa, &c.

Then she became a fly
  A fly all in the air;
And he became a spider,
  And fetched her to his lair,
    Hulloa, &c.

16th Century

The Passionate Man's Pilgrimage

Give me my scallop-shell of quiet,
My staff of faith to walk upon,
My scrip of joy, immortal diet,
My bottle of salvation,
My gown of glory, hope's true gage,
And thus I'll take my pilgrimage.

Blood must be my body's balmer,
No other balm will there be given,
Whilst my soul like a white palmer
Travels to the land of heaven,
Over the silver mountains,
Where spring the nectar fountains;
And there I'll kiss
The bowl of bliss
And drink my eternal fill
On every milken hill.
My soul will be a-dry before,
But after it, will ne'er thirst more.

And by the happy blissful way
More peaceful pilgrims I shall see,
That have shook off their gowns of clay

And go apparelled fresh like me.
I'll bring them first
To slake their thirst,
And then to taste those nectar suckets,
At the clear wells
Where sweetness dwells,
Drawn up by saints in crystal buckets.

And when our bottles and all we
Are filled with immortality,
Then the holy paths we'll travel,
Strewed with rubies thick as gravel,
Ceilings of diamonds, sapphire floors,
High walls of coral and pearl bowers.

From thence to heaven's bribeless hall
Where no corrupted voices brawl,
No conscience molten into gold,
Nor forged accusers bought and sold,
No cause deferred, nor vain-spent journey,
For there Christ is the King's Attorney,
Who pleads for all without degrees,
And he hath angels, but no fees.

When the grand twelve million jury
Of our sins and sinful fury
'Gainst our souls black verdicts give,
Christ pleads his death, and then we live.
Be thou my speaker, taintless pleader,
Unblotted lawyer, true proceeder;
Thou movest salvation even for alms,
Not with a bribed lawyer's palms.

And this is my eternal plea
To him that made heaven, earth, and sea:
Seeing my flesh must die so soon,
And want a head to dine next noon,
Just at the stroke when my veins start and spread,
Set on my soul an everlasting head.
Then am I ready, like a palmer fit,
To tread those blest paths which before I writ.

16th Century

Song

The lowest trees have tops, the ant her gall,
  The fly her spleen, the little spark his heat;
Hairs cast their shadows, though they be but small,
  And bees have stings, although they be not great.
Seas have their source, and so have shallow springs,
And love is love, in beggars and in kings.

The ermine hath the fairest skin on earth,
  Yet doth she choose the weasel for her peer;
The panther hath a sweet perfumed breath,
  Yet doth she suffer apes to draw her near.
No flower more fresh than is the damask rose,
Yet next her side the nettle often grows.

Where waters smoothest run, deep'st are the fords,
  The dial stirs, though none perceive it move;
The fairest faith is in the sweetest words,
  The turtles sing not love, and yet they love.
True hearts have eyes and ears, no tongues to speak,
They hear and see, and sigh, and then they break.

16th Century

A New Courtly Sonnet of the Lady Greensleeves

Greensleeves was all my joy,
  Greensleeves was my delight;
Greensleeves was my heart of gold,
  And who but Lady Greensleeves.

Alas, my love, ye do me wrong
  To cast me off discourteously;
And I have loved you so long,
  Delighting in your company.
    Greensleeves was all my joy, &c.

I have been ready at your hand,
  To grant whatever you would crave;
I have both waged life and land,
  Your love and goodwill for to have.
    Greensleeves was all my joy, &c.

I bought thee kerchers to thy head,
  That were wrought fine and gallantly;
I kept thee both at board and bed,
  Which cost my purse well favouredly
    Greensleeves was all my joy, &c.

I bought thee petticoats of the best,
  The cloth so fine as fine might be;
I gave thee jewels for thy chest,
  And all this cost I spent on thee.
    Greensleeves was all my joy, &c.

Thy smock of silk, both fair and white,
  With gold embroidered gorgeously;
Thy petticoat of sendal right;
  And thus I bought thee gladly.
    Greensleeves was all my joy, &c.

Thy girdle of gold so red,
  With pearls bedecked sumptuously;
The like no other lasses had,
  And yet thou wouldst not love me.
    Greensleeves was all my joy, &c.

Thy purse and eke thy gay gilt knives,
  Thy pincase gallant to the eye;
No better wore the burgess wives,
  And yet thou wouldst not love me.
    Greensleeves was all my joy, &c.

Thy crimson stockings all of silk,
  With gold all wrought above the knee;
Thy pumps as white as was the milk,
  And yet thou wouldst not love me.
    Greensleeves was all my joy, &c.

Thy gown was of the grassy green,
  Thy sleeves of satin hanging by,
Which made thee be our harvest queen,
  And yet thou wouldst not love me.
    Greensleeves was all my joy, &c.

Thy garters fringed with the gold,
  And silver aglets hanging by,
Which made thee blithe for to behold,
  And yet thou wouldst not love me
    Greensleeves was all my joy, &c.

My gayest gelding I thee gave,
  To ride wherever liked thee;
No lady ever was so brave,
  And yet thou wouldst not love me.
    Greensleeves was all my joy, &c.

My men were clothed all in green,
  And they did ever wait on thee;
All this was gallant to he seen,
  And yet thou wouldst not love me.
    Greensleeves was all my joy, &c.

They set thee up, they took thee down.
　　They served thee with humility;
Thy foot might not once touch the ground,
　　And yet thou wouldst not love me.
　　　Greensleeves was all my joy, &c.

For every morning when thou rose,
　　I sent thee dainties orderly,
To cheer thy stomach from all woes,
　　And yet thou wouldst not love me.
　　　Greensleeves was all my joy, &c.

Thou couldst desire no earthly thing
　　But still thou hadst it readily;
Thy music still to play and sing,
　　And yet thou wouldst not love me.
　　　Greensleeves was all my joy, &c.

And who did pay for all this gear
　　That thou didst spend when pleased thee?
Even I that am rejected here,
　　And thou disdain'st to love me.
　　　Greensleeves was all my joy, &c.

Well, I will pray to God on high,
　　That thou my constancy mayst see,
And that yet once before I die,
　　Thou wilt vouchsafe to love me.
　　　Greensleeves was all my joy, &c.

Greensleeves, now farewell! adieu!
　　God I pray to prosper thee;
For I am still thy lover true.
　　Come once again and love me.
　　　Greensleeves was all my joy,
　　　　Greensleeves was my delight;
　　　Greensleeves was my heart of gold,
　　　　And who but Lady Greensleeves.

16th Century (?)

Tom O'Bedlam

The moon's my constant mistress,
　　And the lovely owl my marrow;
　　　The flaming drake,
　　　And the night-crow, make
　　Me music to my sorrow

I know more than Apollo;
　　For oft, when he lies sleeping,
　　　I behold the stars
　　　At mortal wars,
　　And the rounded welkin weeping.

The moon embraces her shepherd,
　　And the Queen of Love her warrior;
　　　While the first does horn
　　　The stars of the morn,
　　And the next the heavenly farrier.

With a heart of furious fancies,
　　Whereof I am commander:
　　　With a burning spear,
　　　And a horse of air,
　　To the wilderness I wander;

With a Knight of ghosts and shadows,
　　I summoned am to Tourney:
　　　Ten leagues beyond
　　　The wide world's end;
　　Methinks it is no journey.

after 1600

The Golden Vanity

1

A ship I have got in the North Country
And she goes by the name of the *Golden Vanity*,
O I fear she'll by taken by a Spanish Ga–la–lee,
    As she sails by the Low–lands low.

2

To the captain then upspake the little cabin-boy,
He said, 'What is my fee, if the galley I destroy?
The Spanish Ga–la–lee, if no more it shall anoy,
    As you sail by the Low–lands low.'

3

'Of silver and of gold I will give to you a store;
And my pretty little daughter that dwelleth on the shore,
Of treasure and of fee as well, I'll give to thee galore,
    As we sail by the Low–lands low.'

4

Then they row'd him up tight in a black bull's skin,
And he held all in his hand an augur sharp and thin,
And he swam until he came to the Spanish Gal–a–lin,
    As she lay by the Low–lands low.

5

He bored with his augur, he bored once and twice,
And some were playing cards, and some were playing
                           dice,
When the water flowèd in it dazzled their eyes,
    And she sank by the Low–lands low.

6

So the cabin-boy did swim all to the larboard side,
Saying, 'Captain! take me in, I am drifting with the tide!'
'I will shoot you! I will kill you!' the cruel Captain cried,
    'You may sink by the Low–lands low.'

7

Then the cabin-boy did swim all to the starboard side,
Saying, 'Messmates, take me in, I am drifting with the tide!'
Then they laid him on the deck, and he closed his eyes
                          and died,
    As they sailed by the Low–lands low.

8

They sewed his body tight in an old cow's hide,
And they cast the gallant cabin-boy out over the ship side,
And left him without more ado to drift with the tide,
    And to sink by the Low–lands low.

Weep you no more, sad fountains;
　What need you flow so fast?
Look how the snowy mountains
　Heaven's sun doth gently waste.
But my sun's heavenly eyes
　View not your weeping,
　That now lies sleeping
Softly, now softly lies
　　Sleeping.

Sleep is a reconciling,
　A rest that peace begets:
Doth not the sun rise smiling
　When fair at even he sets?
Rest you, then, rest sad eyes,
　Melt not in weeping,
　While she lies sleeping
Softly, now softly lies
　　Sleeping.

17th Century

Beauty Extoll'd

Gaze not on swans, in whose soft breast
A full-hatch'd beauty seems to nest,
Nor snow, which falling from the sky,
Hovers in its virginity.

Gaze not on roses, though new-blown,
Grac'd with a fresh complexion;
Nor lilies, which no subtle bee
Hath robb'd by kissing chemistry.

Gaze not on that pure milky way,
Where night vies splendour with the day;
Nor pearl, whose silver walls confine
The riches of an Indian mine.

For it my Empress appears.
Swans moulting die, snow melts to tears;
Roses do blush and hang their heads,
Pale lilies shrink into their beds.

The milky way rides post to shroud
Its baffles glory in a cloud;
And pearls do climb into her ear,
To hang themselves for envy there.

So have I seen stars big with light
Prove lanterns to the moon-eyed night,
Which, when Sol's rays were once display'd,
Sunk in their sockets, and decay'd.

17th Century

The Fire of London

Of Fire, Fire, Fire I sing, that have more cause to cry
In the Great Chamber of the King (a City mounted High);
    Old London that
Hath stood in State above six hundred years,
    In six days space,
Woe and alas! is burned and drowned in tears.

The second of September in the middle time of night,
In Pudding Lane it did begin to burn and blaze out right;
    Where all that gazed,
Were so amazed at such a furious flame,
    They knew not how,
Or what to do that might expel the same.

It swallowed Fishstreet Hill, and straight it licked up Lombard
                                 Street,
Down Canon Street in blazing State it flew with flaming feet;
    Down to the Thames
Whose shrinking streams began to ebb away,
    As thinking that
The power of Fate had brought the latter day . . .

Eurus the God of Eastern Gales was Vulcan's Bellows now,
And did so fill the flagrant dayls that High-built Churches bow;
    The Leads they bear
Drop'd many a Tear, to see their Fabricks burn;
    The Sins of Men,
Made Churches then in Dust and Ashes mourn.

Although the Fire be fully quenched yet of our sins remain,
And that in them we still are drenched, the Fire will rage again;
    Or what is worse,
A heavier Curse in Famine will appear;
    Where shall we tread,
When Want of Bread and Hunger draweth near?
With hand and feet, in every street, they pack up Goods and fly,

Pitch, Tarr and Oyl increase the spoyl old Fish Street 'gins to frye:
    The Fire doth range
Up to the Change, and every King commands,
    But in despight
Of all its might the stout old Founder stands . . .

The Cracking flames do fume and roar, as Billows do retyre,
The City (though upon the shoar) doth seem a sea of fire;
    Where Steeple Spires
Shew in the Fires like Vessels sinking down.
    The open fields
More safety yields, and thither fly the Town . . .

From Sunday morn till Thursday at night it roared about the Town,
There was no way to quell its might but to pull Houses down;
    And so they did.
As they were bid by Charles, His Great Command;
    The Duke of York,
Some say did work, with Bucket in his hand . . .

Many of French and Dutch were stopped and also are confined,
'Tis said that they their Fire balls dropped and this Plot was
                                designed
    By Them and Those
That are our Foes, yet some think nothing so;
    But that our God.
With His flaming Rod, for Sin sends all this woe.

If this do not reform our lives, a worse thing will succeed,
Our kindred, children, and our wives, will dye for want of Bread;
    When famine comes,
'Tis not our Drums, our Ships, our Horse or Foot
    That can defend,
But if we mend, we never shall come to 't.

                              Broadsheet Ballad

18th Century (?)

Barbara Allen's Cruelty

1

In Scarlet town, where I was born,
  There was a fair maid dwellin',
Made every youth cry, 'Well-a-way!'
  Her name was Barbara Allen.

2

All in the merry month of May,
  When green buds they were swellin',
Young Jemmy Grove on his death-bed lay,
  For love of Barbara Allen.

3

He sent his man in to her then,
  To the town where she was dwellin':
'O haste and come to my master dear,
  If your name be Barbara Allen.'

4

So slowly, slowly rase she up,
  And slowly she came nigh him,
And when she drew the curtain by –
  'Young man, I think you're dyin'.'

5

'O it's I am sick and very very sick,
  And it's all for Barbara Allen.' –
'O the better for me ye'se never be,
  Tho' your heart's blood were a-spillin'!

6

'O dinna ye mind, young man,' says she,
  'When the red wine ye were fillin',
That ye made the healths go round and round,
  And slighted Barbara Allen?'

7

He turn'd his face unto the wall,
  And death was with him dealin':
'Adieu, adieu, my dear friends all,
  And be kind to Barbara Allen!'

8

As she was walking o'er the fields,
  She heard the dead-bell knellin';
And every jow the dead-bell gave
  Cried, 'Woe to Barbara Allen.'

9

'O mother, mother, make my bed,
  O make it saft and narrow:
My love has died for me today,
  I'll die for him tomorrow.

10

'Farewell,' she said, 'ye virgins all,
  And shun the fault I fell in:
Henceforth take warning by the fall
  Of cruel Barbara Allen.'

19th Century

God Bless Plimsoll, The Sailors' Friend

Hear a sailor! kind sirs, who made it his glory,
   And when I have ended, your sympathy lend,
O, list for a moment, and hear my sad story,
   Of brave Samuel Plimsoll, the poor sailors' friend.
How many poor tars have of late shipped their cable,
   And gone to their death on a watery main,
Through those rotten ships, to return are unable,
   And friends and relations, they'll ne'er see aga'n.

Of Plimsoll, the poor sailors' friend, I am thinking,
   In St Stephen's he boldly let them understand,
Rotten ships with our tars, every day they are sinking,
   Then cheer for brave Plimsoll, that bold Englishman.

Shall I tell you the sight I've seen on the ocean,
   As, drenched with the spray, on deck I have stood,
It will fill many a landsman's heart with emotion,
   To see mothers and fathers and children good,
Go down in the sea, while he stood uncovered,
   O, hear this now messmates – my Lords understand,
From the sea cries aloud, for I now have discovered,
   Rotten ships they go down, when they leave Britain land.

I can't make it out how these lords of creation,
   On board of that ship *House of Commons* by name,
While he spoke for the rights of the tars of our nation,
   How Englishmen, ever, could brave Plimsoll blame.
He cries, 'See that ship with those brave lads on board?
   She's now overloaded, I tell you, with pain;
Her owners, no doubt, have fully insured her,
   But those gallant men you will ne'er see again.

Cries Plimsoll, 'O, pray give a ear to my warning,
  And let not my bill for our tars be withdrawn,
They go down in the sea, while my words you are scorning,
  And hundreds again will ne'er see the dawn.
See that old rotten ship – and her villainous owner
  On shore stands and rubs his knuckles with glee;
He knows that coffin ship, with her crew, none bolder,
  Will never return, she'll go down in the sea.'

Then God help poor seamen, whose life on the ocean
  Compels them to sail on the wide-raging main
In those death-dealing ships – and I speak with emotion –
  To go down in those coffins we ne'er see again.
O what will they say when they go under hatches,
  Those cruel shipowners, when life it is gone,
For the hundreds of souls, now, whom death often catches,
  To our gallant commander that sits up aloft?

Then here's to brave Plimsoll, the friend of our sailor,
  His conduct, there's no one in England can blame,
He spoke like a man, I know he's no sailor,
  And those cruel shipowners, he put them to shame.
The wrongs of our seamen he wished to see righted,
  Those rotten ships sailing from England's land,
And thousands of lives that at sea have been blighted.
  God bless Samuel Plimsoll, that bold Englishman.

Broadsheet Ballad. *c.*1875

19th Century

Polly Perkins

I am a broken-hearted milkman, in grief I'm arrayed,
Through keeping of the company of a young servant maid,
Who lived on board wages to keep the house clean
In a gentleman's family near Paddington Green.
> *She was as beautiful as a butterfly*
> *And as proud as a Queen*
> *Was pretty Polly Perkins of*
> *Paddington Green.*

Her eyes were as black as the pips of a pear,
No rose in the garden with her cheeks could compare,
Her hair hung in ringlets so beautiful and long,
I thought that she loved me but I found I was wrong.
> *She was as beautiful as a butterfly, &c.*

When I asked her to marry me, she said, 'Oh! what stuff,'
And told me to drop it, for she had quite enough
Of my nonsense – at the same time I'd been very kind,
But to marry a milkman she did not feel inclined.
'Oh, the man that has me must have silver and gold,
A chariot to ride in and be handsome and bold,
His hair must be curly as any watch spring,
And his whiskers as long as a brush for clothing.'
> *She was as beautiful as a butterfly, &c.*

In six months she married, this hard-hearted girl,
But it was not a wicount, and it was not a nearl,
It was not a baronite, but a shade or two wuss,
It was a bow-legged conductor of a twopenny bus.
> *She was as beautiful as a butterfly, &c.*

19th Century

She Will Not Have To Climb the Golden Stairs

The Maybrick trial is over now, there's been a lot of jaw,
    Of doctors' contradiction, and expounding of the law;
She had Sir Charles Russell to defend her as we know,
    But though he tried his very best it all turned out no go.
But Mrs Maybrick will not have to climb the golden stairs;
    The jury found her guilty so she nearly said her prayers;
She's at another kind of mashing and at it she must stop,
    Old Berry is took down a peg with his big long drop.

Now the doctors at the trial had a very gay old time,
    They all told different stories about this cruel crime;
Some said that Mr Maybrick to death had dosed himself,
    While others said it was his wife that put him on the shelf.
But Mrs Maybrick will not have to climb the golden stairs; &c.

Then came the servants' story how the flypapers were found,
    In fact it seems the missis had arsenic all around,
In food and drink of every kind, in cupboard and in box,
    In handkerchiefs, and even in the pockets of her frocks.
But Mrs Maybrick will not have to climb the golden stairs; &c.

Next came the waiter's story about her trip to town,
    Which proved that from the virtue of a woman she'd
                                            come down,
And when a woman like her from her husband goes astray,
    It plainly shows she wishes that he was out of the way.
But Mrs Maybrick will not have to climb the golden stairs; &c.

Then came the fatal letter that fairly cooked her goose,
    It seemed to say to Brierly that she would soon be loose;
And though she made a statement to explain it all away,
    The jury wouldn't have it, she the penalty must pay.
But Mrs Maybrick will not have to climb the golden stairs; &c.

Then to each gay and flirty wife may this a warning be,
   Don't write to any other man or sit upon his knee;
When once you start, like Mrs Maybrick perhaps you couldn't
                                 stop,
   So stick close to your husband and keep clear of Berry's drop.
But Mrs Maybrick will not have to climb the golden stairs; &c.

19th Century

The Owslebury Lads

The thirtieth of November, eighteen hundred and thirty,
The Owslebury lads they did prepare all for the machinery,
And when they did get there, my eye! how they let fly,
The machinery flew to pieces in the twinkling of an eye.
   The mob, such a mob, you had never seen before,
   And if you live for a hundred years you never will no more.

Oh then to Winchester we were sent, our trial for to take,
And if we do have nothing said, our council we shall keep.
When the judges did begin, I'm sorry for to say,
So many there was transported for life and some was cast to die.
   The mob, &c.

Sometimes our parents they comes in all for to see us all,
Sometimes they bring us some baccy or a loaf that is so small,
Then we goes into the kitchen and sits all round about,
There is so many of us that we are very soon all smoked out.
   The mob, &c.

At six o'clock in the morning our turnkey he comes in
With a bunch of keys all in his hands tied up all in a ring,
And we can't get any further than back and forward the yard;
A pound and a half of bread a day, and don't you think it hard?
   The mob, &c.

At six o'clock in evening the turnkey he comes round,
The locks and bolts they rattle like the sounding of a drum,
And we are all locked up all in our cells so high
And there we stay till morning whether we lives or dies.
    The mob, &c.

So now to conclude and finish my new song,
I hope you gentlemen round me will think that I'm not wrong,
And all the poor in Hampshire for rising of their wages –
And I hope that none of our enemies will ever want for places.
    The mob, &c.

Broadsheet Ballad, 1830

19th Century

The Durham Lock-Out

In our Durham County I am sorry for to say,
That hunger and starvation is increasing every day,
For the want of food and coals, we know not what to do,
But with your kind assistance we will stand the struggle through.

I need not state the reason why we have been brought so low,
The masters have behaved unkind, which everyone will know;
Because we won't lie down and let them treat us as they like,
To punish us, they've stopped the pits and caused the present
                           strike.

May every Durham colliery owner that is in the fault,
Receive nine lashes with the rod, and then be rubbed with salt,
May his back be thick with boils so that he may never sit,
And never burst until the wheels go round at every pit.

The pulley wheels have ceased to move which went so swift
                                                around,
The horses and the ponies too all brought from underground,
Our work is taken from us now, they care not if we die,
For they can eat the best of food, and drink the best when dry.

The miner and his wife too, each morning have to roam,
To seek for bread to feed the hungry little ones at home.
The flour barrel is empty now, their true and faithful friend,
Which makes the thousands wish today the strike was at an end.

We have done our very best as honest working men.
To let the pits commence again, we've offered to them ten.
The offer they will not accept, they firmly do demand
Thirteen and a half per cent, or let the collieries stand.

Let them stand or let them lie or do with them as they choose,
To give them thirteen and a half we ever shall refuse.
They're always willing to receive, but not inclined to give.
Very soon they won't allow a working man to live.

With tyranny and capital they never seem content,
Unless they are endeavouring to take from us per cent.
If it was due, what they request, we willingly would grant;
We know it's not, therefore we cannot give them what they
                                                want.

The miners of Northumberland we shall for ever praise,
For being so kind in helping us those tyrannising days.
We thank the other counties too, that have been doing the same,
For every man who hears this song will know we're not to
                                                blame.

Broadsheet Ballad, 1892

LASCELLES ABERCROMBIE
1881–1938

The Nightingale
(from the Old English riddle)

I through my throat the thronging melodies
Delicately devising in divers moods,
Let my little breath lavishly chime,
Still the bestower of unstinted song.
Of old to all men my evening enchantment
Brings blissful ease; they, when I bind them
With my thrilling sweet troubles, enthralled in
     their houses
Lean forward, listening. Learn now my name
Who cry so keenly, such quivering glee
Pealing merrily, and pour such musical
Ringing welcome to returning warriors.

JOSEPH ADDISON
1672–1719

Hymn

1

The spacious firmament on high,
With all the blue ethereal sky,
And spangled heavens, a shining frame,
Their great original proclaim:
Th' unwearied sun, from day to day,
Does his Creator's power display,
And publishes to every land
The work of an almighty hand.

2

Soon as the evening shades prevail,
The moon takes up the wondrous tale,
And nightly to the listening earth
Repeats the story of her birth:
Whilst all the stars that round her burn,
And all the planets in their turn,
Confirm the tidings as they roll,
And spread the truth from pole to pole.

3

What though, in solemn silence, all
Move round the dark terrestrial ball?
What though nor real voice nor sound
Amid their radiant orbs be found?
In reason's ear they all rejoice,
And utter forth a glorious voice,
For ever singing, as they shine,
'The hand that made us is divine.'

WILLIAM ALLINGHAM
1824–1889

The Fairies
(*A child's song*)

Up the airy mountain,
  Down the rushy glen,
We daren't go a-hunting
  For fear of little men;
Wee folk, good folk,
  Trooping all together;
Green jacket, red cap,
  And white owl's feather!

Down along the rocky shore
  Some make their home,
They live on crispy pancakes
  Of yellow-tide foam;
Some in the reeds
  Of the black mountain-lakes,
With frogs for their watch-dogs,
  All night awake.

High on the hilltop
  The old King sits;
He is now so old and grey
  He's nigh lost his wits.
With a bridge of white mist
  Columbkill he crosses,
On his stately journeys
  From Slieveleague to Rosses;
Or going up with music
  On cold starry nights,
To sup with the Queen
  Of the gay Northern Lights.

They stole little Bridget
   For seven years long;
When she came down again
   Her friends were all gone.
They took her lightly back,
   Between the night and morrow,
They thought that she was fast asleep,
   But she was dead with sorrow.
They have kept her ever since
   Deep within the lakes,
On a bed of flag-leaves,
   Watching till she wakes.

By the craggy hillside,
   Through the mosses bare,
They have planted thorn-trees
   For pleasure here and there.
Is any man so daring
   As digs them up in spite,
He shall find their sharpest thorns
   In his bed at night.

Up the airy mountain,
   Down the rushy glen,
We daren't go a-hunting
   For fear of little men;
Wee folk, good folk,
   Trooping all together;
Green jacket, red cap,
   And white owl's feather!

A Wife

The wife sat thoughtfully turning over
  A book inscribed with the schoolgirl's name,
A tear, one tear, fell hot on the cover,
  So quickly closed when her husband came.

He came and he went away, it was nothing;
  With commonplace words upon either side;
But, just with the sound of the room-door shutting,
  A dreadful door in her soul stood wide.

Love she had read of in sweet romances,
  Love that could sorrow, but never fail;
Built her own palace of noble fancies,
  All the wide world like a fairy-tale.

Bleak and bitter and utterly doleful
  Spread to this woman her map of life:
Hour after hour she look'd in her soul, full
  Of deep dismay and turbulent strife.

Face in hands, she knelt on the carpet;
  The cloud was loosen'd, the storm-rain fell.
O! life has so much to wilder and warp it,
  One poor heart's day what poet could tell?

A Memory

Four ducks on a pond,
A grass-bank beyond,
A blue sky of spring,
White clouds on the wing;
What a little thing
To remember for years –
To remember with tears!

MATTHEW ARNOLD
1822–1888

Dover Beach

The sea is calm tonight.
The tide is full, the moon lies fair
Upon the straits; – on the French coast the light
Gleams and is gone; the cliffs of England stand,
Glimmering and vast, out in the tranquil bay.
Come to the window, sweet is the night-air!
Only, from the long line of spray
Where the sea meets the moon-blanch'd land,
Listen! you hear the grating roar
Of pebbles which the waves draw back, and fling,
At their return, up the high strand,
Begin, and cease, and then again begin,
With tremulous cadence slow, and bring
The eternal note of sadness in.

Sophocles long ago
Heard it on the Aegean, and it brought
Into his mind the turbid ebb and flow
Of human misery; we
Find also in the sound a thought,
Hearing it by this distant northern sea.

The Sea of Faith
Was once, too, at the full, and round earth's shore
Lay like the folds of a bright girdle furl'd.
But now I only hear
Its melancholy, long, withdrawing roar,
Retreating, to the breath
Of the night-wind, down the vast edges drear
And naked shingles of the world.

Ah, love, let us be true
To one another! for the world, which seems
To lie before us like a land of dreams,
So various, so beautiful, so new,

Hath really neither joy, nor love, nor light,
Nor certitude, nor peace, nor help for pain;
And we are here as on a darkling plain
Swept with confused alarms of struggle and flight,
Where ignorant armies clash by night.

The Forsaken Merman

Come, dear children, let us away;
Down and away below!
Now my brothers call from the bay,
Now the great winds shoreward blow,
Now the salt tides seaward flow;
Now the wild white horses play.
Champ and chafe and toss in the spray.
Children dear, let us away!
This way, this way!

Call her once before you go –
Call once yet!
In a voice that she will know:
'Margaret! Margaret!'
Children's voices should be dear
(Call once more) to a mother's ear;
Children's voices, wild with pain –
Surely she will come again!
Call her once and come away;
This way, this way!
'Mother dear, we cannot stay!
The wild white horses foam and fret.'
Margaret! Margaret!

Come, dear children, come away down;
Call no more!
One last look at the white-wall'd town
And the little grey church on the windy shore;
Then come down!
She will not come though you call all day;
Come away, come away!

Children dear, was it yesterday
We heard the sweet bells over the bay?
In the caverns where we lay,
Through the surf and through the swell,
The far-off sound of a silver bell?
Sand-strewn caverns, cool and deep,
Where the winds are all asleep;
Where the spent lights quiver and gleam,
Where the salt weed sways in the stream,
Where the sea-beasts, ranged all round,
Feed in the ooze of their pasture-ground;
Where the sea-snakes coil and twine,
Dry their mail and bask in the brine;
Where great whales come sailing by,
Sail and sail, with unshut eye,
Round the world for ever and aye?
When did music come this way?
Children dear, was it yesterday?

Children dear, was it yesterday
(Call yet once) that she went away?
Once she sat with you and me,
On a red gold throne in the heart of the sea,
And the youngest sat on her knee.
She comb'd its bright hair, and she tended it well,
When down swung the sound of a far-off bell.
She sigh'd, she look'd up through the clear green sea;
She said: 'I must go, for my kinsfolk pray
In the little grey church on the shore today.
'Twill be Eastertime in the world – ah me!
And I lose my poor soul, Merman! here with thee.'
I said: 'Go up, dear heart, through the waves;
Say thy prayer, and come back to the kind sea-caves!'
She smiled, she went up through the surf in the bay.
Children dear, was it yesterday?

Children dear, were we long alone?
'The sea grows stormy, the little ones moan;
Long prayers,' I said, 'in the world they say;

Come!' I said; and we rose through the surf in the bay.
We went up the beach, by the sandy down
Where the sea-stocks bloom, to the white-wall'd town;
Through the narrow paved streets, where all was still,
To the little grey church on the windy hill.
From the church came a murmur of folk at their prayers,
But we stood without in the cold blowing airs.
We climb'd on the graves, on the stones worn with rains,
And we gazed up the aisle through the small leaded panes.
She sat by the pillar; we saw her clear:
'Margaret, hist! come quick, we are here!
Dear heart,' I said, 'we are long alone;
The sea grows stormy, the little ones moan.'
But, ah, she gave me never a look,
For her eyes were seal'd to the holy book!
Loud prays the priest; shut stands the door.
Come away, children, call no more!
Come away, come down, call no more!

    Down, down, down!
Down to the depths of the sea!
She sits at her wheel in the humming town,
Singing most joyfully.
Hark what she sings: 'O joy, O joy,
For the humming street, and the child with its toy!
For the priest, and the bell, and the holy well;
For the wheel where I spun,
And the blessed light of the sun!'
And so she sings her fill,
Singing most joyfully,
Till the spindle drops from her hand,
And the whizzing wheel stands still.
She steals to the window, and looks at the sand,
And over the sand at the sea;
And her eyes are set in a stare;
And anon there breaks a sigh,
And anon there drops a tear,
From a sorrow-clouded eye,
And a heart sorrow-laden,
A long, long sigh;

For the cold strange eyes of a little Mermaiden
And the gleam of her golden hair.

   Come away, away children;
Come children, come down!
The hoarse wind blows coldly;
Lights shine in the town.
She will start from her slumber
When gusts shake the door;
She will hear the winds howling,
Will hear the waves roar.
We shall see, while above us
The waves roar and whirl,
A ceiling of amber,
A pavement of pearl.
Singing: 'Here came a mortal,
But faithless was she!
And alone dwell for ever
The kings of the sea.'

But, children, at midnight,
When soft the winds blow,
When clear falls the moonlight,
When springtides are low;
When sweet airs come seaward
From heaths starr'd with broom,
And high rocks throw mildly
On the blanch'd sands a gloom;
Up the still, glistening beaches,
Up the creeks we will hie,
Over banks of bright seaweed
The ebb-tide leaves dry.
We will gaze, from the sand-hills,
At the white, sleeping town;
At the church on the hillside –
And then come back down,
Singing: 'There dwells a loved one,
But cruel is she!
She left lonely for ever
The kings of the sea.'

JOHN BANCKS
1709–1751

London

Houses, churches, mixed together,
Streets unpleasant in all weather;
Prisons, palaces contiguous,
Gates, a bridge, the Thames irriguous.

Gaudy things enough to tempt ye,
Showy outsides, insides empty;
Bubbles, trades, mechanic arts,
Coaches, wheelbarrows and carts.

Warrants, bailiffs, bills unpaid,
Lords of laundresses afraid;
Rogues that nightly rob and shoot men,
Hangmen, aldermen and footmen.

Lawyers, poets, priests, physicians,
Noble, simple, all conditions:
Worth beneath a threadbare cover,
Villainy bedaubed all over.

Women black, red, fair and grey,
Prudes and such as never pray,
Handsome, ugly, noisy, still,
Some that will not, some that will.

Many a beau without a shilling,
Many a widow not unwilling;
Many a bargain, if you strike it:
This is London! How d'ye like it?

RICHARD HARRIS BARHAM
1788–1845

The Jackdaw of Rheims

The Jackdaw sat on the Cardinal's chair!
Bishop and abbot and prior were there;
    Many a monk and many a friar,
    Many a knight and many a squire,
With a great many more of lesser degree –
In sooth a goodly company;
And they served the Lord Primate on bended knee.
    Never I ween
    Was a prouder seen,
Read of in books, or dreamt of in dreams,
Than the Cardinal Lord Archbishop of Rheims!

    In and out
    Through the motley rout,
That little Jackdaw kept hopping about;
    Here and there
    Like a dog in a fair,
    Over comfits and cates,
    And dishes and plates,
Cowl and cope, and rochet and pall,
Mitre and crosier! he hopp'd upon all!
    With saucy air,
    He perch'd on the chair
Where, in state, the great Lord Cardinal sat
In the great Lord Cardinal's great red hat.
    And he peer'd in the face
    Of his Lordship's Grace
With a satisfied look, as if he would say,
'We two are the greatest folks here today!'
    And the priests, with awe,
    As such freaks they saw,
Said, 'The Devil must be in that little Jackdaw!'

The feast was over. The board was clear'd.
The flawns and the custards had all disappear'd.
And six little singing-boys – dear little souls!
In nice clean faces, and nice white stoles,
    Came, in order due,
    Two by two,
Marching that grand refectory through!
A nice little boy held a golden ewer,
Emboss'd and fill'd with water, as pure
As any that flows between Rheims and Namur,
Which a nice little boy stood ready to catch
In a fine golden hand-basin made to match.
Two nice little boys, rather more grown,
Carried lavender-water, and eau de Cologne;
And a nice little boy had a nice cake of soap,
Worthy of washing the hands of the Pope.
    One little boy more
    A napkin bore
Of the best white diaper, fringed with pink,
And a Cardinal's Hat mark'd in permanent ink.

The great Lord Cardinal turns at the sight
Of these nice little boys dress'd all in white.
    From his finger he draws
    His costly turquoise;
And, not thinking at all about little Jackdaws,
    Deposits it straight
    By the side of his plate,
While the nice little boys on his Eminence wait;
Till, when nobody's dreaming of any such thing,
That little Jackdaw hops off with the ring!

    There's a cry and a shout,
    And a deuce of a rout,
And nobody seems to know what they're about,
But the monks have their pockets all turn'd inside out.
    The friars are kneeling,
    And hunting, and feeling
The carpet, the floor, and the walls, and the ceiling.
    The Cardinal drew

Off each plum-colour'd shoe,
And left his red stockings exposed to the view;
He peeps, and he feels
In the toes and the heels.
They turn up the dishes. They turn up the plates.
They take up the poker and poke out the grates.
They turn up the rugs.
They examine the mugs.
But, no! – no such thing;
They can't find the ring!
And the Abbot declared that, 'when nobody twigg'd it,
Some rascal or other had popp'd in, and prigg'd it!'

The Cardinal rose with a dignified look.
He call'd for his candle, his bell, and his book!
In holy anger and pious grief,
He solemnly cursed that rascally thief!
He cursed him at board, he cursed him in bed,
From the sole of his foot to the crown of his head;
He cursed him in sleeping, that every night
He should dream of the Devil, and wake in a fright;
He cursed him in eating, he cursed him in drinking,
He cursed him in coughing, in sneezing, in winking;
He cursed him in sitting, in standing, in lying;
He cursed him in walking, in riding, in flying,
He cursed him in living, he cursed him in dying!
Never was heard such a terrible curse!
But what gave rise
To no little surprise –
Nobody seem'd one penny the worse!

The day was gone.
The night came on.
The monks and the friars they search'd till dawn,
When the Sacristan saw,
On crumpled claw,
Come limping a poor little lame Jackdaw!
No longer gay,
As on yesterday;
His feathers all seem'd to be turn'd the wrong way;

His pinions droop'd – he could hardly stand,
His head was as bald as the palm of your hand;
    His eyes so dim,
    So wasted each limb,
That, heedless of grammar, they all cried, 'That Him!
That's the scamp that has done this scandalous thing!
That's the thief that has got My Lord Cardinal's Ring!'

    The poor little Jackdaw,
    When the monks he saw,
Feebly gave vent to the ghost of a caw;
And turn'd his bald head, as much as to say,
'Pray, be so good as to walk this way!'
    Slower and slower
    He limp'd on before,
Till they came to the back of the belfry door,
    Where the first thing they saw,
    Midst the sticks and the straw,
Was the ring in the nest of that little Jackdaw!

Then the great Lord Cardinal call'd for his book
And off that terrible curse he took.
    The mute expression
    Served in lieu of confession,
And, being thus coupled with full restitution,
The Jackdaw got plenary absolution!
    When those words were heard,
    That poor little bird
Was so changed in a moment, 'twas really absurd.
    He grew sleek, and fat.
    In addition to that,
A fresh crop of feathers came thick as a mat!

    His tail waggled more
    Even than before.
But no longer it wagg'd with an impudent air.
No longer he perch'd on the Cardinal's chair.
    He hopp'd now about
    With a gait devout.
At Matins, at Vespers, he never was out.

And, so far from any more pilfering deeds,
He always seem'd telling the Confessor's beads.
If anyone lied, or if anyone swore,
Or slumber'd in prayer-time and happen'd to snore,
    That good Jackdaw
    Would give a great 'Caw!'
As much as to say, 'Don't do so any more!'
While many remark'd, as his manners they saw,
That they 'never had known such a pious Jackdaw!'
    He long lived the pride
    Of that countryside,
And at last in the odour of sanctity died;
    When, as words were too faint
    His merits to paint,
The Conclave determined to make him a Saint;
And on newly made Saints and Popes, as you know,
It's the custom, at Rome, new names to bestow,
So they canonised him by the name of 'Jim Crow'!

WILLIAM BARNES
1801–1886

Lowshot Light

As I went eastward, while the zun did zet,
His yollow light on bough by bough did sheen.

An' there, among the gil'cups by the knap,
Below the elems, cow by cow did sheen.

While after heäiry-headed horses' heels,
Wi' slowly-rollen wheels, the plough did sheen.

An' up among the vo'k upon the reäves,
One lovely feäce, wi' zunny brow, did sheen.

An' bright, vor that one feäce, the bough, an' cow,
An' plough, in my sweet fancy, now do sheen.

My Orcha'd in Linden Lea

'Ithin the woodlands, flow'ry gleäded,
    By the woak tree's mossy moot,
The sheenen grass-bleädes, timber-sheäded,
    Now do quiver under voot;
An' birds do whissle overhead,
An' water's bubblen in its bed,
An' there vor me the apple tree
Do leän down low in Linden Lea.

When leaves that leätely wer a-springen
    Now do feäde 'ithin the copse,
An' païnted birds do hush their zingen
    Up upon the timber's tops;
An' brown-leav'd fruit's a-turnen red,

In cloudless zunsheen, overhead,
Wi' fruit vor me, the apple tree
Do leän down low in Linden Lea.

Let other vo'k meäke money vaster
   In the aïr o' dark-room'd towns,
I don't dread a peevish meäster;
   Though noo man do heed my frowns,
I be free to goo abrode,
Or teäke ageän my homeward road
To where, vor me, the apple tree
Do leän down low in Linden Lea.

The Zilver-Weed

The zilver-weed upon the green,
   Out where my sons an' daughters plaÿ'd,
Had never time to bloom between
   The litty steps o' bwoy an' maïd.
But rwose-trees down along the wall,
   That then wer all the maïdens' ceäre,
An' all a-trimm'd an' traïn'd, did bear
   Their bloomen buds vrom Spring to Fall.

But now the zilver leaves do show
   To zummer day their goolden crown,
Wi' noo swift shoe-zoles' litty blow,
   In merry plaÿ to beät em down.
An' where vor years zome busy hand
   Did train the rwoses wide an' high;
Now woone by woone the trees do die,
   An' vew of all the row do stand.

RICHARD BARNFIELD
1574–1627

Sonnet

Here, hold this glove, this milk-white cheveril glove,
   Not quaintly overwrought with curious knots,
   Not deck'd with golden spangs nor silver spots,
Yet wholesome for thy hand as thou shalt prove.
Ah no, sweet boy, place this glove near thy heart,
   Wear it and lodge it still within thy breast;
   So shalt thou make me, most unhappy, blest,
So shalt thou rid my pain and ease my smart.
How can that be, perhaps thou wilt reply,
   A glove is for the hand, not for the heart,
   Nor can it well be prov'd by common art,
Nor reason's rule. To this thus answer I:
   If thou from glove dost take away the g
   Then glove is love, and so I send it thee.

THOMAS LOVELL BEDDOES
1803–1849

Dream-Pedlary

If there were dreams to sell,
  What would you buy?
Some cost a passing bell;
  Some a light sigh,
That shakes from Life's fresh crown
Only a roseleaf down.
If there were dreams to sell,
  Merry and sad to tell,
    And the crier rung the bell,
      What would you buy?

A cottage lone and still,
  With bowers nigh,
Shadowy, my woes to still,
  Until I die.
Such pearl from Life's fresh crown
Fain would I shake me down.
  Were dreams to have at will,
  This would best heal my ill,
    This would I buy.

But there were dreams to sell,
  Ill didst thou buy;
Life is a dream, they tell,
  Waking, to die.
Dreaming a dream to prize,
In wishing ghosts to rise;
  And, if I had the spell
  To call the buried, well,
    Which one would I?

If there are ghosts to raise,
   What shall I call,
Out of hell's murky haze,
   Heaven's blue pall?
Raise my loved long-lost boy
To lead me to his joy,
   There are no ghosts to raise;
   Out of death lead no ways;
     Vain is the call.

Know'st thou not ghosts to sue?
   No love thou hast.
Else lie, as I will do,
   And breathe thy last.
So out of Life's fresh crown
Fall like a roseleaf down.
   Thus are the ghosts to woo;
   Thus are all dreams made true,
     Ever to last!

HILAIRE BELLOC
1870–1953

Tarantella

Do you remember an Inn,
Miranda?
Do you remember an Inn?
And the tedding and the spreading
Of the straw for a bedding,
And the fleas that tease in the High Pyrenees,
And the wine that tasted of the tar?
And the cheers and the jeers of the young muleteers
(Under the vine of the dark verandah)?
Do you remember an Inn, Miranda,
Do you remember an Inn?

And the cheers and the jeers of the young muleteers
Who hadn't got a penny,
And who weren't paying any,
And the hammer at the doors and the Din?
And the Hip! Hop! Hap!
Of the clap
Of the hands to the twirl and the swirl
Of the girl gone chancing,
Glancing,
Dancing,
Backing and advancing,
Snapping of the clapper to the spin
Out and in –
And the Ting, Tong, Tang of the Guitar!
Do you remember an Inn,
Miranda?
Do you remember an Inn?

Never more;
Miranda,
Never more.
Only the high peaks hoar:

And Aragon a torrent at the door.
No sound
In the walls of the Halls where falls
The tread
Of the feet of the dead to the ground
No sound:
But the boom
Of the far Waterfall like Doom.

The Python

A Python I should not advise –
It needs a doctor for its eyes
And has the measles yearly.
However, if you feel inclined
To get one (to improve your mind,
And not from fashion merely),
Allow no music near its cage;
And when it flies into a rage
Chastise it, most severely.

I had an aunt in Yucatan
Who bought a Python from a man
    And kept it for a pet.
She died, because she never knew
Those simple little rules and few –
    The Snake is living yet.

On His Book

When I am dead I hope it may be said:
'His sins were scarlet but his books were read.'

On a General Election

The accursed power which stands on Privilege
(And goes with Women, and Champagne and Bridge)
Broke – and Democracy resumed her reign
(Which goes with Bridge, and Women and Champagne).

JOHN PEALE BISHOP
1892–1944

Speaking of Poetry

The ceremony must be found
that will wed Desdemona to the huge Moor.

      It is not enough –
to win the approval of the Senator
or to outwit his disapproval; honest Iago
can manage that: it is not enough. For then,
though she may pant again in his black arms
(his weight resilient as a Barbary stallion's)
she will be found
when the ambassadors of the Venetian state arrive
again smothered. The things have not been changed,
not in three hundred years.

      (Tupping is still tupping
though that particular word is obsolete.
Naturally, the ritual would not be in Latin.)

For though Othello had his blood from kings
his ancestry was barbarous, his ways African,
his speech uncouth. It must be remembered
that though he valued an embroidery –
three mulberries proper on a silk like silver –
it was not for the subtlety of the stitches,
but for the magic in it. Whereas, Desdemona

once contrived to imitate in needlework
her father's shield, and plucked it out
three times, to begin again, each time
with diminished colours. This is a small point
but indicative.

Desdemona was small and fair,
delicate as a grasshopper
at the tag-end of summer: a Venetian
to her noble fingertips.

O, it is not enough
that they should meet, naked, at dead of night
in a small inn on a dark canal. Procurers
less expert than Iago can arrange as much.

The ceremony must be found

Traditional, with all its symbols
ancient as the metaphors in dreams;
strange, with never before heard music; continuous
until the torches deaden at the bedroom door.

WILLIAM BLAKE
1757–1827

The Divine Image

To Mercy, Pity, Peace, and Love
All pray in their distress;
And to these virtues of delight
Return their thankfulness.

For Mercy, Pity, Peace, and Love
Is God, our Father dear,
And Mercy, Pity, Peace, and Love
Is man, His child and care.

For Mercy has a human heart,
Pity a human face,
And Love, the human form divine,
And Peace, the human dress.

Then every man, of every clime,
That prays in his distress,
Prays to the human form divine,
Love, Mercy, Pity, Peace.

And all must love the human form,
In heathen, Turk, or Jew;
Where Mercy, Love, and Pity dwell
There God is dwelling too.

The Tiger

Tiger! Tiger! burning bright
In the forests of the night,
What immortal hand or eye
Could frame thy fearful symmetry?

In what distant deeps or skies
Burnt the fire of thine eyes?
On what wings dare he aspire?
What the hand dare seize the fire?

And what shoulder, and what art,
Could twist the sinews of thy heart?
And when thy heart began to beat,
What dread hand? and what dread feet?

What the hammer? what the chain?
In what furnace was thy brain?
What the anvil? what dread grasp
Dare its deadly terrors clasp?

When the stars threw down their spears,
And water'd heaven with their tears,
Did he smile his work to see?
Did he who made the Lamb make thee?

Tiger! Tiger! burning bright
In the forests of the night,
What immortal hand or eye,
Dare frame thy fearful symmetry?

Infant Joy

'I have no name:
I am but two days old.'
What shall I call thee?
'I happy am,
Joy is my name.'
Sweet joy befall thee!

Pretty Joy!
Sweet Joy, but two days old.
Sweet Joy I call thee
Thou dost smile,
I sing the while,
Sweet joy befall thee!

The Clod and the Pebble

'Love seeketh not itself to please,
Nor for itself hath any care,
But for another gives its ease,
And builds a Heaven in Hell's despair.'

So sung a little Clod of Clay,
Trodden with the cattle's feet,
But a Pebble of the brook
Warbled out these metres meet:

'Love seeketh only Self to please,
To bind another to its delight,
Joys in another's loss of ease,
And builds a Hell in Heaven's despite.'

Eternity

He who bends to himself a Joy
Doth the wingèd life destroy;
But he who kisses the Joy as it flies
Lives in Eternity's sunrise.

A Poison Tree

I was angry with my friend:
I told my wrath, my wrath did end.
I was angry with my foe:
I told it not, my wrath did grow.

And I water'd it in fears,
Night and morning with my tears;
And I sunnèd it with smiles,
And with soft deceitful wiles.

And it grew both day and night,
Till it bore an apple bright;
And my foe beheld it shine,
And he knew that it was mine,

And into my garden stole
When the night had veil'd the pole:
In the morning glad I see
My foe outstretch'd beneath the tree.

The Question Answered

What is it men in women do require?
The lineaments of gratified desire.
What is it women do in men require?
The lineaments of gratified desire.

The Sick Rose

O Rose, thou art sick!
The invisible worm
That flies in the night,
In the howling storm,

Has found out thy bed
Of crimson joy;
And his dark secret love
Does thy life destroy.

London

I wander thro' each charter'd street,
Near where the charter'd Thames does flow,
And mark in every face I meet
Marks of weakness, marks of woe.

In every cry of every Man,
In every Infant's cry of fear,
In every voice, in every ban,
The mind-forg'd manacles I hear.

How the chimney-sweeper's cry
Every black'ning church appals;
And the hapless soldier's sigh
Runs in blood down palace walls.

But most thro' midnight streets I hear
How the youthful harlot's curse
Blasts the new-born infant's tear,
And blights with plagues the marriage hearse.

Ah! Sun-flower

Ah, Sun-flower! weary of time,
Who countest the steps of the sun;
Seeking after that sweet golden clime,
Where the traveller's journey is done;

Where the Youth pined away with desire,
And the pale Virgin shrouded in snow,
Arise from their graves, and aspire
Where my Sun-flower wishes to go.

Auguries of Innocence

To see a World in a grain of sand,
And a Heaven in a wild flower,
Hold Infinity in the palm of your hand,
And Eternity in an hour.
A robin redbreast in a cage
Puts all Heaven in a rage.
A dove-house fill'd with doves and pigeons
Shudders Hell thro' all its regions.
A dog starv'd at his master's gate
Predicts the ruin of the State.
A horse misus'd upon the road
Calls to Heaven for human blood.
Each outcry of the hunted hare

A fibre from the brain does tear.
A skylark wounded in the wing,
A cherubim does cease to sing.
The game-cock clipt and arm'd for fight
Does the rising sun affright.
Every wolf's and lion's howl
Raises from Hell a Human soul.
The wild deer, wandering here and there,
Keeps the Human soul from care.
The lamb misus'd breeds public strife,
And yet forgives the butcher's knife.
The bat that flits at close of eve
Has left the brain that won't believe.
The owl that calls upon the night
Speaks the unbeliever's fright.
He who shall hurt the little wren
Shall never be belov'd by men.
He who the ox to wrath has mov'd
Shall never be by woman lov'd.
The wanton boy that kills the fly
Shall feel the spider's enmity.
He who torments the chafer's sprite
Weaves a bower in endless night.
The caterpillar on the leaf
Repeats to thee thy mother's grief.
Kill not the moth nor butterfly,
For the Last Judgement draweth nigh.
He who shall train the horse to war
Shall never pass the polar bar.
The beggar's dog and widow's cat,
Feed them, and thou wilt grow fat.
The gnat that sings his summer's song
Poison gets from Slander's tongue.
The poison of the snake and newt
Is the sweat of Envy's foot.
The poison of the honey-bee
Is the artist's jealousy.
The prince's robes and beggar's rags
Are toadstools on the miser's bags.
A truth that's told with bad intent

Beats all the lies you can invent.
It is right it should be so;
Man was made for joy and woe;
And when this we rightly know,
Thro' the world we safely go.
Joy and woe are woven fine,
A clothing for the soul divine;
Under every grief and pine
Runs a joy with silken twine.
The babe is more than swaddling-bands;
Throughout all these human lands
Tools were made, and born were hands,
Every farmer understands.
Every tear from every eye
Becomes a babe in Eternity;
This is caught by Females bright,
And return'd to its own delight.
The bleat, the bark, bellow, and roar
Are waves that beat on Heaven's shore.
The babe that weeps the rod beneath
Writes revenge in realms of death.
The beggar's rags, fluttering in air,
Does to rags the heavens tear.
The soldier, arm'd with sword and gun,
Palsied strikes the summer's sun.
The poor man's farthing is worth more
Than all the gold on Afric's shore.
One mite wrung from the labourer's hands
Shall buy and sell the miser's lands
Or, if protected from on high,
Does that whole nation sell and buy.
He who mocks the infant's faith
Shall be mock'd in Age and Death.
He who shall teach the child to doubt
The rotting grave shall ne'er get out.
He who respects the infant's faith
Triumphs over Hell and Death.
The child's toys and the old man's reasons
Are the fruits of the two seasons.
The questioner, who sits so sly,

Shall never know how to reply.
He who replies to words of Doubt
Doth put the light of knowledge out.
The strongest poison ever known
Came from Caesar's laurel crown.
Nought can deform the human race
Like to the armour's iron brace.
When gold and gems adorn the plough
To peaceful arts shall Envy bow.
A riddle, or the cricket's cry,
Is to Doubt a fit reply.
The emmet's inch and eagle's mile
Make lame Philosophy to smile.
He who doubts from what he sees
Will ne'er believe, do what you please.
If the Sun and Moon should doubt,
They'd immediately go out.
To be in a passion you good may do,
But no good if a passion is in you.
The whore and gambler, by the state
Licensed, build that nation's fate.
The harlot's cry from street to street
Shall weave Old England's winding-sheet.
The winner's shout, the loser's curse,
Dance before dead England's hearse.
Every night and every morn
Some to misery are born.
Every morn and every night
Some are born to sweet delight.
Some are born to sweet delight,
Some are born to endless night.
We are led to believe a lie
When we see not thro' the eye,
Which was born in a night, to perish in a night,
When the Soul slept in beams of light.
God appears, and God is Light,
To those poor souls who dwell in Night;
But does a Human Form display
To those who dwell in realms of Day.

EDMUND BLUNDEN
1896–1974

The Midnight Skaters

The hop-poles stand in cones,
   The icy pond lurks under,
The pole-tops steeple to the thrones
   Of stars, sound gulfs of wonder;
But not the tallest there, 'tis said,
Could fathom to this pond's black bed.

Then is not death at watch
   Within those secret waters?
What wants he but to catch
   Earth's heedless sons and daughters?
With but a crystal parapet
Between, he has his engines set.

Then on, blood shouts, on, on,
   Twirl, wheel and whip above him,
Dance on this ball-floor thin and wan,
   Use him as though you love him;
Court him, elude him, reel and pass,
And let him hate you through the glass.

EDMUND BOLTON
c.1575–c.1633

A Palinode

As withereth the primrose by the river,
   As fadeth summer's sun from gliding fountains,
As vanisheth the light-blown bubble ever,
   As melteth snow upon the mossy mountains:
So melts, so vanisheth, so fades, so withers
   The rose, the shine, the bubble, and the snow

Of praise, pomp, glory, joy (which short life gathers),
  Fair praise, vain pomp, sweet glory, brittle joy.
The withered primrose by the mourning river,
  The faded summer's sun from weeping fountains,
The light-blown bubble vanished for ever,
  The molten snow upon the naked mountains,
Are emblems that the treasures we up-lay
Soon wither, vanish, fade, and melt away.

For as the snow, whose lawn did overspread
  The ambitious hills, which giant-like did threat
To pierce the heaven with their aspiring head,
  Naked and bare doth leave their craggy seat;
Whenas the bubble, which did empty fly
  The dalliance of the undiscerned wind,
On whose calm rolling waves it did rely,
  Hath shipwreck made, where it did dalliance find;
And when the sunshine which dissolved the snow,
  Coloured the bubble with a pleasant vary,
And made the rathe and timely primrose grow,
  Swarth clouds withdrawn (which longer time do tarry);
O, what is praise, pomp, glory, joy, but so
As shine by fountains, bubbles, flowers, or snow?

FRANCIS WILLIAM BOURDILLON
1852–1921

The night has a thousand eyes,
  And the day but one;
Yet the light of the bright world dies
  With the dying sun.

The mind has a thousand eyes,
  And the heart but one;
Yet the light of a whole life dies,
  When love is done.

NICHOLAS BRETON
*c.*1555–1626

In the merry month of May,
In a morn by break of day,
Forth I walked by the wood side,
Whereas May was in his pride.
There I spied all alone
Phyllida and Corydon.
Much ado there was, God wot,
He would love and she would not.
She said, never man was true;
He said none was false to you.
He said he had loved her long;
She said, love should have no wrong.
Corydon would kiss her then;
She said, maids must kiss no men,
Till they did for good and all.
Then she made the shepherd call
All the heavens to witness truth,
Never loved a truer youth.
Thus with many a pretty oath,
Yea and nay, and faith and troth,
Such as silly shepherds use,
When they will not love abuse,
Love, which had been long deluded,
Was with kisses sweet concluded:
And Phyllida with garlands gay
Was made the Lady of the May.

ROBERT BRIDGES
1844–1939

A Passer-by

Whither, O splendid ship, thy white sails crowding,
　　Leaning across the bosom of the urgent West,
That fearest nor sea rising nor sky clouding,
　　Whither away, fair rover, and what thy quest?
　　Ah! soon, when Winter has all our vales opprest,
When skies are cold and misty, and hail is hurling,
　　Wilt thou glide on the blue Pacific or rest
In a summer haven asleep, thy white sails furling.

I there before thee, in the country that well thou knowest,
　　Already arrived am inhaling the odorous air:
I watch thee enter unerringly where thou goest
　　And anchor, queen of the strange shipping there,
　　Thy sails for awnings spread, thy masts bare;
Nor is aught from the foaming reef to the snow-capped grandest
　　Peak, that is over the feathery palms more fair
Than thou, so upright, so stately, and still thou standest.

And yet, O splendid ship, unhailed and nameless,
　　I know not if, aiming a fancy, I rightly divine
That thou hast a purpose joyful, a courage blameless,
　　Thy port assured in a happier land than mine.
But for all I have given thee, beauty enough is thine,
As thou, aslant with trim tackle and shrouding,
　　From the proud nostril curve of a prow's line
In the offing scatterest foam, thy white sails crowding.

Awake, My Heart, To Be Loved, Awake, Awake!

Awake, my heart, to be loved, awake, awake!
The darkness silvers away, the morn doth break,
It leaps in the sky: unrisen lustres slake
The o'ertaken moon. Awake, O heart, awake!

She too that loveth awaketh and hopes for thee;
Her eyes already have sped the shades that flee,
Already they watch the path thy feet shall take:
Awake, O heart, to be loved, awake, awake!

And if thou tarry from her – if this could be –
She cometh herself, O heart, to be loved, to thee;
For thee would unashamèd herself forsake:
Awake to be loved, my heart, awake, awake!

Awake, the land is scattered with light, and see,
Uncanopied sleep is flying from field and tree:
And blossoming boughs of April in laughter shake;
Awake, O heart, to be loved, awake, awake!

Lo all things wake and tarry and look for thee:
She looketh and saith, 'O sun, now bring him to me.
Come more adored, O adored, for his coming's sake,
And awake my heart to be loved: awake, awake!'

I Love All Beauteous Things

I love all beauteous things,
    I seek and adore them;
God hath no better praise,
And man in his hasty days
    Is honoured for them.

I too will something make
    And joy in the making;
Altho' tomorrow it seem
Like the empty words of a dream
    Remembered on waking.

EMILY BRONTË
1818–1848

Shall Earth no more inspire thee,
Thou lonely dreamer now?
Since passion may not fire thee
Shall Nature cease to bow?

Thy mind is ever moving
In regions dark to thee;
Recall its useless roving –
Come back and dwell with me –

I know my mountain breezes
Enchant and soothe thee still.
l know my sunshine pleases
Despite thy wayward will –

When day with evening blending
Sinks from the summer sky,
I've seen thy spirit bending
In fond idolatry –

I've watched thee every hour.
I know my mighty sway –
l know my magic power
To drive thy griefs away –

Few hearts to mortals given
On earth so wildly pine
Yet none would ask a Heaven
More like the Earth than thine.

Then let my winds caress thee –
Thy comrade let me be.
Since nought beside can bless thee
Return and dwell with me –

No Coward Soul is Mine

No coward soul is mine,
No trembler in the world's storm-troubled sphere:
I see Heaven's glories shine,
And Faith shines equal, arming me from fear.

O God within my breast,
Almighty, ever-present Deity!
Life – that in me has rest,
As I – undying Life – have power in thee!

Vain are the thousand creeds
That move men's hearts, unutterably vain;
Worthless as withered weeds
Or idlest froth amid the boundless main

To waken doubt in one
Holding so fast by thy infinity;
So surely anchored on
The steadfast rock of Immortality.

With wide-embracing love
Thy spirit animates eternal years,
Pervades and broods above,
Changes, sustains, dissolves, creates and rears.

Though earth and moon were gone,
And suns and universe ceased to be,
And thou were left alone,
Every existence would exist in thee.

There is not room for Death,
Nor atom that his might could render void:
Since thou art Being and Breath,
And what thou art may never be destroyed.

RUPERT BROOKE
1887–1915

The Great Lover

I have been so great a lover: filled my days
So proudly with the splendour of Love's praise,
The pain, the calm, and the astonishment,
Desire illimitable, and still content,
And all dear names men use, to cheat despair,
For the perplexed and viewless streams that bear
Our hearts at random down the dark of life.
Now, ere the unthinking silence on that strife
Steals down, I would cheat drowsy Death so far,
My night shall be remembered for a star
That outshone all the suns of all men's days.
Shall I not crown them with immortal praise
Whom I have loved, who have given me, dared with me
High secrets, and in darkness knelt to see
The inenarrable godhead of delight?
Love is a flame – we have beaconed the world's night.
A city – and we have built it, these and I.
An emperor – we have taught the world to die.
So, for their sakes I loved, ere I go hence,
And the high cause of Love's magnificence,
And to keep loyalties young, I'll write those names
Golden for ever, eagles, crying flames,
And set them as a banner, that men may know,
To dare the generations, burn, and blow
Out on the wind of Time, shining and streaming . . .

These I have loved:
                    White plates and cups, clean-gleaming,
Ringed with blue lines; and feathery, faery dust;
Wet roofs, beneath the lamp-light; the strong crust
Of friendly bread; and many-tasting food;
Rainbows; and the blue bitter smoke of wood;
And radiant raindrops couching in cool flowers;

And flowers themselves, that sway through sunny hours,
Dreaming of moths that drink them under the moon;
Then, the cool kindliness of sheets, that soon
Smooth away trouble; and the rough male kiss
Of blankets; grainy wood; live hair that is
Shining and free; blue-massing clouds; the keen
Unpassioned beauty of a great machine;
The benison of hot water; furs to touch;
The good smell of old clothes; and other such –
The comfortable smell of friendly fingers,
Hair's fragrance, and the musty reek that lingers
About dead leaves and last year's ferns . . .
                                                    Dear names,
And a thousand others throng to me! Royal flames;
Sweet water's dimpling laugh from tap or spring;
Holes in the ground; and voices that do sing;
Voices in laughter, too; and body's pain,
Soon turned to peace; and the deep-panting train;
Firm sands; the little dulling edge of foam
That browns and dwindles as the wave goes home;
And washen stones, gay for an hour; the cold
Graveness of iron; moist black earthen mould;
Sleep; and high places; footprints in the dew;
And oaks; and brown horse-chestnuts, glossy-new;
And new-peeled sticks; and shining pools on grass –
All these have been my loves. And these shall pass,
Whatever passes not, in the great hour,
Nor all my passion, all my prayers, have power
To hold them with me through the gate of Death.
They'll play deserter, turn with the traitor breath,
Break the high bond we made, and sell Love's trust
And sacramented covenant to the dust.
Oh, never a doubt but, somewhere, I shall wake,
And give what's left of love again, and make
New friends, now strangers . . .
                                        But the best I've known
Stays here, and changes, breaks, grows old, is blown
About the winds of the world, and fades from brains
Of living men, and dies.
                                        Nothing remains

O dear my loves, O faithless, once again
This one last gift I give: that after men
Shall know, and later lovers, far-removed,
Praise you, 'All these were lovely'; say, 'He loved.'

The Soldier

If I should die, think only this of me:
   That there's some corner of a foreign field
That is for ever England. There shall be
   In that rich earth a richer dust concealed;
A dust whom England bore, shaped, made aware,
   Gave, once, her flowers to love, her ways to roam,
A body of England's, breathing English air,
   Washed by the rivers, blest by suns of home.

And think, this heart, all evil shed away,
   A pulse in the eternal mind, no less
      Gives somewhere back the thoughts by England given;
Her sights and sounds; dreams happy as her day;
   And laughter, learnt of friends; and gentleness,
      In hearts at peace, under an English heaven.

The Old Vicarage, Grantchester
(Café des Westens, Berlin, May 1912)

Just now the lilac is in bloom,
All before my little room;
And in my flower-beds, I think,
Smile the carnation and the pink;
And down the borders, well I know,
The poppy and the pansy blow . . .
Oh! there the chestnuts, summer through,
Beside the river make for you
A tunnel of green gloom, and sleep
Deeply above; and green and deep
The stream mysterious glides beneath,
Green as a dream and deep as death.
– Oh, damn! I know it! and I know
How the May fields all golden show,
And when the day is young and sweet,
Gild gloriously the bare feet
That run to bathe . . .
                              Du lieber Gott!

Here am I, sweating, sick, and hot,
And there the shadowed waters fresh
Lean up to embrace the naked flesh.
Temperamentvoll German Jews
Drink beer around – and *there* the dews
Are soft beneath a morn of gold.
Here tulips bloom as they are told;
Unkempt about those hedges blows
An English unofficial rose;
And there the unregulated sun
Slopes down to rest when day is done,
And wakes a vague unpunctual star,
A slippered Hesper; and there are
Meads towards Haslingfield and Coton
Where *das Betreten's* not *verboten*.

εἴθε γενοίμην . . would I were
In Grantchester, in Grantchester! –
Some, it may be, can get in touch
With Nature there, or Earth, or such.
And clever modern men have seen
A Faun a-peeping through the green,
And felt the Classics were not dead,
To glimpse a Naiad's reedy head,
Or hear the Goat-foot piping low . . .
But these are things I do not know.
I only know that you may lie
Day long and watch the Cambridge sky,
And, flower-lulled in sleepy grass,
Hear the cool lapse of hours pass,
Until the centuries blend and blur
In Grantchester, in Grantchester . . .
Still in the dawnlit waters cool
His ghostly Lordship swims his pool,
And tries the strokes, essays the tricks
Long learnt on Hellespont, or Styx.
Dan Chaucer hears his river still
Chatter beneath a phantom mill.
Tennyson notes, with studious eye,
How Cambridge waters hurry by . . .
And in that garden, black and white,
Creep whispers through the grass all night;
And spectral dance, before the dawn,
A hundred Vicars down the lawn;
Curates, long dust, will come and go
On lissom, clerical, printless toe;
And oft between the boughs is seen
The sly shade of a Rural Dean . . .
Till, at a shiver in the skies,
Vanishing with Satanic cries,
The prim ecclesiastic rout
Leaves but a startled sleeper-out,
Grey heavens, the first bird's drowsy calls,
The falling house that never falls.

God! I will pack, and take a train,
And get me to England once again!
For England's the one land, I know,
Where men with Splendid Hearts may go;
And Cambridgeshire, of all England,
The shire for Men who Understand;
And of *that* district I prefer
The lovely hamlet Grantchester.
For Cambridge people rarely smile,
Being urban, squat, and packed with guile;
And Royston men in the far South
Are black and fierce and strange of mouth;
At Over they fling oaths at one,
And worse than oaths at Trumpington,
And Ditton girls are mean and dirty,
And there's none in Harston under thirty,
And folks in Shelford and those parts
Have twisted lips and twisted hearts,
And Barton men make Cockney rhymes,
And Coton's full of nameless crimes,
And things are done you'd not believe
At Madingley, on Christmas Eve.
Strong men have run for miles and miles,
When one from Cherry Hinton smiles;
Strong men have blanched, and shot their wives,
Rather than send them to St Ives;
Strong men have cried like babes, bydam,
To hear what happened at Babraham.
But Grantchester! ah, Grantchester!
There's peace and holy quiet there,
Great clouds along pacific skies,
And men and women with straight eyes,

Lithe children lovelier than a dream,
A bosky wood, a slumbrous stream,
And little kindly winds that creep
Round twilight corners, half asleep.
In Grantchester their skins are white;
They bathe by day, they bathe by night;

The women there do all they ought;
The men observe the Rules of Thought.
They love the Good; they worship Truth;
They laugh uproariously in youth;
(And when they get to feeling old,
They up and shoot themselves, I'm told) . . .

Ah God! to see the branches stir
Across the moon at Grantchester!
To smell the thrilling-sweet and rotten
Unforgettable, unforgotten
River-smell, and hear the breeze
Sobbing in the little trees.
Say, do the elm-clumps greatly stand
Still guardians of that holy land?
The chestnuts shade, in reverend dream,
The yet unacademic stream?
Is dawn a secret shy and cold
Anadyomene, silver-gold?
And sunset still a golden sea
From Haslingfield to Madingley?
And after, ere the night is born,
Do hares come out about the corn?
Oh, is the water sweet and cool,
Gentle and brown, above the pool?
And laughs the immortal river still
Under the mill, under the mill?
Say, is there Beauty yet to find?
And Certainty? and Quiet kind?
Deep meadows yet, for to forget
The lies, and truths, and pain? . . . oh! yet
Stands the Church clock at ten to three?
And is there honey still for tea?

ELIZABETH BARRETT BROWNING
1806–1861

from *Sonnets from the Portuguese*

1

I thought once how Theocritus had sung
Of the sweet years, the dear and wished-for years,
Who each one in a gracious hand appears
To bear a gift for mortals, old or young:
And, as I mused it in his antique tongue,
I saw, in gradual vision through my tears,
The sweet, sad years, the melancholy years,
Those of my own life, who by turns had flung
A shadow across me. Straightway I was 'ware,
So weeping, how a mystic Shape did move
Behind me, and drew me backward by the hair;
And a voice said in mystery, while I strove –
'Guess now who holds thee?' – 'Death,' I said. But, there,
The silver answer rang – 'Not Death, but Love.'

14

If thou must love me, let it be for nought
Except for love's sake only. Do not say,
'I love her for her smile – her look – her way
Of speaking gently – for a trick of thought
That falls in well with mine, and certes brought
A sense of pleasant ease on such a day' –
For these things in themselves, belovèd, may
Be changed, or change for thee – and love, so wrought,
May be unwrought so. Neither love me for
Thine own dear pity's wiping my cheeks dry –
A creature might forget to weep, who bore
Thy comfort long, and lose thy love thereby!
But love me for love's sake, that evermore
Thou may'st love on, through love's eternity.

43

How do I love thee? Let me count the ways.
I love thee to the depth and breadth and height
My soul can reach, when feeling out of sight
For the ends of Being and ideal Grace.
I love thee to the level of everyday's
Most quiet need, by sun and candlelight.
I love thee freely, as men strive for Right;
I love thee purely, as they turn from Praise.
I love thee with the passion put to use
In my old griefs, and with my childhood's faith.
I love thee with a love I seemed to lose
With my lost saints – I love thee with the breath,
Smiles, tears, of all my life! – and, if God choose,
I shall but love thee better after death.

ROBERT BROWNING
1812–1889

Home Thoughts from Abroad

1

Oh, to be in England
Now that April's there,
And whoever wakes in England
Sees, some morning, unaware,
That the lowest boughs and the brushwood sheaf
Round the elm-tree bole are in tiny leaf,
While the chaffinch sings on the orchard bough
In England – now!

2

And after April, when May follows,
And the whitethroat builds, and all the swallows –
Hark! where my blossomed pear-tree in the hedge
Leans to the field and scatters on the clover
Blossoms and dewdrops – at the bent spray's edge –
That's the wise thrush; he sings each song twice over,
Lest you should think he never could recapture
The first fine careless rapture!
And though the fields look rough with hoary dew,
All will be gay when noontide wakes anew
The buttercups, the little children's dower,
 – Far brighter than this gaudy melon-flower!

Home Thoughts from the Sea

Nobly, nobly Cape Saint Vincent to the north-west died
    away;
Sunset ran, one glorious blood-red, reeking into Cadiz Bay;
Bluish 'mid the burning water, full in face Trafalgar lay;
In the dimmest north-east distance, dawned Gibraltar grand
    and grey;
'Here and here did England help me – how can I help
    England?' – say,
Whoso turns as I, this evening, turn to God to praise and
    pray,
While Jove's planet rises yonder, silent over Africa.

My Last Duchess

FERRARA

That's my last Duchess painted on the wall,
Looking as if she were alive; I call
That piece a wonder, now: Frà Pandolf's hands
Worked busily a day, and there she stands.
Will't please you sit and look at her? I said
'Frà Pandolf' by design, for never read
Strangers like you that pictured countenance,
The depth and passion of its earnest glance,
But to myself they turned (since none puts by
The curtain I have drawn for you, but I)
And seemed as they would ask me, if they durst,
How such a glance came there; so, not the first
Are you to turn and ask thus. Sir, 'twas not
Her husband's presence only, called that spot
Of joy into the Duchess' cheek: perhaps
Frà Pandolf chanced to say, 'Her mantle laps
Over my lady's wrist too much,' or, 'Paint
Must never hope to reproduce the faint
Half-flush that dies along her throat;' such stuff
Was courtesy, she thought, and cause enough

For calling up that spot of joy. She had
A heart . . . how shall I say? . . too soon made glad,
Too easily impressed; she liked whate'er
She looked on, and her looks went everywhere.
Sir, 'twas all one! My favour at her breast,
The dropping of the daylight in the west,
The bough of cherries some officious fool
Broke in the orchard for her, the white mule
She rode with round the terrace – all and each
Would draw from her alike the approving speech,
Or blush, at least. She thanked men – good; but thanked
Somehow . . . I know not how . . . as if she ranked
My gift of a nine-hundred-years-old name
With anybody's gift. Who'd stoop to blame
This sort of trifling? Even had you skill
In speech – (which I have not) – to make your will
Quite clear to such an one, and say, 'Just this
Or that in you disgusts me; here you miss,
Or there exceed the mark' – and if she let
Herself be lessoned so, nor plainly set
Her wits to yours, forsooth, and made excuse
 – E'en then would be some stooping; and I choose
Never to stoop. Oh, sir, she smiled, no doubt
Whene'er I passed her; but who passed without
Much the same smile? This grew; I gave commands;
Then all smiles stopped together. There she stands
As if alive. Will't please you rise? We'll meet
The company below, then. I repeat,
The Count your master's known munificence
Is ample warrant that no just pretence
Of mine for dowry will be disallowed;
Though his fair daughter's self, as I avowed
At starting, is my object. Nay, we'll go
Together down, sir! Notice Neptune, tho',
Taming a sea-horse, thought a rarity,
Which Claus of Innsbruck cast in bronze for me.

PORPHYRIA'S LOVER

The rain set early in tonight,
    The sullen wind was soon awake,
It tore the elm-tops down for spite,
    And did its worst to vex the lake,
I listened with heart fit to break;
When glided in Porphyria: straight
    She shut the cold out and the storm,
And kneeled and made the cheerless grate
    Blaze up, and all the cottage warm;
Which done, she rose, and from her form
Withdrew the dripping cloak and shawl,
    And laid her soiled gloves by, untied
Her hat and let the damp hair fall,
    And, last, she sat down by my side
And called me. When no voice replied,
She put my arm about her waist,
    And made her smooth white shoulder bare,
And all her yellow hair displaced,
    And, stooping, made my cheek lie there,
And spread o'er all her yellow hair,
Murmuring how she loved me; she
    Too weak, for all her heart's endeavour,
To set its struggling passion free
    From pride, and vainer ties dissever,
And give herself to me for ever:
But passion sometimes would prevail,
    Nor could tonight's gay feast restrain
A sudden thought of one so pale
    For love of her, and all in vain;
So, she was come through wind and rain.
Be sure I looked up at her eyes
    Proud, very proud; at last I knew
Porphyria worshipped me; surprise
    Made my heart swell, and still it grew
While I debated what to do.
That moment she was mine, mine, fair,
    Perfectly pure and good: I found
A thing to do, and all her hair

In one long yellow string I wound
Three times her little throat around,
And strangled her. No pain felt she;
    I am quite sure she felt no pain.
As a shut bud that holds a bee
    I warily oped her lids; again
Laughed the blue eyes without a stain.
And I untightened next the tress
    About her neck; her cheek once more
Blushed bright beneath my burning kiss:
    I propped her head up as before,
Only, this time *my* shoulder bore
Her head, which droops upon it still:
    The smiling rosy little head,
So glad it has its utmost will,
    That all it scorned at once is fled,
And I, its love, am gained instead!
Porphyria's love: she guessed not how
    Her darling one wish would be heard.
And thus we sit together now,
    And all night long we have not stirred,
And yet God has not said a word!

Meeting at Night

1

The grey sea and the long black land;
And the yellow half-moon large and low;
And the startled little waves that leap
In fiery ringlets from their sleep,
As I gain the cove with pushing prow,
And quench its speed in the slushy sand.

2

Then a mile of warm sea-scented beach;
Three fields to cross till a farm appears;
A tap at the pane, the quick sharp scratch

And blue spurt of a lighted match,
And a voice less loud, thro' its joys and fears,
Than the two hearts beating each to each!

Parting at Morning

Round the cape of a sudden came the sea,
And the sun looked over the mountain's rim –
And straight was a path of gold for him,
And the need of a world of men for me.

To Edward FitzGerald

I chanced upon a new book yesterday:
I opened it, and where my finger lay
    'Twixt page and uncut page these words I read –
Some six or seven at most – and learned thereby
that you, FitzGerald, whom by ear and eye
    She never knew, 'thanked God my wife was dead'.

Ay, dead! and were yourself alive, good Fitz,
How to return you thanks would task my wits:
    Kicking you seems the common lot of curs –
While more appropriate greeting lends you grace:
Surely to spit there glorifies your face –
    Spitting – from lips once sanctified by Hers.

Rhyme for a Child Viewing a Naked Venus in a Painting of 'The Judgement of Paris'

He gazed and gazed and gazed and gazed,
Amazed, amazed, amazed, amazed.

JOHN BUNYAN
1628–1688

Valiant's Song

Who would true valour see,
Let him come hither;
One here will constant be,
Come wind, come weather.
There's no discouragement
Shall make him once relent
His first avowed intent
To be a pilgrim.

Whoso beset him round
With dismal stories
Do but themselves confound:
His strength the more is.
No lion can him fright,
He'll with a giant fight,
But he will have a right
To be a pilgrim.

Hobgoblin nor foul fiend
Can daunt his spirit;
He knows he at the end
Shall life inherit.
Then fancies fly away,
He'll fear not what men say,
He'll labour night and day
To be a pilgrim.

ROBERT BURNS
1759–1796

To a Mouse

Wee, sleekit, cow'rin', tim'rous beastie,
O what a panic's in thy breastie!
Thou need no start awa' sae hasty,
   Wi' bickering brattle![1]
I wad be laith to rin an' chase thee
   Wi' murd'ring pattle![2]

I'm truly sorry man's dominion
Has broken Nature's social union,
An' justifies that ill opinion
   Which mak's thee startle
At me, thy poor earth-born companion,
   An' fellow-mortal!

I doubt na, whiles, but thou may thieve;
What then? poor beastie, thou maun live!
A daimen-icker[3] in a thrave[4]
   'S a sma' request:
I'll get a blessin' wi' the lave,[5]
   And never miss't!

Thy wee bit housie, too, in ruin!
Its silly wa's the win's are strewin'!
An' naething, now, to big a new ane,
   O' foggage[6] green!
An' bleak December's winds ensuin',
   Baith snell[7] an' keen!

---

1 scurrying rush   2 plough-spade   3 odd ear of corn   4 two dozen sheaves
   5 remainder   6 aftermath   7 biting

Thou saw the fields laid bare and waste,
An' weary winter comin' fast,
An' cozie here, beneath the blast,
       Thou thought to dwell,
Till crash! the cruel coulter pass'd
       Out thro' thy cell.

That wee bit heap o' leaves an' stibble
Has cost thee mony a weary nibble!
Now thou's turn'd out, for a' thy trouble,
       But[8] house or hald,[9]
To thole[10] the winter's sleety dribble,
       An' cranreuch cauld![11]

But, Mousie, thou art no thy lane[12]
In proving foresight may be vain:
The best laid schemes o' mice an' men
       Gang aft a-gley,[13]
An' lea'e us nought but grief an' pain
       For promis'd joy.

Still thou art blest, compar'd wi' me!
The present only toucheth thee:
But, och! I backward cast my ee
       On prospects drear!
An' forward tho' I canna see,
       I guess an' fear!

8 without   9 shelter   10 bear   11 hoar-frost   12 alone   13 awry

Auld Lang Syne

Should auld acquaintance be forgot
 And never brought to mind?
Should auld acquaintance be forgot,
 And auld lang syne!
For auld lang syne, my dear,
 For auld lang syne,
We'll tak a cup o' kindness yet
 For auld lang syne.

And surely ye'll be your pint stowp![1]
 And surely I'll be mine!
And we'll tak a cup o' kindness yet,
 For auld lang syne.
For auld lang syne, my dear, &c.

We twa hae run about the braes,
 And pou'd[2] the gowans[3] fine;
But we've wander'd mony a weary fitt,[4]
 Sin auld lang syne.
For auld lang syne, my dear, &c.

We twa hae paidl'd in the burn,
 Frae morning sun till dine;[5]
But seas between us braid hae roar'd,
 Sin auld lang syne.
For auld lang syne, my dear, &c.

And there's a hand, my trusty fiere![6]
 And gie's a hand o' thine!
And we'll tak a right gude-willie waught,[7]
 For auld lang syne.
For auld lang syne, my dear, &c.

1 pay for your own drink 2 pulled 3 daisies 4 foot 5 dinnertime
6 companion 7 a drink of goodwill or friendship

To a Haggis

Fair fa'[1] your honest, sonsie[2] face,
Great Chieftain o' the Puddin-race!
Aboon them a' ye tak your place,
          Painch,[3] tripe, or thairm:[4]
Weel are ye wordy[5] of a grace
          As lang's my arm.

The groaning trencher there ye fill,
Your hurdies[6] like a distant hill,
Your pin wad help to mend a mill
          In time o' need,
While thro' your pores the dews distil
          Like amber bead.

His knife see Rustic-labour dight,[7]
An' cut you up wi' ready slight,[8]
Trenching your gushing entrails bright
          Like onie ditch;
And then, O what a glorious sight,
          Warm-reekin, rich!

Then, horn[9] for horn they stretch an' strive,
Deil tak the hindmost, on they drive,
Till a' their weel-swall'd kytes[10] belyve[11]
          Are bent like drums;
Then auld Guidman, maist like to rive,[12]
          Bethankit hums.

Is there that owre his French *ragout,*
Or *olio* that wad staw[13] a sow,
Or *fricassee* wad mak her spew
          Wi' perfect sconner[14]
Looks down wi' sneering, scornfu' view
          On sic a dinner?

1 blessings on   2 jolly   3 paunch   4 small guts   5 worthy   6 buttocks
7 wipe   8 skill   9 horn-spoon   10 well-swelled stomachs   11 by and by
12 burst   13 surfeit   14 disgust

Poor devil! see him owre his trash,
As feckless as a wither'd rash,[15]
His spindle shank a guid whiplash,
       His nieve[16] a nit;[17]
Thro' bluidy flood or field to dash,
       O how unfit!

But mark the Rustic, haggis-fed,
The trembling earth resounds his tread,
Clap in his walie nieve[18] a blade,
       He'll mak it whissle;
An' legs, an' arms, an' heads will sned,[19]
       Like taps o' thrissle.[20]

Ye Pow'rs wha mak mankind your care,
And dish them out their bill o' fare,
Auld Scotland wants nae skinking[21] ware,
       That jaups[22] in luggies;[23]
But, if ye wish her gratefu' prayer,
       Gie her a Haggis!

15 rush   16 fist   17 nut   18 ample fist   19 lop   20 tops of thistle
21 watery   22 splashes   23 wooden bowls

Tam o' Shanter
A Tale

Of Brownyis and of Bogillis full is this buke.

GAWIN DOUGLAS

When chapman billies[1] leave the street,
And drouthy[2] neebors, neebors meet,
As market-days are wearing late,
An' folk begin to tak the gate;[3]
While we sit bousing at the nappy,[4]
An' getting fou[5] and unco[6] happy,
We think na[7] on the lang Scots miles,
The mosses, waters, slaps,[8] and styles,
That lie between us and our hame,
Whare sits our sulky sullen dame,
Gathering her brows like gathering storm,
Nursing her wrath to keep it warm.

    This truth fand[9] honest Tam o' Shanter,
As he frae Ayr ae night did canter
(Auld Ayr, wham ne'er a town surpasses,
For honest men and bonny lasses).

    O Tam! had'st thou but been sae wise,
As ta'en thy ain wife Kate's advice!
She tauld thee weel thou was a skellum,[10]
A blethering,[11] blustering, a drunken blellum;[12]
That frae November till October,
Ae market-day thou was nae sober;
That ilka melder,[13] wi' the miller,
Thou sat as lang as thou had siller;
That ev'ry naig was ca'ed a shoe on,[14]
The smith and thee got roaring fou on;
That at the Lord's house, even on Sunday,
Thou drank wi' Kirkton Jean till Monday
She prophesied that, late or soon,

1 packman fellows   2 thirsty   3 road   4 ale   5 drunk   6 extra   7 not
8 gaps in walls   9 found   10 rogue   11 chattering   12 boaster
13 every meal-grinding   14 every horse shod

Thou would be found deep drown'd in Doon;
Or catch'd wi' warlocks in the mirk,
By Alloway's auld haunted kirk.

    Ah, gentle dames! it gars[1] me greet,[2]
To think how mony counsels sweet,
How mony lengthen'd sage advices,
The husband frae the wife despises!

    But to our tale: Ae market-night,
Tam had got planted unco right;
Fast by an ingle, bleezing finely,
Wi' reaming swats,[3] that drank divinely;
And at his elbow, Souter[4] Johnny,
His ancient, trusty, drouthy[5] crony;
Tam lo'ed him like a vera brither;
They had been fou for weeks thegither.
The night drave on wi' sangs and clatter;[6]
And ay the ale was growing better:
The landlady and Tam grew gracious,
Wi' favours, secret, sweet, and precious:
The Souter tauld his queerest stories;
The landlord's laugh was ready chorus:
The storm without might rair and rustle,
Tam did na mind the storm a whistle.

    Care, mad to see a man sae happy,
E'en drown'd himsel amang the nappy:[7]
As bees flee hame wi' lades o' treasure,
The minutes wing'd their way wi' pleasure:
Kings may be blest, but Tam was glorious,
O'er a' the ills o' life victorious!

    But pleasures are like poppies spread,
You seize the flow'r, its bloom is shed;
Or like the snow falls in the river,
A moment white – then melts for ever;
Or like the borealis race,
That flit ere you can point their place;
Or like the rainbow's lovely form

1 makes   2 weep   3 frothing ale   4 cobbler   5 thirsty   6 gossip
7 drink

Evanishing amid the storm.
Nae man can tether time or tide;
The hour approaches Tam maun ride;
That hour, o' night's black arch the key-stane,
That dreary hour he mounts his beast in;
And sic a night he taks the road in,
As ne'er poor sinner was abroad in.

   The wind blew as 'twad[1] blawn its last;
The rattling showers rose on the blast;
The speedy gleams the darkness swallow'd;
Loud, deep, and lang the thunder bellow'd:
That night, a child might understand,
The Deil had business on his hand.

   Weel mounted on his grey mare, Meg,
A better never lifted leg,
Tam skelpit[2] on thro' dub[3] and mire,
Despising wind, and rain, and fire;
Whiles holding fast his gude blue bonnet;
Whiles crooning o'er some auld Scots sonnet;[4]
Whiles glowring[5] round wi' prudent cares,
Lest bogles catch him unawares:
Kirk-Alloway was drawing nigh,
Whare ghaists and houlets[6] nightly cry.

   By this time he was cross the ford,
Whare, in the snaw, the chapman smoor'd;[7]
And past the birks[8] and meikle stane,
Whare drunken Charlie brak's neck-bane;
And thro' the whins,[9] and by the cairn,
Whare hunters fand the murder'd bairn;
And near the thorn, aboon the well,
Whare Mungo's mither hang'd hersel.
Before him Doon pours all his floods;
The doubling storm roars thro' the woods;
The lightnings flash from pole to pole;
Near and more near the thunders roll:
When, glimmering thro' the groaning trees,

1 as if it would blow 2 dashed 3 puddle 4 song 5 staring 6 owls
7 smothered 8 birches 9 furze

Kirk-Alloway seem'd in a bleeze;
Thro' ilka bore[1] the beams were glancing;
And loud resounded mirth and dancing. –
    Inspiring bold John Barleycorn!
What dangers thou can make us scorn!
Wi' tippeny,[2] we fear nae evil;
Wi' usquabae,[3] we'll face the devil!
The swats sae ream'd in Tammy's noddle,
Fair play, he car'd na deils a boddle.[4]
But Maggie stood right sair astonish'd,
Till, by the heel and hand admonish'd,
She ventur'd forward on the light;
And, wow! Tam saw an unco sight!
Warlocks and witches in a dance;
Nae cotillion, brent[5] new frae France,
But hornpipes, jigs, strathspeys, and reels,
Put life and mettle in their heels.
A winnock-bunker[6] in the east,
There sat auld Nick, in shape o' beast;
A towzie tyke,[7] black, grim, and large,
To gie them music was his charge:
He screw'd the pipes and gart[8] them skirl,
Till roof and rafters a' did dirl.[9]
Coffins stood round, like open presses,
That shaw'd the dead in their last dresses;
And by some devilish cantraip slight[10]
Each in its cauld hand held a light –
By which heroic Tam was able
To note upon the haly[11] table,
A murderer's banes in gibbet airns;[12]
Twa span-lang, wee, unchristen'd bairns;
A thief, new-cutted frae the rape,[13]
Wi' his last gasp his gab did gape;
Five tomahawks, wi' blude red-rusted;
Five scymitars, wi' murder crusted;
A garter, which a babe had strangled;

1 chink 2 ale 3 whisky 4 farthing 5 brand 6 window-seat
7 shaggy dog 8 made 9 rattle 10 weird trick 11 holy 12 irons
13 rope

A knife, a father's throat had mangled,
Whom his ain son o' life bereft,
The grey hairs yet stack to the heft;
Wi' mair o' horrible and awefu',
Which even to name wad be unlawfu'.

   As Tammie glower'd, amaz'd, and curious,
The mirth and fun grew fast and furious:
The piper loud and louder blew;
The dancers quick and quicker flew;
They reel'd, they set, they cross'd, they cleekit,[1]
Till ilka carlin[2] swat and reekit,[3]
And coost[4] her duddies[5] to the wark,
And linket[6] at it in her sark![7]

   Now, Tam, O Tam! had thae[8] been queans,[9]
A' plump and strapping in their teens,
Their sarks, instead o' creeshie[10] flannen,
Been snaw-white seventeen hunder linnen!
Thir[11] breeks o' mine, my only pair,
That ance[12] were plush, o' gude blue hair,
I wad hae gi'en them off my hurdies,[13]
For ae blink[14] o' the bonie burdies!

   But wither'd beldams, auld and droll,
Rigwoodie[15] hags wad spean[16] a foal,
Lowping[17] and flinging on a crummock,[18]
I wonder didna turn thy stomach.

   But Tam kend what was what fu' brawlie,[19]
There was ae winsome wench and wawlie,[20]
That night enlisted in the core,[21]
Lang after kend on Carrick shore!
(For mony a beast to dead she shot
And perish'd mony a bonnie boat,
And shook baith[22] meikle[23] corn and bear,[24]
And kept the countryside in fear.)
Her cutty sark,[25] o' Paisley harn,[26]

---

1 joined hands   2 witch   3 sweated and steamed   4 cast off   5 rags
6 tripped   7 shift   8 those   9 girls   10 greasy   11 these   12 once
13 buttocks   14 one glimpse   15 scraggy   16 wean   17 leaping   18 staff
19 well   20 choice   21 company   22 both   23 much   24 barley
25 short shift   26 coarse cloth

That while a lassie she had worn,
In longitude tho' sorely scanty,
It was her best, and she was vauntie.[1]
Ah! little kend thy reverend grannie,
That sark she coft[2] for her wee Nannie,
Wi' twa pund[3] Scots ('twas a' her riches),
Wad ever grac'd a dance of witches!

But here my Muse her wing maun cour;[4]
Sic flights are far beyond her pow'r;
To sing how Nannie lap and flang[5]
(A souple[6] jade she was, and strang),
And how Tam stood, like ane bewitch'd,
And thought his very een enrich'd;
Even Satan glowr'd, and fidg'd fu' fain,[7]
And hotch'd[8] and blew wi' might and main:
Till first ae caper, syne[9] anither,
Tam tint[10] his reason a' thegither,
And roars out, 'Weel done, Cutty-sark!'
And in an instant all was dark:
And scarcely had he Maggie rallied,
When out the hellish legion sallied.

As bees bizz out wi' angry fyke,[11]
When plundering herds[12] assail their byke;[13]
As open pussie's[14] mortal foes,
When, pop! she starts before their nose;
As eager runs the market-crowd,
When 'Catch the thief!' resounds aloud;
So Maggie runs, the witches follow,
Wi' mony an eldritch skreech[15] and hollow.

Ah, Tam! Ah, Tam! thou'll get thy fairin![16]
In hell they'll roast thee like a herrin'!
In vain thy Kate awaits thy comin'!
Kate soon will be a woefu' woman!
Now, do thy speedy utmost, Meg,

---

1 proud   2 brought   3 pounds   4 stoop   5 leaped and kicked   6 supple
7 wriggled with delight   8 jerked   9 then   10 lost   11 fret   12 shepherds
13 hive   14 the hare   15 unearthly yell   16 deserts

And win the key-stane* of the brig;
There at them thou thy tail may toss,
A running stream they dare na cross.
But ere the key-stane she could make
The fient[1] a tail she had to shake!
For Nannie, far before the rest,
Hard upon noble Maggie prest,
And flew at Tam wi' furious ettle;[2]
But little wist she Maggie's mettle –
Ae spring brought off her master hale,[3]
But left behind her ain grey tail:
The carlin claught[4] her by the rump,
And left poor Maggie scarce a stump.

   Now, wha this tale o' truth shall read,
Ilk man and mother's son take heed:
Whene'er to drink you are inclin'd,
Or cutty-sarks run in your mind,
Think, ye may buy the joys o'er dear,
Remember Tam o' Shanter's mare.

* It is a well-known fact that witches, or any evil spirits, have no power to follow
a poor wight any farther than the middle of the next running stream. It may be
proper likewise to mention to the benighted traveller, that when he falls in with
bogles, whatever danger may be in his going forward, there is much more hazard
in turning back. (Burns's note)

1 devil   2 intent   3 whole   4 clutched

John Anderson My Jo

John Anderson my jo, John,
    When we were first acquent,
Your locks were like the raven,
    Your bonnie brow was brent;
But now your brow is beld, John,
    Your locks are like the snaw;
But blessings on your frosty pow,
    John Anderson my jo.

John Anderson my jo, John,
    We clamb the hill thegither;
And mony a canty day, John,
    We've had wi' ane anither:

Now we maun totter down, John,
    And hand in hand we'll go;
And sleep thegither at the foot,
    John Anderson my jo.

Song

Ae fond kiss, and then we sever;
Ae fareweel, and then for ever!
Deep in heart-wrung tears I'll pledge thee,
Warring sighs and groans I'll wage thee.

Who shall say that Fortune grieves him,
While the star of hope she leaves him?
Me, nae cheerful twinkle lights me;
Dark despair around benights me.

I'll ne'er blame my partial fancy,
Naething could resist my Nancy:
But to see her was to love her;
Love but her, and love for ever.

Had we never loved sae kindly,
Had we never loved sae blindly!
Never met – or never parted,
We had ne'er been broken-hearted.

Fare thee weel, thou first and fairest!
Fare thee weel, thou best and dearest!
Thine be ilka joy and treasure,
Peace, enjoyment, love and pleasure!

Ae fond kiss, and then we sever!
Ae fareweel, alas, for ever!
Deep in heart- wrung tears I'll pledge thee,
Warring sighs and groans I'll wage thee.

For a' that and a' that

Is there, for honest poverty
    That hings his head, and a' that;
The coward-slave, we pass him by,
    We dare be poor for a' that!
For a' that, and a' that,
    Our toils obscure, and a' that,
The rank is but the guinea's stamp,
    The man's the gowd[1] for a' that.

What though on hamely fare we dine,
    Wear hoddin[2] grey, and a' that.
Gie fools their silks, and knaves their wine,
    A man's a man for a' that.
For a' that, and a' that,
    Their tinsel show, and a' that;
The honest man, though e'er sae poor,
    Is king o' men for a' that.

1 gold   2 homespun cloth

Ye see yon birkie[3] ca'd a lord,
　　Wha struts, and stares, and a' that,
Though hundreds worship at his word,
　　He's but a coof[4] for a' that.
For a' that, and a' that,
　　His ribband, star and a' that,
The man of independent mind,
　　He looks and laughs at a' that.

A prince can mak a belted knight,
　　A marquis, duke, and a' that;
But an honest man's aboon his might,
　　Gude faith he mauna fa'[5] that!
For a' that, and a' that,
　　Their dignities, and a' that,
The pith o' sense, and pride o' worth
　　Are higher rank than a' that.

Then let us pray that come it may,
　　As come it will for a' that,
That sense and worth, o'er a' the earth,
　　Shall bear the gree,[6] and a' that.
For a' that, and a' that,
　　It's comin yet for a' that,
That man to man the warld o'er,
　　Shall brothers be for a' that.

3 dandy　　4 fool　　5 obtain　　6 come off best

A Poet's Welcome to His Love-Begotten Daughter
The first instance that entitled him to the venerable appellation of Father.

Thou's welcome, wean![1] Mischanter[2] fa' me,
If thoughts o' thee, or yet thy mammie,
Shall ever daunton[3] me or awe me,
   My bonnie lady;
Or if I blush when thou shalt ca' me
   Tyta,[4] or daddie.

Though now they ca' me fornicator,
And tease my name in kintra clatter,[5]
The mair they talk, I'm kend the better;
   E'en let them clash!
An auld wife's tongue's a feckless[6] matter
   To gie ane fash.

Welcome! My bonnie, sweet, wee dochter!
Though ye come here a wee unsought for;
And though your comin I hae fought for,
   Baith kirk and queir;
Yet by my faith, ye're no unwrought for,
   That I shall swear!

Wee image o' my bonnie Betty,
As fatherly I kiss and daut[7] thee,
As dear and near my heart I set thee,
   Wi' as gude will,
As a' the priests had seen me get thee
   That's out o' hell.

Sweet fruit o' monie a merry dint,
My funny toil is no a' tint;[8]
Though ye come to the warld asklent,[9]
   Which fools may scoff at,
In my last plack[10] your part's be in't,
   The better half o't.

---

1 child 2 mishap 3 subdue 4 pet name for father 5 country gossip
6 worthless 7 fondle 8 lost 9 on the side 10 coin

Though I should be the waur bestead,[1]
Thou's be as braw and bienly[2] clad,
And thy young years as nicely bred
            Wi' education,
As any brat o' wedlock's bed,
            In a' thy station.

Lord grant that thou may ay inherit
Thy mither's looks an' gracefu' merit;
An' thy poor, worthless daddie's spirit,
            Without his failins!
'Twad please me mair to see thee heir it
            Than stocked mailins![3]

For if thou be, what I wad hae thee,
And tak the counsel I shall gie thee,
I'll never rue my trouble wi' thee,
            The cost nor shame o't,
But be a loving father to thee,
            And brag the name o't.

1 worse placed   2 warmly   3 smallholdings

The Banks o' Doon

Ye banks and braes o' bonie Doon,
    How can ye bloom sae fresh and fair;
How can ye chant, ye little birds,
    And I sae weary, fu' o' care!
Thou'll break my heart, thou warbling bird,
    That wantons through the flowering thorn:
Thou minds me o' departed joys,
    Departed, never to return.

Oft hae I roved by bonnie Doon,
    To see the rose and woodbine twine;
And ilka bird sang o' its luve,
    And fondly sae did I o' mine.
Wi' lightsome heart I pu'd a rose,
    Fu' sweet upon its thorny tree;
And my fause luver staw my rose,
    But, ah! he left the thorn wi' me.

A Red, Red Rose

O my luve's like a red, red rose,
    That's newly sprung in June;
O my luve's like the melodie
    That's sweetly played in tune.

As fair art thou, my bonnie lass,
    So deep in luve am I;
And I will love thee still, my dear,
    Till a' the seas gang dry.

Till a' the seas gang dry, my dear,
    And the rocks melt wi' the sun:
I will love thee still, my dear,
    While the sands o' life shall run.

And fare thee weel, my only luve!
    And fare thee weel, a while!
And I will come again, my luve,
Though it were ten thousand mile!

JOHN BYROM
1692–1763

Epigram on the Feuds between Handel and Bononcini

Some say, compared to Bononcini,
That Mynheer Handel's but a ninny;
Others aver that he to Handel
Is scarcely fit to hold a candle:
Strange all this difference should be
'Twixt Tweedle-dum and Tweedle-dee!

GEORGE GORDON, LORD BYRON
1788–1824

She Walks in Beauty

She walks in beauty, like the night
    Of cloudless climes and starry skies;
And all that's best of dark and bright
    Meeting in her aspect and her eyes:
Thus mellowed to that tender light
    Which heaven to gaudy day denies.

One shade the more, one ray the less,
    Had half impaired the nameless grace,
Which waves in every raven tress,
    Or softly lightens o'er her face;
Where thoughts serenely sweet express,
    How pure, how dear their dwelling-place.

And on the cheek, and o'er that brow,
   So soft, so calm, yet eloquent,
The smiles that win, the tints that glow,
   But tell of days in goodness spent,
A mind at peace with all below,
   A heart whose love is innocent!

When We Two Parted

When we two parted
   In silence and tears,
Half broken-hearted
   To sever for years,
Pale grew thy cheek and cold,
   Colder thy kiss;
Truly that hour foretold
   Sorrow to this.

The dew of the morning
   Sunk chill on my brow –
It felt like the warning
   Of what I feel now,
Thy vows are all broken,
   And light is thy fame;
I hear thy name spoken,
   And share in its shame.

They name thee before me,
   A knell to mine ear;
A shudder comes o'er me –
   Why wert thou so dear?
They know not I knew thee,
   Who knew thee too well –
Long, long shall I rue thee,
   Too deeply to tell.

In secret we met –
　　In silence I grieve,
That thy heart could forget,
　　Thy spirit deceive.
If I should meet thee
　　After long years,
How should I greet thee?
　　With silence and tears.

The Destruction of Sennacherib

The Assyrian came down like a wolf on the fold,
And his cohorts were gleaming in purple and gold;
And the sheen of their spears was like stars on the sea,
When the blue wave rolls nightly on deep Galilee.

Like the leaves of the forest when summer is green.
That host with their banners at sunset were seen;
Like the leaves of the forest when autumn hath blown,
That host on the morrow lay withered and strown.

For the Angel of Death spread his wings on the blast,
And breathed in the face of the foe as he passed;
And the eyes of the sleepers waxed deadly and chill,
And their hearts but once heaved, and for ever grew still!

And there lay the steed with his nostril all wide,
But through it there rolled not the breath of his pride;
And the foam of his gasping lay white on the turf,
And cold as the spray of the rock-beating surf.

And there lay the rider distorted and pale,
With the dew on his brow, and the rust on his mail;
And the tents were all silent, the banners alone,
The lances unlifted, the trumpet unblown.

And the widows of Ashur are loud in their wail,
And the idols are broke in the temple of Baal;
And the might of the Gentile, unsmote by the sword,
Hath meted like snow in the glance of the Lord!

Remember Thee! Remember Thee!

Remember thee! remember thee!
  Till Lethe quench life's burning stream
Remorse and Shame shall cling to thee,
  And haunt thee like a feverish dream!

Remember thee! Aye, doubt it not.
  Thy husband too shall think of thee:
By neither shalt thou be forgot,
  Thou *false* to him, thou *fiend* to me!

Stanzas for Music

There be none of beauty's daughters
  With a magic like thee;
And like music on the waters
  Is thy sweet voice to me:
When, as if its sound were causing
The charmèd ocean's pausing,
The waves lie still and gleaming,
And the lulled winds seem dreaming:

And the midnight moon is weaving
  Her bright chain o'er the deep;
Whose breast is gently heaving,
  As an infant's asleep:
So the spirit bows before thee,
To listen and adore thee;
With a full but soft emotion,
Like the swell of summer's ocean.

So We'll Go No More a-Roving

So we'll go no more a-roving
    So late into the night,
Though the heart be still as loving,
    And the moon be still as bright.

For the sword outwears its sheath,
    And the soul wears out the breast,
And the heart must pause to breathe,
    And love itself have rest.

Though the night was made for loving,
    And the day returns too soon,
Yet we'll go no more a-roving
    By the light of the moon.

The Isles of Greece

I

The isles of Greece, the isles of Greece!
    Where burning Sappho loved and sung,
Where grew the arts of war and peace,
    Where Delos rose, and Phoebus sprung!
Eternal summer gilds them yet,
But all, except their sun, is set.

2

The Scian and the Teian muse,
    The hero's harp, the lover's lute,
Have found the fame your shores refuse;
    Their place of birth alone is mute
To sounds which echo further west
Than your sires' 'Islands of the Blest'.

3

The mountains look on Marathon –
   And Marathon looks on the sea;
And musing there an hour alone,
   I dreamed that Greece might still be free;
For standing on the Persians' grave,
I could not deem myself a slave.

4

A king sat on the rocky brow
   Which looks o'er sea-born Salamis;
And ships, by thousands, lay below,
   And men in nations – all were his!
He counted them at break of day –
And when the sun set where were they?

5

And where are they? and where art thou,
   My country? On thy voiceless shore
The heroic lay is tuneless now –
   The heroic bosoms beats no more!
And must thy lyre, so long divine,
Degenerate into hands like mine?

6

'Tis something in the dearth of fame,
   Though linked among a fettered race,
To feel at least a patriot's shame,
   Even as I sing, suffuse my face;
For what is left the poet here?
For Greeks a blush – for Greece a tear.

7

Must *we* but weep o'er days more blest?
   Must *we* but blush? – Our fathers bled.
Earth! render back from out thy breast
   A remnant of our Spartan dead!
Of the three hundred grant but three,
To make a new Thermopylae!

8

What, silent still? and silent all?
    Ah! no – the voices of the dead
Sound like a distant torrent's fall,
    And answer, 'Let one living head,
But one arise – we come, we come!'
'Tis but the living who are dumb.

9

In vain – in vain; strike other chords;
    Fill high the cup with Samian wine!
Leave battles to the Turkish hordes,
    And shed the blood of Scio's vine!
Hark! rising to the ignoble call –
How answers each bold Bacchanal!

10

You have the Pyrrhic dance as yet,
    Where is the Pyrrhic phalanx gone?
Of two such lessons, why forget
    The nobler and the manlier one?
You have the letters Cadmus gave –
Think ye he meant them for a slave?

11

Fill high the bowl with Samian wine!
    We will not think the themes like these!
It made Anacreon's song divine:
    He served – but served Polycrates –
A tyrant; but our masters then
Were still, at least, our countrymen.

12

The tyrant of the Chersonese
    Was freedom's best and bravest friend;
That tyrant was Miltiades!
    Oh! that the present hour would lend
Another despot of the kind!
Such chains as his were sure to bind.

13

Fill high the bowl with Samian wine!
On Suli's rock, and Parga's shore,
Exists the remnant of a line
Such as the Doric mothers bore;
And there, perhaps some seed is sown,
The Heracleidan blood might own.

14

Trust not for freedom to the Franks –
    They have a king who buys and sells:
In native swords, and native ranks,
    The only hope of courage dwells;
But Turkish force, and Latin fraud,
Would break your shield, however broad.

15

Fill high the bowl with Samian wine!
    Our virgins dance beneath the shade –
I see their glorious black eyes shine;
    But gazing on each glowing maid,
My own the burning tear-drop laves,
To think such breasts must suckle slaves.

16

Place me on Sunium's marbled steep,
    Where nothing, save the waves and I,
May hear our mutual murmurs sweep;
    There, swan-like, let me sing and die:
A land of slaves shall ne'er be mine –
Dash down yon cup of Samian wine!

THOMAS CAMPION
1567–1620

Song

Follow your saint, follow with accents sweet;
Haste you, sad notes, fall at her flying feet.
There, wrapped in cloud of sorrow, pity move,
And tell the ravisher of my soul I perish for her love.
But if she scorns my never-ceasing pain,
Then burst with sighing in her sight, and ne'er return again.

All that I sung still to her praise did tend.
Still she was first, still she my songs did end.
Yet she my love and music both doth fly,
The music that her echo is, and beauty's sympathy.
Then let my notes pursue her scornful flight;
It shall suffice that they were breathed, and died for her
   delight

Song

When thou must home to shades of underground,
   And there arrived, a new admired guest,
The beauteous spirits do engirt thee round,
   White Iope, blithe Helen and the rest,
To hear the stories of thy finished love
From that smooth tongue, whose music hell can move:

Then wilt thou speak of banqueting delights,
   Of masks and revels which sweet youth did make,
Of tourneys and great challenges of knights,
   And all these triumphs, for thy beauty's sake.
When thou hast told these honours done to thee,
Then tell, O! tell, how thou didst murder me.

Song

Follow thy fair sun, unhappy shadow.
  Though thou be black as night,
  And she made all of light,
Yet follow thy fair sun, unhappy shadow.

Follow her whose light thy light depriveth.
  Though here thou liv'st disgraced,
  And she in heaven is placed,
Yet follow her whose light the world reviveth.

Follow those pure beams whose beauty burneth,
  That so have scorchèd thee
  As thou still black must be
Till her kind beams thy black to brightness turneth.

Follow her while yet her glory shineth,
  There comes a luckless night,
  That will dim all her light;
And this the black unhappy shade divineth.

Follow still, since so thy fates ordainèd.
  The sun must have his shade,
  Till both at once do fade,
The sun still proud, the shadow still disdainèd.

Song

Now winter nights enlarge
  The number of their hours,
And clouds their storms discharge
  Upon the airy towers.
Let now the chimneys blaze
  And cups o'erflow with wine;
Let well-tuned words amaze
  With harmony divine.
Now yellow waxen lights
  Shall wait on honey love
While youthful revels, masques, and courtly sights
  Sleep's leaden spells remove.

This time doth well dispense
   With lovers' long discourse:
Much speech hath some defence,
   Though beauty no remorse.
All do not all things well:
   Some measures comely tread,
Some knotted riddles tell,
   Some poems smoothly read.
The summer hath his joys,
   And winter his delights.
Though love and all his pleasures are but toys,
   They shorten tedious nights.

HENRY CAREY
*c.*1687–1743

The Ballad of Sally in Our Alley

Of all the girls that are so smart
   There's none like pretty Sally;
She is the darling of my heart,
   And she lives in our alley.
There is no lady in the land
   Is half so sweet as Sally;
She is the darling of my heart,
   And she lives in our alley.

Her father he makes cabbage-nets,
   And through the streets does cry 'em;
Her mother she sells laces long
   To such as please to buy 'em;
But sure such folks could ne'er beget
   So sweet a girl as Sally!
She is the darling of my heart,
   And she lives in our alley.

When she is by I leave my work
   (I love her so sincerely);

My master comes like any Turk
   And bangs me most severely;
But let him bang his bellyfull,
   I'll bear it all for Sally;
She is the darling of my heart,
   And she lives in our alley.

Of all the days that's in the week
   I dearly love but one day,
And that's the day that comes betwixt
   A Saturday and Monday;
For then I'm dressed all in my best
   To walk abroad with Sally;
She is the darling of my heart,
   And she lives in our alley.

My master carries me to church,
   And often am I blamed
Because I leave him in the lurch
   As soon as text is named;
I leave the church in sermon time
   And slink away to Sally;
She is the darling of my heart,
   And she lives in our alley.

When Christmas comes about again,
   O then I shall have money;
I'll hoard it up, and box and all
   I'll give it to my honey;
And would it were ten thousand pounds,
   I'd give it all to Sally;
She is the darling of my heart,
   And she lives in our alley.

My master and the neighbours all
   Make game of me and Sally;
And, but for her, I'd better be
   A slave and row a galley;
But when my seven long years are out,
   O, then I'll marry Sally!
O then we'll wed, and then we'll bed,
   But not in our alley.

A Lilliputian Ode on
Their Majesties' Accession

Smile, smile,
Blest isle!
Grief past,
At last,
Halcyon
Comes on.
New King,
Bells ring;
New Queen,
Blest scene!
Britain
Again
Revives
And thrives.
Fear flies,
Stocks rise;
Wealth flows,
Art grows.
Strange pack
Sent back;
Own folks
Crack jokes.
Those out
May pout;
Those in
Will grin.

Great, small,
Pleased all.

God send
No end
To line
Divine
Of George and Caroline!

LEWIS CARROLL
(Charles Lutwidge Dodgson)
1832–1898

How doth the little crocodile
   Improve his shining tail,
And pour the waters of the Nile
   On every golden scale!

How cheerfully he seems to grin,
   How neatly spreads his claws,
And welcomes little fishes in,
   With gently smiling jaws!

Jabberwocky

’Twas brillig, and the slithy toves
   Did gyre and gimble in the wabe:
All mimsy were the borogoves,
   And the mome raths outgrabe.

’Beware the Jabberwock, my son!
   The jaws that bite, the claws that catch!
Beware the Jubjub bird, and shun
   The frumious Bandersnatch!’

He took his vorpal sword in hand:
   Long time the manxome foe he sought –
So rested he by the Tumtum tree,
   And stood awhile in thought.

And, as in uffish thought he stood,
   The Jabberwock, with eyes of flame,
Came whiffling through the tulgey wood,
   And burbled as it came!

One, two! One, two! And through and through
   The vorpal blade went snicker-snack!
He left it dead, and with its head
   He went galumphing back.

'And hast thou slain the Jaberwock?
   Come to my arms, my beamish boy!
O frabjous day! Callooh! Callay!'
   He chortled in his joy.

'Twas brillig, and the slithy toves
   Did gyre and gimble in the wabe:
All mimsy were the borogoves,
   And the mome raths outgrabe.

GEOFFREY CHAUCER
c.1343–1400

Merciless Beauty
A Triple Roundel

1   CAPTIVITY

Your two eyes will destroy me suddenly:
I can the beauty of them not sustain;
It sendeth through my heart a wound so keen.

And if you will not succour hastily
That stricken heart while yet the wound is green,
   Your two eyes will destroy me suddenly:
   I can the beauty of them not sustain.

Upon the truth I tell you honestly
That of my life or death you are the queen;
And should I die, that truth will then be seen.
   Your two eyes will destroy me suddenly:
   I can the beauty of them not sustain;
   It sendeth through my heart a wound so keen.

2 REJECTION

So hath your beauty rid your heart of rue
That all my lamentations are but vain:
For your proud mind holds pity on a chain.

Thus you decree a guiltless death my due;
And that is truth – I have no need to feign;
So hath your beauty rid your heart of rue
That all my lamentations are but vain.

Alas, that nature should have formed in you
Beauty so great that no man may attain
To mercy, though he starve away for pain.
So hath your beauty rid your heart of rue
That all my lamentations are but vain.
For your proud mind holds pity on a chain.

3 ESCAPE

Since I from Love escapèd am so fat,
I'll never enter more his prison lean!
Since I am free, I count him not a bean.

Let him reply, and tell me this or that:
I do not care; I speak out what I mean.
Since I from Love escapèd am so fat,
I'll never enter more his prison lean!

Love has struck out my name from off his slate,
And from my own book his have I struck clean
For evermore: the only way, I ween.
Since I from Love escaped am so fat,
I'll never enter more his prison lean;
Since I am free, I count him not a bean!

THE EARL OF CHESTERFIELD
1694–1773

Epigram

In Flavia's eye is every grace,
She's handsome as she could be:
With Jacob's beauty in her face
And Esau's where it should be.

G. K. CHESTERTON
1874–1936

The Donkey

When fishes flew and forests walked
    And figs grew upon thorn,
Some moment when the moon was blood
    Then surely I was born;

With monstrous head and sickening cry
    And ears like errant wings,
The devil's walking parody
    On all four-footed things.

The tattered outlaw of the earth,
    Of ancient crooked will;
Starve, scourge, deride me: I am dumb,
    I keep my secret still.

Fools! For I also had my hour;
    One far fierce hour and sweet:
The was a shout about my ears,
    And palms before my feet.

The Rolling English Road

Before the Roman came to Rye or out to Severn strode,
The rolling English drunkard made the rolling English road.
A reeling road, a rolling road, that rambles round the shire,
And after him the parson ran, the sexton and the squire;
A merry road, a mazy road, and such as we did tread
The night we went to Birmingham by way of Beachy Head.

I knew no harm of Bonaparte and plenty of the Squire,
And for to fight the Frenchman I did not much desire;
But I did bash their baggonets because they came arrayed
To straighten out the crooked road an English drunkard
                                             made,
Where you and I went down the lane with ale-mugs in our
                                             hands,
The night we went to Glastonbury by way of Goodwin Sands.

His sins they were forgiven him; or why do flowers run
Behind him; and the hedges all strengthening in the sun?
The wild thing went from left to right and knew not which
                                             was which,
But the wild rose was above him when they found him in
                                             the ditch.
God pardon us, nor harden us; we did not see so clear
The night we went to Bannockburn by way of Brighton Pier.

My friends, we will not go again or ape an ancient rage,
Or stretch the folly of our youth to be the shame of age,
But walk with clearer eyes and cars this path that wandereth,
And see undrugged in evening light the decent inn of death;
For there is good news yet to hear and fine things to be seen
Before we go to Paradise by way of Kensal Green.

LADY MARY CHUDLEIGH
1656–1710

To the Ladies

Wife and servant are the same,
But only differ in the name:
For when that fatal knot is tied,
Which nothing, nothing can divide,
When she the word *Obey* has said,
And man by law supreme has made,
Then all that's kind is laid aside,
And nothing left but state and pride.
Fierce as an eastern prince he grows,
And all his innate rigour shows:
Then but to look, to laugh, or speak,
Will the nuptial contract break.
Like mutes, she signs alone must make,
And never any freedom take,
But still be governed by a nod,
And fear her husband as her god:
Him still must serve, him still obey,
And nothing act, and nothing say,
But what her haughty lord thinks fit,
Who, with the power, has all the wit.
Then shun, oh! shun that wretched state,
And all the fawning flatt'rers hate.
Value yourselves, and men despise:
You must be proud, if you'll be wise.

JOHN CLARE
1793–1864

Early Images

Come, early morning, with thy mealy grey,
Moist grass, and fitful gales that winnow soft
And frequent, I'll be up with early day
And roam the social way, there passing oft
The milking maid who greets the pleasant morn,
And shepherd with his crook in folded arm
Rocking along across the bended corn;
And hear the many sounds from distant farm,
Of cackling hens and turkeys gobbling loud,
And teams just plodding on their way to plough
Down russet tracks that strip the closen green,
And hear the mellow low of distant cow,
And see the mist upcreeping like a cloud
From hollow places in the early scene.

First Love

No single hour can pass for naught,
   No moment-hand can move,
But calendars an aching thought
   Of my first lonely love.

Where silence doth the loudest call
   My secret to betray,
As moonlight holds the night in thrall,
   As suns reveal the day,

I hide it in the silent shades,
   Till silence finds a tongue;
I make its grave where time invades,
   Till time becomes a song.

I bid my foolish heart be still,
　But hopes will not be chid:
My heart will beat, and burn, and chill,
　First love will not be hid.

When summer ceases to be green,
　And winter bare and blea,
Death may forget what I have been
　When I shall cease to be.

When words refuse before the crowd
　My Mary's name to give,
The muse in silence sings aloud:
　And there my love will live.

Summer Evening

The frog, half fearful, jumps across the path,
And little mouse that leaves its hole at eve
Nimbles with timid dread beneath the swath;
My rustling steps awhile their joys deceive,
Till past – and then the cricket sings more strong,
And grasshoppers in merry moods still wear
The short night weary with their fretting song.
Up from behind the mole-hill jumps the hare,
Cheat of his chosen bed, and from the bank
The yellowhammer flutters in short fears
From off its nest hid in the grasses rank,
And drops again when no more noise it hears.
Thus nature's human link and endless thrall,
Proud man, still seems the enemy of all.

Nutting

The sun had stooped, his westward clouds to win,
Like weary traveller seeking for an inn,
When from the hazelly wood we glad descried
The ivied gateway by the pastureside.
Long had we sought for nuts amid the shade,
Where silence fled the rustle that we made;
When torn by briers and brushed by sedges rank,
We left the wood, and on the velvet bank
Of short-sward pasture-ground we sat us down
To shell our nuts before we reached the town.
The near-hand stubble-field, with mellow glower,
Showed the dimmed blaze of poppies still in flower;
And sweet the mole-hills smelt we sat upon –
Again the thyme's in bloom, but where is pleasure gone?

Winter

The small wind whispers through the leafless hedge
   Most sharp and chill, where the light snowy flakes
Rest on each twig and spike of wither'd sedge,
   Resembling scatter'd feathers; vainly breaks
The pale split sunbeam through the frowning cloud,
   On Winter's frowns below – from day to day
Unmelted still he spreads his hoary shroud,
   In dithering pride on the pale traveller's way,
Who, croodling, hastens from the storm behind
Fast gathering deep and black, again to find
   His cottage fire and corner's sheltering bounds;
Where, haply, such uncomfortable days
   Make musical the wood-sap's frizzling sounds,
And hoarse loud bellows puffing up the blaze.

The Flight of Birds

The crow goes flopping on from wood to wood,
The wild duck wherries to the distant flood,
The starnels hurry o'er in merry crowds,
And overhead whew by like hasty clouds;
The wild duck from the meadow-water plies
And dashes up the water as he flies;
The pigeon suthers by on rapid wing,
The lark mounts upward at the call of spring.
In easy flights above the hurricane
With doubled neck high sails the noisy crane.
Whizz goes the pewit o'er the ploughman's team,
With many a whew and whirl and sudden scream;
And lightly fluttering to the tree just by,
In chattering journeys whirls the noisy pie;
From bush to bush slow swees the screaming jay,
With one harsh note of pleasure all the day.

The Yellow-Hammer's Nest

Just by the wooden bridge a bird flew up,
Frit by the cow-boy, as he scrambled down
To reach the misty dewberry. Let us stoop,
And seek its nest. The brook we need not dread –
'Tis scarcely deep enough a bee to drown,
As it sings harmless o'er its pebbly bed.
Ay, here it is! stuck close beside the bank,
Beneath the bunch of grass, that spindles rank
Its husk-seeds tall and high: 'tis rudely planned
Of bleachèd stubbles, and the withered fare
That last year's harvest left upon the land –
Lined thinly with the horse's sable hair.
Five eggs, pen-scribbled o'er with ink their shells
Resembling writing-scrawls, which fancy reads
As nature's poesy, and pastoral spells –
They are the yellow-hammer's, and she dwells,

Most poet-like, where brooks and flowery weeds
As sweet as Castaly her fancy deems;
And that old mole-hill is Parnassus Hill,
On which her partner haply sits and dreams
O'er all his joys of song. Let's leave it still
A happy home of sunshine, flowers, and streams.
Yet is the sweetest place exposed to ill,
A noisome weed that burthens every soil;
For snakes are known, with chill and deadly coil,
To watch such nests and seize the helpless young;
And like as if the plague became a guest,
To leave a houseless home, a ruined nest:
Ay! mournful hath the little warbler sung
When suchlike woes have rent his gentle breast.

Pleasant Sounds

The rustling of leaves under the feet in woods and under
        hedges;
The crumping of cat-ice and snow down wood-rides, narrow
        lanes, and every street causeway;
Rustling through a wood or rather rushing, while the wind
        halloos in the oak-top like thunder;
The rustle of birds' wings startled from their nests or flying
        unseen into the bushes;
The whizzing of larger birds overhead in a wood, such as
        crows, puddocks, buzzards;
The trample of robins and woodlarks on the brown leaves, and
        the patter of squirrels on the green moss;
The fall of an acorn on the ground, the pattering of nuts on the
        hazel branches as they fall from ripeness;
The flirt of the groundlark's wing from the stubbles – how
        sweet such pictures on dewy mornings, when the dew
        flashes from its brown feathers!

I Am

I am: yet what I am none cares or knows,
 My friends forsake me like a memory lost;
I am the self-consumer of my woes,
 They rise and vanish in oblivious host,
Like shades in love and death's oblivion lost;
And yet I am, and live with shadows tost

Into the nothingness of scorn and noise,
 Into the living sea of waking dreams,
Where there is neither sense of life nor joys,
 But the vast shipwreck of my life's esteems;
And e'en the dearest – that I loved the best –
Are strange – nay, rather stranger than the rest.

I long for scenes where man has never trod,
 A place where woman never smiled or wept;
There to abide with my Creator, God,
 And sleep as I in childhood sweetly slept:
Untroubling and untroubled where I lie,
  The grass below – above the vaulted sky.

John Clare

I feel I am, I only know I am,
And plod upon the earth as dull and void;
Earth's prison chilled my body with its dram
Of dullness, and my soaring thoughts destroyed.
I fled to solitude from passion's dream,
But strife pursued: I only know I am.
I was a being created in the race
Of men, disdaining bounds of place and time;
A spirit that could travel o'er the space
Of earth and heaven like a thought sublime;
Tracing creation, like my Maker free,
A soul unshackled like eternity:
Spurning earth's vain and soul-debasing thrall –
But now I only know I am, that's all.

The Eternity of Song
[In one manuscript this stanza stands alone]

The eternity of song
  Liveth here;
Nature's universal tongue
  Singeth here
Songs I've heard and felt and seen
  Everywhere;
Songs like the grass are evergreen:
  The giver
Said 'Live and be' – and they have been,
  For ever.

ARTHUR HUGH CLOUGH
1819–1861

Say Not the Struggle Nought Availeth

Say not the struggle nought availeth,
  The labour and the wounds are vain,
The enemy faints not, nor faileth,
  And as things have been, things remain.

If hopes were dupes, fears may be liars;
  It may be, in yon smoke concealed,
Your comrades chase e'en now the fliers,
  And, but for you, possess the field.

For while the tired waves, vainly breaking,
  Seem here no painful inch to gain,
Far back through creeks and inlets making
  Came, silent, flooding in, the main,

And not by eastern windows only,
  When daylight comes, comes in the light,
In front the sun climbs slow, how slowly,
  But westward, look, the land is bright.

The Latest Decalogue

Thou shalt have one God only; who
Would be at the expense of two?
No graven images may be
Worshipped, except the currency;
Swear not at all: for, for thy curse
Thine enemy is none the worse;
At church on Sunday to attend
Will serve to keep the world thy friend;
Honour thy parents: that is, all
From whom advancement may befall;
Thou shalt not kill: but need'st not strive
Officiously to keep alive;
Do not adultery commit:
Advantage rarely comes of it;
Thou shalt not steal: an empty feat,
When it's so lucrative to cheat;
Bear not false witness: let the lie
Have time on its own wings to fly;
Thou shalt not covet, but tradition
Approves all forms of competition.

SAMUEL TAYLOR COLERIDGE
1772–1834

Kubla Khan

In Xanadu did Kubla Khan
A stately pleasure dome decree:
Where Alph, the sacred river, ran
Through caverns measureless to man
   Down to a sunless sea.
So twice five miles of fertile ground
With walls and towers were girdled round:
And there were gardens bright with sinuous rills,
Where blossomed many an incense-bearing tree;
And here were forests ancient as the hills,
Enfolding sunny spots of greenery.

But oh! that deep romantic chasm which slanted
Down the green hill athwart a cedarn cover!
A savage place! as holy and enchanted
As e'er beneath a waning moon was haunted
By woman waiting for her demon lover!
And from this chasm, with ceaseless turmoil seething,
As if this earth in fast thick pants were breathing,
A mighty fountain momently was forced:
Amid whose swift half-intermitted burst
Huge fragments vaulted like rebounding hail,
Or chaffy grain beneath the thresher's flail:
And 'mid these dancing rocks at once and ever
It flung up momently the sacred river.
Four miles meandering with a mazy motion
Through wood and dale the sacred river ran,
Then reached the caverns measureless to man,
And sank in tumult to a lifeless ocean:
And 'mid this tumult Kubla heard from far
Ancestral voices prophesying war!

The shadow of the dome of pleasure
Floated midway on the waves;
Where was heard the mingled measure
From the fountain and the caves.
It was a miracle of rare device,
A sunny pleasure-dome with caves of ice!

A damsel with a dulcimer
In a vision once I saw:
It was an Abyssinian maid,
And on her dulcimer she played,
Singing of Mount Abora.
Could I revive within me
Her symphony and song,
  To such a deep delight 'twould win me,
That with music loud and long,
I would build that dome in air,
That sunny dome! those caves of ice!
And all who heard should see them there,
And all should cry, Beware! Beware!
His flashing eyes, his floating hair!
Weave a circle round him thrice,
And close your eyes with holy dread,
For he on honey dew hath fed,
And drunk the milk of Paradise.

Frost at Midnight

The Frost performs its secret ministry,
Unhelped by any wind. The owlet's cry
Came loud – and hark, again! loud as before.
The inmates of my cottage, all at rest,
Have left me to that solitude, which suits
Abstruser musings; save that at my side
My cradled infant slumbers peacefully.
'Tis calm indeed! so calm, that it disturbs

And vexes meditation with its strange
And extreme silentness. Sea, hill, and wood,
This populous village! Sea, and hill, and wood,
With all the numberless goings-on of life,
Inaudible as dreams! the thin blue flame
Lies on my low-burnt fire, and quivers not;
Only the film, which fluttered on the grate,
Still flutters there, the sole unquiet thing.
Methinks, its motion in this hush of nature
Gives it dim sympathies with me who live,
Making it a companionable form,
Whose puny flaps and freaks the idling Spirit
By its own moods interprets, everywhere
Echo or mirror seeking of itself,
And makes a toy of Thought.

                           But O! how oft,
How oft, at school, with most believing mind,
Presageful, have I gazed upon the bars,
To watch that fluttering *stranger*! and as oft
With unclosed lids, already had I dreamt
Of my sweet birthplace, and the old church-tower,
Whose bells, the poor man's only music, rang
From morn to evening, all the hot Fair-day,
So sweetly, that they stirred and haunted me
With a wild pleasure, falling on mine ear
Most like articulate sounds of things to come!
So gazed I, till the soothing things I dreamt
Lulled me to sleep, and sleep prolonged my dreams!
And so I brooded all the following morn,
Awed by the stern preceptor's face, mine eye
Fixed with mock study on my swimming book:
Save if the door half opened, and I snatched
A hasty glance, and still my heart leaped up,
For still I hoped to see the *stranger*'s face,
Townsman, or aunt, or sister more beloved,
My playmate when we both were clothed alike!

    Dear Babe, that sleepest cradled by my side,
Whose gentle breathings, heard in this deep calm,

Fill up the interspersed vacancies
And momentary pauses of the thought!
My babe so beautiful! it thrills my heart
With tender gladness, thus to look at thee,
And think that thou shalt learn far other lore,
And in far other scenes! For I was reared
In the great city, pent 'mid cloisters dim,
And saw nought lovely but the sky and stars.
But thou, my babe! shalt wander like a breeze
By lakes and sandy shores, beneath the crags
Of ancient mountain, and beneath the clouds,
Which image in their bulk both lakes and shores
And mountain crags: so shalt thou see and hear
The lovely shapes and sounds intelligible
Of that eternal language, which thy God
Utters, who from eternity doth teach
Himself in all, and all things in himself.
Great universal Teacher! he shall mould
Thy spirit, and by giving make it ask.

   Therefore all seasons shall be sweet to thee,
Whether the summer clothe the general earth
With greenness, or the redbreast sit and sing
Betwixt the tufts of snow on the bare branch
Of mossy apple-tree, while the nigh thatch
Smokes in the sun-thaw; whether the eave-drops fall
Heard only in the trances of the blast,
Or if the secret ministry of frost
Shall hang them up in silent icicles,
Quietly shining to the quiet Moon.

On Donne's Poetry

With Donne, whose muse on dromedary trots,
Wreathe iron pokers into true-love knots;
Rhyme's sturdy cripple, fancy's maze and clue,
Wit's forge and fire-blast, meaning's press and screw.

The Homeric Hexameter
Described and Exemplified

Strongly it bears us along in swelling and limitless billows,
Nothing before and nothing behind but the sky and the ocean.

The Ovidian Elegiac Metre
Described and Exemplified

In the hexameter rises the fountain's silvery column;
In the pentameter aye falling in melody back.

This Lime-Tree Bower My Prison

In the June of 1797 some long-expected friends paid a visit to the
author's cottage; and on the morning of their arrival, he met with
an accident, which disabled him from walking during the whole
time of their stay. One evening, when they had left him for a few
hours, he composed the following lines in the garden-bower.

Well, they are gone, and here must I remain,
This lime-tree bower my prison! I have lost
Beauties and feelings, such as would have been
Most sweet to my remembrance even when age
Had dimmed mine eyes to blindness! They, meanwhile,
Friends, whom I never more may meet again,
On springy heath, along the hilltop edge,
Wander in gladness, and wind down, perchance,
To that still roaring dell, of which I told;
The roaring dell, o'erwooded, narrow, deep,
And only speckled by the midday sun;

Where its slim trunk the ash from rock to rock
Flings arching like a bridge – that branchless ash,
Unsunned and damp, whose few poor yellow leaves
Ne'er tremble in the gale, yet tremble still,
Fanned by the waterfall! and there my friends
Behold the dark green file of long lank weeds,
That all at once (a most fantastic sight!)
Still nod and drip beneath the dripping edge
Of the blue clay-stone.

        Now, my friends emerge,
Beneath the wide wide Heaven – and view again
The many-steepled tract magnificent
Of hilly fields and meadows, and the sea,
With some fair bark, perhaps, whose sails light up
The slip of smooth clear blue betwixt two Isles
Of purple shadow! Yes! they wander on
In gladness all; but thou, methinks, most glad,
My gentle-hearted Charles! for thou hast pined
And hungered after Nature, many a year,
In the great City pent, winning thy way
With sad yet patient soul, through evil and pain
And strange calamity! Ah! slowly sink
Behind the western ridge, thou glorious Sun!
Shine in the slant beams of the sinking orb,
Ye purple heath-flowers! richlier burn, ye clouds!
Live in the yellow light, ye distant groves!
And kindle, thou blue Ocean! So my friend
Struck with deep joy may stand, as I have stood,
Silent with swimming sense; yea, gazing round
On the wide landscape, gaze till all doth seem
Less gross than bodily; and of such hues
As veil the Almighty Spirit, when yet he makes
Spirits perceive his presence.

        A delight
Comes sudden on my heart, and I am glad
As I myself were there! Nor in this bower,
This little lime-tree bower, have I not marked
Much that has soothed me. Pale beneath the blaze
Hung the transparent foliage; and I watched

Some broad and sunny leaf, and loved to see
The shadow of the leaf and stem above
Dappling its sunshine! And that walnut tree
Was richly tinged, and a deep radiance lay
Full on the ancient ivy, which usurps
Those fronting elms, and now, with blackest mass
Makes their dark branches gleam a lighter hue
Through the late twilight: and though now the bat
Wheels silent by, and not a swallow twitters,
Yet still the solitary humble-bee
Sings in the bean-flower! Henceforth I shall know
That Nature ne'er deserts the wise and pure;
No plot so narrow, be but Nature there,
No waste so vacant, but may well employ
Each faculty of sense, and keep the heart
Awake to Love and Beauty! and sometimes
'Tis well to be bereft of promised good,
That we may lift the soul, and contemplate
With lively joy the joys we cannot share.
My gentle-hearted Charles! when the last rook
Beat its straight path along the dusky air
Homewards, I blest it! deeming its black wing
(Now a dim speck, now vanishing in light)
Had crossed the mighty Orb's dilated glory,
While thou stood'st gazing or, when all was still,
Flew creeking o'er thy head, and had a charm
For thee, my gentle-hearted Charles, to whom
No sound is dissonant which tells of Life.

The Devil's Thoughts

1

From his brimstone bed at break of day
A-walking the Devil is gone,
To visit his snug little farm the earth,
And see how his stock goes on.

2

Over the hill and over the dale,
And he went over the plain,
And backward and forward he switched his long tail
As a gentleman switches his cane.

3

And how then was the Devil drest?
Oh! he was in his Sunday's best:
His jacket was red and his breeches were blue,
And there was a hole where the tail came through.

4

He saw a Lawyer killing a Viper
On a dunghill hard by his own stable;
And the Devil smiled, for it put him in mind
Of Cain and his brother, Abel.

5

He saw an Apothecary on a white horse
   Ride by on his vocations,
And the Devil thought of his old Friend
   Death in the Revelations.

6

He saw a cottage with a double coach-house,
   A cottage of gentility;
And the Devil did grin, for his darling sin
   Is pride that apes humility.

7

He peeped into a rich bookseller's shop,
   Quoth he! we are both of one college!
For I sat myself, like a cormorant, once,
   Hard by the tree of knowledge.

8

Down the river did glide, with wind and tide,
   A pig with vast celerity;
And the Devil looked wise as he saw how the while,
It cut its own throat. 'There!' quoth he with a smile,
   'Goes "England's commercial prosperity".'

9

As he went through Cold-Bath Fields he saw
  A solitary cell;
And the Devil was pleased, for it gave him a hint
  For improving his prisons in Hell.

10

He saw a Turnkey in a trice
  Fetter a troublesome blade;
'Nimbly,' quoth he, 'do the fingers move
  If a man be but used to his trade.'

11

He saw the same Turnkey unfetter a man,
  With but little expedition,
Which put him in mind of the long debate
  On the slave-trade abolition.

12

He saw an old acquaintance
  As he passed by a Methodist meeting;
She holds a consecrated key,
  And the Devil nods her a greeting.

13

She turned up her nose, and said,
  'Avaunt! my name's Religion,'
And she looked to Mr —
  And leered like a love-sick pigeon.

14

He saw a certain minister
  (A minister to his mind)
Go up into a certain House,
  With a majority behind.

15

The Devil quoted Genesis
  Like a very learned clerk,
How 'Noah and his creeping things
  Went up into the Ark.'

16

He took from the poor,
   And he gave to the rich,
And he shook hands with a Scotchman,
   For he was not afraid of the —

17

General — burning face
   He saw with consternation,
And back to hell his way did he take,
For the Devil thought by a slight mistake
   It was general conflagration.

Dejection: An Ode

Late, late yestreen I saw the new Moon,
With the old Moon in her arms;
And I fear, I fear, my Master dear!
We shall have a deadly storm.

Ballad of Sir Patrick Spence

1

Well, if the bard was weather-wise, who made
The grand old ballad of Sir Patrick Spence,
This night, so tranquil now, will not go hence
Unroused by winds, that ply a busier trade
Than those which mould yon cloud in lazy flakes,
Or the dull sobbing draft, that moans and rakes
Upon the strings of this Aeolian lute,
   Which better far were mute.
  For lo! the New-moon winter-bright!
  And overspread with phantom light
  (With swimming phantom light o'erspread,
   But rimmed and circled by a silver thread),
I see the old Moon in her lap, foretelling
  The coming on of rain and squally blast.
And oh! that even now the gust were swelling,
  And the slant night-shower driving loud and fast!

Those sounds that oft have raised me, whilst they awed,
    And sent my soul abroad,
Might now perhaps their wonted impulse give,
Might startle this dull pain and make it move and live!

2

A grief without a pang, void, dark and drear,
  A stifled, drowsy, unimpassioned grief,
  Which finds no natural outlet, no relief,
    In word, or sigh, or tear –
Oh Lady! in this wan and heartless mood,
To other thoughts by yonder throstle wooed,
  All this long eve, so balmy and serene,
 Have I been gazing on the western sky,
  And its peculiar tint of yellow-green:
And still I gaze – and with how blank an eye!
And those thin clouds above, in flakes and bars,
That give away their motion to the stars;
Those stars, that glide behind them, or between,
Now sparkling, now bedimmed, but always seen:
Yon crescent Moon, as fixed as if it grew
In its own cloudless, starless lake of blue;
I see them all so excellently fair,
I see, not feel, how beautiful they are!

3

    My genial spirits fail;
    And what can these avail
To lift the smothering weight from off my breast?
    It were a vain endeavour,
    Though I should gaze for ever
On that green light that lingers in the west:
I may not hope from outward forms to win
The passion and the life whose fountains are within.

4

O Lady! we receive but what we give,
And in our life alone does Nature live:
Ours is her wedding garment, ours her shroud!
  And would we aught behold, of higher worth,
Than that inanimate cold world allowed

To the poor loveless ever-anxious crowd,
   Ah! from the soul itself must issue forth
A light, a glory, a fair luminous cloud
     Enveloping the Earth –
And from the soul itself must there be sent
   A sweet and potent voice, of its own birth,
Of all sweet sounds the life and element!

5

O pure of heart! thou need'st not ask of me
What this strong music in the soul may be!
What, and wherein it doth exist,
This light, this glory, this fair luminous mist,
This beautiful and beauty-making power.
   Joy, virtuous Lady! Joy that ne'er was given,
Save to the pure, and in their purest hour,
Life and Life's effluence, cloud at once and shower,
Joy, Lady! is the spirit and the power,
Which wedding Nature to us gives in dower
   A new Earth and new Heaven,
Undreamt of by the sensual and the proud –
Joy is the sweet voice, Joy the luminous cloud –
     We in ourselves rejoice!
And thence flows all that charms or ear or sight,
   All melodies the echoes of that voice,
All colours a suffusion from that light.

6

There was a time when, though my path was rough,
   This joy within me dallied with distress,
And all misfortunes were but as the stuff
   Whence Fancy made me dreams of happiness:
For hope grow round me, like the twining vine,
And fruits and foliage, not my own, seemed mine.
But now afflictions bow me down to earth:
Nor care I that they rob me of my mirth;
     But oh! each visitation
Suspends what nature gave me at my birth,
   My shaping spirit of Imagination.
For not to think of what I needs must feel,

But to be still and patient all I can;
And haply by abstruse research to steal
    From my own nature all the natural man –
    This was my sole resource, my only plan:
Till that which suits a part infects the whole,
And now is almost grown the habit of my soul.

7

Hence, viper thoughts, that coil around my mind,
    Reality's dark dream!
I turn from you, and listen to the wind,
    Which long has raved unnoticed. What a scream
Of agony by torture lengthened out
That lute sent forth! Thou Wind, that rav'st without,
    Bare crag, or mountain tairn, or blasted tree,
Or pine grove whither woodman never clomb,
Or lonely house, long held the witches' home,
    Methinks were fitter instruments for thee,
Mad Lutanist! who in this month of showers,
Of dark brown gardens, and of peeping flowers,
Mak'st devils' yule, with worse than wintry song,
The blossoms, buds, and timorous leaves among.
    Thou actor, perfect in all tragic sounds!
Thou mighty poet, e'en to frenzy bold!
        What tell'st thou now about?
        'Tis of the rushing of an host in rout,
    With groans of trampled men, with smarting wounds –
At once they groan with pain, and shudder with the cold!
But hush! there is a pause of deepest silence!
    And all that noise, as of a rushing crowd,
With groans and tremulous shudderings – all is over –
    It tells another tale, with sounds less deep and loud!
        A tale of less affright,
        And tempered with delight,
As Otway's self head framed the tender lay –
        'Tis of a little child
        Upon a lonesome wild,
Not far from home, but she hath lost her way:
And now moans low in bitter grief and fear,
And now screams loud, and hopes to make her mother hear.

8

'Tis midnight, but small thoughts have I of sleep:
Full seldom may my friend such vigils keep!
Visit her, gentle Sleep! with wings of healing,
  And may this storm be but a mountain-birth,
May all the stars hang bright above her dwelling,
    Silent as though they watched the sleeping Earth!
      With light heart may she rise,
        Gay fancy, cheerful eyes,
      Joy lift her spirit, joy attune her voice;
  To her may all things live, from pole to pole,
  Their life the eddying of her living soul!
    O simple spirit, guided from above,
Dear Lady! friend devoutest of my choice,
Thus may'st thou ever, evermore rejoice.

The Rime of the Ancient Mariner

1

It is an ancient Mariner,
And he stoppeth one of three.
'By thy long gray beard and glittering eye,
Now wherefore stopp'st thou me?

The Bridegroom's doors are opened wide,
And I am next of kin;
The guests are met, the feast is set;
May'st hear the merry din.'

He holds him with his skinny hand,
'There was a ship,' quoth he.
'Hold off! unhand me, grey-beard loon!'
Eftsoons his hand dropped he.

He holds him with his glittering eye –
The Wedding-Guest stood still,
And listens like a three years' child:
The Mariner hath his will.

The Wedding-Guest sat on a stone:
He cannot choose but hear;
And thus spake on that ancient man,
The bright-eyed Mariner.

'The ship was cheered, the harbour cleared,
Merrily did we drop
Below the kirk, below the hill,
Below the lighthouse top.

The Sun came up upon the left,
Out of the sea came he!
And he shone bright, and on the right
Went down into the sea.

Higher and higher every day,
Till over the mast at noon – '
The Wedding-Guest here beat his breast,
For he heard the loud bassoon.

The bride hath paced into the hall,
Red as a rose is she;
Nodding their heads before her goes
The merry minstrelsy.

The Wedding-Guest he beat his breast,
Yet he cannot choose but hear;
And thus spake on that ancient man,
The bright-eyed Mariner.

'And now the Storm-Blast came, and he
Was tyrannous and strong:
He struck with his o'ertaking wings,
And chased us south along.

With sloping masts and dipping prow,
As who pursued with yell and blow
Still treads the shadow of his foe,

And forward bends his head,
The ship drove fast, loud roared the blast,
And southward aye we fled.

And now there came both mist and snow,
And it grew wondrous cold:
And ice, mast-high, came floating by,
As green as emerald.

And through the drifts the snowy clifts
Did send a dismal sheen:
Nor shapes of men nor beasts we ken –
The ice was all between.

The ice was here, the ice was there,
The ice was all around:
It cracked and growled, and roared and howled,
Like noises in a swound!

At length did cross an Albatross,
Thorough the fog it came;
As if it had been a Christian soul,
We hailed it in God's name.

It ate the food it ne'er had eat,
And round and round it flew.
The ice did split with a thunder-fit;
The helmsman steered us through!

And a good south wind sprung up behind;
The Albatross did follow,
And every day, for food or play,
Came to the mariner's hollo!

In mist or cloud, on mast or shroud,
It perched for vespers nine;
Whiles all the night, through fog-smoke white,
Glimmered the white moonshine.'

'God save thee, ancient Mariner!
From the fiends, that plague thee thus! –
Why look'st thou so?' – 'With my crossbow
I shot the Albatross.

2

The Sun now rose upon the right:
Out of the sea came he,
Still hid in mist, and on the left
Went down into the sea.

And the good south wind still blew behind,
But no sweet bird did follow,
Nor any day for food or play
Came to the mariners' hollo!

And I had done a hellish thing,
And it would work 'em woe:
For all averred, I had killed the bird
That made the breeze to blow.
Ah wretch! said they, the bird to slay,
That made the breeze to blow!

Nor dim nor red, like God's own head,
That glorious Sun uprist:
Then all averred, I had killed the bird
That brought the fog and mist.
'Twas right, said they, such birds to slay,
That bring the fog and mist.

The fair breeze blew, the white foam flew,
The furrow followed free;
We were the first that ever burst
Into that silent sea.

Down dropped the breeze, the sails dropped down,
'Twas sad as sad could be;
And we did speak only to break
The silence of the sea!

All in a hot and copper sky,
The bloody Sun, at noon,
Right up above the mast did stand,
No bigger than the Moon.

Day after day, day after day,
We stuck, nor breath nor motion;
As idle as a painted ship
Upon a painted ocean.

Water, water, everywhere,
And all the boards did shrink;
Water, water, everywhere,
Nor any drop to drink.

The very deep did rot: O Christ!
That ever this should be!
Yea, slimy things did crawl with legs
Upon the slimy sea.

About, about, in reel and rout
The death-fires danced at night;
The water, like a witch's oils,
Burnt green, and blue and white.

And some in dreams assured were
Of the Spirit that plagued us so;
Nine fathom deep he had followed us
From the land of mist and snow.

And every tongue, through utter drought,
Was withered at the root;
We could not speak, no more than if
We had been choked with soot.

Ah! well-a-day! what evil looks
Had I from old and young!
Instead of the cross, the Albatross
About my neck was hung.

3

There passed a weary time. Each throat
Was parched, and glazed each eye.
A weary time! a weary time!
How glazed each weary eye,
When looking westward, I beheld
A something in the sky.

At first it seemed a little speck,
And then it seemed a mist;
It moved and moved, and took at last
A certain shape, I wist.

A speck, a mist, a shape, I wist!
And still it neared and neared:
As if it dodged a water-sprite,
It plunged and tacked and veered.

With throats unslaked, with black lips baked,
We could nor laugh nor wail;
Through utter drought all dumb we stood!
I bit my arm, I sucked the blood,
And cried, A sail! a sail!

With throats unslaked, with black lips baked,
Agape they heard me call:
Gramercy! they for joy did grin,
And all at once their breath drew in,
As they were drinking all.

See! see! (I cried) she tacks no more!
Hither to work us weal;
Without a breeze, without a tide,
She steadies with upright keel!

The western wave was all aflame.
The day was well nigh done!
Almost upon the western wave
Rested the broad bright sun;
When that strange shape drove suddenly
Betwixt us and the Sun.

And straight the Sun was flecked with bars
(Heaven's Mother send us grace!),
As if through a dungeon grate he peered
With broad and burning face.

Alas! (thought I, and my heart beat loud)
How fast she nears and nears!
Are those her sails that glance in the Sun,
Like restless gossameres?

Are those her ribs through which the Sun
Did peer, as through a grate?
And is that Woman all her crew?
Is that a Death? and are there two?
Is Death that woman's mate?

Her lips were red, her looks were free,
Her locks were yellow as gold:
Her skin was as white as leprosy,
The Nightmare Life-in-Death was she,
Who thicks man's blood with cold.

The naked hulk alongside came,
And the twain were casting dice;
'The game is done! I've won! I've won!'
Quoth she, and whistled thrice.

The Sun's rim dips; the stars rush out:
At one stride comes the dark;
With far-heard whisper, o'er the sea,
Off shot the spectre-bark.

We listened and looked sideways up!
Fear at my heart, as at a cup,
My lifeblood seemed to sip!
The stars were dim, and thick the night,
The steersman's face by his lamp gleamed white;
From the sails the dew did drip –
Till clomb above the eastern bar
The horned Moon, with one bright star
Within the nether tip.

One after one, by the star-dogged Moon,
Too quick for groan or sigh,
Each turned his face with a ghastly pang,
And cursed me with his eye.

Four times fifty living men
(And I heard nor sigh nor groan),
With heavy thump, a lifeless lump,
They dropped down one by one.

The souls did from their bodies fly –
They fled to bliss or woe!
And every soul, it passed me by,
Like the whizz of my crossbow!'

4

'I fear thee, ancient Mariner!
I fear thy skinny hand!
And thou art long, and lank, and brown,
As in the ribbed sea-sand.

I fear thee and thy glittering eye,
And thy skinny hand, so brown.' –
'Fear not, fear not, thou Wedding-Guest!
This body dropped not down.

Alone, alone, all, all alone,
Alone on a wide wide sea!
And never a saint took pity on
My soul in agony.

The many men, so beautiful!
And they all dead did lie:
And a thousand thousand slimy things
Lived on; and so did I.

I looked upon the rotting sea,
And drew my eyes away;
I looked upon the rotting deck,
And there the dead men lay.

I looked to heaven, and tried to pray;
But or ever a prayer had gushed,
A wicked whisper came, and made
My heart as dry as dust.

I closed my lids, and kept them close,
And the balls like pulses beat;
For the sky and the sea, and the sea and the sky
Lay like a load on my weary eye,
And the dead were at my feet.

The cold sweat melted from their limbs,
Nor rot nor reek did they:
The look with which they looked on me
Had never passed away.

An orphan's curse would drag to hell
A spirit from on high;
But oh! more horrible than that
Is the curse in a dead man's eye!
Seven days, seven nights, I saw that curse,
And yet I could not die.

The moving Moon went up the sky,
And nowhere did abide:
Softly she was going up,
And a star or two beside –

Her beams bemocked the sultry main,
Like April hoar-frost spread;
But where the ship's huge shadow lay,
The charmed water burnt alway
A still and awful red.

Beyond the shadow of the ship,
I watched the water snakes:
They moved in tracks of shining white,
And when they reared, the elfish light
Fell off in hoary flakes.

Within the shadow of the ship
I watched their rich attire:
Blue, glossy green, and velvet black,
They coiled and swam; and every track
Was a flash of golden fire.

O happy living things! no tongue
Their beauty might declare:
A spring of love gushed from my heart,
And I blessed them unaware:
Sure my kind saint look pity on me,
And I blessed them unaware.

The self-same moment I could pray;
And from my neck so free
The Albatross fell off, and sank
Like lead into the sea.

5

Oh sleep! it is a gentle thing,
Beloved from pole to pole!
To Mary Queen the praise be given!
She sent the gentle sleep from Heaven,
That slid into my soul.

The silly buckets on the deck,
That had so long remained,
I dreamt that they were filled with dew;
And when I awoke, it rained.

My lips were wet, my throat was cold,
My garments all were dank;
Sure I had drunken in my dreams,
And still my body drank.

I moved, and could not feel my limbs:
I was so light – almost
I thought that I had died in sleep,
And was a blessed ghost.

And soon I heard a roaring wind:
It did not come anear;
But with its sound it shook the sails,
That were so thin and sere.

The upper air burst into life!
And a hundred fire-flags sheen,
To and fro they were hurried about!
And to and fro, and in and out,
The wan stars danced between.

And the coming wind did roar more loud,
And the sails did sigh like sedge;
And the rain poured down from one black cloud;
The Moon was at its edge.

The thick black cloud was cleft, and still
The Moon was at its side:
Like waters shot from some high crag,
The lightning fell with never a jag,
A river steep and wide.

The loud wind never reached the ship,
Yet now the ship moved on!
Beneath the lightning and the Moon
The dead men gave a groan.

They groaned, they stirred, they all uprose,
Nor spake, nor moved their eyes;
It had been strange, even in a dream,
To have seen those dead men rise.

The helmsman steered, the ship moved on;
Yet never a breeze up-blew;
The mariners all 'gan work the ropes,
Where they were wont to do;
They raised their limbs like lifeless tools —
We were a ghastly crew.

The body of my brother's son
Stood by me, knee to knee:
The body and I pulled at one rope,
But he said nought to me.'

'I fear thee, ancient Mariner!'
'Be calm, thou Wedding-Guest!
'Twas not those souls that fled in pain,
Which to their corses came again,
But a troop of spirits blest:

For when it dawned — they dropped their arms,
And clustered round the mast;
Sweet sounds rose slowly through their mouths,
And from their bodies passed.

Around, around, flew each sweet sound,
Then darted to the Sun;
Slowly the sounds came back again,
Now mixed, now one by one.

Sometimes a-dropping from the sky
I heard the skylark sing;
Sometimes all little birds that are,
How they seemed to fill the sea and air
With their sweet jargoning!

And now 'twas like all instruments,
Now like a lonely flute;
And now it is an angel's song,
That makes the heavens be mute.

It ceased; yet still the sails made on
A pleasant noise till noon,
A noise like of a hidden brook
In the leafy month of June,
That to the sleeping woods all night
Singeth a quiet tune.

Till noon we quietly sailed on,
Yet never a breeze did breathe:
Slowly and smoothly went the ship,
Moved onward from beneath.

Under the keel nine fathom deep,
From the land of mist and snow,
The spirit slid: and it was he
That made the ship to go.
The sails at noon left off their tune,
And the ship stood still also.

The Sun, right up above the mast,
Had fixed her to the ocean:
But in a minute she 'gan stir,
With a short uneasy motion –
Backwards and forwards half her length
With a short, uneasy motion.

Then like a pawing horse let go,
She made a sudden bound:
It flung the blood into my head,
And I fell down in a swound.

How long in that same fit I lay,
I have not to declare;
But ere my living life returned,
I heard and in my soul discerned
Two voices in the air.

'Is it he?' quoth one, 'Is this the man?
By him who died on cross,
With his cruel bow he laid full low
The harmless Albatross.

The spirit who bideth by himself
In the land of mist and snow,
He loved the bird that loved the man
Who shot him with his bow.'

The other was a softer voice,
As soft as honeydew:
Quoth he, 'The man hath penance done,
And penance more will do.'

6

First Voice
'But tell me, tell me! speak again,
Thy soft response renewing –
What makes that ship drive on so fast?
What is the ocean doing?'

Second Voice
'Still as a slave before his lord,
The ocean hath no blast;
His great bright eye most silently
Up to the Moon is cast –

If he may know which way to go;
For she guides him, smooth or grim.
See, brother, see! how graciously
She looketh down on him.'

First Voice
'But why drives on that ship so fast,
Without or wave or wind?'

Second Voice
'The air is cut away before,
And closes from behind.

Fly, brother, fly! more high, more high!
Or we shall be belated:

For slow and slow that ship will go,
When the Mariner's trance is abated.'

I woke, and we were sailing on
As in a gentle weather:
'Twas night, calm night, the moon was high;
The dead men stood together.

All stood together on the deck,
For a charnel-dungeon fitter:
All fixed on me their stony eyes,
That in the Moon did glitter.

The pang, the curse, with which they died,
Had never passed away:
I could not draw my eyes from theirs,
Nor turn them up to pray.

And now this spell was snapped: once more
I viewed the ocean green,
And looked far forth, yet little saw
Of what had else been seen –

Like one, that on a lonesome road
Doth walk in fear and dread,
And having once turned round walks on,
And turns no more his head;
Because he knows, a frightful fiend
Doth close behind him tread.

But soon there breathed a wind on me,
Nor sound nor motion made:
Its path was not upon the sea,
In ripple or in shade.

It raised my hair, it fanned my cheek
Like a meadow-gale of spring –
It mingled strangely with my fears,
Yet it felt like a welcoming.

Swiftly, swiftly flew the ship,
Yet she sailed softly too:
Sweetly, sweetly blew the breeze –
On me alone it blew.

Oh! dream of joy! is this indeed
The lighthouse top I see?
Is this the hill? is this the kirk?
Is this mine own countree?

We drifted o'er the harbour bar,
And I with sobs did pray –
O let me be awake, my God!
Or let me sleep alway.

The harbour bay was clear as glass,
So smoothly it was strewn!
And on the bay the moonlight lay,
And the shadow of the Moon.

The rock shone bright, the kirk no less,
That stands above the rock:
The moonlight steeped in silentness
The steady weathercock.

And the bay was white with silent light,
Till rising from the same,
Full many shapes, that shadows were,
In crimson colours came.

A little distance from the prow
Those crimson shadows were:
I turned my eyes upon the deck –
Oh, Christ! what saw I there!

Each corse lay flat, lifeless and flat,
And, by the holy rood!
A man all light, a seraph man,
On every corse there stood.

This seraph band, each waved his hand:
It was a heavenly sight!
They stood as signals to the land,
Each one a lovely light;

This seraph band, each waved his hand,
No voice they did impart –
No voice; but oh! the silence sank
Like music on my heart.

But soon I heard the clash of oars,
I heard the Pilot's cheer;
My head was turned perforce away
And I saw a boat appear.

The Pilot and the Pilot's boy,
I heard them coming fast:
Dear Lord in Heaven! it was a joy
The dead men could not blast.

I saw a third – I heard his voice:
It is the Hermit good!
He singeth loud his goodly hymns
That he makes in the wood.
He'll shrieve my soul, he'll wash away
The Albatross's blood.

7

This Hermit good lives in that wood
Which slopes down to the sea.
How loudly his sweet voice he rears!
He loves to talk with mariners
That come from a far countree.

He kneels at morn, and noon, and eve –
He hath a cushion plump:
It is the moss that wholly hides
The rotted old oak-stump.

The skiff-boat neared: I heard them talk,
'Why, this is strange, I trow!
Where are those lights, so many and fair,
That signal made but now?'

'Strange, by my faith!' the Hermit said –
'And they answered not our cheer!
The planks looked warped! and see those sails
How thin they are and sere!
I never saw aught like to them,
Unless perchance it were

Brown skeletons of leaves that lag
My forest-brook along;
When the ivy-tod is heavy with snow,
And the owlet whoops to the wolf below
That eats the she-wolf's young.'

'Dear Lord! it hath a fiendish look'
(The Pilot made reply),
'I am a-feared.' – 'Push on, push on!'
Said the Hermit cheerily.

The boat came closer to the ship,
But I nor spake nor stirred;
The boat came close beneath the ship,
And straight a sound was heard.

Under the water it rumbled on,
Still louder and more dread:
It reached the ship, it split the bay;
The ship went down like lead.

Stunned by that loud and dreadful sound,
Which sky and ocean smote,
Like one that hath been seven days drowned
My body lay afloat;
But, swift as dreams, myself I found
Within the Pilot's boat.

Upon the whirl, where sunk the ship,
The boat spun round and round;
And all was still, save that the hill
Was telling of the sound.

I moved my lips – the Pilot shrieked
And fell down in a fit;
The holy Hermit raised his eyes,
And prayed where he did sit.

I took the oars: the Pilot's boy,
Who now doth crazy go,
Laughed loud and long, and all the while,
His eyes went to and fro.
'Ha! ha!' quoth he, 'full plain I see,
The Devil knows how to row.'

And now, all in my own countree,
I stood on the firm land!
The Hermit stepped forth from the boat,
And scarcely he could stand.

'O shrieve me, shrieve me, holy man!'
The Hermit crossed his brow.
'Say quick,' quoth he, 'I bid thee say –
What manner of man art thou?'

Forthwith this frame of mine was wrenched
With a woeful agony,
Which forced me to begin my tale;
And then it left me free.

Since then, at an uncertain hour,
That agony returns:
And till my ghastly tale is told,
This heart within me burns.

I pass, like night, from land to land;
I have strange power of speech;
That moment that his face I see,
I know the man that must hear me:
To him my tale I teach.

What loud uproar bursts from that door!
That wedding-guests are there:
But in the garden-bower the bride
And bride-maids singing are:
And hark the little vesper bell,
Which biddeth me to prayer!

O Wedding-Guest! this soul hath been
Alone on a wide wide sea:
So lonely 'twas, that God himself
Scarce seemed there to be.

O sweeter than the marriage feast,
'Tis sweeter far to me,
To walk together to the kirk
With a goodly company! –

To walk together to the kirk,
And all together pray,
While each to his great Father bends,
Old men, and babes, and loving friends,
And youths and maidens gay!

Farewell, farewell! but this I tell
To thee, thou Wedding-Guest!
He prayeth well, who loveth well
Both man and bird and beast.

He prayeth best, who loveth best
All things both great and small;
For the dear God who loveth us,
He made and loveth all.'

The Mariner, whose eye is bright,
Whose beard with age is hoar,
Is gone: and now the Wedding-Guest
Turned from the bridegroom's door.

He went like one that hath been stunned,
And is of sense forlorn:
A sadder and a wiser man,
He rose the morrow morn.

FRANCES CORNFORD
1886–1960

To a Fat Lady Seen from a Train

O why do you walk through the fields in gloves,
    Missing so much and so much?
O fat white woman whom nobody loves,
Why do you walk through the fields in gloves,
When the grass is soft as the breast of doves
    And shivering-sweet to the touch?
O why do you walk through the fields in gloves,
    Missing so much and so much?

WILLIAM CORNISH
d. 1523

You and I and Amyas

You and I and Amyas,
Amyas and you and I,
To the green wood must we go, alas!
You and I, my life, and Amyas.

The knight knocked at the castle gate;
The lady marvelled who was thereat.

To call the porter he would not blin;
The lady said he should not come in.

The portress was a lady bright;
Strangeness that lady hight.

She asked him what was his name:
He said 'Desire, your man, Madame.'

She said, 'Desire, what do ye here?'
He said, 'Madame, as your prisoner.'

He was counselled to brief a bill,
And show my lady his own will.

'Kindness,' said she, 'would it bear,'
'And Pity,' said she, 'would be there.'

Thus how they did we cannot say;
We left them there and went our way.

WILLIAM JOHNSON CORY
1823–1892

Heraclitus

They told me, Heraclitus, they told me you were dead,
They brought me bitter news to hear and bitter tears to shed.
I wept as I remember'd how often you and I
Had tired the sun with talking and sent him down the sky.
And now that thou art lying, my dear old Carian guest,
A handful of grey ashes, long, long ago at rest,
Still are thy pleasant voices, thy nightingales, awake;
For Death, he taketh all away, but them he cannot take.

WILLIAM COWPER
1731–1800

Hymn

God moves in a mysterious way,
    His wonders to perform;
He plants his footsteps in the sea,
    And rides upon the storm.

Deep in unfathomable mines
    Of never-failing skill
He treasures up his bright designs,
    And works his sovereign will.

Ye fearful saints fresh courage take,
    The clouds ye so much dread
Are big with mercy, and shall break
    In blessings on your head.

Judge not the Lord by feeble sense,
    But trust him for his grace;
Behind a frowning providence,
    He hides a smiling face.

His purposes will ripen fast,
    Unfolding ev'ry hour;
The bud may have a bitter taste,
    But sweet will be the flow'r.

Blind unbelief is sure to err,
    And scan his work in vain;
God is his own interpreter,
    And he will make it plain.

ADELAIDE CRAPSEY
1878–1914

Cinquains

1

Triad

These be
Three silent things:
The falling snow . . . the hour
Before the dawn . . . the mouth of one
Just dead.

2
Moon Shadows

Still as
On windless nights
The moon-cast shadows are,
So still will be my heart when I
Am dead.

3
Susanna and the Elders

'Why do
You thus devise
Evil against her?' 'For that
She is beautiful, delicate;
Therefore.'

4
Night Winds

The old
Old winds that blew
When chaos was, what do
They tell the clattered trees that I
Should weep?

5
Amaze

I know
Not these hands
And yet I think there was
A woman like me once had hands
Like these.

6
The Warning

Just now,
Out of the strange
Still dusk . . . as strange, as still . . .
A white moth flew . . Why am I grown
So cold?

RICHARD CRASHAW
c.1612–1649

Easter Day

Rise, heir of fresh Eternity,
   From Thy virgin tomb:
Rise, mighty Man of wonders, and Thy world with Thee,
   Thy tomb, the universal East,
   Nature's new womb,
Thy tomb, fair Immortality's perfumèd nest.

Of all the glories make noon gay
   This is the morn.
This rock buds forth the fountain of the streams of day.
   In joy's white annals live this hour,
   When life was born,
No cloud scowl on His radiant lids, no tempest lower.

Life, by this light's nativity
   All creatures have.
Death only by this day's just doom is forc'd to die;
   Nor is death forc'd; for may he lie
   Thron'd in Thy grave;
Death will on this condition be content to die.

e. e. cummings
1894–1962

'next to of course god america i
love you land of the pilgrims' and so forth oh
say can you see by the dawn's early my
country 'tis of centuries come and go
and are no more what of it we should worry
in every language even deafanddumb
thy sons acclaim your glorious name by gorry
by jingo by gee by gosh by gum
why talk of beauty what could be more beaut-
iful than these heroic happy dead
who rushed like lions to the roaring slaughter
they did not stop to think they died instead
then shall the voice of liberty be mute?'

He spoke. And drank rapidly a glass of water

SAMUEL DANIEL
1563–1619

Sonnet

Care-charmer Sleep, son of the sable Night,
   Brother to Death, in silent darkness born,
Relieve my languish, and restore the light,
   With dark forgetting of my cares return.
And let the day be time enough to mourn
   The shipwreck of my ill-adventured youth;
Let waking eyes suffice to wail their scorn,
   Without the torment of the night's untruth.
Cease, dreams, the images of day-desires,
   To model forth the passions of the morrow;
Never let rising sun approve you liars,
   To add more grief to aggravate my sorrow.
      Still let me sleep, embracing clouds in vain;
      And never wake to feel the day's disdain.

SIR WILLIAM DAVENANT
1606–1668

Song

The lark now leaves his watery nest,
    And climbing, shakes his dewy wings:
He takes this window for the east;
    And to implore your light, he sings.
Awake, awake, the morn will never rise
Till she can dress her beauty at your eyes.

The merchant bows unto the seaman's star,
    The ploughman from the sun his season takes;
But still the lover wonders what they are,
    Who look for day before his mistress wakes.
Awake, awake, break through your veils of lawn!
Then draw your curtains, and begin the dawn.

W. H. DAVIES
1871–1940

Leisure

What is this life if, full of care,
We have no time to stand and stare.

No time to stand beneath the boughs
And stare as long as sheep or cows.

No time to see, when woods we pass,
Where squirrels hide their nuts in grass.

No time to see, in broad daylight,
Streams full of stars, like skies at night.

No time to turn at Beauty's glance,
And watch her feet, how they can dance.

No time to wait till her mouth can
Enrich that smile her eyes began.

A poor life this if, full of care,
We have no time to stand and stare.

CHARLES DIBDIN
1745–1814

Poor Tom

Here, a sheer hulk, lies poor Tom Bowling,
    The darling of our crew,
No more he'll hear the tempest howling,
    For death has broached him to.
His form was of the manliest beauty,
    His heart was kind and soft,
Faithful below he did his duty,
    But now he's gone aloft.

Tom never from his word departed,
    His virtues were so rare,
His friends were many, and true-hearted,
    His Poll was kind and fair:
And then he'd sing so blithe and jolly,
    Ah many's the time and oft!
But mirth is turned to melancholy,
    For Tom is gone aloft.

Yet shall poor Tom find pleasant weather,
    When he, who all commands,
Shall give, to call life's crew together,
    The word to pipe all hands.
Thus death, who kings and tars despatches,
    In vain Tom's life has doffed,
For though his body's under hatches,
    His soul is gone aloft.

The Lady's Diary

Lectured by Pa and Ma o'er night,
Monday at ten quite vexed and jealous,
Resolved in future to be right,
And never listen to the fellows:
Stitched half a wristband, read the text,
Received a note from Mrs Racket:
I hate that woman, she sat next
All church-time to sweet Captain Clackit.

Tuesday got scolded, did not care,
The toast was cold, 'twas past eleven;
I dreamed the Captain through the air
On Cupid's wings bore me to heaven;
Pouted and dined, dressed, looked divine,
Made an excuse, got Ma to back it;
Went to the play, what joy was mine!
Talked loud and laughed with Captain Clackit.

Wednesday came down no lark so gay,
'The girl's quite altered,' said my mother;
Cried Dad, 'I recollect the day
When, dearee, thou wert such another.'
Danced, drew a landscape, skimmed a play,
In the paper read that widow Flackit
To Gretna Green had run away,
The forward minx, with Captain Clackit.

Thursday fell sick: 'Poor soul she'll die.'
Five doctors came with lengthened faces;
Each felt my pulse; 'Ah me,' cried I,
'Are these my promised loves and graces?'
Friday grew worse; cried Ma, in pain,
'Our day was fair, heaven do not black it;
Where's your complaint, love?' – 'In my brain.'
'What shall I give you?' – 'Captain Clackit.'

Early next morn a nostrum came
Worth all their cordials, balms and spices;
A letter, I had been to blame;
The Captain's truth brought on a crisis.
Sunday, for fear of more delays,
Of a few clothes I made a packet,
And Monday morn stepped in a chaise
And ran away with Captain Clackit.

EMILY DICKINSON
1830–1886

Drowning is not so pitiful
     As the attempt to rise.
Three times, 'tis said, a sinking man
     Comes up to face the skies,
And then declines forever
     To that adhorred abode
Where hope and he part company –
     For he is grasped of God.
The Maker's cordial visage,
     However good to see,
Is shunned, we must admit it,
     Like an adversity.

Parting

My life closed twice before its close;
     It yet remains to see
If Immortality unveil
     A third event to me.

So huge, so hopeless to conceive,
     As these that twice befell.
Parting is all we know of heaven,
     And all we need of hell.

The Railway Train

I like to see it lap the miles,
And lick the valleys up,
And stop to feed itself at tanks;
And then, prodigious, step

Around a pile of mountains,
And, supercilious, peer
In shanties by the sides of roads;
And then a quarry pare

To fit its sides, and crawl between,
Complaining all the while
In horrid, hooting stanza;
Then chase itself downhill

and neigh like Boanerges;
Then, punctual as a star,
Stop – docile and omnipotent –
At its own stable door.

The Snake

A narrow fellow in the grass
Occasionally rides;
You may have met him – did you not,
His notice sudden is.

The grass divides as with a comb,
A spotted shaft is seen;
And then it closes at your feet
And opens further on.

He likes a boggy acre,
A floor too cool for corn.
Yet when a child, and barefoot,
I more than once, at morn,

Have passed, I thought, a whiplash
Unbraiding in the sun –
When, stooping to secure it,
It wrinkled, and was gone.

Several of nature's people
I know, and they know me;
I feel for them a transport
Of cordiality;

But never met this fellow,
Attended or alone,
Without a tighter breathing,
And zero at the bone.

Safe in their Alabaster Chambers

Safe in their alabaster chambers,
Untouched by morning and untouched by noon,
Sleep the meek members of the resurrection,
Rafter of satin, and roof of stone.

Light laughs the breeze in her castle of sunshine;
Babbles the bee in a stolid ear;
Pipe the sweet birds in ignorant cadence –
Ah, what sagacity perished here!

Grand go the years in the crescent above them;
Worlds scoop their arcs, and firmaments row,
Diadems drop and Doges surrender,
Soundless as dots on a disk of snow.

Surgeons Must be Very Careful

Surgeons must be very careful
When they take the knife!
Underneath their fine incisions
Stirs the Culprit – *Life*.

JOHN DONNE
1572–1631

Song

Go, and catch a falling star,
   Get with child a mandrake root,
Tell me where all past years are,
   Or who cleft the Devil's foot,
Teach me to hear mermaids singing,
   Or to keep off envy's stinging,
        And find
        What wind
Serves to advance an honest mind.

If thou be'est born to strange sights,
   Things invisible to see,
Ride ten thousand days and nights,
   Till age snow white hairs on thee,
Thou, when thou return'st, wilt tell me
All strange wonders that befell thee,
        And swear
        Nowhere
Lives a woman true, and fair.

If thou find'st one, let me know,
   Such a pilgrimage were sweet,
Yet do not, I would not go,
   Though at next door we might meet,
Though she were true, when you met her,
And last, till you write your letter,
        Yet she
        Will be
False, ere I come, to two, or three.

The Flea

Mark but this flea, and mark in this,
How little that which thou deny'st me is;
Me it sucked first, and now sucks thee,
And in this flea, our two bloods mingled be;
Confess it, this cannot be said
A sin, or shame, or loss of maidenhead,
   Yet this enjoys before it woo,
     And pampered swells with one blood made of two,
     And this, alas, is more than we would do.

Oh stay, three lives in one flea spare,
Where we almost, nay more than married are.
This flea is you and I, and this
Our marriage bed, and marriage temple is;
Though parents grudge, and you, we are met,
And cloistered in these living walls of jet.
     Though use make you apt to kill me,
     Let not to this, self murder added be,
     And sacrilege, three sins in killing three.

Cruel and sudden, hast thou since
Purpled thy nail, in blood of innocence?
In what could this flea guilty be,
Except in that drop which it sucked from thee?
Yet thou triumph'st, and say'st that thou
Find'st not thyself, nor me the weaker now;
   'Tis true, then learn how false, fears be;
     Just so much honour, when thou yield'st to me,
     Will waste, as this flea's death took life from thee.

The Ecstasy

Where, like a pillow on a bed,
   A pregnant bank swelled up, to rest
The violet's reclining head,
   Sat we two, one another's best;

Our hands were firmly cemented
   With a fast balm, which thence did spring;
Our eye-beams twisted, and did thread
   Our eyes, upon one double string;

So to intergraft our hands, as yet
   Was all our means to make us one,
And pictures in our eyes to get
   Was all our propagation.

As 'twixt two equal armies, Fate
   Suspends uncertain victory,
Our souls (which to advance their state,
   Were gone out) hung 'twixt her and me.

And whilst our souls negotiate there,
   We like sepulchral statues lay;
All day, the same our postures were,
   And we said nothing, all the day.

If any, so by love refined
   That he soul's language understood,
And by good love were grown all mind,
   Within convenient distance stood,

He (though he knew not which soul spake
   Because both meant, both spake the same)
Might thence a new concoction take,
   And part far purer than he came.

This ecstasy doth unperplex

(We said) and tell us what we love,
We see by this, it was not sex,
    We see, we saw not what did move:

But as all several souls contain
    Mixture of things, they know not what,
Love, these mixed souls doth mix again,
    And makes both one, each this and that.

A single violet transplant,
    The strength, the colour, and the size
(All which before was poor, and scant),
    Redoubles still, and multiplies.

When love, with one another so
    Interinanimates two souls,
That abler soul, which thence doth flow,
    Defects of loneliness controls.

We then who are this new soul, know,
    Of what we are composed and made,
For, th' atomies of which we grow,
    Are souls, whom no change can invade.

But O alas, so long, so far
    Our bodies why do we forbear?
They are ours, though they are not we, we are
    The intelligences, they the sphere.

We owe them thanks because they thus
    Did us, to us, at first convey,
Yielded their forces, sense, to us,
    Nor are dross to us, but allay.

On man heaven's influence works not so,
    But that it first imprints the air,
So soul into the soul may flow,
    Though it to body first repair.

As our blood labours to beget
   Spirits, as like souls as it can,
Because such fingers need to knit
   That subtle knot, which makes us man:

So must pure lovers' souls descend
   To affections, and to faculties,
Which sense may reach and apprehend,
   Else a great prince in prison lies.

To our bodies turn we then, that so
   Weak men on love revealed may look;
Love's mysteries in souls do grow,
   But yet the body is his book.

And if some lover, such as we,
   Have heard this dialogue of one,
Let him still mark us, he shall see
   Small change, when we're to bodies gone.

The Sun Rising

Busy old fool, unruly Sun,
Why dost thou thus,
Through windows, and through curtains all on us?
Must to thy motions lovers' seasons run?
Saucy pedantic wretch, go chide
Late schoolboys and sour 'prentices,
Go tell court-huntsmen that the King will ride,
Call country ants to harvest offices;
Love, all alike, no season knows, nor clime,
Nor hours, days, months, which are the rags of time.

Thy beams so reverend, and strong
Why shouldst thou think?
I could eclipse and cloud them with a wink,
But that I would not lose her sight so long:
If her eyes have not blinded thine,
Look, and tomorrow late, tell me,
Whether both the Indias of spice and mine
Be where thou left'st them, or lie here with me.
Ask for those kings whom thou saw'st yesterday,
And thou shalt hear, 'All here in one bed lay.'

She's all states, and all princes I,
Nothing else is.
Princes do but play us; compared to this,
All honour's mimic; all wealth alchemy.
Thou, Sun, art half as happy as we,
In that the world's contracted thus;
Thine age asks ease, and since thy duties be
To warm the world, that's done in warming us.
Shine here to us, and thou art everywhere;
This bed thy centre is, these walls thy sphere.

A Valediction: Forbidding Mourning

As virtuous men pass mildly away,
    And whisper to their souls to go,
Whilst some of their sad friends do say,
    'The breath goes now,' and some say, 'No':

So let us melt, and make no noise,
    No tear-floods, nor sigh-tempests move,
'Twere profanation of our joys
    To tell the laity our love.

Moving of the earth brings harms and fears,
    Men reckon what it did and meant,
But trepidation of the spheres,
    Though greater far, is innocent.

Dull sublunary lovers' love
    (Whose soul is sense) cannot admit
Absence, because it doth remove
    Those things which elemented it.

But we by a love, so much refined,
    That ourselves know not what it is,
Inter-assurèd of the mind,
    Care less, eyes, lips and hands to miss.

Our two souls therefore, which are one,
    Though I must go, endure not yet
A breach, but an expansion,
    Like gold to aery thinness beat.

If they be two, they are two so
    As stiff twin compasses are two,
Thy soul, the fixed foot, makes no show
    To move, but doth, if the other do.

And though it in the centre sit,
    Yet when the other far doth roam,
It leans, and hearkens after it,
    And grows erect, as it comes home.

Such wilt thou be to me, who must
   Like the other foot, obliquely run;
Thy firmness makes my circle just,
   And makes me end where I begun.

To His Mistress Going to Bed

Come, Madam, come, all rest my powers defy,
Until I labour, I in labour lie.
The foe oft-times having the foe in sight,
Is tired with standing though they never fight.
Off with that girdle, like heaven's zone glistering,
But a far fairer world encompassing.
Unpin that spangled breastplate which you wear,
That the eyes of busy fools may be stopped there.
Unlace yourself, for that harmonious chime,
Tells me from you, that now 'tis your bedtime.
Off with that happy busk, which I envy,
That still can be, and still can stand so nigh.
Your gown going off, such beauteous state reveals,
As when from flowery meads the hill's shadow steals.
Off with that wiry coronet and show
The hairy diadem which on you doth grow;
Now off with those shoes, and then safely tread
In this love's hallowed temple, this soft bed.
In such white robes heaven's angels used to be
Received by men; thou angel bring'st with thee
A heaven like Mahomet's paradise; and though
Ill spirits walk in white, we easily know
By this these angels from an evil sprite,
Those set our hairs, but these our flesh upright.
   Licence my roving hands, and let them go
Before, behind, between, above, below.
O my America, my new-found land,
My kingdom, safeliest when with one man manned,
My mine of precious stones; my empery,
How blessed am I in this discovering thee!
To enter in these bonds is to be free;

Then where my hand is set, my seal shall be.
　Full nakedness, all joys are due to thee.
As souls unbodied, bodies unclothed must be,
To taste whole joys. Gems which you women use
Are like Atlanta's balls, cast in men's views,
That when a fool's eye lighteth on a gem,
His earthly soul may covet theirs, not them.
Like pictures, or like books' gay coverings made
For laymen, are all women thus arrayed;
Themselves are mystic books, which only we
Whom their imputed grace will dignify
Must see revealed. Then since that I may know,
As liberally, as to a midwife, show
Thyself: cast all, yea, this white linen hence,
Here is no penance, much less innocence.
　To teach thee, I am naked first, why then
What needst thou have more covering than a man.

At the Round Earth's Imagined Corners

At the round earth's imagined corners, blow
Your trumpets, angels, and arise, arise
From death, you numberless infinities
Of souls, and to your scattered bodies go,
All whom the flood did, and fire shall o'erthrow,
All whom war, dearth, age, agues, tyrannies,
Despair, law, chance, hath slain, and you whose eyes
Shall behold God, and never taste death's woe.
But let them sleep, Lord, and me mourn a space,
For, if above all these, my sins abound,
'Tis late to ask abundance of thy grace,
When we are there; here on this lowly ground,
Teach me how to repent; for that's as good
As if thou hadst sealed my pardon, with thy blood.

Death, Be Not Proud

Death, be not proud, though some have called thee
Mighty and dreadful, for thou art not so,
For those whom thou think'st thou dost overthrow,
Die not, poor Death, nor yet canst thou kill me;
From rest and sleep, which but thy pictures be,
Much pleasure, then from thee, much more must flow,
And soonest our best men with thee do go,
Rest of their bones, and soul's delivery.
Thou art slave to fate, chance, kings and desperate men,
And dost with poison, war and sickness dwell,
And poppy or charms can make us sleep as well,
And better than thy stroke; why swell'st thou then?
One short sleep past, we wake eternally,
And death shall be no more. Death, thou shalt die.

Batter My Heart, Three-Personed God

Batter my heart, three-personed God; for you
As yet but knock, breathe, shine, and seek to mend;
That I may rise, and stand, o'erthrow me and bend
Your force, to break, blow, burn and make me new.
I, like an usurped town, to another due,
Labour to admit you, but oh, to no end,
Reason your viceroy in me, me should defend,
But is captived, and proves weak or untrue.
Yet dearly I love you, and would be loved fain,
But am betrothed unto your enemy.
Divorce me, untie, or break that knot again,
Take me to you, imprison me, for I,
Except you enthral me, never shall be free,
Nor ever chaste, except you ravish me.

ERNEST DOWSON
1867–1900

Non Sum Qualis Eram Bonae
Sub Regno Cynarae

Last night, ah, yesternight, betwixt her lips and mine
There fell thy shadow, Cynara! thy breath was shed
Upon my soul between the kisses and the wine;
And I was desolate and sick of an old passion,
    Yea, I was desolate and bow'd my head:
I have been faithful to thee, Cynara! in my fashion.

All night upon mine heart I felt her warm heart beat,
Night-long within mine arms in love and sleep she lay;
Surely the kisses of her bought red mouth were sweet;
But I was desolate and sick of an old passion,
    When I awoke and found the dawn was grey:
I have been faithful to thee, Cynara! in my fashion.

I have forgot much, Cynara! gone with the wind,
Flung roses, roses riotously with the throng,
Dancing, to put thy pale, lost lilies out of mind;
But I was desolate and sick of an old passion,
    Yea, all the time, because the dance was long:
I have been faithful to thee, Cynara! in my fashion.

I cried for madder music and for stronger wine,
But when the feast is finish'd and the lamps expire,
Then falls thy shadow, Cynara! the night is thine;
And I am desolate and sick of an old passion,
    Yea, hungry for the lips of my desire:
I have been faithful to thee, Cynara! in my fashion.

MICHAEL DRAYTON
1563–1631

Sonnet

How many paltry foolish painted things,
That now in coaches trouble every street,
Shall be forgotten, whom no poet sings,
Ere they be well wrapped in their winding-sheet!
Where I to thee eternity shall give,
When nothing else remaineth of these days,
And queens hereafter shall be glad to live
Upon the alms of thy superfluous praise.
Virgins and matrons, reading these my rhymes,
Shall be so much delighted with thy story,
That they shall grieve thy lived not in these times,
To have seen thee, their sex's only glory:
   So shalt thou fly above the vulgar throng,
   Still to survive in my immortal song.

Sonnet

Since there's no help, come let us kiss and part.
   Nay, I have done; you get no more of me,
And I am glad, yea, glad with all my heart,
   That thus so cleanly I myself can free;
Shake hands for ever, cancel all our vows.
   And when we meet at any time again,
Be it not seen in either of our brows
   That we one jot of former love retain.
Now at the last gasp of Love's latest breath,
   When, his pulse failing, Passion speechless lies,
When Faith is kneeling by his bed of death,
   And Innocence is closing up his eyes,
     Now if thou wouldst, when all have given him over,
     From death to life thou mightst him yet recover.

WILLIAM DRUMMOND OF HAWTHORNDEN
1585–1649

Madrigal

This world a hunting is,
The prey poor man, the Nimrod fierce is death;
His speedy greyhounds are
Lust, sickness, envy, care,
Strife that ne'er falls amiss,
With all those ills which haunt us while we breathe.
Now, if by chance we fly
Of these the eager chase,
Old age with stealing pace
Casts up his nets, and there we panting die.

Madrigal

Like the Idalian queen
Her hair about her eyne,
With her neck and breasts' ripe apples to be seen,
At first glance of the morn
In Cyprus gardens gathering those fair flowers
Which of her blood were born,
I saw, but fainting saw, my paramours,
The Graces naked danc'd about the place,
The winds and trees amaz'd
With silence on her gaz'd,
The flowers did smile, like those upon her face,
And as their aspen stalks those fingers band
(That she might read my case)
A hyacinth I wish'd me in her hand.

Attributed to SIR EDWARD DYER
1543–1607

In Praise of a Contented Mind

My mind to me a kingdom is.
  Such perfect joy therein I find
That it excels all other bliss
  That world affords or grows by kind.
    Though much I want which most men have,
    Yet still my mind forbids to crave.

No princely pomp, no wealthy store,
  No force to win the victory,
No wily wit to salve a sore,
  No shape to feed each gazing eye;
    To none of these I yield as thrall,
    For why? my mind doth serve for all.

I see how plenty suffers oft,
  And hasty climbers soon do fall;
I see that those that are aloft
  Mishap doth threaten most of all;
    They get with toil, they keep with fear;
    Such cares my mind could never bear.

Content I live, this is my stay,
  I seek no more than may suffice;
I press to bear no haughty sway;
  Look, what I lack my mind supplies.
    Lo! thus I triumph like a king,
    Content with that my mind doth bring.

Some have too much, yet still do crave;
  I little have, and seek no more.
They are but poor, though much they have,
  And I am rich with little store.
    They poor, I rich; they beg, I give;
    They lack, I leave; they pine, I live.

I laugh not at another's loss;
  I grudge not at another's gain;
No worldly waves my mind can toss;
  My state at one doth still remain.
    I fear no foe nor fawning friend;
    I loathe not life, nor dread my end.

Some weigh their pleasure by their lust,
  Their wisdom by their rage of will;
Their treasure is their only trust,
    And cloaked craft their store of skill:
    But all the pleasure that I find
    Is to maintain a quiet mind.

My wealth is health and perfect ease,
  My conscience clear my chief defence;
I neither seek by bribes to please,
  Nor by desert to breed offence.
    Thus do I live; thus will I die;
    Would all did so as well as I!

QUEEN ELIZABETH I
1533–1603

The doubt of future foes exiles my present joy,
And wit me warns to shun such snares as threaten mine annoy;
For falsehood now doth flow, and subjects' faith doth ebb,
Which should not be if reason ruled or wisdom weaved the web.
But clouds of joys untried do cloak aspiring minds,
Which turn to rain of late repent by changed course of winds.
The top of hope supposed the root upreared shall be,
And fruitless all their grafted guile, as shortly ye shall see.
The dazzled eyes with pride, which great ambition blinds,
Shall be unseeled by worthy wights whose foresight falsehood
                                            finds.
The daughter of debate that discord aye doth sow
Shall reap no gain where former rule still peace hath taught to
                                            know.
No foreign banished wight shall anchor in this port;
Our realm brooks not seditious sects, let them elsewhere resort.
My rusty sword through rest shall first his edge employ
To poll their tops that seek such change or gape for future joy.

Attributed to
QUEEN ELIZABETH I

On being Questioned about the Nature of the Sacrament

Christ was the Word and spake it;
He took the bread and brake it;
And what the Word did make it,
That I believe and take it.

RALPH WALDO EMERSON
1803–1882

Quatrains

ORATOR

He who has no hands
Perforce must use his tongue:
Foxes are so cunning
Because they are not strong.

POET

To clothe the fiery thought
In simple words succeeds,
For still the craft of genius is
To mask a king in weeds.

GARDENER

True Brahmin, in the morning meadows wet,
Expound the Vedas of the violet,
Or, hid in vines, peeping through many a loop,
See the plum redden, and the *beurré* stoop.

Forebearance

Hast thou named all the birds without a gun?
Loved the wood-rose, and left it on its stalk?
At rich men's tables eaten bread and pulse?
Unarmed, faced danger with a heart of trust?
And loved so well a high behaviour,
In man or maid, that thou from speech refrained,
Nobility more nobly to repay?
O, be my friend, and teach me to be thine!

THOMAS FLATMAN
1637–1688

An Appeal to Cats in the Business of Love

Ye Cats that at midnight spit love at each other,
Who best feel the pangs of a passionate lover,
I appeal to your scratches and your tattered fur,
If the business of love be no more than to purr.
Old Lady Grimalkin with her gooseberry eyes,
Knew something when a kitten, for why she was wise;
You find by experience, the love-fit's soon o'er,
Puss! Puss! lasts not long, but turns to *Cat-whore!*
    Men ride many miles,
    Cats tread many tiles,
  Both hazard their necks in the fray;
    Only Cats, when they fall
    From a house or a wall,
  Keep their feet, mount their tails, and away.

JAMES ELROY FLECKER
1884–1915

A Ship, an Isle, a Sickle Moon

A ship, an isle, a sickle moon –
With few but with how splendid stars
The mirrors of the sea are strewn
Between their silver bars!

An isle beside an isle she lay,
The pale ship anchored in the bay,
While in the young moon's port of gold
A star-ship – as the mirrors told –
Put forth its great and lonely light
To the unreflecting Ocean, Night.
And still, a ship upon her seas,
The isle and the island cypresses
Went sailing on without the gale:
And still there moved the moon so pale,
A crescent ship without a sail!

The Old Ships

I have seen old ships sail like swans asleep
Beyond the village which men still call Tyre,
With leaden age o'ercargoed, dipping deep
For Famagusta and the hidden sun
That rings black Cyprus with a lake of fire;
And all those ships were certainly so old,
Who knows how oft with squat and noisy gun,
Questing brown slaves or Syrian oranges,
The pirate Genoese
Hell-raked them till they rolled
Blood, water, fruit and corpses up the hold.
But now through friendly seas they softly run,
Painted the mid-sea blue or shore-sea green,
Still patterned with the vine and grapes in gold.

But I have seen,
Pointing her shapely shadows from the dawn
An image tumbled on a rose-swept bay,
A drowsy ship of some yet older day;
And, wonder's breath indrawn,
Thought I – who knows – who knows – but in that same
(Fished up beyond Aeaea, patched up new
– Stern painted brighter blue –)
That talkative, bald-headed seaman came
(Twelve patient comrades sweating at the oar)
From Troy's doom-crimson shore,
And with great lies about his wooden horse
Set the crew laughing, and forgot his course.

It was so old a ship – who knows, who knows?
 – And yet so beautiful, I watched in vain
To see the mast burst open with a rose,
And the whole deck put on its leaves again.

JOHN FLETCHER
1579–1625

Song from Henry VIII

Orpheus with his lute made trees,
And the mountain tops that freeze
    Bow themselves when he did sing.
To his music, plants and flowers
Ever sprung, as sun and showers
    There had made a lasting spring.
Everything that heard him play,
Even the billows of the sea,
    Hung their heads, and then lay by.
In sweet music is such art,
Killing care and grief of heart
    Fall asleep, or hearing, die.

ROBERT FROST
1874–1963

Stopping by Woods on a Snowy Evening

Whose woods these are I think I know.
His house is in the village though;
He will not see me stopping here
To watch his woods fill up with snow.

My little horse must think it queer
To stop without a farmhouse near
Between the woods and frozen lake
The darkest evening of the year.

He gives his harness bells a shake
To ask if there is some mistake.
The only other sound's the sweep
Of easy wind and downy flake.

The woods are lovely, dark and deep,
But I have promises to keep,
And miles to go before I sleep,
And miles to go before I sleep.

Fire and Ice

Some say the world will end in fire,
Some say in ice.
From what I've tasted of desire
I hold with those who favour fire.
But if it had to perish twice,
I think I know enough of hate
To say that for destruction ice
Is also great
And would suffice.

The Road Not Taken

Two roads diverged in a yellow wood,
And sorry I could not travel both
And be one traveller, long I stood
And looked down one as far as I could
To where it bent in the undergrowth;

Then took the other, as just as fair,
And having perhaps the better claim,
Because it was grassy and wanted wear;
Though as for that the passing there
Had worn them really about the same,

And both that morning equally lay
In leaves no step had trodden black.
Oh, I kept the first for another day!
Yet knowing how way leads on to way,
I doubted if I should ever come back.

I shall be telling this with a sigh
Somewhere ages and ages hence:
Two roads diverged in a wood, and I –
I took the one less travelled by,
And that has made all the difference.

DAVID GARRICK
1717–1779

Heart of Oak

Come cheer up my lads, 'tis to glory we steer,
To add something more to this wonderful year.
To honour we call you, not press you like slaves,
For who are so free as we sons of the waves?
　　Heart of oak are our ships, heart of oak are our men;
　　We always are ready – steady, boys, steady –
　　We'll fight and we'll conquer again and again.

We ne'er see our foes but we wish 'em to stay.
They never see us but they wish us away.
If they run, why, we follow and run 'em ashore,
For if they won't fight us, we cannot do more.
　　Heart of oak, &c

They swear they'll invade us, these terrible foes.
They frighten our women, our children and beaux.
But should their flat-bottoms in darkness get o'er,
Still Britons they'll find to receive them on shore.
　　Heart of oak, &c

We'll still make 'em run and we'll still make 'em sweat,
In spite of the devil and *Brussels Gazette*.
Then cheer up my lads, with one heart let us sing
Our soldiers, our sailors, our statesmen and King.
　　Heart of oak, &c

GEORGE GASCOIGNE
c.1534–1577

Gascoigne's Lullaby

Sing lullaby, as women do,
    Wherewith they bring their babes to rest,
And lullaby can I sing too
    As womanly as can the best.
        With lullaby they still the child,
        And if I be not much beguiled,
        Full many wanton babes have I
        Which must be stilled with lullaby.

First lullaby my youthful years.
    It is now time to go to bed,
For crooked age and hoary hairs
    Have won the haven within my head.
        With lullaby then youth be still,
        With lullaby content thy will,
        Since courage quails and comes behind,
        Go sleep, and so beguile thy mind.

Next lullaby my gazing eyes,
    Which wonted were to glance apace:
For every glass may now suffice
    To show the furrows in my face.
        With lullaby then wink a while,
        With lullaby your looks beguile.
        Let no fair face nor beauty bright
        Entice you eft with vain delight.

And lullaby my wanton will.
    Let reason's rule now reign thy thought,
Since all too late I find by skill
    How dear I have thy fancies bought.
        With lullaby now take thine ease,
        With lullaby thy doubts appease:
        For trust to this, if thou be still,
        My body shall obey thy will.

Eke lullaby my loving boy:
     My little Robin take thy rest;
Since age is cold and nothing coy,
     Keep close thy coin, for so is best.
     With lullaby be thou content,
     With lullaby thy lusts relent;
     Let others pay which have more pence,
     Thou art too poor for such expense.

Then lullaby my youth, mine eyes,
     My will, my ware, and all that was.
I can no more delays devise,
     But welcome pain, let pleasure pass.
          With lullaby now take your leave,
          With lullaby your dreams deceive;
          And when you rise with waking eye,
          Remember Gascoigne's Lullaby.

JOHN GAY
1685–1732

To a Young Lady with Some Lampreys

With lovers 'twas of old the fashion
By presents to convey their passion:
No matter what the gift they sent,
The lady saw that love was meant.
Fair Atalanta, as a favour,
Took the boar's head her hero gave her;
Nor could the bristly thing affront her,
'Twas a fit present from a hunter.
When squires send woodcocks to the dame,
It serves to show their absent flame;
Some by a snip of woven hair
In posied lockets bribe the fair;
How many mercenary matches
Have sprung from di'mond-rings and watches!

But hold – a ring, a watch, a locket,
Would drain at once a poet's pocket;
He should send songs that cost him nought,
Nor ev'n be prodigal of thought.

    Why then send lampreys? fie, for shame!
'Twill set a virgin's blood on flame.
This to fifteen a proper gift!
It might lend sixty-five a lift.

    I know your maiden aunt will scold,
And think my present somewhat bold.
I see her lift her hands and eyes:
    'What, eat it, niece? eat Spanish flies!
Lamprey's a most immodest diet:
You'll neither wake nor sleep in quiet.
Should I tonight eat sago cream,
'Twould make me blush to tell my dream;
If I eat lobster, 'tis so warming
That ev'ry man I see looks charming;
Wherefore had not the filthy fellow
Laid Rochester upon your pillow?
I vow and swear, I think the present
Had been as modest and as decent.

    'Who has her virtue in her power?
Each day has its unguarded hour;
Always in danger of undoing,
A prawn, a shrimp may prove our ruin!

    'The shepherdess, who lives on salad,
To cool her youth controls her palate;
Should Dian's maids turn liqu'rish livers,
And of huge lampreys rob the rivers,
Then all beside each glade and visto,
You'd see nymphs lying like Calisto.

    'The man who meant to heat your blood,
Needs not himself such vicious food – '

    In this, I own, your aunt is clear,
I sent you what I well might spare:
For when I see you (without joking),
Your eyes, lips, breasts are so provoking,
They set my heart more cock-a-hoop
Than could whole seas of crawfish soup.

Sweet William's Farewell
to Black-Eyed Susan

A BALLAD

All in the Downs the fleet was moored,
    The streamers waving in the wind,
When black-eyed Susan came aboard.
    'Oh! where shall I my true love find?
Tell me, ye jovial sailors, tell me true,
If my sweet William sails among the crew.'

William, who, high upon the yard,
    Rocked with the billow to and fro,
Soon as her well-known voice he heard,
    He sighed and cast his eyes below:
The cord slides swiftly through his glowing hands,
And (quick as lightning) on the deck he stands.

So the sweet lark, high-poised in air,
    Shuts close his pinions to his breast
(If, chance, his mate's shrill call he hear)
    And drops at once into her nest.
The noblest captain in the British fleet
Might envy William's lip those kisses sweet.

'O Susan, Susan, lovely dear,
    My vows shall ever true remain;
Let me kiss off that falling tear,
    We only part to meet again.
Change, as ye list, ye winds; my heart shall be
The faithful compass that still points to thee.

'Believe not what the landmen say,
    Who tempt with doubts thy constant mind:
They'll tell thee, sailors, when away,
    In ev'ry port a mistress find.
Yes, yes, believe them when they tell thee so,
For thou art present wheresoe'er I go.

'If to far India's coast we sail,
　　Thy eyes are seen in di'monds bright,
　Thy breath is Africk's spicy gale,
　　Thy skin is ivory, so white.
Thus ev'ry beauteous object that I view
Wakes in my soul some charm of lovely Sue.

'Though battle call me from thy arms,
　　Let not my pretty Susan mourn;
　Though cannons roar, yet safe from harms
　　William shall to his dear return.
Love turns aside the balls that round me fly,
Lest precious tears should drop from Susan's eye.'

The boatswain gave the dreadful word,
　　The sails their swelling bosom spread,
　No longer must she stay aboard:
　　They kissed, she sighed, he hung his head.
Her less'ning boat unwilling rows to land:
'Adieu!' she cries; and waves her lily hand.

My Own Epitaph

Life is a jest, and all things show it;
I thought so once, but now I know it.

OLIVER GOLDSMITH
1728–1774

Songs

When lovely woman stoops to folly,
  And finds too late that men betray,
What charm can soothe her melancholy,
  What art can wash her guilt away?

The only art her guilt to cover,
  To hide her shame from every eye,
To give repentance to her lover,
  And wring his bosom – is to die.

THOMAS GRAY
1716–1771

On the Death of a Favourite Cat, Drowned in a Tub of Gold Fishes

'Twas on a lofty vase's side,
Where China's gayest art had dyed
  The azure flowers that blow;
Demurest of the tabby kind,
The pensive Selima, reclined,
  Gazed on the lake below.

Her conscious tail her joy declared;
The fair round face, the snowy beard,
  The velvet of her paws,
Her coat that with the tortoise vies,
Her ears of jet, and emerald eyes –
  She saw; and purred applause.

Still had she gazed; but midst the tide
Two angel forms were seen to glide,
    The genii of the stream:
Their scaly armour's Tyrian hue
Through richest purple to the view
    Betrayed a golden gleam.

The hapless nymph with wonder saw:
A whisker first, and then a claw,
    With many an ardent wish,
She stretched, in van, to reach the prize,
What female heart can gold despise?
    What cat's averse to fish?

Presumptuous maid! with looks intent
Again she stretched, again she bent,
    Nor knew the gulf between.
(Malignant Fate sat by, and smiled.)
The slippery verge her feet beguiled,
    She tumbled headlong in.

Eight times emerging from the flood
She mewed to every watery god,
    Some speedy aid to send.
No Dolphin came, no Nereid stirred:
Nor cruel Tom, nor Susan heard –
    A favourite has no friend!

From hence ye beauties undeceived,
Know, one false step is ne'er retrieved,
    And be with caution bold:
Not all that tempts your wandering eyes
And heedless hearts is lawful prize,
    Nor all that glisters gold.

Elegy Written in a Country Churchyard

The curfew tolls the knell of parting day,
The lowing herd wind slowly o'er the lea,
The ploughman homeward plods his weary way,
And leaves the world to darkness and to me.

Now fades the glimmering landscape on the sight,
And all the air a solemn stillness holds,
Save where the beetle wheels his droning flight
And drowsy tinklings lull the distant folds;

Save that from yonder ivy-mantled tower
The moping owl does to the moon complain
Of such as, wand'ring near her secret bower,
Molest her ancient solitary reign.

Beneath those rugged elms, that yew tree's shade,
Where heaves the turf in many a mouldering heap,
Each in his narrow cell for ever laid,
The rude forefathers of the hamlet sleep.

The breezy call of incense-breathing morn,
The swallow twittering from the straw-built shed,
The cock's shrill clarion or the echoing horn,
No more shall rouse them from their lowly bed.

For them no more the blazing hearth shall burn,
Or busy housewife ply her evening care:
No children run to lisp their sire's return,
Or climb his knees the envied kiss to share.

Oft did the harvest to their sickle yield,
Their furrow oft the stubborn glebe has broke;
How jocund did they drive their team afield!
How bowed the woods beneath their sturdy stroke!

Let not Ambition mock their useful toil,
Their homely joys and destiny obscure;
Nor Grandeur hear, with a disdainful smile,
The short and simple annals of the poor.

The boast of heraldry, the pomp of power,
And all that beauty, all that wealth e'er gave,
Awaits alike the inevitable hour.
The paths of glory lead but to the grave.

Nor you, ye Proud, impute to these the fault,
If Memory o'er their tomb no trophies raise,
Where through the long-drawn aisle and fretted vault
The pealing anthem swells the note of praise.

Can storied urn or animated bust
Back to its mansion call the fleeting breath?
Can Honour's voice provoke the silent dust,
Or Flattery soothe the dull cold ear of Death?

Perhaps in this neglected spot is laid
Some heart once pregnant with celestial fire;
Hands that the rod of empire might have swayed,
Or waked to ecstasy the living lyre.

But Knowledge to their eyes her ample page
Rich with the spoils of time did ne'er unroll;
Chill Penury repressed their noble rage,
And froze the genial current of the soul.

Full many a gem of purest ray serene
The dark unfathomed caves of ocean bear:
Full many a flower is born to blush unseen,
And waste its sweetness on the desert air.

Some village-Hampden that with dauntless breast
The little tyrant of his fields withstood;
Some mute inglorious Milton here may rest,
Some Cromwell guiltless of his country's blood.

The applause of listening senates to command,
The threats of pain and ruin to despise,
To scatter plenty o'er a smiling land,
And read their history in a nation's eyes,

Their lot forbade: nor circumscribed alone
Their growing virtues, but their crimes confined;
Forbade to wade through slaughter to a throne,
And shut the gates of mercy on mankind,

The struggling pangs of conscious truth to hide,
To quench the blushes of ingenuous shame,
Or heap the shrine of Luxury and Pride
With incense kindled at the Muse's flame.

Far from the madding crowd's ignoble strife
Their sober wishes never learned to stray;
Along the cool sequestered vale of life
They kept the noiseless tenor of their way.

Yet ev'n these bones from insult to protect
Some frail memorial still erected nigh,
With uncouth rhymes and shapeless sculpture decked,
Implores the passing tribute of a sigh.

Their name, their years, spelt by the unlettered muse,
The place of fame and elegy supply:
And many a holy text around she strews,
That teach the rustic moralist to die.

For who to dumb Forgetfulness a prey,
This pleasing anxious being e'er resigned,
Left the warm precincts of the cheerful day,
Nor cast one longing lingering look behind?

On some fond breast the parting soul relies,
Some pious drops the closing eye requires;
Even from the tomb the voice of Nature cries,
Even in our ashes live their wonted fires.

For thee who, mindful of the unhonoured dead,
Dost in these lines their artless tale relate;
If chance, by lonely Contemplation led,
Some kindred spirit shall inquire thy fate,

Haply some hoary-headed swain may say,
'Oft have we seen him at the peep of dawn
Brushing with hasty steps the dews away
To meet the sun upon the upland lawn.

'There at the foot of yonder nodding beech
That wreathes its old fantastic roots so high,
His listless length at noontide would he stretch,
And pore upon the brook that babbles by.

'Hard by yon wood, now smiling as in scorn,
Muttering his wayward fancies he would rove,
Now drooping, woeful wan, like one forlorn,
Or crazed with care, or crossed in hopeless love.

'One morn I missed him on the customed hill,
Along the heath and near his favourite tree;
Another came; nor yet beside the rill,
Nor up the lawn, nor at the wood was he;

'The next with dirges due in sad array
Slow through the church-way path we saw him borne.
Approach and read (for thou canst read) the lay,
Graved on the stone beneath yon aged thorn.'

THE EPITAPH

Here rests his head upon the lap of earth
A youth to fortune and to fame unknown.
Fair Science frowned not on his humble birth,
And Melancholy marked him for her own.

Large was his bounty and his soul sincere,
Heaven did a recompense as largely send:
He gave to Misery all he hand, a tear,
He gained from heaven ('twas all he wished) a friend.

No farther seek his merits to disclose,
Or draw his frailties from their dread abode
(There they alike in trembling hope repose),
The bosom of his Father and his God.

FULKE GREVILLE, LORD BROOKE
1554–1628

O wearisome condition of humanity!
Born under one law, to another bound;
Vainly begot, and yet forbidden vanity,
Created sick, commanded to be sound.
What meaneth Nature by these diverse laws?
Passion and reason self-division cause.

It is the mark and majesty of power
To make offences that it may forgive.
Nature herself doth her own self deflower,
To hate those errors she herself doth give.
For how should man think that he may not do,
If Nature did not fail and punish too?

Tyrant to others, to herself unjust,
Only commands things difficult and hard,
Forbids us all things which it knows is lust,
Makes easy pains, impossible reward.
If Nature did not take delight in blood,
She would have made more easy ways to good.

We that are bound by vows and by promotion,
With pomp of holy sacrifice and rites,
To teach belief in God and still devotion,
To preach of Heaven's wonders and delights,
Yet, when each of us in his own heart looks,
He finds the God there far unlike his books.

CAPTAIN H—
18th Century

An Imitation of Martial
Book II, Epistle 105

Sweet spouse, you must presently troop and be gone,
    Or fairly submit to your betters;
Unless for the faults that are past you atone,
    I must knock off my conjugal fetters.

When at night I am paying the tribute of love –
    You know well enough what's my meaning –
You scorn to assist my devotions, or move,
    As if all the while you were dreaming.

At cribbage and put and all-fours I have seen
    A porter more passion expressing
Than thou, wicked Kate, in the rapturous scene,
    And the height of the amorous blessing.

Then say I to myself, 'Is my wife made of stone,
    Or does the old serpent possess her?'
Better motion and vigour by far might be shown
    By dull spouse of a German professor.

So, Kate, take advice and reform in good time,
    And while I'm performing my duty,
Come in for your club, and repent of the crime
    Of paying all scores with your beauty.

All day thou may'st cant, and look grave as a nun,
    And run after Burgess the surly;
Or see that the family business be done,
    And chide all thy servants demurely.

But when you're in bed with your master and king,
    That tales out of school ne'er does trumpet,
Move, wriggle, heave, pant, clip round like a ring:
    In short, be as lewd as a strumpet.

JOHN HALL
1627–1656

An Epicurean Ode

Since that this thing we call the world
By chance on atoms is begot,
Which though in daily motions hurled
   Yet weary not,
   How doth it prove
Thou art so fair, and I in love?

Since that the soul doth only lie
Immersed in matter, chained in sense,
How can, Romira, thou and I
   With both dispense,
   And thus ascend
In higher flights than wings can lend?

Since man's but pasted up of earth,
And ne'er was cradled in the skies,
What *terra lemnia* gave thee birth?
   What diamond, eyes?
   Or thou alone,
To tell what others were, came down?

THOMAS HARDY
1840–1928

Heredity

I am the family face;
Flesh perishes, I live on,
Projecting trait and trace
Through time to times anon,
And leaping from place to place
Over oblivion.

The years-heired feature that can
In curve and voice and eye
Despise the human span
Of durance – that is I;
The eternal thing in man,
That heeds no call to die.

The Oxen

Christmas eve, and twelve of the clock.
  'Now they are all on their knees,'
An elder said as we sat in a flock
  By the embers in hearthside ease.

We pictured the meek mild creatures where
  They dwelt in their strawy pen,
Nor did it occur to one of us there
  To doubt they were kneeling then.

So fair a fancy few would weave
  In these years! Yet, I feel,
If someone said on Christmas Eve,
  'Come; see the oxen kneel

'In the lonely barton by yonder coomb
   Our childhood used to know,'
I should go with him in the gloom,
   Hoping it might be so.

The Self-Unseeing

Here is the ancient floor,
Footworn and hollowed and thin,
Here was the former door
Where the dead feet walked in.

She sat here in her chair,
Smiling into the fire;
He who played stood there,
Bowing it higher and higher.

Childlike, I danced in a dream;
Blessings emblazoned that day;
Everything glowed with a gleam;
Yet we were looking away!

Midnight on the Great Western

In the third-class seat sat the journeying boy,
   And the roof-lamp's oily flame
Played down on his listless form and face,
Bewrapt past knowing to what he was going,
   Or whence he came.

In the band of his hat the journeying boy
   Had a ticket stuck; and a string
Around his neck bore the key of his box,
That twinkled gleams of the lamp's sad beams
   Like a living thing.

What past can be yours, O journeying boy,
    Towards a world unknown,
Who calmly, as if uncurious quite
On all at stake, can undertake
        This plunge alone?

Knows your soul a sphere, O journeying boy,
    Our rude realms far above,
Whence with spacious vision you mark and mete
This region of sin that you find you in,
        But are not of?

I Look into My Glass

I look into my glass,
And view my wasting skin,
And say, 'Would God it came to pass
My heart had shrunk as thin!'

For then, I, undistrest
By hearts grown cold to me.
Could lonely wait my endless rest
With equanimity.

But Time, to make me grieve.
Part steals, lets part abide;
And shakes this fragile frame at eve
With throbbings of noontide.

The Ruined Maid

'O 'Melia, my dear, this does everything crown!
Who could have supposed I should meet you in Town?
And whence such fair garments, such prosperi–ty?' –
'Oh didn't you know I'd been ruined?' said she.

– 'You left us in tatters, without shoes or socks,
Tired of digging potatoes, and spudding up docks;
And now you've gay bracelets and bright feathers three!' –
'Yes: that's how we dress when we're ruined,' said she.

– 'At home in the barton you said "thee" and "thou",
And "thik oon", and "theäs oon", and "t'other"; but now
Your talking quite fits 'ee for high compa–ny!' –
'Some polish is gained with one's ruin,' said she.

– 'Your hands were like paws then, your face blue and bleak,
But now I'm bewitched by your delicate cheek.
And your little gloves fit as on any la–dy!' –
'We never do work when we're ruined,' said she.

– 'You used to call home-life a hag-ridden dream.
And you'd sigh, and you'd sock; but at present you seem
To know not of megrims or melancho–ly!' –
'True. One's pretty lively when ruined,' said she

– 'I wish I had feathers, a fine sweeping gown,
And a delicate face, and could strut about Town!' –
'My dear – a raw country girl, such as you be,
Cannot quite expect that. You ain't ruined,' said she.

The Darkling Thrush

I leant upon a coppice gate
    When Frost was spectre-grey,
And Winter's dregs made desolate
    The weakening eye of day.
The tangled bine-stems scored the sky
    Like strings of broken lyres,
And all mankind that haunted nigh
    Had sought their household fires.

The land's sharp features seemed to be
    The Century's corpse outleant,
His crypt the cloudy canopy,
    The wind his death-lament.
The ancient pulse of germ and birth
    Was shrunken hard and dry,
And every spirit upon earth
    Seemed fervourless as I.

At once a voice arose among
    The bleak twigs overhead
In a full-hearted evensong
    Of joy illimited;
An aged thrush, frail, gaunt and small,
    In blast-beruffled plume,
Had chosen thus to fling his soul
    Upon the growing gloom.

So little cause for carolings
    Of such ecstatic sound
Was written on terrestrial things
    Afar or nigh around,
That I could think there trembled through
    His happy good-night air
Some blessed Hope, whereof he knew
    And I was unaware.

31 December 1900

The Haunter

He does not think that I haunt here nightly:
    How shall I let him know
That whither his fancy sets him wandering
    I, too, alertly go?
Hover and hover a few feet from him
    Just as I used to do,
But cannot answer the words he lifts me –
    Only listen thereto!

When I could answer he did not say them:
    When I could let him know
How I would like to join in his journeys,
    Seldom he wished to go.
Now that he goes and wants me with him
    More than he used to do,
Never he sees my faithful phantom,
    Though he speaks thereto.

Yes, I companion him to places
    Only dreamers know,
Where the shy hares print long paces,
    Where the night rooks go;
Into old aisles where the past is all to him,
    Close as his shade can do,
Always lacking the power to call to him,
    Near as I reach thereto!

What a good haunter I am, O tell him!
    Quickly make him know
If he but sigh since my loss befell him
    Straight to his side I go.
Tell him a faithful one is doing
    All that love can do
Still that his path may be worth pursuing,
    And to bring peace thereto.

The Voice

Woman much missed, how you call to me, call to me,
Saying that now you are not as you were
When you had changed from the one who was all to me,
But as at first, when our day was fair.

Can it be you that I hear? Let me view you, then,
Standing as when I drew near to the town
Where you would wait for me: yes, as I knew you then,
Even to the original air-blue gown!

Or is it only the breeze, in its listlessness
Travelling across the wet mead to me here,
You being ever dissolved to wan wistlessness,
Heard no more again far or near?

Thus I; faltering forward,
Leaves around me falling,
Wind oozing thin through the thorn from norward,
And the woman calling.

I Found Her Out There

I found her out there
On a slope few see,
That falls westwardly
To the salt-edged air,
Where the ocean breaks
On the purple strand,
And the hurricane shakes
The solid land.

I brought her here,
And have laid her to rest
In a noiseless nest
No sea beats near.

She will never be stirred
In her loamy cell
By the waves long heard
And loved so well.

So she does not sleep
By those haunted heights
The Atlantic smites
And the blind gales sweep,
Whence she often would gaze
At Dundagel's famed head.
While the dipping blaze
Dyed her face fire-red;

And would sigh at the tale
Of sunk Lyonesse,
As a wind-tugged tress
Flapped her cheek like a flail;
Or listen at whiles
With a thought-bound brow
To the murmuring miles
She is far from now.

Yet her shade, maybe,
Will creep underground
Till it catch the sound
Of that western sea
As it swells and sobs
Where she once domiciled,
And joy in its throbs
With the heart of a child.

The Choirmaster's Burial

He often would ask us
That, when he died,
After playing so many
To their last rest,
If out of us any
Should here abide,
And it would not task us,
We would with our lutes
Play over him
By his grave-brim
The psalm he liked best –
The one whose sense suits
'Mount Ephraim' –
And perhaps we should seem
To him, in Death's dream,
Like the seraphim.

As soon as I knew
That his spirit was gone
I thought this his due,
And spake thereupon.
'I think,' said the vicar,
'A read service quicker
Than viols out-of-doors
In these frosts and hoars.
That old-fashioned way
Requires a fine day,
And it seems to me
It had better not be.'

Hence, that afternoon,
Though never knew he
That his wish could not be,
To get through it faster
They buried the master
Without any tune.
But 'twas said that, when

At the dead of next night
The vicar looked out,
There struck on his ken
Thronged roundabout,
Where the frost was greying
The headstoned grass,
A band all in white
Like the saints in church-glass,
Singing and playing
The ancient stave
By the choirmaster's grave.

Such the tenor man told
When he had grown old.

In Time of 'The Breaking of Nations'

1

Only a man harrowing clods
 In a slow silent walk
With an old horse that stumbles and nods
 Half asleep as they stalk.

2

Only thin smoke without flame
 From the heaps of couch-grass;
Yet this will go onward the same
 Though Dynasties pass.

3

Yonder a maid and her wight
 Come whispering by:
War's annals will cloud into night
 Ere their story die.

Afterwards

When the Present has latched its postern behind my tremulous
                                        stay,
  And the May month flaps its glad green leaves like wings,
Delicate-filmed as new-spun silk, will the neighbours say,
    'He was a man who used to notice such things'?

If it be in the dusk when like an eyelid's soundless blink,
  The dewfall-hawk comes crossing the shades to alight
Upon the wind-warped upland thorn, a gazer may think,
      'To him this must have been a familiar sight.'

If I pass during some nocturnal blackness, mothy and warm,
  When the hedgehog travels furtively over the lawn,
One may say, 'He strove that such innocent creatures, should
                                        come to no harm,
  But he could do little for them; and now he is gone.'

If, when hearing that I have been stilled at last, they stand at the
                                        door,
  Watching the full-starred heavens that winter sees,
Will this thought rise on those who will meet my face no more,
    'He was one who had an eye for such mysteries'?

And will any say when my bell of quittance is heard in the
                                        gloom,
  And a crossing breeze cuts a pause in its outrollings,
Till they rise again, as they were a new bell's boom,
    'He hears it not now, but used to notice such things'?

SIR JOHN HARINGTON
1561–1612

Epigram of Treason

Treason doth never prosper – what's the reason?
For if it prosper, none dare call it treason.

Attributed to
KING HENRY VIII
1491–1547

Pastime with good company
I love and shall, until I die.
Grudge who list, but none deny:
So God be pleased, thus live will I.
 For my pastance,
 Hunt, sing and dance,
 My heart is set.
  All goodly sport
  For my comfort
Who shall me let?

Youth must have some dalliance,
Of good or ill some pastance.
Company me thinks the best,
All thoughts and fancies to digest;
 For idleness
 Is chief mistress
 Of vices all.
  Then who can say
  But mirth and play
Is best of all?

Company with honesty
Is virtue, vices to flee;
Company is good and ill,
But every man has his free will.
　　The best ensue,
　　The worst eschew!
　　My mind shall be,
　　　Virtue to use,
　　　Vice to refuse;
　　Thus shall I use me.

LORD HERBERT OF CHERBURY
1582–1648

Kissing

Come hither womankind, and all their worth:
Give me thy kisses as I call them forth.
Give me the billing-kiss, that of the dove,
　　A kiss of love;
The melting-kiss, a kiss that doth consume
　　To a perfume;
The extract-kiss, of every sweet a part,
　　A kiss of art;
The kiss which ever stirs some new delight,
　　A kiss of might;
The twaching smacking kiss, and when you cease
　　A kiss of peace;
The music-kiss, crotchet and quaver time,
　　The kiss of rhyme;
The kiss of eloquence, which doth belong
　　Unto the tongue;
The kiss of all the sciences in one,
　　The kiss alone.
So 'tis enough.

GEORGE HERBERT
1596–1633

Virtue

Sweet day, so cool, so calm, so bright,
The bridal of the earth and sky;
The dew shall weep thy fall tonight,
    For thou must die.

Sweet rose, whose hue angry and brave
Bids the rash gazer wipe his eye,
Thy root is ever in its grave,
    And thou must die.

Sweet spring, full of sweet days and roses,
A box where sweets compacted lie;
My music shows ye have your closes,
    And all must die.

Only a sweet and virtuous soul,
Like season'd timber, never gives;
But though the whole world turn to coal,
    Then chiefly lives.

The Quip

The merry world did on a day
With his train-bands and mates agree
To meet together, where I lay,
And all in sport to jeer at me.

First, Beauty crept into a rose,
Which when I pluck'd not, 'Sir,' said she,
'Tell me, I pray, whose hands are those?'
But Thou shalt answer, Lord, for me.

Then Money came, and chinking still,
'What tune is this, poor man?' said he:

'I heard in music you had skill:'
But Thou shalt answer, Lord, for me.

Then came brave Glory puffing by
In silks that whistled, who but he?
He scarce allowed me half an eye.
But Thou shalt answer, Lord, for me.

Then came quick Wit and Conversation,
And he would needs a comfort be,
And, to be short, make an oration.
But Thou shalt answer, Lord, for me.

Yet when the hour of Thy design
To answer these fine things shall come,
Speak not at large; say, 'I am Thine,'
And then they have their answer home.

Easter Wings

Lord, Who createdst man in wealth and store,
Though foolishly he lost the same,
Decaying more and more,
Till he became
Most poor:
With Thee
O let me rise,
As larks, harmoniously,
And sing this day Thy victories:
Then shall the fall further the flight in me.

My tender age in sorrow did begin;
And still with sicknesses and shame
Thou didst so punish sin,
That I became
Most thin.
With Thee
Let me combine,
And feel this day Thy victory;
For, if I imp my wing on Thine,
Affliction shall advance the flight in me.

Love

Love bade me welcome; yet my soul drew back,
      Guilty of dust and sin.
But quick-eyed Love, observing me grow slack
      From my first entrance in,
Drew nearer to me, sweetly questioning
      If I lack'd anything.

'A guest,' I answered, 'worthy to be here.'
      Love said, 'You shall be he.'
'I, the unkind, ungrateful? Ah, my dear,
      I cannot look on thee.'
Love took my hand, and smiling did reply,
      'Who made the eyes but I?'

'Truth, Lord; but I have marr'd them; let my shame
      Go where it doth deserve.'
'And know you not,' says Love, 'Who bore the blame?'
      'My dear, then I will serve.'
'You must sit down,' says Love, 'and taste my meat.'
      So I did sit and eat.

The Flower

    How fresh, O Lord, how sweet and clean
Are Thy returns! Even as the flowers in spring,
    To which, besides their own demesne,
The late-past frosts tributes of pleasure bring,
      Grief melts away,
      Like snow in May,
    As if there were no such cold thing.

    Who would have thought my shrivelled heart
Could have recovered greenness? It was gone
    Quite underground; as flowers depart
To see their mother-root, when they have blown;
      Where they together
      All the hard weather,
Dead to the world, keep house unknown.

These are Thy wonders, Lord of power,
Killing and quick'ning, bringing down to Hell
   And up to Heaven in an hour;
Making a chiming of a passing-bell.
     We say amiss
     This or that is;
   Thy word is all, if we could spell.

O that I once past changing were,
Fast in Thy Paradise, where no flower can wither!
   Many a spring I shoot up fair,
Off'ring at Heav'n, growing and groaning thither;
     Nor doth my flower
     Want a spring shower,
   My sins and I joining together.

But while I grow in a straight line,
Still upwards bent, as if Heav'n were mine own,
   Thy anger comes, and I decline.
What frost to that? What pole is not the zone
     Where all things burn,
     When Thou dost turn,
   And the least frown of Thine is shown?

And now in age I bud again,
After so many deaths I live and write;
   I once more smell the dew and rain,
And relish versing: O, my only Light,
     It cannot be
     That I am he
   On whom Thy tempests fell all night.

These are Thy wonders, Lord of love,
To make us see we are but flowers that glide;
   Which when we once can find and prove,
Thou hast a garden for us, where to bide;
     Who would be more,
     Swelling through store,
   Forfeit their Paradise by their pride.

Redemption

Having been tenant long to a rich Lord,
    Not thriving, I resolved to be bold,
    And make a suit unto Him, to afford
A new small-rented lease, and cancel the old.

In heaven, at His manor, I Him sought.
    They told me there, that He was lately gone
    About some land, which he had dearly bought
Long since on earth, to take possession.

I straight return'd, and knowing His great birth,
    Sought Him accordingly in great resorts –
    In cities, theatres, gardens, parks, and courts:
At length I heard a ragged noise and mirth
    Of thieves and murderers; there I Him espied,
    Who straight, 'Your suit is granted,' said, and died.

The Answer

My comforts drop and melt away like snow;
I shake my head, and all the thoughts and ends,
Which my fierce youth did bandy, fall and flow
Like leaves about me, or like summer-friends,
Flies of estates and sunshine. But to all
Who think me eager, hot and undertaking,
But in my prosecutions slack and small –
As a young exhalation, newly waking,
Scorns his first bed of dirt, and means the sky,
But cooling by the way, grows pursy and slow,
And settling to a cloud, doth live and die
In that dark state of tears – to all that so
Show me and set me, I have one reply,
Which they that know the rest know more than I.

The Foil

If we could see below
The sphere of virtue and each shining grace
As plainly as that above doth show,
This were the better sky, the brighter place.

God hath made stars the foil
To set off virtues, griefs to set off sinning;
Yet in this wretched world we toil,
As if grief were not foul, nor virtue winning.

The Pulley

When God at first made man,
Having a glass of blessings standing by,
'Let us,' said He, 'pour on him all we can;
Let the world's riches, which disperséd lie,
Contract into a span.'

So strength first made a way;
Then beauty flow'd, then wisdom, honour, pleasure;
When almost all was out, God made a stay,
Perceiving that, alone of all His treasure,
Rest in the bottom lay.

'For if I should,' said He,
'Bestow this jewel also on My creature,
He would adore My gifts instead of Me,
And rest in Nature, not the God of Nature:
So both should losers be.

'Yet let him keep the rest,
But keep them with repining restlessness;
Let him be rich and weary, that at least,
If goodness lead him not, yet weariness
May toss him to My breast.'

The Collar

I struck the board, and cried; 'No more;
        I will abroad.'
  What, shall I ever sigh and pine?
My lines and life are free; free as the road,
    Loose as the wind, as large as store.
        Shall I be still in suit?
    Have I no harvest but a thorn
    To let me blood, and not restore
    What I have lost with cordial fruit?
        Sure there was wine
Before my sighs did dry it; there was corn
    Before my tears did drown it.
  Is the year only lost to me?
    Have I no bays to crown it,
No flowers, no garlands gay? All blasted,
        All wasted?
    Not so, my heart: but there is fruit,
        And thou hast hands.
    Recover all thy sigh-blown age
On double pleasures; leave thy cold dispute
Of what is fit and not; forsake thy cage,
        Thy rope of sands,
Which petty thoughts have made; and made to thee
    Good cable, to enforce and draw,
        And be thy law,
    While thou didst wink and would'st not see.
        Away! take heed;
        I will abroad.
Call in thy death's-head there, tie up thy fears;
        He that forbears
    To suit and serve his need
        Deserves his load.
But as I rav'd and grew more fierce and wild
        At every word,
    Methought I heard one calling, '*Child!*'
        And I replied, 'My Lord.'

ROBERT HERRICK
1591–1674

Delight in Disorder

A sweet disorder in the dress
Kindles in clothes a wantonness:
A lawn about the shoulders thrown
Into a fine distraction;
An erring lace, which here and there
Enthrals the crimson stomacher;
A cuff neglectful, and thereby
Ribbands to flow confusedly;
A winning wave (deserving note)
In the tempestuous petticoat;
A careless shoestring, in whose tie
I see a wild civility:
Do more bewitch me, than when art
Is too precise in every part.

The Lily in a Crystal

You have beheld a smiling rose
    When virgins' hands have drawn
    O'er it a cobweb-lawn;
And here, you see, this lily shows,
    Tombed in a crystal stone,
More fair in this transparent case
    Than when it grew alone,
    And had but single grace.

You see how cream but naked is,
    Nor dances in the eye
    Without a strawberry;
Or some fine tincture, like to this,

Which draws the sight thereto
More by that wantoning with it
   Than when the paler hue
   No mixture did admit.

You see how amber through the streams
   More gently strokes the sight,
   With some concealed delight,
Than when he darts his radiant beams
   Into the boundless air:
Where either too much light his worth
   Doth all at once impair
   Or set it little forth.

Put purple grapes or cherries in
   To glass, and they will send
   More beauty to commend
Them, from that clean and subtile skin,
   Than if they naked stood,
And had no other pride at all
   But their own flesh and blood
   And tinctures natural.

Thus lily, rose, grape, cherry, cream
   And strawberry do stir
   More love, when they transfer
A weak, a soft, a broken beam,
   Than if they should discover
At full their proper excellence,
   Without some scene cast over
   To juggle with the sense.

Thus let this crystalled lily be
   A rule, how far to teach,
   Your nakedness must reach;
And that, no further than we see
   Those glaring colours laid
By art's wise hand, but to this end
   They should obey a shade,
   Lest they too far extend.

So though you're white as swan, or snow,
   And have the power to move
   A world of men to love:
Yet, when your lawns and silks shall flow,
   And that white cloud divide
Into a doubtful twilight, then,
   Then will your hidden pride
   Raise greater fires in men.

To the Virgins, to Make Much of Time

Gather ye rosebuds while ye may,
   Old Time is still a flying;
And this same flower that smiles today,
   Tomorrow will be dying.

The glorious lamp of heaven, the sun,
   The higher he's a-getting;
The sooner will his race be run,
   And nearer he's to setting.

That age is best which is the first,
   When youth and blood are warmer;
But being spent, the worse, and worst
   Times, still succeed the former.

Then be not coy, but use your time,
   And while ye may, go marry;
For having lost but once your prime,
   You may for ever tarry.

His Poetry his Pillar

Only a little more
   I have to write,
   Then I'll give o'er,
And bid the world goodnight.

'Tis but a flying minute
   That I must stay
   Or linger in it;
And then I must away.

O time that cutst down all!
   And scarce leav'st here
   Memorial
Of any men that were.

How many lie forgot
   In vaults beneath?
   And piecemeal rot
Without a fame in death?

Behold this living stone
   I rear for me,
   Ne'er to be thrown
Down, envious time, by thee.

Pillars let some set up
   If so they please;
   Here is my hope
And my pyrámidès.

To Daffodils

Fair daffadils, we weep to see
   You haste away so soon:
As yet the early-rising sun
   Has not attained his noon.
     Stay, stay,
   Until the hasting day
      Has run
   But to the evensong,
And, having prayed together, we
   Will go with you along.

We have short time to stay as you,
   We have as short a spring;
As quick a growth to meet decay
   As you, or anything.
     We die,
   As your hours do, and dry
      Away,
   Like to the summer's rain,
Or as the pearls of morning's dew,
   Ne'er to be found again.

The Nightpiece, to Julia

Her eyes the glow-worm lend thee,
The shooting stars attend thee;
   And the elves also,
   Whose little eyes glow
Like the sparks of fire, befriend thee.

No will-o'-the-wisp mislight thee,
Nor snake or slow-worm bite thee;
   But on, on thy way
   Not making a stay,
Since ghost there's none to affright thee.

Let not the dark thee cumber;
What though the moon does slumber?
   The stars of the night
   Will lend thee their light,
Like tapers clear without number.

Then Julia let me woo thee,
Thus, thus to come unto me;
   And when I shall meet
   Thy silvery feet,
My soul I'll pour into thee.

Upon Julia's Clothes

Whenas in silks my Julia goes,
Then, then (methinks) how sweetly flows
That liquefaction of her clothes.

Next, when I cast mine eyes and see
That brave vibration each way free,
Oh how that glittering taketh me!

RALPH HODGSON
1871–1962

Reason has moons, but moons not hers,
   Lie mirror'd on her sea,
Confounding her astronomers,
   But, O! delighting me.

GERARD MANLEY HOPKINS
1844–1889

The Wreck of the Deutschland

To the happy memory of five Franciscan nuns, exiles by the Falck
Laws, drowned between midnight and morning of 7 December 1875

PART THE FIRST

1

Thou mastering me
God! giver of breath and bread;
World's strand, sway of the sea;
Lord of living and dead;
Thou hast bound bones and veins in me, fastened me flesh,
And after it almost unmade, what with dread,
Thy doing: and dost thou touch me afresh?
Over again I feel thy finger and find thee.

2

I did say yes
O at lightning and lashed rod;
Thou heardst me truer than tongue confess
Thy terror, O Christ, O God;
Thou knowest the walls, altar and hour and night:
The swoon of a heart that the sweep and the hurl of thee trod
Hard down with a horror of height:
And the midriff astrain with leaning of, laced with fire of stress.

3

The frown of his face
Before me, the hurtle of hell
Behind, where, where was a, where was a place?
I whirled out wings that spell
And fled with a fling of the heart to the heart of the Host.
My heart, but you were dovewinged, I can tell,
Carrier-witted, I am bold to boast,
To flash from the flame to the flame then, tower from the grace
to the grace.

4

I am soft sift
In an hourglass – at the wall
Fast, but mined with a motion, a drift,
And it crowds and it combs to the fall;
I steady as a water in a well, to a poise, to a pane,
But roped with, always, all the way down from the tall
Fells or flanks of the voel, a vein
Of the gospel proffer, a pressure, a principle, Christ's gift.

5

I kiss my hand
To the stars, lovely-asunder
Starlight, wafting him out of it; and
Glow, glory in thunder;
Kiss my hand to the dappled-with-damson west:
Since, tho' he is under the world's splendour and wonder,
His mystery must be instressed, stressed;
For I greet him the days I meet him, and bless when I understand.

6

Not out of his bliss
Springs the stress felt
Nor first from heaven (and few know this)
Swings the stroke dealt –
Stroke and a stress that stars and storms deliver,
That guilt is hushed by, hearts are flushed by and melt –
But it rides time like riding a river
(And here the faithful waver, the faithless fable and miss).

7

It dates from day
Of his going in Galilee;
Warm-laid grave of a womb-life grey;
Manger, maiden's knee;
The dense and the driven Passion, and frightful sweat:
Thence the discharge of it, there its swelling to be,
Though felt before, though in high flood yet –
What none would have known of it, only the heart, being
                                        hard at bay,

8

Is out with it! Oh,
We lash with the best or worst
Word last! How a lush-kept plush-capped sloe
Will, mouthed to flesh-burst,
Gush! – flush the man, the being with it, sour or sweet,
Brim, in a flash, full! – Hither then, last or first,
To hero of Calvary, Christ,'s feet –
Never ask if meaning it, wanting it, warned of it – men go.

9

Be adored among men,
God, three-numberèd form;
Wring thy rebel, dogged in den,
Man's malice, with wrecking and storm.
Beyond saying sweet, past telling of tongue,
Thou art lightning and love, I found it, a winter and warm;
Father and fondler of heart thou hast wrung:
Hast thy dark descending and most art merciful then.

10

With an anvil-ding
And with fire in him forge thy will
Or rather, rather then, stealing as Spring
Through him, melt him but master him still:
Whether at once, as once at a crash Paul,
Or as Austin, a lingering-out swéet skíll,
Make mercy in all of us, out of us all
Mastery, but be adored, but be adored King.

PART THE SECOND

11

'Some find me a sword; some
The flange and the rail; flame,
Fang, or flood' goes Death on drum,
And storms bugle his fame.
But wé dream we are rooted in earth – Dust!
Flesh falls within sight of us, we, though our flower the same,
Wave with the meadow, forget that there must
The sour scythe cringe, and the blear share come.

12

On Saturday sailed from Bremen,
    American-outward-bound,
  Take settler and seamen, tell men with women,
    Two hundred souls in the round –
O Father, not under thy feathers nor ever as guessing
 The goal was a shoal, of a fourth the doom to he drowned;
   Yet did the dark side of the bay of thy blessing
Not vault them, the million of rounds of thy mercy not reeve
                                    even them in?

13

Into the snows she sweeps,
    Hurling the haven behind,
  The *Deutschland*, on Sunday; and so the sky keeps,
    For the infinite air is unkind,
 And the sea flint-flake, black-backed in the regular blow
 Sitting Eastnortheast, in cursed quarter, the wind;
   Wiry and white-fiery and whirlwind-swivellèd snow
Spins to the widow-making unchilding unfathering deeps.

14

She drove in the dark to leeward,
    She struck – not a reef or a rock
  But the combs of a smother of sand: night drew her
    Dead to the Kentish Knock;
 And she beat the bank down with her bows and the ride
                                    of her keel:
  The breakers rolled on her beam with ruinous shock;
    And canvas and compass, the whorl and the wheel
Idle for ever to waft her or wind her with, these she endured.

15

Hope had grown grey hairs,
    Hope had mourning on,
  Trenched with tears, carved with cares,
    Hope was twelve hours gone;
 And frightful a nightfall folded rueful a day
 Nor rescue, only rocket and lightship, shone,
   And lives at last were washing away:
To the shrouds they took, – they shook in the hurling and
                                    horrible airs.

16

One stirred from the rigging to save
The wild woman-kind below,
With a rope's end round the man, handy and brave –
He was pitched to his death at a blow,
For all his dreadnought breast and braids of thew:
They could tell him for hours, dandled the to and fro
Through the cobbled foam-fleece. What could he do
With the burl of the fountains of air, buck and the flood of
the wave?

17

They fought with God's cold –
And they could not and fell to the deck
(Crushed them) or water (and drowned them) or rolled
With the sea-romp over the wreck.
Night roared, with the heart-break hearing a heart-broke
rabble,
The woman's wailing, the crying of child without check –
Till a lioness arose breasting the babble,
A prophetess towered in the tumult, a virginal tongue told.

18

Ah, touched in your bower of bone,
Are you! turned for an exquisite smart,
Have you! make words break from me here all alone,
Do you! – mother of being in me, heart.
O unteachably after evil, but uttering truth,
Why, tears! is it? tears; such a melting, a madrigal start!
Never-eldering revel and river of youth,
What can it be, this glee? the good you have there of your own?

19

Sister, a sister calling
A master, her master and mine! –
And the inboard seas run swirling and hawling;
The rash smart sloggering brine
Blinds her; but she that weather sees one thing, one;
Has one fetch in her: she rears herself to divine
Ears, and the call of the tall nun
To the men in the tops and the tackle rode over the storm's
brawling.

20

She was first of a five and came
Of a coifèd sisterhood.
(O *Deutschland*, double a desperate name!
O world wide of its good!
But Gertrude, lily, and Luther, are two of a town,
Christ's lily and beast of the waste wood:
From life's dawn it is drawn down,
Abel is Cain's brother and breasts they have sucked the same.)

21

Loathed for a love men knew in them,
Banned by the land of their birth,
Rhine refused them, Thames would ruin them;
Surf, snow, river and earth
Gnashed: but thou art above, thou Orion of light;
Thy unchancelling poising palms were weighing the worth,
Thou martyr-master: in thy sight
Storm flakes were scroll-leaved flowers, lily showers – sweet
heaven was astrew in them.

22

Five! the finding and sake
And cipher of suffering Christ.
Mark, the mark is of man's make
And the word of it Sacrificed.
But he scores it in scarlet himself on his own bespoken,
Before-time-taken, dearest prizèd and priced –
Stigma, signal, cinquefoil token
For lettering of the lamb's fleece, ruddying of the rose-flake.

23

Joy fall to thee, father Francis,
Drawn to the Life that died;
With the gnarls of the nails in thee, niche of the lances his
Lovescape crucified
And seal of his seraph-arrival! and these thy daughters
And five-livèd and leavèd favour and pride,
Are sisterly sealed in wild waters,
To bathe in his fall-gold mercies, to breathe in his all-fire
glances.

24

Away in the loveable west,
  On a pastoral forehead of Wales,
I was under a roof here, I was at rest,
  And they the prey of the gales;
She to the black-about air, to the breaker, the thickly
Falling flakes, to the throng that catches and quails
  Was calling, 'O Christ, Christ, come quickly';
The cross to her she calls Christ to her, christens her wild-worst
                                        Best.

25

The majesty! what did she mean?
  Breathe, arch and original Breath.
Is it love in her of the being as her lover had been?
  Breathe, body of lovely Death.
They were else-minded then, altogether, the men
Woke thee with a *We are perishing* in the weather of
                                        Gennesareth.
  Or is it that she cried for the crown then,
The keener to come at the comfort for feeling the combating keen?

26

For how to the heart's cheering
  The down-dugged ground-hugged grey
Hovers off, the jay-blue heavens appearing
  Of pied and peeled May!
Blue-beating and hoary-glow height; or night, still higher,
With belled fire and the moth-soft Milky Way,
  What by your measure is the heaven of desire,
The treasure never eyesight got, nor was ever guessed what for
                                        the hearing?

27

No, but it was not these.
  The jading and jar of the cart,
Time's tasking, it is fathers that asking for ease
  Of the sodden-with-its-sorrowing heart,
Not danger, electrical horror; then further it finds
The appealing of the Passion is tenderer in prayer apart:
  Other, I gather, in measure her mind's
Burden, in wind's burly and beat of endragonèd seas.

28

But how shall I . . . make me room there:
　　Reach me a . . . Fancy, come faster –
　Strike you the sight of it? Look at it loom there,
　　Thing that she . . . there then! the Master,
Ipse, the only one, Christ, King, Head:
　He was to cure the extremity where he had cast her;
　　Do, deal, lord it with living and dead;
Let him ride, her pride, in his triumph, despatch and have done
　　　　　　　　　　　　　　with his doom there.

29

Ah! there was a heart right!
　　There was single eye!
　Read the unshapeable shock night
　　And knew the who and the why;
　Wording it how but by him that present and past,
　Heaven and earth are word of, worded by? –
　　The Simon Peter of a soul! to the blast
Tarpeïan-fast, but a blown beacon of light.

30

Jesu, heart's light,
　　Jesu, maid's son,
　What was the feast followed the night
　　Thou hadst glory of this nun? –
　Feast of the one woman without stain.
　For so conceivèd, so to conceive thee is done;
　　But here was heart-throe, birth of a brain,
Word, that heard and kept thee and uttered thee outright.

31

Well, she has thee for the pain, for the
　　Patience; but pity of the rest of them!
　Heart, go and bleed at a bitterer vein for the
　　Comfortless unconfessed of them –
　No not uncomforted: lovely-felicitous Providence
　Finger of a tender of, O of a feather delicacy, the breast of the
　　　　Maiden could obey so, be a bell to, ring of it, and
Startle the poor sheep back! is the shipwrack then a harvest,
　　　　　　　　　　　does tempest carry the grain for thee?

32

I admire thee, master of the tides,
　　Of the Yore-flood, of the year's fall;
The recurb and the recovery of the gulf's sides,
　　The girth of it and the wharf of it and the wall;
Stanching, quenching ocean of a motionable mind;
Ground of being, and granite of it: past all
　　Grasp God, throned behind
Death with a sovereignty that heeds but hides, bodes but abides;

33

With a mercy that outrides
　　The all of water, an ark
For the listener; for the lingerer with a love glides
　　Lower than death and the dark;
A vein for the visiting of the past-prayer, pent in prison,
The-last-breath penitent spirits – the uttermost mark
　　Our passion-plungèd giant risen,
The Christ of the Father compassionate, fetched in the storm of
　　　　　　　　　　　　　　　　　　his strides.

34

Now burn, new born to the world,
　　Double-naturèd name,
The heaven-flung, heart-fleshed, maiden-furled
　　Miracle-in-Mary-of-flame,
Mid-numberèd he in three of the thunder-throne!
Not a dooms-day dazzle in his coming nor dark as he came;
　　Kind, but royally reclaiming his own;
A released shower, let flash to the shire, not a lightning of fire
　　　　　　　　　　　　　　　　　　hard-hurled.

35

Dame, at our door
　　Drowned, and among our shoals,
Remember us in the roads, the heaven-haven of the reward:
　　Our King back, Oh, upon English souls!
Let him easter in us, be a dayspring to the dimness of us, be a
　　　　　　　　　　　　　　　　crimson-cresseted east,
More brightening her, rare-dear Britain, as his reign rolls,
　　Pride, rose, prince, hero of us, high-priest,
Our hearts' charity's hearth's fire, our thoughts' chivalry's
　　　　　　　　　　　　　　　　　　throng's Lord.

Spring

Nothing is so beautiful as Spring –
    When weeds, in wheels, shoot long and lovely and lush;
    Thrush's eggs look little low heavens, and thrush
Through the echoing timber does so rinse and wring
The ear, it strikes like lightnings to hear him sing;
    The glassy peartree leaves and blooms, they brush
    The descending blue; that blue is all in a rush
With richness; the racing lambs too have fair their fling.

What is all this juice and all this joy?
    A strain of the earth's sweet being in the beginning
In Eden garden. – Have, get, before it cloy,
    Before it cloud, Christ, lord, and sour with sinning,
Innocent mind and Mayday in girl and boy,
    Most, O maid's child, thy choice and worthy the winning.

The Windhover
To Christ Our Lord

I caught this morning morning's minion, king-
    dom of daylight's dauphin, dapple-dawn-drawn Falcon, in his riding
    Of the rolling level underneath him steady air, and striding
High there, how he rung upon the rein of a wimpling wing
In his ecstasy! then off, off forth on swing,
    As a skate's heel sweeps smooth on a bow-bend: the hurl and gliding
    Rebuffed the big wind. My heart in hiding
Stirred for a bird, – the achieve of, the mastery of the thing!

Brute beauty and valour and act, oh, air, pride, plume, here
    Buckle! AND the fire that breaks from thee then, a billion
Times told lovelier, more dangerous, O my chevalier!

    No wonder of it: shéer plód makes plough down sillion
Shine, and blue-bleak embers, ah my dear,
    Fall, gall themselves, and gash gold-vermilion.

Pied Beauty

Glory be to God for dappled things –
   For skies of couple-colour as a brinded cow;
     For rose-moles all in stipple upon trout that swim;
Fresh-firecoal chestnut-falls; finches' wings;
   Landscape plotted and pieced – fold, fallow, and plough;
     And áll trádes, their gear and tackle and trim.

All things counter, original, spare, strange;
   Whatever is fickle, freckled (who knows how?)
     With swift, slow; sweet, sour; adazzle, dim;
He fathers-forth whose beauty is past change:
       Praise him.

Spring and Fall
To a Young Child

Márgarét, áre you gríeving
Over Goldengrove unleaving?
Leaves, like the things of man, you
With your fresh thoughts care for, can you?
Ah! as the heart grows older
It will come to such sights colder
By and by, nor spare a sigh
Though worlds of wanwood leafmeal lie;
And yet you *will* weep and know why.
Now no matter, child, the name:
Sórrow's spríngs áre the same.
Nor mouth had, no nor mind, expressed
What heart heard of, ghost guessed:
It ís the blight man was born for,
It is Margaret you mourn for.

Sonnet

No worst, there is none. Pitched past pitch of grief,
More pangs will, schooled at forepangs, wilder wring.
Comforter, where, where is your comforting?
Mary, mother of us, where is your relief?
My cries heave, herds-long; huddle in a main, a chief-
Woe, world-sorrow; on an age-old anvil wince and sing –
Then lull, then leave off. Fury had shrieked, 'No ling-
ering! Let me be fell: force I must be brief.'
O the mind, mind has mountains; cliffs of fall
Frightful, sheer, no-man-fathomed. Hold them cheap
May who ne'er hung there. Nor does long our small
Durance deal with that steep or deep. Here! creep,
Wretch, under a comfort serves in a whirlwind: all
Life death does end and each day dies with sleep.

Sonnet

I wake and feel the fell of dark not day.
What hours, O what black hoürs we have spent
This night! what sights you, heart, saw; ways you went!
And more must, in yet longer light's delay.

With witness I speak this. But where I say
Hours I mean years, mean life. And my lament
Is cries countless, cries like dead letters sent
To dearest him that lives alas! away.

I am gall, I am heartburn. God's most deep decree
Bitter would have me taste: my taste was me;
Bones built in me, flesh filled, blood brimmed the curse.

Selfyeast of spirit a dull dough sours. I see
The lost are like this, and their scourge to be
As I am mine, their sweating selves; but worse.

In Honour of St Alphonsus Rodriguez
Laybrother of the Society of Jesus

Honour is flashed off exploit, so we say;
And those strokes once that gashed flesh or galled shield
Should tongue that time now, trumpet now that field,
And, on the fighter, forge his glorious day.
On Christ they do and on the martyr may;
But be the war within, the brand we wield
Unseen, the heroic breast not outward-steeled,
Earth hears no hurtle then from fiercest fray.

Yet God (that hews mountain and continent,
Earth, all, out; who, with trickling increment,
Veins violets and tall trees makes more and more)
Could crows career with conquest while there went
Those years and years by of world without event
That in Majorca Alfonso watched the door.

A. E. HOUSMAN
1859–1936

Her strong enchantments failing,
    Her towers of fear in wreck,
Her limbecks dried of poisons
    And the knife at her neck,

The Queen of air and darkness
    Begins to shrill and cry,
'O young man, O my slayer,
    Tomorrow you shall die.'

O Queen of air and darkness,
    I think 'tis truth you say,
And I shall die tomorrow;
    But you will die today.

Into My Heart an Air that Kills

Into my heart an air that kills
    From yon far country blows:
What are those blue remembered hills,
    What spires, what farms are those?

That is the land of lost content,
    I see it shining plain,
The happy highways where I went
    And cannot come again.

Bredon Hill

In summertime on Bredon
    The bells they sound so clear;
Round both the shires they ring them
    In steeples far and near,
    A happy noise to hear.

Here of a Sunday morning
    My love and I would lie,
And see the coloured counties,
    And hear the larks so high
    About us in the sky.

The bells would ring to call her
    In valleys miles away:
'Come all to church, good people;
    Good people, come and pray.'
    But here my love would stay.

And I would turn and answer
    Among the springing thyme,
'Oh, peal upon our wedding,
    And we will hear the chime,
    And come to church in time.'

But when the snows at Christmas
  On Bredon top were strown,
My love rose up so early
  And stole out unbeknown
  And went to church alone.

They tolled the one bell only,
  Groom there was none to see,
The mourners followed after,
  And so to church went she,
  And would not wait for me.

The bells they sound on Bredon,
  And still the steeples hum.
'Come all to church, good people,'
  Oh, noisy bells, be dumb;
  I hear you, I will come.

Loveliest of Trees

Loveliest of trees, the cherry now
Is hung with bloom along the bough,
And stands about the woodland ride
Wearing white for Eastertide.

Now, of my threescore years and ten,
Twenty will not come again,
And take from seventy springs a score,
It only leaves me fifty more.

And since to look at things in bloom
Fifty springs are little room,
About the woodlands I will go
To see the cherry hung with snow.

The Fairies Break Their Dances

The fairies break their dances
  And leave the printed lawn,
And up from India glances
  The silver sail of dawn.

The candles burn their sockets,
  The blinds let through the day,
The young man feels his pockets
  And wonders what's to pay.

Epitaph on an Army of Mercenaries

These, in the day when heaven was falling,
  The hour when earth's foundations fled,
Followed their mercenary calling
  And took their wages and are dead.

Their shoulders held the sky suspended;
  They stood, and earth's foundations stay;
What God abandoned, these defended,
  And saved the sum of things for pay.

LEIGH HUNT
1784–1859

Abou Ben Adhem

Abou Ben Adhem (may his tribe increase!)
Awoke one night from a deep dream of peace,
And saw, within the moonlight in his room,
Making it rich and like a lily in bloom,
An angel writing in a book of gold:
Exceeding peace had made Ben Adhem bold,
And to the presence in the room he said,
'What writest thou?' – The vision raised its head,
And with a look made of all sweet accord,
Answered, 'The names of those who love the Lord.'
'And is mine one?' said Abou. 'Nay, not so,'
Replied the angel. Abou spoke more low,
But cheerly still, and said, 'I pray thee, then,
Write me as one that loves his fellow men.'
The angel wrote, and vanished. The next night
It came again with a great wakening light,
And showed the names whom love of God had blest,
And lo! Ben Adhem's name led all the rest.

Rondeau

Jenny kissed me when we met,
    Jumping from the chair she sat in;
Time, you thief! who love to get
    Sweets into your list, put that in.
Say I'm weary, say I'm sad;
    Say that health and wealth have missed me;
Say I'm growing old, but add –
        Jenny kissed me!

ALDOUS HUXLEY
1894–1963

Fifth Philosopher's Song

A million million spermatozoa,
    All of them alive:
Out of their cataclysm but one poor Noah
    Dare hope to survive.

And among that billion minus one
    Might have chanced to be
Shakespeare, another Newton, a new Donne –
    But the One was Me.

Shame to have ousted your betters thus,
    Taking ark while the others remained outside!
Better for all of us, froward Homunculus,
    If you'd quietly died!

DR SAMUEL JOHNSON
1709–1784

An Epitaph on Claudy Phillips, a Musician

Phillips! whose touch harmonious could remove
The pangs of guilty power and hapless love,
Rest here, distressed by poverty no more,
Here find that calm thou gav'st so oft before;
Sleep undisturbed within this peaceful shrine,
Till angels wake thee with a note like thine.

BEN JONSON
1573–1637

Epitaph for My First Son

Farewell, thou child of my right hand, and joy;
My sin was too much hope of thee, loved boy.
Seven years thou wert lent to me, and I thee pay,
Exacted by thy fate, on the just day.
Oh, could I lose all father now! For why
Will man lament the state he should envy?
To have so soon 'scaped world's and flesh's rage,
And, if no other misery, yet age!
Rest in soft peace, and, asked, say here doth lie
Ben Jonson, his best piece of poetry;
For whose sake, henceforth, all his vows be such,
As what he loves may never like too much.

Echo's Song

Slow, slow, fresh fount, keep time with my salt tears;
    Yet slower yet, oh faintly, gentle springs;
List to the heavy part the music bears:
    Woe weeps out her division when she sings.
      Droop, herbs and flowers,
      Fall, grief, in showers;
      Our beauties are not ours:
        Oh, I could still,
Like melting snow upon some craggy hill,
    Drop, drop, drop, drop,
Since nature's pride is now a withered daffodil.

Hymn to Cynthia

Queen and huntress, chaste and fair,
Now the sun is laid to sleep,
Seated in thy silver chair,
State in wonted manner keep:
    Hesperus entreats thy light,
    Goddess excellently bright.

Earth, let not thy envious shade
Dare itself to interpose;
Cynthia's shining orb was made
Heaven to clear, when day did close:
        Bless us then with wishèd sight
        Goddess excellently bright.

Lay thy bow of pearl apart,
And thy crystal-shining quiver;
Give unto the flying hart
Space to breathe, how short soever:
        Thou that mak'st a day of night,
        Goddess excellently bright.

Her Triumph

See the chariot at hand here of Love,
    Wherein my lady rideth!
Each that draws is a swan or a dove,
    And well the car Love guideth.
As she goes, all hearts do duty
        Unto her beauty;
And enamoured, do wish, so they might
        But enjoy such a sight,
That they still were to run by her side,
Through swords, through seas, whither she would ride.

Do but look on her eyes, they do light
   All that Love's world compriseth!
Do but look on her hair, it is bright
   As Love's star when it riseth!
Do but mark, her forehead's smoother
     Than words that soothe her!
And from her arched brows, such a grace
     Sheds itself through the face,
As alone there triumphs to the life
All the gain, all the good, of the elements' strife.

Have you seen but a bright lily grow,
   Before rude hands have touched it?
Have you marked but the fall o' the snow
   Before the soil hath smutched it?
Have you felt the wool o' the beaver?
     Or swan's down ever?
Or have smelt o' the bud o' the briar?
     Or the nard in the fire?
Or have tasted the bag o' the bee?
Oh so white! Oh so soft! Oh so sweet is she!

JOHN KEATS
1795–1821

On First Looking into Chapman's Homer

Much have I travelled in the realms of gold,
    And many goodly states and kingdoms seen;
    Round many western islands have I been
Which bards in fealty to Apollo hold.
Oft of one wide expanse had I been told
    That deep-brow'd Homer ruled as his demesne:
    Yet did I never breathe its pure serene
Till I heard Chapman speak out loud and bold:
Then felt I like some watcher of the skies
    When a new planet swims into his ken;
Or like stout Cortez, when with eagle eyes
    He stared at the Pacific – and all his men
Looked at each other with a wild surmise –
    Silent, upon a peak in Darien.

La Belle Dame Sans Merci

'O what can ail thee, knight-at-arms,
    Alone and palely loitering?
The sedge is withered from the lake,
    And no birds sing.

'O what can ail thee, knight-at-arms,
    So haggard and so woebegone?
The squirrel's granary is full,
    And the harvest's done.

'I see a lily on thy brow
    With anguish moist and fever dew;
And on thy check a fading rose
    Fast withereth too.'

'I met a lady in the meads,
   Full beautiful – a faery's child,
Her hair was long, her foot was light,
   And her eyes were wild.

'I made a garland for her head,
   And bracelets too, and fragrant zone;
She looked at me as she did love,
   And made sweet moan.

'I set her on my pacing steed
   And nothing else saw all day long,
For sideways would she lean, and sing
   A faery's song.

'She found me roots of relish sweet,
   And honey wild and manna dew,
And sure in language strange she said,
   "I love thee true!"

'She took me to her elfin grot,
   And there she wept and sighed full sore;
And there I shut her wild, wild eyes
   With kisses four.

'And there she lullèd me asleep,
   And there I dreamed – Ah! woe betide!
The latest dream I ever dreamed
   On the cold hill's side.

'I saw pale kings and princes too,
   Pale warriors, death-pale were they all;
Who cried – "La belle Dame sans Merci
   Hath thee in thrall!"

'I saw their starved lips in the gloam
   With horrid warning gapèd wide,
And I awoke and found me here
   On the cold hill's side.

'And this is why I sojourn here
   Alone and palely loitering,
Though the sedge is withered from the lake,
   And no birds sing.'

Ode to a Nightingale

1

My heart aches, and a drowsy numbness pains
  My sense, as though of hemlock I had drunk
Or emptied some dull opiate to the drains
  One minute past, and Lethe-wards had sunk:
'Tis not through envy of thy happy lot,
  But being too happy in thy happiness,
    That thou, light-wingèd Dryad of the trees,
      In some melodious plot
Of beechen green, and shadows numberless,
  Singest of summer in full-throated ease.

2.

O for a draught of vintage! that hath been
  Cooled a long age in the deep-delvèd earth,
Tasting of Flora and the country-green,
  Dance, and Provençal song, and sunburnt mirth!
O for a beaker full of the warm South!
Full of the true, the blushful Hippocrene,
  With beaded bubbles winking at the brim,
    And purple-stainèd mouth;
That I might drink, and leave the world unseen,
  And with thee fade away into the forest dim:

3

Fade far away, dissolve, and quite forget
  What thou among the leaves hast never known,
The weariness, the fever, and the fret
  Here, where men sit and hear each other groan;
Where palsy shakes a few, sad, last grey hairs,
  Where youth grows pale, and spectre-thin, and dies;
    Where but to think is to be full of sorrow
      And leaden-eyed despairs;
  Where beauty cannot keep her lustrous eyes,
    Or new Love pine at them beyond tomorrow.

4

Away! away! for I will fly to thee,
  Not charioted by Bacchus and his pards,

But on the viewless wings of Poesy,
    Though the dull brain perplexes and retards:
Already with thee! tender is the night,
    And haply the Queen-Moon is on her throne,
        Cluster'd around by all her starry Fays;
            But here there is no light,
Save what from heaven is with the breezes blown
        Through verdurous glooms and winding mossy ways.

5

I cannot see what flowers are at my feet,
    Nor what soft incense hangs upon the boughs,
But, in embalmèd darkness, guess each sweet
    Wherewith the seasonable month endows
The grass, the thicket, and the fruit-tree wild;
    White hawthorn, and the pastoral eglantine;
        Fast-fading violets cover'd up in leaves;
            And mid-May's eldest child,
    The coming musk-rose, full of dewy wine,
        The murmurous haunt of flies on summer eves.

6

Darkling I listen; and for many a time
    I have been half in love with easeful Death,
Call'd him soft names in many a musèd rhyme,
    To take into the air my quiet breath;
Now more than ever seems it rich to die,
    To cease upon the midnight with no pain,
        While thou art pouring forth thy soul abroad
            In such an ecstasy!
    Still wouldst thou sing, and I have ears in vain –
        To thy high requiem become a sod.

7

Thou wast not born for death, immortal Bird!
    No hungry generations tread thee down;
The voice I hear this passing night was heard
    In ancient days by emperor and clown:
Perhaps the self-same song that found a path
    Through the sad heart of Ruth, when, sick for home,
        She stood in tears amid the alien corn;

The same that oft-times hath
Charmed magic casements, opening on the foam
Of perilous seas, in faery lands forlorn.

8

Forlorn! the very word is like a bell
To toll me back from thee to my sole self!
Adieu! the fancy cannot cheat so well
As she is famed to do, deceiving elf.
Adieu! adieu! thy plaintive anthem fades
Past the near meadows, over the still stream,
Up the hillside; and now 'tis buried deep
In the next valley-glades:
Was it a vision, or a waking dream?
Fled is that music – do I wake or sleep?

Ode on a Grecian Urn

1

Thou still unravished bride of quietness!
Thou foster-child of Silence and slow Time,
Sylvan historian, who canst thus express
A flowery tale more sweetly than our rhyme:
What leaf-fringed legend haunts about thy shape
Of deities or mortals, or of both,
In Tempe or the dales of Arcady?
What men or gods are these? What maidens loth?
What mad pursuit? What struggle to escape?
What pipes and timbrels? What wild ecstasy?

2

Heard melodies are sweet, but those unheard
Are sweeter; therefore, ye soft pipes, play on;
Not to the sensual ear, but, more endeared,
Pipe to the spirit ditties of no tone:
Fair youth, beneath the trees, thou canst not leave
Thy song, nor ever can those trees be bare;

Bold Lover, never, never canst thou kiss,
   Though winning near the goal – yet, do not grieve;
She cannot fade, though thou hast not thy bliss,
   For ever wilt thou love, and she be fair!

3

Ah, happy, happy boughs! that cannot shed
   Your leaves, nor ever bid the Spring adieu;
And, happy melodist, unwearièd.
   Forever piping songs forever new;
More happy love! more happy, happy love!
   Forever warm and still to be enjoyed.
      Forever panting and forever young;
   All breathing human passion far above,
That leaves a heart high-sorrowful and cloyed,
      A burning forehead, and a parching tongue.

4

Who are these coming to the sacrifice?
   To what green altar, O mysterious priest,
Lead'st thou that heifer lowing at the skies.
   And all her silken flanks with garlands drest?
What little town by river or sea-shore,
   Or mountain-built with peaceful citadel,
      Is emptied of its folk, this pious morn?
   And, little town, thy streets for evermore
Will silent be; and not a soul, to tell
      Why thou art desolate, can e'er return.

5

O Attic shape! Fair attitude! with brede
   Of marble men and maidens overwrought,
With forest branches and the trodden weed;
   Thou, silent form! dost tease us out of thought
As doth eternity. Cold Pastoral!
   When old age shall this generation waste,
      Thou shalt remain, in midst of other woe
   Than ours, a friend to man, to whom thou say'st,
'Beauty is truth, truth beauty – that is all
      Ye know on earth, and all ye need to know.'

To Autumn

1

Season of mists and mellow fruitfulness!
   Close bosom-friend of the maturing sun;
Conspiring with him how to load and bless
   With fruit the vines that round the thatch-eaves run;
To bend with apples the mossed cottage-trees,
   And fill all fruit with ripeness to the core;
     To swell the gourd, and plump the hazel shells
   With a sweet kernel; to set budding more,
And still more, later flowers for the bees,
Until they think warm days will never cease,
     For Summer has o'er-brimmed their clammy cells.

2

Who hath not seen thee oft amid thy store?
   Sometimes whoever seeks abroad may find
Thee sitting careless on a granary floor,
   Thy hair soft-lifted by the winnowing wind,
Or on a half-reaped furrow sound asleep,
   Drowsed with the fume of poppies, while thy hook
     Spares the next swath and all its twinèd flowers;
And sometimes like a gleaner thou dost keep
   Steady thy laden head across a brook;
   Or by a cider-press, with patient look,
     Thou watchest the last oozings hours by hours.

3

Where are the songs of Spring? Ay, where are they?
   Think not of them, thou hast thy music too –
While barred clouds bloom the soft-dying day,
   And touch the stubble-plains with rosy hue;
Then in a wailful choir the small gnats mourn
   Among the river sallows, borne aloft
     Or sinking as the light wind lives or dies;
And full-grown lambs loud bleat from hilly bourn;
   Hedge-crickets sing; and now with treble soft
   The redbreast whistles from a garden-croft;
     And gathering swallows twitter in the skies.

Written on a Blank Page in Shakespeare's Poems

Bright star, would I were steadfast as thou art –
   Not in lone splendour hung aloft the night,
And watching, with eternal lids apart,
   Like Nature's patient sleepless Eremite,
The moving waters at their priest-like task
   Of pure ablution round earth's human shores,
Or gazing on the new soft-fallen mask
   Of snow upon the mountains and the moors –
No – yet still steadfast, still unchangeable,
   Pillowed upon my fair love's ripening breast,
To feel for ever its soft fall and swell,
   Awake for ever in a sweet unrest,
Still, still to hear her tender-taken breath,
And so live ever – or else swoon to death.

When I Have Fears that I May Cease To Be

When I have fears that I may cease to be
   Before my pen has gleaned my teeming brain,
Before high-pilèd books, in charactery,
   Hold like full garners the full-ripenèd grain;
When I behold, upon the night's starrèd face,
   Huge cloudy symbols of a high romance,
And feel that I may never live to trace
   Their shadows, with the magic hand of chance;
And when I feel, fair creature of an hour!
   That I shall never look upon thee more,
Never have relish in the faery power
   Of unreflecting love – then on the shore
Of the wide world I stand alone, and think,
Till Love and Fame to nothingness do sink.

THOMAS KEN
1637–1711

A Morning Hymn

Awake, my soul, and with the sun
Thy daily stage of duty run;
Shake off dull sloth, and early rise
To pay thy morning sacrifice.

Redeem thy misspent time that's past;
Live this day as if 'twere thy last;
T' improve thy talent take due care:
'Gainst the great day thyself prepare.

Let all thy converse be sincere
Thy conscience as the noonday clear;
Think how all-seeing God thy ways
And all thy secret thoughts surveys.

Influenced by the light divine
Let thy own light in good works shine:
Reflect all heaven's propitious ways,
In ardent love and cheerful praise.

Wake, and lift up thyself, my heart,
And with the angels bear thy part,
Who all night long unwearied sing
Glory to the eternal king.

I wake, I wake, ye heavenly choir;
May your devotion me inspire,
That I like you my age may spend,
Like you may on my God attend.

May I like you in God delight,
Have all day long my God in sight,
Perform like you my maker's will;
Oh may I never more do ill!

Had I your wings, to heaven I'd fly;
But God shall that defect supply,
And my soul, winged with warm desire,
Shall all day long to heaven aspire.

Glory to thee who safe has kept,
And hath refreshed me whilst I slept.
Grant, Lord, when I from death shall wake,
I may of endless light partake.

I would not wake, nor rise again,
Even heaven itself I would disdain,
Wert not thou there to be enjoyed,
And I in hymns to be employed.

Heaven is, dear Lord, where'er thou art:
Oh never, then, from me depart;
For to my soul 'tis hell to be
But for one moment without thee.

Lord, I my vows to thee renew;
Disperse my sins as morning dew;
Guard my first springs of thought and will,
And with thyself my spirit fill.

Direct, control, suggest, this day,
All I design, or do, or say,
That all my powers, with all their might,
In thy sole glory may unite.

HENRY KING
1592–1669

The Exequy

Accept, thou shrine of my dead saint,
Instead of dirges, this complaint;
And for sweet flowers to crown thy hearse
Receive a strew of weeping verse
From thy griev'd friend, whom thou mightst see
Quite melted into tears for thee.

Dear loss! since thy untimely fate,
My talk hath been to meditate
On thee, on thee; thou art the book,
The library whereon I look
Though almost blind. For thee, loved clay,
I languish out, not live the day.
Using no other exercise.
But what I practise with my eyes:
By which wet glasses I find out
How lazily time creeps about
To one that mourns: this, only this,
My exercise and business is:
So I compute the weary hours
With sighs dissolved into showers.

Nor wonder if my time go thus
Backward and most preposterous;
Thou hast benighted me, thy set
This eve of blackness did beget,
Who wast my day (though overcast
Before thou hadst thy noontide past),
And I remember must in tears,
Thou scarce hadst seen so many years
As day tells hours. By thy clear sun
My love and fortune first did run;
But thou wilt never more appear

Folded within my hemisphere,
Since both thy light and motion
Like a fled star is fall'n and gone,
And 'twixt me and my soul's dear wish
The earth now interposed is,
Which such a strange eclipse doth make
As ne'er was read in almanac.

I could allow thee for a time
To darken me and my sad clime,
Were it a month, a year, or ten,
I would thy exile live till then;
And all that space my mirth adjourn,
So thou wouldst promise to return;
And putting off thy ashy shroud
At length disperse this sorrow's cloud.

But woe is me! the longest date
Too narrow is to calculate
These empty hopes; never shall I
Be so much blest as to descry
A glimpse of thee, till that day come
Which shall the earth to cinders doom,

And a fierce fever must calcine
The body of this world like thine
(My little world!); that fit of fire
Once off, our bodies shall aspire
To our souls' bliss: then we shall rise,
And view ourselves with clearer eyes
In that calm region where no night
Can hide us from each other's sight.

Meantime, thou hast her, earth; much good
May my harm do thee. Since it stood
With Heaven's will I might not call
Her longer mine, I give thee all
My short-lived right and interest
In her, whom living I loved best:
With a most free and bounteous grief,

I give thee what I could not keep.
Be kind to her, and prithee look
Thou write into thy doomsday book
Each parcel of this rarity
Which in thy casket shrin'd doth lie.
See that thou make thy reck'ning straight,
And yield her back again by weight;
For thou must audit on thy trust
Each grain and atom of this dust,
As thou wilt answer Him that lent,
Not gave thee, my dear monument.

So close the ground, and 'bout her shade
Black curtains draw; my bride is laid.

Sleep on, my love, in thy cold bed
Never to be disquieted!
My last good-night! Thou wilt not wake
Till I thy fate shall overtake:
Till age, or grief, or sickness must
Marry my body to that dust
It so much loves; and fill the room
My heart keeps empty in thy tomb.
Stay for me there; I will not fail
To meet thee in that hollow vale.
And think not much of my delay;
I am already on the way,
And follow thee with all the speed
Desire can make, or sorrows breed.

Each minute is a short degree,
And ev'ry hour a step towards thee.
At night when I betake to rest,
Next morn I rise nearer my west
Of life, almost by eight hours' sail,
Than when sleep breath'd his drowsy gale.

Thus from the sun my bottom steers,
And my day's compass downward bears:
Nor labour I to stem the tide
Through which to thee I swiftly glide.

'Tis true, with shame and grief I yield,
Thou like the van first took'st the field,
And gotton hast the victory
In thus adventuring to die
Before me, whose more years might crave
A just precedence in the grave.
But hark! my pulse, like a soft drum,
Beats my approach, tells thee I come;

And slow howe'er my marches be,
I shall at last sit down by thee.

The thought of this bids me go on,
And wait my dissolution
With hope and conform. Dear (forgive
The crime), I am content to live
Divided, with but half a heart,
Till we shall meet and never part.

Sic Vita

Like to the falling of a star;
Or as the flights of eagles are;
Or like the fresh Spring's gaudy hue;
Or silver drops of morning dew;
Or like a wind that chafes the flood;
Or bubbles which on water stood;
Even such is man, whose borrow'd light
Is straight called in, and paid to night.

The wind blows out; the bubble dies;
The Spring entombed in Autumn lies;
The dew dries up; the star is shot;
The flight is past; and man forgot.

RUDYARD KIPLING
1865–1936

Recessional

God of our fathers, known of old,
Lord of our far-flung battle-line,
Beneath whose awful Hand we hold
 Dominion over palm and pine –
Lord God of Hosts, be with us yet,
Lest we forget – lest we forget!

The tumult and the shouting dies;
 The Captains and the Kings depart:
Still stands Thine ancient sacrifice,
 An humble and a contrite heart.
Lord God of Hosts, be with us yet,
Lest we forget – lest we forget!

Far-called, our navies melt away;
 On dune and headland sinks the fire:
Lo, all our pomp of yesterday
 Is one with Nineveh and Tyre!
Judge of the Nations, spare us yet,
Lest we forget – lest we forget!

If, drunk with sight of power, we loose
 Wild tongues that have not Thee in awe,
Such boastings as the Gentiles use,
 Or lesser breeds without the Law –
Lord God of Hosts, be with us yet,
Lest we forget – lest we forget!

For heathen heart that puts her trust
 In reeking tube and iron shard,
All valiant dust that builds on dust,
 And guarding, calls not Thee to guard,
For frantic boast and foolish word –
Thy mercy on Thy People, Lord!

Mandalay

By the old Moulmein Pagoda, lookin' lazy at the sea,
There's a Burma girl a-settin', and I know she thinks o' me;
For the wind is in the palm-trees, and the temple-bells they say:
'Come you back, you British soldier; come you back to Mandalay!'
       Come you back to Mandalay,
      Where the old Flotilla lay:
      Can't you 'ear their paddles chunkin' from
                    Rangoon to Mandalay?
      On the road to Mandalay,
      Where the flyin'-fishes play,
      An' the dawn comes up like thunder outer China 'crost
                    the Bay!

'Er petticoat was yaller an' 'er little cap was green,
An' 'er name was Supi-yaw-lat – jes' the same as Theebaw's Queen,
An' I seed her first a-smokin' of a whackin' white cheroot,
An' a-wastin' Christian kisses on an 'eathen idol's foot:
      Bloomin' idol made o' mud –
      Wot they called the Great Gawd Budd –
      Plucky lot she cared for idols when I kissed 'er
                  where she stud!
      On the road to Mandalay, &c.

When the mist was on the rice-fields an' the sun was droppin' slow,
She'd git 'er little banjo an' she'd sing '*Kulla-lo-lo!*'
With 'er arm upon my shoulder an' 'er cheek agin my cheek
We useter watch the steamers an' the *hathis* pilin' teak.
      Elephints a-pilin' teak
      In the sludgy, squdgy creek,
      Where the silence 'ung that 'eavy you was 'arf
                afraid to speak!
      On the road to Mandalay, &c.

But that's all shove be'ind me – long ago an' fur away,
An' there ain't no 'buses runnin' from the Bank to Mandalay;
An' I'm learnin' 'ere in London what the ten-year soldier tells:
'If you've 'eard the East a-callin', you won't never 'eed naught else.'

No! you won't 'eed nothin' else
But them spicy garlic smells,
An' the sunshine an' the palm-trees an' the tinkly
                                        temple-bells;
On the road to Mandalay, &c.

I am sick o' wastin' leather on these gritty pavin'-stones,
An' the blasted English drizzle wakes the fever in my bones;
Tho' I walks with fifty 'ousemaids outer Chelsea to the Strand,
An' they talks a lot o' lovin', but wot do they understand?
Beefy face an' grubby 'and –
Law! wot do they understand?
I've a neater, sweeter maiden in a cleaner, greener
                                        land!
On the road to Mandalay, &c.

Ship me somewheres east of Suez, where the best is like the worst,
Where there aren't no Ten Commandments an' a man can raise a
                                        thirst;
For the temple-bells are callin', an' it's there that I would be –
By the old Moulmein Pagoda, lookin' lazy at the sea;
On the road to Mandalay,
Where the old Flotilla lay,
With our sick beneath the awnings when we went
                                        to Mandalay!
O the road to Mandalay,
Where the flyin'-fishes play,
An' the dawn comes up like thunder outer China 'crost
                                        the Bay!

The Way Through the Woods

They shut the road through the woods
Seventy years ago.
Weather and rain have undone it again,
And now you would never know
There was once a road through the woods
Before they planted the trees.
It is underneath the coppice and heath
And the thin anemones.
Only the keeper sees
That, where the ring-dove broods,
And the badgers roll at ease,
There was once a road through the woods.

Yet, if you enter the woods
Of a summer evening late,
When the night-air cools on the trout-ringed pools
Where the otter whistles his mate
(They fear not men in the woods,
Because they see so few),
You will hear the beat of a horse's feet,
And the swish of a skirt in the dew,
Steadily cantering through
The misty solitudes,
As though they perfectly knew
The old lost road through the woods . . .
But there is no road through the woods.

Danny Deever

'What are the bugles blowin' for?' said Files-on-Parade.
'To turn you out, to turn you out,' the Colour-Sergeant said.
'What makes you look so white, so white?' said Files-on-Parade.
'I'm dreadin' what I've got to watch,' the Colour-Sergeant said.
　For they're hangin' Danny Deever, you can hear the
　　Dead March play,
　The Regiment's in 'ollow square – they're hangin' him today;
　They've taken of his buttons off an' cut his stripes away,
　An' they're hangin' Danny Deever in the mornin'.

'What makes the rear-rank breathe so 'ard?' said Files-on-Parade.
'It's bitter cold, it's bitter cold,' the Colour-Sergeant said.
'What makes that front-rank man fall down?' said Files-on-Parade.
'A touch o' sun, a touch o' sun,' the Colour-Sergeant said.
　They are hangin' Danny Deever, they are marchin' of 'im round,
　They 'ave 'alted Danny Deever by 'is coffin on the ground;
　An' 'e'll swing in 'arf a minute for a sneakin' shootin' hound –
　O they're hangin' Danny Deever in the mornin'!

' 'Is cot was right-'and cot to mine,' said Files-on-Parade.
' 'E's sleepin' out an' far tonight,' the Colour-Sergeant said.
'I've drunk 'is beer a score o' times,' said Files-on-Parade.
' 'E's drinkin' bitter beer alone,' the Colour-Sergeant said.
　They are hangin' Danny Deever, you must mark 'im to 'is place.
　For 'e shot a comrade sleepin' – you must look 'im in the face;
　Nine 'undred of 'is county an' the Regiment's disgrace,
　While they're hangin' Danny Deever in the mornin'.

'What's that so black agin the sun?' said Files-on-Parade.
'It's Danny fightin' 'ard for life,' the Colour-Sergeant said.
'What's that that whimpers over'ead?' said Files-on-Parade.
'It's Danny's soul that's passin' now,' the Colour-Sergeant said.
　For they're done with Danny Deever, you can 'ear the
　　quickstep play,
　The Regiment's in column, an' they're marchin' us away;
　Ho! the young recruits are shakin', an' they'll want their
　　beer today,
　After hangin' Danny Deever in the mornin'!

If

If you can keep your head when all about you
    Are losing theirs and blaming it on you,
If you can trust yourself when all men doubt you,
    But make allowance for their doubting too;
If you can wait and not be tired by waiting,
    Or being lied about, don't deal in lies,
Or being hated, don't give way to hating,
    And yet don't look too good, nor talk too wise:

If you can dream – and not make dreams your master;
    If you can think – and not make thoughts your aim;
If you can meet with Triumph and Disaster
    And treat those two impostors just the same;
If you can bear to hear the truth you've spoken
    Twisted by knaves to make a trap for fools,
Or watch the things you gave your life to, broken,
    And stoop and build 'em up with worn-out tools:

If you can make one heap of all your winnings
    And risk it on one turn of pitch-and-toss,
And lose, and start again at your beginnings
    And never breathe a word about your loss;
If you can force your heart and nerve and sinew
    To serve your turn long after they are gone,
And so hold on when there is nothing in you
    Except the Will which says to than: 'Hold on!'

If you can talk with crowds and keep your virtue,
    Or walk with Kings – nor lose the common touch,
If neither foes nor loving friends can hurt you,
    If all men count with you, but none too much;
If you can fill the unforgiving minute
    With sixty seconds' worth of distance run,
Yours is the Earth and everything that's in it,
    And – which is more – you'll be a Man, my son!

The Glory of the Garden

Our England is a garden that is full of stately views,
Of borders, beds and shrubberies and lawns and avenues,
With statues on the terraces and peacocks strutting by;
But the Glory of the Garden lies in more than meets the eye.

For where the old thick laurels grow, along the thin red wall,
You find the tool- and potting-sheds which are the heart of all;
The cold-frames and the hot-houses, the dungpits and the tanks,
The rollers, carts and drainpipes, with the barrows and the
                                                    planks.

And there you'll see the gardeners, the men and 'prentice boys
Told off to do as they are bid and do it without noise;
For, except when seeds are planted and we shout to scare the
                                                    birds,
The Glory of the Garden it abideth not in words.

And some can pot begonias and some can bud a rose,
And some are hardly fit to trust with anything that grows;
But they can roll and trim the lawns and sift the sand and loam,
For the Glory of the Garden occupieth all who come.

Our England is a garden, and such gardens are not made
By singing: 'Oh, how beautiful!' and sitting in the shade,
While better men than we go out and start their working lives
At grubbing weeds from gravel-paths with broken dinner-knives.

There's not a pair of legs so thin, there's not a head so thick,
There's not a hand so weak and white, nor yet a heart so sick,
But it can find some needful job that's crying to be done,
For the Glory of the Garden glorifieth everyone.

Then seek your job with thankfulness and work till further
                                                    orders,
If it's only netting strawberries or killing slugs on borders;
And when your back stops aching and your hands begin to
                                                    harden,
You will find yourself a partner in the Glory of the Garden.

Oh, Adam was a gardener, and God who made him sees
That half a proper gardener's work is done upon his knees,
So when your work is finished, you can wash your hands and
                                                    pray
For the Glory of the Garden, that it may not pass away!
And the Glory of the Garden, it shall never pass away!

The Gods of the Copybook Headings

As I pass through my incarnations in every age and race,
I make my proper prostrations to the Gods of the Market-Place.
Peering through reverent fingers I watch them flourish and fall,
And the Gods of the Copybook Headings, I notice, outlast
    them all.

We were living in trees when they met us. They showed us each
    in turn
That Water would certainly wet us, as Fire would certainly burn:
But we found them lacking in Uplift, Vision and Breadth of
    Mind,
So we left them to teach the Gorillas while we followed the
    March of Mankind.

We moved as the Spirit listed. *They* never altered their pace,
Being neither cloud nor wind-borne like the Gods of the
    Market-Place;
But they always caught up with our progress, and presently
    word would come
That a tribe had been wiped off its icefield, or the lights had
    gone out in Rome.

With the Hopes that our World is built on they were utterly out
    of touch,
They denied that the Moon was Stilton; they denied she was
    even Dutch.

They denied that Wishes were Horses; they denied that a
    Pig had Wings.
So we worshipped the Gods of the Market, Who promised these
    beautiful things.

When the Cambrian measures were forming, They promised
    perpetual peace.
They swore, if we gave them our weapons, that the wars of the
    tribes would cease.
But when we disarmed, They sold us and delivered us bound to
    our foe,
And the Gods of the Copybook Headings said: '*Stick to
the Devil you know.*'

On the first Feminian Sandstones we were promised the Fuller
    Life
(Which started by loving our neighbour and ended by loving his
    wife),
Till our women had no more children and the men lost reason
    and faith,
And the Gods of the Copybook Headings said: '*The Wages
of Sin is Death.*'

In the Carboniferous Epoch we were promised abundance for all,
By robbing selected Peter to pay for collective Paul;
But, though we had plenty of money, there was nothing our
    money could buy,
And the Gods of the Copybook Headings said: '*If you don't
work, you die.*'

Then the Gods of the Market tumbled, and their smooth-
    tongued wizards withdrew,
And the hearts of the meanest were humbled and began to
    believe it was true
That All is not Gold that Glitters, and Two and Two make Four –
And the Gods of the Copybook Headings limped up to explain it
    once more.

As it will be in the future, it was at the birth of Man –
There are only four things certain since Social Progress began:

That the Dog returns to his Vomit and the Sow returns to her
    Mire,
And the burnt Fool's bandaged finger goes wabbling back to
    the Fire;

And that after this is accomplished, and the brave new world
    begins,
When all men are paid for existing and no man must pay for his
    sins,
As surely as Water will wet us, as surely as Fire will burn,
The Gods of the Copybook Headings with terror and slaughter
    return!

WALTER SAVAGE LANDOR
1775–1864

Finis

I strove with none, for none was worth my strife.
    Nature I loved and, next to Nature, Art:
I warmed both hands before the fire of life;
    It sinks, and I am ready to depart.

EDWARD LEAR
1812–1888

Limericks

There was an old man with a beard
Who said, 'It is just as I feared! –
   Two owls and a hen,,
   Four larks and a wren
Have all built their nests in my beard!'

There was a young person of Smyrna
Whose grandmother threatened to burn her,
   But she seized on the cat,
   And said, 'Granny, burn that!
You incongruous old woman of Smyrna.'

The Jumblies

1

They went to sea in a sieve, they did,
  In a sieve they went to sea:
In spite of all their friends could say,
On a winter's morn, on a stormy day,
  In a sieve they went to sea!
And when the sieve turned round and round,
And everyone cried, 'You'll all be drowned!'
They called aloud, 'Our sieve ain't big,
But we don't care a button! we don't care a fig!
  In a sieve we'll go to sea!'
    Far and few, far and few,
     Are the lands where the Jumblies live;
     Their heads are green, and their hands are blue,
      And they went to sea in a sieve.

2

They sailed away in a sieve, they did,
     In a sieve they sailed so fast,
With only a beautiful pea-green veil
Tied with a riband by way of a sail,
     To a small tobacco-pipe mast;
And everyone said, who saw them go,
'O won't they be soon upset, you know!
For the sky is dark, and the voyage is long,
And happen what may, it's extremely wrong
     In a sieve to sail so fast!'
          Far and few, far and few,
               Are the lands where the Jumblies live;
          Their heads are green, and their hands are blue,
               And they went to sea in a sieve.

3

The water it soon came in, it did,
     The water it soon came in;
So to keep them dry, they wrapped their feet
In a pinky paper, all folded neat,
     And they fastened it down with a pin.
And they passed the night in a crockery-jar,
And each of them said, 'How wise we are!
Though the sky be dark, and the voyage be long,
Yet we never can think we were rash or wrong,
     While round in our sieve we spin!'
          Far and few, far and few,
               Are the lands where the Jumblies live;
          Their heads are green, and their hands are blue,
               And they went to sea in a sieve.

4

And all night long they sailed away;
     And when the sun went down,
They whistled and warbled a moony song
To the echoing sound of a coppery gong,
     In the shade of the mountains brown.
'O Timballo! How happy we are,
When we live in a sieve and a crockery-jar,

And all night long in the moonlight pale,
We sail away with a pea-green sail,
  In the shade of the mountains brown!'
    Far and few, far and few,
      Are the lands where the Jumblies live;
     Their heads are green, and their hands are blue,
      And they went to sea in a sieve.

5

They sailed to the Western Sea, they did,
  To a land all covered with trees,
And they bought an Owl, and a useful Cart,
And a pound of Rice, and a Cranberry Tart,
  And a hive of silvery Bees.
And they bought a Pig, and some green Jackdaws,
And a lovely Monkey with lollipop paws,
And forty bottles of Ring-Bo-Ree,
  And no end of Stilton Cheese.
    Far and few, far and few,
      Are the lands where the Jumblies live;
     Their heads are green, and their hands are blue,
      And they went to sea in a sieve.

6

And in twenty years they all came back,
  In twenty years or more,
And everyone said, 'How tall they've grown!
For they've been to the Lakes, and the Torrible Zone,
  And the hills of the Chankly Bore.'
And they drank their health, and gave them a feast
Of dumplings made of beautiful yeast;
And everyone said, 'If we only live,
We too will go to sea in a sieve,
  To the hills of the Chankly Bore!'
    Far and few, far and few,
      Are the lands where the Jumblies live;
     Their heads are green, and their hands are blue,
      And they went to sea in a sieve.

The Owl and the Pussy Cat

The Owl and the Pussy Cat went to sea
   In a beautiful pea-green boat.
They took some honey, and plenty of money
   Wrapped up in a five-pound note.
The Owl looked up to the stars above,
   And sang to a small guitar,
'O lovely Pussy! O Pussy, my love,
What a beautiful Pussy you are,
       You are,
       You are!
What a beautiful Pussy you are!'

Pussy said to the Owl, 'You elegant fowl!'
   How charmingly sweet you sing!
O let us be married! too long we have tarried:
   But what shall we do for a ring?'
They sailed away, for a year and a day,
   To the land where the Bong-tree grows,
And there in a wood a Piggy-wig stood,
With a ring at the end of his nose,
       His nose,
       His nose!
With a ring at the end of his nose.

'Dear Pig, are you willing to sell for one shilling
   Your ring?' Said the Piggy, 'I will.'
So they took it away, and were married next day
   By the Turkey who lives on the hill.
They dined on mince, and slices of quince,
   Which they ate with a runcible spoon;
And hand in hand, on the edge of the sand
   They danced by the light of the moon,
       The moon,
       The moon,
They danced by the light of the moon.

NICHOLAS VACHEL LINDSAY
1879–1931

General William Booth Enters into Heaven

1

Booth led boldly with his big bass drum –
(Are you washed in the blood of the Lamb?)
The Saints smiled gravely and they said: 'He's come.'
(Are you washed in the blood of the Lamb?)
Walking lepers followed, rank on rank,
Lurching bravoes from the ditches dank,
Drabs from the alleyways and drug fiends pale –
Minds still passion-ridden, soul-powers frail –
Vermin-eaten saints with mouldy breath,
Unwashed legions with the ways of Death –
(Are you washed in the blood of the Lamb?)

Every slum had sent its half-a-score
The round world over. (Booth had groaned for more.)
Every banner that the wide world flies
Bloomed with glory and transcendent dyes.
Big-voiced lasses made their banjos bang,
Tranced, fanatical they shrieked and sang:
'Are you washed in the blood of the Lamb?'
Hallelujah! It was queer to see
Bull-necked convicts with that land make free.
Loons with trumpets blowed a blare, blare, blare
On, on upward thro' the golden air!
(Are you washed in the blood of the Lamb?)

2

Booth died blind and still by Faith he trod,
Eyes still dazzled by the ways of God.
Booth led boldly, and he looked the chief
Eagle countenance in sharp relief,
Heard a-flying, air of high command
Unabated in that hold land.

Jesus came from out the court-house door,
Stretched his hands above the passing poor.
Booth saw not, but led his queer ones there,
Round and round the mighty court-house square.
Yet in an instant all that blear review
Marched on spotless, clad in raiment new.
The lame were straightened, withered limbs uncurled
And blind eyes opened on a new, sweet world.
Drabs and vixens in a flash made whole!
Gone was the weasel-head, the snout, the jowl!
Sages and sibyls now, and athletes clean,
Rulers of empires, and of forests green!

The hosts were sandalled, and their wings were fire!
(Are you washed in the blood of the Lamb?)
But their noise played havoc with the angel-choir.
(Are you washed in the blood of the Lamb?)
O, shout salvation! It was good to see
Kings and Princes by the Lamb set free.
The banjos rattled and the tambourines
Jing-jing-jingled in the hands of Queens.

And when Booth halted by the curb for prayer
He saw his Master thro' the flag-filled air.
Christ came gently with a robe and crown
For Booth the soldier, while the throng knelt down.
He saw King Jesus. They were face to face,
And he knelt a-weeping in that holy place.
Are you washed in the blood of the lamb?

WILLIAM JAMES LINTON
1812–1898

Faint Heart

Faint heart wins not lady fair:
Victory smiles on those who dare,
There is but one way to woo –
Think thy Mistress willing too!
Leave her never chance to choose,
Hold her powerless to refuse.

If she answers thee with No,
Wilt thou bow and let her go? –
When, most like, her 'No' is meant
But to make more sweet consent;
So thy suit may longer be
For so much she liketh thee.

Never heed her pretty airs!
He's no lover who despairs;
He's no warrior whom a frown
Drives from his beleaguered town;
And no hunter he who stops
Till his stricken quarry drops.

Aim as certain not to miss;
Take her as thou would'st a kiss!
Or ask once, and if in vain,
Ask her twice, and thrice again:
Sure of this when all is said –
They lose most who are afraid.

HENRY WADSWORTH LONGFELLOW
1808–1882

The Arrow and the Song

I shot an arrow into the air,
It fell to earth, I knew not where;
For, so swiftly it flew, the sight
Could not follow it in its flight.

I breathed a song into the air,
It fell to earth, I knew not where;
For who has sight so keen and strong
That it can follow the flight of song?

Long, long afterward, in an oak
I found the arrow, still unbroke;
And the song, from beginning to end,
I found again in the heart of a friend.

Paul Revere's Ride

Listen, my children, and you shall hear
Of the midnight ride of Paul Revere,
On the eighteenth of April, in 'seventy-five;
Hardly a man is now alive
Who remembers that famous day and year.

He said to his friend, 'If the British march
By land or sea from the town tonight,
Hang a lantern aloft in the belfry arch
Of the North Church tower as a signal light –
One, if by land, and two, if by sea;
And I on the opposite shore will be,
Ready to ride and spread the alarm
Through every Middlesex village and farm,
For the country folk to be up and to arm.'

Then he said, 'Good-night!' and with muffled oar
Silently rowed to the Charlestown shore,
Just as the moon rose over the bay,
Where swinging wide at her moorings lay
The *Somerset*, British man-of-war,
A phantom ship, with each mast and spar
Across the moon like a prison bar,
And a huge black hulk, that was magnified
By its own reflection in the tide.

Meanwhile, his friend, through alley and street,
Wanders and watches with eager ears,
Till in the silence around him he hears
The muster of men at the barrack door,
The sound of arms, and the tramp of feet,
And the measured tread of the grenadiers,
Marching down to their boats on the shore.

Then he climbed the tower of the Old North Church,
By the wooden stairs, with stealthy tread,
To the belfry-chamber overhead,
And startled the pigeons from their perch
On the sombre rafters, that round him made
Masses and moving shapes of shade –
By the trembling ladder, steep and tall,
To the highest window in the wall,
Where he paused to listen and look down
A moment on the roofs of the town,
And the moonlight flowing over all.

Beneath, in the churchyard, lay the dead,
In their night-encampment on the hill,
Wrapped in silence so deep and still
That he could hear, like a sentinel's tread,
The watchful night-wind, as it went
Creeping along from tent to tent,
And seeming to whisper, 'All is well!'
A moment only he feels the spell
Of the place and the hour, and the secret dread
Of the lonely belfry and the dead;

For suddenly all his thoughts are bent
On a shadowy something far away,
Where the river widens to meet the bay –
A line of black that bends and floats
On the rising tide, like a bridge of boats.

Meanwhile, impatient to mount and ride,
Booted and spurred, with a heavy stride
On the opposite shore walked Paul Revere.
Now he patted his horse's side,
Now gazed at the landscape far and near,
Then, impetuous, stamped the earth,
And turned and tightened his saddle-girth;
But mostly he watched with eager search
The belfry-tower of the Old North Church,
As it rose above the graves on the hill,
Lonely and spectral and sombre and still.
And lo! as he looks, on the belfry's height
A glimmer, and then a gleam of light!
He springs to the saddle, the bridle he turns,
But lingers and gazes, till full on his sight
A second lamp in the belfry burns!

A hurry of hoofs in a village street,
A shape in the moonlight, a bulk in the dark,
And beneath, from the pebbles, in passing, a spark
Struck out by a steed flying fearless and fleet:
That was all! And yet, through the gloom and the light,
The fate of a nation was riding that night;
And the spark struck out by that steed, in his flight,
Kindled the land into flame with its heat.

He has left the village and mounted the steep,
And beneath him, tranquil and broad and deep,
Is the Mystic, meeting the ocean tides;
And under the alders that skirt its edge,
Now soft on the sand, now loud on the ledge,
Is heard the tramp of his steed as he rides.

It was twelve by the village clock,
When he crossed the bridge into Medford town.
He heard the crowing of the cock,
And the barking of the farmer's dog,
And felt the damp of the river fog
That rises after the sun goes down.

It was one by the village clock,
When he galloped into Lexington.
He saw the gilded weathercock
Swim in the moonlight as he passed,
And the meeting-house windows, blank and bare,
Gaze at him with a spectral glare,
As if they already stood aghast
At the bloody work they would look upon.

It was two by the village clock,
When he came to the bridge in Concord town.
He heard the bleating of the flock,
And the twitter of birds among the trees,
And felt the breath of the morning breeze
Blowing over the meadows brown.

And one was safe and asleep in his bed
Who at the bridge would be first to fall,
Who that day would be lying dead,
Pierced by a British musket ball.

You know the rest. In the books you have read,
How the British Regulars fired and fled –
How the farmers gave them ball for ball
From behind each fence and farmyard wall,
Chasing the redcoats down the lane,
Then crossing the fields to emerge again
Under the trees at the turn of the road,
And only pausing to fire and load.

So through the night rode Paul Revere;
And so through the night went his cry of alarm
To every Middlesex village and farm –

A cry of defiance and not of fear,
A voice in the darkness, a knock at the door,
And a word that shall echo forevermore!
For, borne on the night-wind of the past,
Through all our history, to the last,
In the hour of darkness and peril and need,
The people will waken and listen to hear
The hurrying hoof-beats of that steed,
And the midnight message of Paul Revere.

RICHARD LOVELACE
1618–c.1657

To Lucasta,
Going to the Wars

Tell me not, sweet, I am unkind,
    That from the nunnery
Of thy chaste breast and quiet mind
    To war and arms I fly.

True: a new mistress now I chase,
    The first foe in the field;
And with a stronger faith embrace
    A sword, a horse, a shield.

Yet this inconstancy is such
    As you too shall adore;
I could not love thee, dear, so much,
    Loved I not honour more.

AMY LOWELL
1874–1925

Patterns

I walk down the garden paths,
And all the daffodils
Are blowing, and the bright blue squills.
I walk down the patterned garden paths
In my stiff, brocaded gown.
With my powdered hair and jewelled fan,
I too am a rare
Pattern. As I wander down
The garden paths.

My dress is richly figured,
And the train
Makes a pink and silver stain
On the gravel, and the thrift
Of the borders.
Just a plate of current fashion,
Tripping by in high-heeled, ribboned shoes.
Not a softness anywhere about me,
Only whalebone and brocade.
And I sink on a seat in the shade
Of a lime tree. For my passion
Wars against the stiff brocade.
The daffodils and squills
Flutter in the breeze
As they please.
And I weep;
For the lime tree is in blossom
And one small flower has dropped upon my bosom.

And the plashing of waterdrops
In the marble fountain
Comes down the garden paths.
The dripping never stops.
Underneath my stiffened gown
Is the softness of a woman bathing in a marble basin,

A basin in the midst of hedges grown
So thick, she cannot see her lover hiding,
But she guesses he is near,
And the sliding of the water
Seems the stroking of a dear
Hand upon her.
What is Summer in a fine brocaded gown!
I should like to see it lying in a heap upon the ground.
All the pink and silver crumpled up on the ground.

I would be the pink and silver as I ran along the paths,
And he would stumble after,
Bewildered by my laughter.
I should see the sun flashing from his sword-hilt and the
    buckles on his shoes.
I would choose
To lead him in a maze along the patterned paths,
A bright and laughing maze for my heavy-booted lover.
Till he caught me in the shade,
And the buttons of his waistcoat bruised my body as he
    clasped me,
Aching, melting, unafraid.
With the shadows of the leaves and the sundrops,
And the plopping of the waterdrops,
All about us in the open afternoon –
I am very like to swoon
With the weight of this brocade,
For the sun sifts through the shade.

Underneath the fallen blossom
In my bosom
Is a letter I have hid.
It was brought to me this morning by a rider from the Duke.
'Madam, we regret to inform you that Lord Hartwell
Died in action Thursday sennight.'
As I read it in the white, morning sunlight,
The letters squirmed like snakes.
'Any answer, Madam?' said my footman.
'No,' I told him.
'See that the messenger takes some refreshment.
No, no answer.'

And I walked into the garden,
Up and down the patterned paths,
In my stiff, correct brocade.
The blue and yellow flowers stood up proudly in the sun
Each one.
I stood upright too,
Held rigid to the pattern
By the stiffness of my gown;
Up and down I walked,
Up and down.

In a month he would have been my husband.
In a a month, here, underneath this lime,
We would have broke the pattern;
He for me, and I for him,
He as Colonel, I as Lady,
On this shady seat.
He had a whim
That sunlight carried blessing.
And I answered, 'It shall be as you have said.'
Now he is dead.

In Summer and Winter I shall walk
Up and down
The patterened garden paths
In my stiff, brocade gown.
The squills and daffodils
Will give place to pillared roses, and to asters, and to
    snow.
I shall go
Up and down
In my gown.
Gorgeously arrayed,
Boned and stayed.
And the softness of my body will be guarded from
    embrace
By each button, hook and lace.
For the man who should loose me is dead,
Fighting with the Duke in Flanders,
In a pattern called a war.
Christ! What are patterns for?

CHRISTOPHER MARLOWE
1564–1593

The Passionate Shepherd to his Love

Come live with me, and be my love,
And we wilt all the pleasures prove,
That valleys, groves, hills and fields,
Woods, or steepy mountain yields.

And we will sit upon the rocks,
Seeing the shepherds feed their flocks
By shallow rivers, to whose falls
Melodious birds sing madrigals.

And I will make thee beds of roses,
And a thousand fragrant posies,
A cap of flowers and a kirtle
Embroidered all with leaves of myrtle.

A gown made of the finest wool
Which from our pretty lambs we pull,
Fair lined slippers for the cold,
With buckles of the purest gold;

A belt of straw and ivy-buds,
With coral clasps and amber studs,
And if these pleasures may thee move,
Come live with me, and be my love.

The shepherd swains shall dance and sing
For thy delight each May-morning,
If these delights thy mind may move;
Then live with me, and be my love

Elegia V

Corinnae concubitus

FROM OVID'S *Amores*

In summer's heat, and mid-time of the day,
To rest my limbs upon a bed I lay;
One window shut, the other open stood,
Which gave such light as twinkles in a wood,
Like twilight glimpse at selling of the sun,
Or night being past, and yet not day begun.
Such light to shamefast maidens must be shown
Where they may sport, and seem to be unknown.
Then came Corinna in a long loose gown,
Her white neck hid with tresses hanging down,
Resembling fair Semiramis going to bed,
Or Lais of a thousand wooers sped.
I snatched her gown; being thin, the harm was small;
Yet strived she to be covered therewithal;
And striving thus as one that would be cast,
Betrayed herself, and yielded at the last.
Stark naked as she stood before mine eye,
Not one wen in her body could I spy.
What arms and shoulders did I touch and see,
How apt her breasts were to be pressed by me!
How smooth a belly under her waist saw I,
How large a leg, and what a lusty thigh!
To leave the rest, all liked me passing well;
I clinged her naked body, down she fell;
Judge you the rest: being tired she bade me kiss.
Jove send me more such afternoons as this.

ANDREW MARVELL
1621–1678

To His Coy Mistress

Had we but world enough, and time,
This coyness, lady, were no crime.
We would sit down, and think which way
To walk, and pass our long love's day.
Thou by the Indian Ganges' side
Should'st rubies find: I by the tide
Of Humber would complain. I would
Love you ten years before the Flood,
And you should, if you please, refuse
Till the conversion of the Jews.
My vegetable love should grow
Vaster than empires and more slow;
An hundred years should go to praise
Thine eyes, and on thy forehead gaze;
Two hundred to adore each breast,
But thirty thousand to the rest;
An age at least to every part,
And the last age should show your heart.
For, lady, you deserve this state,
Nor would I love at lower rate.
  But at my back I always hear
Time's wingèd chariot hurrying near,
And yonder all before us lie
Deserts of vast eternity.
Thy beauty shall no more be found,
Nor, in thy marble vault, shall sound
My echoing song; then worms shall try
That long-preserved virginity,
And your quaint honour turn to dust,
And into ashes all my lust:
The grave's a fine and private place,
But none, I think, do there embrace.
  Now therefore, while the youthful hue

Sits on thy skin like morning dew,
And while thy willing soul transpires
At every pore with instant fires,
Now let us sport us while we may,
And now, like amorous birds of prey,
Rather at once our time devour
Than languish in his slow-chapt power.
Let us roll all our strength and all
Our sweetness up into one ball,
And tear our pleasures with rough strife,
Thorough the iron gates of life;
Thus, though we cannot make our sun
Stand still, yet we will make him run.

The Definition of Love

My Love is of a birth as rare
As 'tis for object strange and high:
It was begotten by Despair,
Upon Impossibility.

Magnanimous Despair alone
Could show me so divine a thing,
Where feeble Hope could ne'er have flown,
But vainly flapped its tinsel wing.

And yet I quickly might arrive
Where my extended soul is fixed;
But Fate does iron wedges drive,
And always crowds itself betwixt.

For Fate with jealous eye does see
Two perfect loves; nor lets them close:
Their union would her ruin be,
And her tyrannic power depose.

And therefore her decrees of steel
Us as the distant poles have placed
(Though Love's whole world on us doth wheel),
Not by themselves to be embraced,

Unless the giddy heaven fall,
And earth some new convulsion tear;
And, us to join, the world should all
Be cramped into a planisphere.

As lines, so loves oblique, may well
Themselves in every angle greet:
But ours, so truly parallel,
Though infinite, can never meet.

Therefore the love which us doth bind,
But Fate so enviously debars,
Is the conjunction of the mind,
And opposition of the stars.

The Garden

How vainly men themselves amaze
To win the palm, the oak, or bays;
And their incessant labours see
Crowned from some single herb, or tree;
Whose short and narrow-vergèd shade
Does prudently their toils upbraid;
While all the flowers and trees do close,
To weave the garlands of repose!

Fair Quiet, have I found thee here,
And Innocence, thy sister dear?
Mistaken long, I sought you then
In busy companies of men.
Your sacred plants, if here below,
Only among the plants will grow;
Society is all but rude,
To this delicious solitude.

No white nor red was ever seen
So amorous as this lovely green.
Fond lovers, cruel as their flame,
Cut in these trees their mistress' name:
Little, alas! they know or heed
How far these beauties hers exceed!
Fair trees! wheresoe'er your bark I wound,
No name shall but your own be found.

When we have run our passions' heat,
Love hither makes his best retreat.
The gods that mortal beauty chase,
Still in a tree did end their race;
Apollo hunted Daphne so,
Only that she might laurel grow;
And Pan did after Syrinx speed,
Not as a nymph, but for a reed.

What wondrous life is this I lead!
Ripe apples drop about my head;
The luscious clusters of the vine
Upon my mouth do crush their wine;
The nectarine, and curious peach,
Into my hands themselves do reach;
Stumbling on melons, as I pass,
Ensnared with flowers, I fall on grass.

Meanwhile the mind, from pleasure less,
Withdraws into its happiness:
The mind, that ocean where each kind
Does straight its own resemblance find;
Yet it creates, transcending these,
Far other worlds, and other seas,
Annihilating all that's made
To a green thought in a green shade.

Here at the fountain's sliding foot,
Or at some fruit tree's mossy root,
Casting the body's vest aside,
My soul into the boughs does glide:

There, like a bird, it sits and sings,
Then whets and combs its silver wings,
And, till prepared for longer flight,
Waves in its plumes the various light.

Such was that happy garden-state,
While man there walked without a mate:
After a place so pure and sweet,
What other help could yet be meet!
But 'twas beyond a mortal's share
To wander solitary there:
Two paradises 'twere in one
To live in paradise alone.

How well the skilful gardener drew
Of flowers and herbs this dial new;
Where, from above, the milder sun
Does through a fragrant zodiac run,
And, as it works, the industrious bee
Computes its time as well as we!
How could such sweet and wholesome hours
Be reckoned but with herbs and flowers?

The Mower to the Glow-worms

Ye living lamps, by whose dear light
The nightingale does sit so late,
And studying all the summer night,
Her matchless songs does meditate;

Ye country comets, that portend
No war nor prince's funeral,
Shining unto no higher end
Than to presage the grass's fall;

Ye glow-worms, whose officious flame
To wandering mowers shows the way,
That in the night have lost their aim,
And after foolish fires do stray;

Your courteous lights in vain you waste,
Since Juliana here is come,
For she my mind hath so displaced
That I shall never find my home.

Bermudas

Where the remote Bermudas ride,
In the ocean's bosom unespied,
From a small boat, that rowed along,
The listening winds received this song:

 'What should we do but sing His praise,
That led us through the watery maze,
Unto an isle so long unknown,
And yet far kinder than our own?
Where He the huge sea-monsters wracks,
That lift the deep upon their backs;
He lands us on a grassy stage,
Safe from the storms, and prelate's rage.
He gave us this eternal spring,
Which here enamels everything,
And sends the fowls to us in care,
On daily visits through the air;
He hangs in shades the orange bright,
Like golden lamps in a green night,
And does in the pomegranates close
Jewels more rich than Ormus shows;
He makes the figs our mouths to meet,
And throws the melons at our feet;
But apples plants of such a price,
No tree could ever bear them twice;
With cedars chosen by His hand,

From Lebanon, He stores the land,
And makes the hollow seas, that roar,
Proclaim the ambergris on shore;
He cast (of which we rather boast)
The Gospel's pearl upon our coast,
And in these rocks for us did frame
A temple where to sound His name.
Oh! let our voice His praise exalt,
Till it arrive at Heaven's vault,
Which thence (perhaps) rebounding, may
Echo beyond the Mexique Bay.'

Thus sung they, in the English boat,
An holy and a cheerful note;
And all the way, to guide their chime,
With falling oars they kept the time.

JOHN MASEFIELD
1878–1967

Sea Fever

I must go down to the seas again, to the lonely sea and the sky,
And all I ask is a tall ship and a star to steer her by;
And the wheel's kick and the wind's song and the white sail's
                                                shaking,
And a grey mist on the sea's face, and a grey dawn breaking.

I must go down to the seas again, for the call of the running tide
Is a wild call and a clear call that may not be denied;
And all I ask is a windy day with the white clouds flying,
And the flung spray and the blown spume, and the seagulls crying.

I must go down to the seas again, to the vagrant gypsy life,
To the gull's way and the whale's way where the wind's like a
                                                whetted knife;
And all I ask is a merry yarn from a laughing fellow-rover,
And quiet sleep and a sweet dream when the long trick's over.

Cargoes

Quinquireme of Nineveh from distant Ophir
Rowing home to haven in sunny Palestine,
With a cargo of ivory,
And apes and peacocks,
Sandalwood, cedarwood, and sweet white wine.

Stately Spanish galleon coming from the Isthmus,
Dipping through the Tropics by the palm-green shores,
With a cargo of diamonds,
Emeralds, amethysts,
Topazes, and cinnamon, and gold moidores.

Dirty British coaster with a salt-caked smoke-stack,
Butting through the Channel in the mad March days,
With a cargo of Tyne coal,
Road-rails, pig-lead,
Firewood, iron-ware, and cheap tin trays.

HERMAN MELVILLE
1819–1891

The Portent – 1859

Hanging from the beam,
Slowly swaying (such the law),
Gaunt the shadow on your green,
 Shenandoah!
The cut is on the crown
(Lo, John Brown),
And the stabs shall heal no more.

Hidden in the cap
 Is the anguish none can draw;
So your future veils its face,
 Shenandoah!
But the streaming beard is shown
(Weird John Brown),
The meteor of the war.

The Maldive Shark

About the Shark, phlegmatical one,
Pale sot of the Maldive sea,
The sleek little pilot-fish, azure and slim,
How alert in attendance be.
From his saw-pit of mouth, from his charnel of maw,
They have nothing of harm to dread,
Put liquidly glide on his ghastly flank
Or before his Gorgonian head;
Or lurk in the port of serrated teeth
In white triple tiers of glittering gates,
And there find a haven when peril's abroad,
And asylum in jaws of the Fates!
They are friends; and friendly they guide him to prey,
Yet never partake of the treat –
Eyes and brains to the dotard lethargic and dull,
Pale ravener of horrible meat.

GEORGE MEREDITH
1828–1909

from *Modern Love*

1

By this he knew she wept with waking eyes:
That, at his hand's light quiver by her head,
The strange low sobs that shook their common bed,
Were called into her with a sharp surprise,
And strangled mute, like little gaping snakes,
Dreadfully venomous to him. She lay
Stone-still, and the long darkness flowed away
With muffled pulses. Then, as midnight makes
Her giant heart of Memory and Tears
Drink the pale drug of silence, and so beat
Sleep's heavy measure, they from head to feet
Were moveless, looking through their dead black years,
By vain regret scrawled over the blank wall.
Like sculptured effigies they might be seen
Upon their marriage-tomb, the sword between;
Each wishing for the sword that severs all.

6

It chanced his lips did meet her forehead cool.
She had no blush, but slanted down her eye.
Shamed nature, then, confesses love can die:
And most she punishes the tender fool
Who will believe what honours her the most!
Dead! is it dead? She has a pulse, and flow
Of tears, the price of blood-drops, as I know,
For whom the midnight sobs around Love's ghost,
Since then I heard her, and so will sob on.
The love is here; it has but changed its aim.
O bitter barren woman! what's the name?
The name, the name, the new name thou hast won?
Behold me striking the world's coward stroke!

That will I not do, though the sting is dire.
– Beneath the surface this, while by the fire
They sat, she laughing at a quiet joke.

7

She issues radiant from her dressing-room,
Like one prepared to scale an upper sphere:
– By stirring up a lower, much I fear!
How deftly that oiled barber lays his bloom!
That long-shanked dapper Cupid with frisked curls,
Can make known women torturingly fair;
The gold-eyed serpent dwelling in rich hair
Awakes beneath his magic whisks and twirls.
His art can take the eyes from out my head,
Until I see with eyes of other men;
While deeper knowledge crouches in its den,
And sends a spark up – is it true we are wed?
Yea! filthiness of body is most vile,
But faithlessness of heart I do hold worse.
The former, it were not so great a curse
To read on the steel-mirror of her smile.

16

In our old shipwrecked days there was an hour,
When in the firelight steadily aglow,
Joined slackly, we beheld the red chasm grow
Among the clicking coals. Our library-bower
That eve was left to us: and hushed we sat
As lovers to whom Time is whispering.
From sudden-opened doors we heard them sing:
The nodding elders mixed good wine with chat.
Well knew we that Life's greatest treasure lay
With us, and of it was our talk. 'Ah, yes!
Love does!' I said: I never thought it less.
She yearned to me that sentence to unsay.
Then when the fire domed blackening, I found
Her cheek was salt against my kiss, and swift
Up the sharp scale of sobs her breast did lift –
Now am I haunted by that taste! that sound!

17

At dinner, she is hostess, I am host.
Went the feast ever cheerfuller? She keeps
The Topic over intellectual deeps
In buoyancy afloat. They see no ghost.
With sparkling surface-eyes we ply the ball:
It is in truth a most contagious game:
Hiding the Skeleton shall be its name.
Such play as this, the devils might appal!
But here's the greater wonder: in that we
Enamoured of an acting nought can tire,
Each other, like true hypocrites, admire;
Warm-lighted looks, Love's ephemerioe,
Shoot gaily o'er the dishes and the wine.
We waken envy of our happy lot.
Fast, sweet, and golden, shows the marriage-knot.
Dear guests, you now have seen Love's corpse-light shine.

25

You like not that French novel? Tell me why.
You think it quite unnatural. Let us see.
The actors are, it seems, the usual three:
Husband, and wife, and lover. She – but fie!
In England we'll not hear of it. Edmond,
The lover, her devout chagrin doth share;
Blancmange and absinthe are his penitent fare,
Till his pale aspect makes her over-fond:
So, to preclude fresh sin, he tries rosbif.
Meantime the husband is no more abused:
Auguste forgives her ere the tear is used.
Then hangeth all on one tremendous IF –
If she will choose between them. She does choose:
And takes her husband, like a proper wife.
Unnatural? My dear, these things are life:
And life, some think, is worthy of the Muse.

47

We saw the swallows gathering in the sky,
And in the osier-isle we heard them noise.
We had not to look back on summer joys,
Or forward to a summer of bright dye:
But in the largeness of the evening earth
Our spirits grew as we went side by side.
The hour became her husband and my bride.
Love that had robbed us so, thus blessed our dearth!
The pilgrims of the year waxed very loud
In multitudinous chatterings, as the flood
Full brown came from the West, and like pale blood
Expanded to the upper crimson cloud.
Love that had robbed us of immortal things,
This little moment mercifully gave,
Where I have seen across the twilight wave
The swan sail with her young beneath her wings.

50

Thus piteously Love closed what he begat:
The union of this ever-diverse pair!
These two were rapid falcons in a snare,
Condemned to do the flitting of the bat.
Lovers beneath the singing sky of May,
They wandered once; clear as the dew on flowers:
But they fed not on the advancing hours:
Their hearts held cravings for the buried day.
Then each applied to each that fatal knife,
Deep questioning, which probes to endless dole.
Ah, what a dusty answer gets the soul
When hot for certainties in this our life! –
In tragic hints here see what evermore
Moves dark as yonder midnight ocean's force,
Thundering like ramping hosts of warrior horse,
To throw that faint thin line upon the shore!

Lucifer in Starlight

On a starred night Prince Lucifer uprose.
Tired of his dark dominion swung the fiend
Above the rolling ball in cloud part screened,
Where sinners hugged their spectre of repose.
Poor prey to his hot fit of pride were those.
And now upon his western wing he leaned,
Now his huge bulk o'er Afric's sands careened,
Now the black planet shadowed Arctic snows.
Soaring through wider zones that pricked his scars
With memory of the old revolt from Awe,
He reached a middle height, and at the stars,
Which are the brain of heaven, he looked, and sank.
Around the ancient track marched, rank on rank,
The army of unalterable law.

When I Would Image

When I would image her features,
     Comes up a shrouded head:
I touch the outlines, shrinking;
     She seems of the wandering dead.

But when love asks for nothing,
     And lies on his bed of snow,
The face slips under my eyelids,
     All in its living glow.

Like a dark cathedral city,
     Whose spires, and domes, and towers
Quiver in violet lightnings,
     My soul basks on for hours.

CHARLOTTE MEW
1869–1928

Beside the Bed

Someone has shut the shining eyes, straightened and folded
   The wandering hands quietly covering the unquiet breast:
So, smoothed and silenced you lie, like a child, not again to be
                                  questioned or scolded;
   But, for you, not one of us believes that this is rest.

Not so to close the windows down can cloud and deaden
   The blue beyond: or to screen the wavering flame subdue its
                                      breath:
Why, if I lay my cheek to your cheek, your grey lips, like dawn,
                            would quiver and redden,
   Breaking into the old, odd smile at this fraud of death.

Because all night you have not turned to us or spoken
   It is time for you to wake; your dreams were never very deep:
I, for one, have seen the thin, bright, twisted threads of them
                           dimmed suddenly and broken,
   This is only a most piteous pretence of sleep!

A Quoi Bon Dire

      Seventeen years ago you said
    Something that sounded like Goodbye;
        And everybody thinks that you are dead,
        But I.

      So I, as I grow stiff and cold,
    To this and that say Goodbye too;
        And everybody sees that I am old,
        But you.

And one fine morning in a sunny lane
Some boy and girl will meet and kiss and swear
That nobody can love their way again,
          While over there
You will have smiled, I shall have tossed your hair.

EDNA ST VINCENT MILLAY
1892–1950

Passer Mortuus Est

Death devours all lovely things:
    Lesbia with her sparrow
Shares the darkness – presently
    Every bed is narrow.

Unremembered as old rain
    Dries the sheer libation;
And the little petulant hand
    Is an annotation.

After all, my erstwhile dear,
    My no longer cherished,
Need we say it was not love,
    Just because it perished?

*

My candle burns at both ends;
    It will not last the night;
But ah, my foes, and oh, my friends –
    It gives a lovely light!

JOHN MILTON
1608–1674

At a Solemn Music

Blest pair of Sirens, pledges of Heaven's joy,
Sphere-born harmonious sisters, Voice and Verse,
Wed your divine sounds; and mixed power employ
Dead things with inbreathed sense able to pierce,
And to our high-raised phantasy present
That undisturbed song of pure consent,
Ay sung before the sapphire-coloured throne
To Him that sits thereon,
With saintly shout and solemn jubilee;
Where the bright seraphim in burning row
Their loud uplifted angel-trumpets blow,
And the cherubic host in thousand quires
Touch their immortal harps of golden wires,
With those just spirits that wear victorious palms,
Hymns devout and holy psalms
Singing everlastingly;
That we on earth with undiscording voice
May rightly answer that melodious noise:
 As once we did, till disproportioned sin
Jarred against nature's chime, and with harsh din
Broke the fair music that all creatures made
To their great Lord; whose love their motion swayed
In perfect diapason, whilst they stood
In first obedience and their state of good.
O may we soon again renew that song,
And keep in tune with Heaven, till God ere long
To His celestial consort us unite,
To live with Him, and sing in endless morn of light.

L'Allegro

Hence, loathed Melancholy,
    Of Cerberus and blackest Midnight born
In Stygian cave forlorn
    'Mongst horrid shapes, and shrieks, and sights unholy!
Find out some uncouth cell,
    Where brooding Darkness spreads his jealous wings,
And the night-raven sings;
    There, under ebon shades and low-browed rocks,
As ragged as thy locks,
    In dark Cimmerian desert ever dwell.
But come, thou Goddess fair and free,
In heaven yclept Euphrosyne,
And by men heart-easing Mirth;
Whom lovely Venus, at a birth,
With two sister Graces more,
To ivy-crowned Bacchus bore:
Or whether (as some sager sing)
The frolic wind that breathes the spring,
Zephyr, with Aurora playing,
As he met her once a-Maying,
There, on beds of violets blue,
And fresh-blown roses washed in dew,
Filled her with thee, a daughter fair,
So buxom, blithe, and debonair.
    Haste thee, Nymph, and bring with thee
Jest, and youthful Jollity,
Quips and Cranks and wanton Wiles,
Nods and Becks and wreathed Smiles,
Such as hang on Hebe's cheek,
And love to live in dimple sleek;
Sport that wrinkled Care derides,
And Laughter holding both his sides.
Come, and trip it, as you go,
On the light fantastic toe;
And in thy right hand lead with thee
The mountain-nymph, sweet Liberty;

And, if I give thee honour due,
Mirth, admit me of thy crew,
To live with her, and live with thee,
In unreproved pleasures free;
To hear the lark begin his flight,
And, singing, startle the dull night,
From his watch-tower in the skies,
Till the dappled dawn doth rise;
Then to come, in spite of sorrow,
And at my window bid good morrow,
Through the sweet-briar or the vine,
Or the twisted eglantine;
While the cock, with lively din,
Scatters the rear of darkness thin;
And to the stack, or the barn door,
Stoutly struts his dames before:
Oft list'ning how the hounds and horn
Cheerly rouse the slumb'ring morn,
From the side of some hoar hill,
Through the high wood echoing shrill:
Sometime walking, not unseen,
By hedgerow elms, on hillocks green,
Right against the eastern gate
Where the great Sun begins his state,
Robed in flames and amber light,
The clouds in thousand liveries dight;
While the ploughman, near at hand,
Whistles o'er the furrowed land,
And the milkmaid singeth blithe,
And the mower whets his scythe,
And every shepherd tells his tale
Under the hawthorn in the dale.
Straight mine eye hath caught new pleasures,
Whilst the landskip round it measures:
Russet lawns, and fallows grey,
Where the nibbling flocks do stray;
Mountains on whose barren breast
The labouring clouds do often rest;
Meadows trim with daisies pied;
Shallow brooks, and rivers wide;

Towers and battlements it sees
Bosomed high in tufted trees,
Where perhaps some beauty lies,
The cynosure of neighbouring eyes.
Hard by a cottage chimney smokes
From betwixt two aged oaks,
Where Corydon and Thyrsis met
Are at their savoury dinner set
Of herbs and other country messes,
Which the neat-handed Phillis dresses;
And then in haste her bower she leaves,
With Thestylis to bind the sheaves;
Or, if the earlier season lead,
To the tanned haycock in the mead.
Sometimes, with secure delight,
The upland hamlets will invite,
When the merry bells ring round,
And the jocund rebecks sound
To many a youth and many a maid
Dancing in the chequered shade,
And young and old come forth to play
On a sunshine holiday,
Till the livelong daylight fail:
Then to the spicy nut-brown ale,
With stories told of many a feat,
How Faëry Mab the junkets eat.
She was pinched and pulled, she said;
And by the Friars' lantern led,
Tells how the drudging goblin sweat
To earn his cream-bowl duly set,
When in one night, ere glimpse of morn,
His shadowy flail hath threshed the corn
That ten day-labourers could not end;
Then lies him down the lubber fiend,
And, stretched out all the chimney's length,
Basks at the fire his hairy strength,
And crop-full out of doors he flings,
Ere the first cock his matin rings.
Thus done the tales, to bed they creep,
By whispering winds soon lulled asleep.

Towered cities please us then,
And the busy hum of men,
Where throngs of knights and barons bold,
In weeds of peace, high triumphs hold,
With store of ladies, whose bright eyes
Rain influence, and judge the prize
Of wit or arms, while both contend
To win her grace whom all commend.
There let Hymen oft appear
In saffron robe, with taper clear,
And pomp, and feast, and revelry,
With mask and antique pageantry;
Such sights as youthful poets dream
On summer eves by haunted stream.
Then to the well-trod stage anon,
If Jonson's learned sock be on,
Or sweetest Shakespeare, Fancy's child,
Warble his native wood-notes wild,
    And ever, against eating cares,
Lap me in soft Lydian airs,
Married to immortal verse,
Such as the meeting soul may pierce,
In notes with many a winding bout
Of linked sweetness long drawn out
With wanton heed and giddy cunning,
The melting voice through mazes running,
Untwisting all the chains that tie
The hidden soul of harmony;
That Orpheus' self may heave his head
From golden slumber on a bed
Of heaped Elysian flowers, and hear
Such strains as would have won the ear
Of Pluto to have quite set free
His half-regained Eurydice.
    These delights if thou canst give,
Mirth, with thee I mean to live.

Il Penseroso

Hence, vain deluding Joys,
   The brood of Folly without father bred!
How little you bested,
   Or fill the fixed mind with all your toys!
Dwell in some idle brain,
   And fancies fond with gaudy shapes possess,
As thick and numberless
   As the gay motes that people the sunbeams,
Or likest hovering dreams,
   The fickle pensioners of Morpheus' train.
But, hail! thou Goddess sage and holy,
Hail, divinest Melancholy!
Whose saintly visage is too bright
To hit the sense of human sight,
And therefore to our weaker view
O'erlaid with black, staid Wisdom's hue;
Black, but such as in esteem
Prince Memnon's sister might beseem,
Or that starred Ethiop queen that strove
To set her beauty's praise above
The Sea-Nymphs, and their powers offended.
Yet thou art higher far descended:
Thee bright-haired Vesta long of yore
To solitary Saturn bore;
His daughter she; in Saturn's reign
Such mixture was not held a stain.
Oft in glimmering bowers and glades
He met her, and in secret shades
Of woody Ida's inmost grove,
Whilst yet there was no fear of Jove.
   Come, pensive Nun, devout and pure,
Sober, steadfast, and demure,
All in a robe of darkest grain,
Flowing with majestic train,
And sable stole of cypress lawn
Over thy decent shoulders drawn.
Come, but keep thy wonted state,

With even step, and musing gait,
And looks commercing with the skies,
Thy rapt soul sitting in thine eyes:
There, held in holy passion still,
Forget thyself to marble, till
With a sad leaden downward cast
Thou fix them on the earth as fast.
And join with thee calm Peace and Quiet,
Spare Fast, that oft with gods doth diet,
And hears the Muses in a ring
Ay round about Jove's altar sing;
And add to these retired Leisure,
That in trim gardens takes his pleasure;
But, first and chiefest, with thee bring
Him that yon soars on golden wing,
Guiding the fiery-wheeled throne,
The Cherub Contemplation;
And the mute Silence hist along,
'Less Philomel will deign a song,
In her sweetest, saddest plight,
Smoothing the rugged brow of Night,
While Cynthia checks her dragon yoke
Gently o'er th' accustomed oak.
Sweet bird, that shunn'st the noise of folly,
Most musical, most melancholy!
Thee, chauntress, oft the woods among
I woo, to hear thy even-song;
And, missing thee, I walk unseen
On the dry smooth-shaven green,
To behold the wand'ring moon,
Riding near her highest noon,
Like one that had been led astray
Through the heaven's wide pathless way,
And oft, as if her head she bowed,
Stooping through a fleecy cloud.
    Oft, on a plat of rising ground,
I hear the far-off curfew sound,
Over some wide-watered shore,
Swinging slow with sullen roar;
Or, if the air will not permit,

Some still removed place will fit,
Where glowing embers through the room
Teach light to counterfeit a gloom,
Far from all resort of mirth,
Save the cricket on the hearth,
Or the bellman's drowsy charm
To bless the doors from nightly harm.
Or let my lamp, at midnight hour,
Be seen in some high lonely tower,
Where I may oft outwatch the Bear,
With thrice great Hermes, or unsphere
The spirit of Plato, to unfold
What worlds or what vast regions hold
The immortal mind that hath forsook
Her mansion in this fleshly nook;
And of those demons that are found
In fire, air, flood, or underground,
Whose power hath a true consent
With planet or with element.
Sometime let gorgeous Tragedy
In sceptred pall come sweeping by,
Presenting Thebes, or Pelops' line,
Or the tale of Troy divine,
Or what (though rare) of later age
Ennobled hath the buskined stage.
   But, O sad Virgin! that thy power
Might raise Musaeus from his bower;
Or bid the soul of Orpheus sing
Such notes as, warbled to the string,
Drew iron tears down Pluto's cheek,
And made Hell grant what love did seek;
Or call up him that left half-told
The story of Cambuscan bold,
Of Camball, and of Algarsife,
And who had Canace to wife,
That owned the virtuous ring and glass,
And of the wondrous horse of brass
On which the Tartar king did ride;
And if aught else great bards beside
In sage and solemn tunes have sung,

Of tourneys, and of trophies hung,
Of forests, and enchantments drear,
Where more is meant than meets the ear.
    Thus, Night, oft see me in thy pale career,
Till civil-suited Morn appear,
Not tricked and frounced, as she was wont
With the Attic boy to hunt,
But kerchief in a comely cloud,
While rocking winds are piping loud,
Or ushered with a shower still,
When the gust hath blown his fill,
Ending on the rustling leaves,
With minute drops from off the eaves.
And, when the sun begins to fling
His flaring beams, me, Goddess, bring
To arched walks of twilight groves,
And shadows brown, that Sylvan loves,
Of pine, or monumental oak,
Where the rude axe with heaved stroke
Was never heard the nymphs to daunt,
Or fright them from their hallowed haunt.
There, in close covert, by some brook,
Where no profaner eye may look,
Hide me from day's garish eye,
While the bee with honied thigh,
That at her flowery work doth sing.
And the waters murmuring,
With such consort as they keep,
Entice the dewy-feathered Sleep.
And let some strange mysterious dream
Wave at his wings, in airy stream
Of lively portraiture displayed,
Softly on my eyelids laid;
And, as I wake, sweet music breathe
Above, about, or underneath,
Sent by some Spirit to mortals good,
Or th' unseen Genius of the wood.
    But let my due feet never fail
To walk the studious cloister's pale,
And love the high embowèd roof,

With antique pillars massy-proof,
And storied windows richly dight,
Casting a dim religious light.
There let the pealing organ blow,
To the full-voiced quire below,
In service high and anthems clear,
As may with sweetness, through mine ear,
Dissolve me into ecstasies,
And bring all Heaven before mine eyes.
   And may at last my weary age
Find out the peaceful hermitage,
The hairy gown and mossy cell,
Where I may sit and rightly spell
Of every star that heaven doth shew,
And every herb that sips the dew,
Till old experience do attain
To something like prophetic strain.
   These pleasures, Melancholy, give;
And I with thee will choose to live.

On Being Arrived at
Twenty-Three Years of Age

How soon hath Time, the subtle thief of youth,
   Stolen on his wing my three-and-twentieth year!
   My hasting days fly on with full career,
   But my late spring no bud or blossom shew'th.
Perhaps my semblance might deceive the truth
   That I to manhood am arrived so near;
   And inward ripeness doth much less appear,
   That some more timely-happy spirits indu'th.
Yet, be it less or more, or soon or slow,
   It shall be still in strictest measure even
   To that same lot, however mean or high,
Toward which Time leads me, and the will of Heaven.
   All is, if I have grace to use it so,
   As ever in my great Task-Master's eye.

The Fifth Ode of Horace

BOOK 1
Quis multa gracilis te puer in rosa

Rendered almost word for word, without rhyme, according
to the Latin measure, as near as the language will permit.

> What slender youth, bedewed with liquid odours,
> Courts thee on roses in some pleasant cave,
>   Pyrrha? For whom bind'st thou
>   In wreaths thy golden hair,
> Plain in thy neatness? Oh, how oft shall he
> On faith and changed gods complain, and seas
>   Rough with black winds and storms
>   Unwonted shall admire!
> Who now enjoys thee credulous, all gold;
> Who always vacant, always amiable,
>   Hopes thee, of flattering gales
>   Unmindful. Hapless they
> To whom thou untried seem'st fair! Me, in my vowed
> Picture, the sacred wall declares t' have hung
>   My dank and dropping weeds
>   To the stern God of Sea.

Lycidas

In this monody the author bewails a learned friend, unfortu-
nately drowned, in his passage from Chester, on the Irish Seas
in 1637; and, by occasion, foretells the ruin of our corrupted
clergy, then in their height.

> Yet once more, O ye laurels, and once more,
> Ye myrtles brown, with ivy never sere,
> I come to pluck your berries harsh and crude,
> And with forced fingers rude
> Shatter your leaves before the mellowing year.
> Bitter constraint and sad occasion dear

Compels me to disturb your season due;
For Lycidas is dead, dead ere his prime,
Young Lycidas, and hath not left his peer.
Who would not sing for Lycidas? he knew
Himself to sing, and build the lofty rhyme.
He must not float upon his watery bier
Unwept, and welter to the parching wind,
Without the meed of some melodious tear.

   Begin, then, Sisters of the sacred well
That from beneath the seat of Jove doth spring;
Begin, and somewhat loudly sweep the string;
Hence with denial vain and coy excuse.
So may some gentle Muse
With lucky words favour my destined urn,
And as he passes, turn
And bid fair peace be to my sable shroud!

   For we were nursed upon the self-same hill,
Fed the same flock, by fountain, shade, and rill;
Together both, ere the high lawns appeared
Under the opening eyelids of the Morn,
We drove a-field, and both together heard
What time the grey-fly winds her sultry horn,
Batt'ning our flocks with the fresh dews of night,
Oft till the star that rose at evening bright
Toward heaven's descent had sloped his westering wheel.
Meanwhile the rural ditties were not mute,
Tempered to th' oaten flute;
Rough Satyrs danced, and Fauns with cloven heel
From the glad sound would not be absent long;
And old Damætas loved to hear our song.

   But, oh! the heavy change, now thou art gone,
Now thou art gone, and never must return!
Thee, Shepherd, thee the woods, and desert caves,
With wild thyme and the gadding vine o'ergrown,
And all their echoes, mourn.
The willows, and the hazel copses green,
Shall now no more be seen,
Fanning their joyous leaves to thy soft lays.
As killing as the canker to the rose,
Or taint-worm to the weanling herds that graze,

Or frost to flowers, that their gay wardrobe wear,
When first the whitethorn blows;
Such, Lycidas, thy loss to shepherd's ear.
　　Where were ye, Nymphs, when the remorseless deep
Closed o'er the head of your loved Lycidas?
For neither were ye playing on the steep,
Where your old bards, the famous Druids, lie,
Nor on the shaggy top of Mona high,
Nor yet where Deva spreads her wizard stream.
Ay me! I fondly dream
Had ye been there . . . for what could that have done?
What could the Muse herself that Orpheus bore,
The Muse herself, for her enchanting son,
Whom universal nature did lament,
When, by the rout that made the hideous roar,
His gory visage down the stream was sent,
Down the swift Hebrus to the Lesbian shore?
　　Alas! what boots it with incessant care
To tend the homely, slighted, shepherd's trade,
And strictly meditate the thankless Muse?
Were it not better done, as others use,
To sport with Amaryllis in the shade,
Or with the tangles of Neæra's hair?
Fame is the spur that the clear spirit doth raise
(That last infirmity of noble mind)
To scorn delights, and live laborious days;
But the fair guerdon when we hope to find,
And think to burst out into sudden blaze,
Comes the blind Fury with th' abhorrèd shears,
And slits the thin-spun life. 'But not the praise,'
Phœbus replied, and touched my trembling ears:
'Fame is no plant that grows on mortal soil,
Nor in the glistering foil
Set off to the world, nor in broad rumour lies,
But lives and spreads aloft by those pure eyes
And perfect witness of all-judging Jove;
As he pronounces lastly on each deed,
Of so much fame in heaven expect thy meed.'
　　O fountain Arethuse, and thou honoured flood,
Smooth-sliding Mincius, crowned with vocal reeds!

That strain I heard was of a higher mood.
But now my oat proceeds,
And listens to the Herald of the Sea
That came in Neptune's plea.
He asked the waves, and asked the felon winds,
What hard mishap hath doomed this gentle swain?
And questioned every gust of rugged wings
That blows from off each beakèd promontory.
They knew not of his story;
And sage Hippotades their answer brings;
That not a blast was from his dungeon strayed,
The air was calm, and on the level brine
Sleek Panope with all her sisters played.
It was that fatal and perfidious bark,
Built in th' eclipse, and rigged with curses dark,
That sunk so low that sacred head of thine.
    Next, Camus, reverend sire, went footing slow,
His mantle hairy, and his bonnet sedge,
Inwrought with figures dim, and on the edge
Like to that sanguine flower inscribed with woe.
'Ah! who hath reft,' quoth be, 'my dearest pledge?'
Last came, and last did go,
The Pilot of the Galilean Lake;
Two massy keys he bore of metals twain
(The golden opes, the iron shuts amain).
He shook his mitred locks, and stern bespake:
'How well could I have spared for thee, young swain,
Enow of such as, for their bellies' sake,
Creep, and intrude, and climb into the fold!
Of other care they little reckoning make
Than how to scramble at the shearers' feast,
And shove away the worthy bidden guest.
Blind mouths! that scarce themselves know how to hold
A sheep-hook, or have learned aught else the least
That to the faithful herdman's art belongs!
What recks it them? What need they? They are sped;
And, when they list, their lean and flashy songs
Grate on their scrannel pipes of wretched straw;
The hungry sheep look up, and are not fed
But, swol'n with wind and the rank mist they draw,

Rot inwardly, and foul contagion spread:
Besides what the grim wolf with privy paw
Daily devours apace, and nothing said.
But that two-handed engine at the door
Stands ready to smite once, and smite no more.'
    Return, Alpheus the dread voice is past
That shrunk thy streams; return, Sicilian Muse,
And call the vales, and bid them hither cast
Their bells and flowrets of a thousand hues.
Ye valleys low, where the mild whispers use
Of shades, and wanton winds, and gushing brooks,
On whose fresh lap the swart star sparely looks,
Throw hither all your quaint enamelled eyes,
That on the green turf suck the honied showers,
And purple all the ground with vernal flowers.
Bring the rathe primrose that forsaken dies,
The tufted crow-toe, and pale jessamine,,
The white pink, and the pansy freaked with jet,
The glowing violet,
The musk-rose, and the well-attired woodbine,
With cowslips wan that hang the pensive head,
And every flower that sad embroidery wears:
Bid amaranthus all his beauty shed,
And daffadillies fill their cups with tears,
To strew the laureate hearse where Lycid lies.
For so, to interpose a little ease,
Let our frail thoughts dally with false surmise.
Ay me! whilst thee the shores and sounding seas
Wash far away, where'er thy bones are hurled;
Whether beyond the stormy Hebrides,
Where thou perhaps under the whelming tide
Visit'st the bottom of the monstrous world;
Or whether thou, to our moist vows denied,
Sleep'st by the fable of Bellerus old,
Where the great Vision of the guarded mount
Looks toward Namancos, and Bayona's hold.
Look homeward, Angel, now, and melt with ruth:
And, O ye dolphins, waft the hapless youth!
    Weep no more, woeful shepherds, weep no more,
For Lycidas, your sorrow, is not dead,

Sunk though he be beneath the wat'ry floor.
So sinks the day-star in the ocean bed,
And yet anon repairs his drooping head,
And tricks his beams, and with new-spangled ore
Flames in the forehead of the morning sky:
So Lycidas sunk low, but mounted high,
Through the dear might of Him that walked the waves;
Where, other groves and other streams along,
With nectar pure his oozy locks he laves,
And hears the unexpressive nuptial song,
In the blest kingdoms meek of joy and love.
There entertain him all the Saints above,
In solemn troops, and sweet societies,
That sing, and singing in their glory move,
And wipe the tears for ever from his eyes.
Now, Lycidas, the shepherds weep no more;
Henceforth thou art the Genius of the shore,
In thy large recompense, and shalt be good
To all that wander in that perilous flood.
    Thus sang the uncouth swain to th' oaks and rills,
While the still morn went out with sandals grey:
He touched the tender stops of various quills,
With eager thought warbling his Doric lay:
And now the sun had stretched out all the hills,
And now was dropt into the western bay;
At last he rose, and twitched his mantle blue:
Tomorrow to fresh woods, and pastures new.

On His Blindness

When I consider how my light is spent
    Ere half my days in this dark world and wide,
    And that one talent which is death to hide
    Lodged with me useless, though my soul more bent
To serve therewith my Maker, and present
    My true account, lest He returning chide;
    'Doth God exact day-labour, light denied?'
    I fondly ask: but Patience, to prevent
That murmur, soon replies, 'God doth not need
    Either man's work or his own gifts. Who best
    Bear his mild yoke, they serve him best; his state
    Is kingly: thousands at his bidding speed,
And post o'er land and ocean without rest;
They also serve who only stand and wait.'

SIR THOMAS MORE
*c.*1477–1535

Epigram

Between a Tyrant and a King
    Would you the difference have?
The King each subject counts his child,
    The Tyrant each his slave.

WILLIAM MORRIS
1834–1896

The Haystack in the Floods

Had she come all the way for this,
To part at last without a kiss?
Yea, had she borne the dirt and rain
That her own eyes might see him slain
Beside the haystack in the floods?

Along the dripping leafless woods,
The stirrup touching either shoe,
She rode astride as troopers do;
With kirtle kilted to her knee,
To which the mud splashed wretchedly;
And the wet dripped from every tree
Upon her head and heavy hair,
And on her eyelids broad and fair;
The tears and rain ran down her face.
By fits and starts they rode apace,
And very often was his place
Far off from her; he had to ride
Ahead, to see what might betide
When the roads crossed; and sometimes, when
There rose a murmuring from his men,
Had to turn back with promises;
Ah me! she had but little ease;
And often for pure doubt and dread
She sobb'd, made giddy in the head
By the swift riding; while, for cold,
Her slender fingers scarce could hold
the wet reins; yea, and scarcely, too,
She felt the foot within her shoe
Against the stirrup; all for this,
To part at last without a kiss
Beside the haystack in the floods.

For when they near'd that old soak'd hay,
They saw across the only way
That Judas, Godmar, and the three
Red running lions dismally
Grinned from his pennon, under which,
In one straight line along the ditch,
They counted thirty heads.
                              So then,
While Robert turned round to his men,
She saw at once the wretched end,
And, stooping down, tried hard to rend
Her coif the wrong way from her head,
And hid her eyes; while Robert said:
'Nay, love, 'tis scarcely two to one –
Like Poitiers where we made them run
So fast – why, sweet my love, good cheer.
The Gascon frontier is so near,
Nought after this.'
                              But, 'O,' she said,
'My God! my God! I have to tread
The long way back without you; then
The court at Paris; those six men;
The gratings of the Châtelet;
The swift Seine on some rainy day
Like this, and people standing by,
And laughing, while my weak hands try
To recollect how strong men swim,
All this, or else a life with him,
For which I should be damned at last,
Would God that this next hour were past!'
He answer'd not, but cried his cry,
'St George for Marny!' cheerily;
And laid his hand upon her rein.
Alas! no man of all his train
Gave back that cheery cry again;
And, while for rage his thumb beat fast
Upon his sword-hilt, someone cast
About his neck a kerchief long,
And bound him.

                              Then they went along
To Godmar; who said: 'Now, Jehane,
Your lover's life is on the wane
So fast, that, if this very hour
You yield not as my paramour,
He will not see the rain leave off –
Nay, keep your tongue from gibe and scoff,
Sir Robert, or I slay you now.'
She laid her hand upon her brow,
Then gazed upon the palm, as though
She thought her forehead bled, and – 'No,'
She said and turned her head away,
As there were nothing else to say,
And everything were settled: red
Grew Godmar's face from chin to head:
'Jehane, on yonder hill there stands
My castle, guarding well my lands:
What hinders me from taking you,
And doing that I list to do
To your fair wilful body, while
Your knight lies dead?'
                              A wicked smile
Wrinkled her face, her lips grew thin,
A long way out she thrust her chin:
'You know that I should strangle you
While you were sleeping; or bite through
Your throat, by God's help – ah!' she said,
'Lord Jesus, pity your poor maid!
For in such wise they hem me in,
I cannot choose but sin and sin,
Whatever happens; yet I think
They could not make me eat or drink,
And so should I just reach my rest.'
'Nay, if you do not my behest,
O Jehane! though I love you well,'
Said Godmar, 'would I fail to tell
All that know.' 'Foul lies,' she said,
'Eh? lies, my Jehane? by God's head,
At Paris folks would deem them true!
Do you know, Jehane, they cry for you,

"Jehane the brown! Jehane the brown!
Give us Jehane to burn or drown!" –
Eh – gag me Robert! – sweet, my friend,
This were indeed a piteous end
For those long fingers, and long feet,
And long neck, and smooth shoulders sweet;
An end that few men would forget
That saw it – So, an hour yet:
Consider, Jehane, which to take
Of life or death!'

             So, scarce awake,
Dismounting, did she leave that place,
And totter some yards: with her face
Turn'd upward to the sky she lay,
Her head on a wet heap of hay,
And fell asleep; and while she slept,
And did not dream, the minutes crept
Round to the twelve again; but she,
Being waked at last, sighed quietly,
And strangely childlike came, and said:
'I will not.' Straightway Godmar's head,
As though it hung on strong wires, turned
Most sharply round, and his face burned.
For Robert – both his eyes were dry,
He could not weep, but gloomily
He seemed to watch the rain; yea, too,
His lips were firm; he tried once more
To touch her lips; she reached out, sore
And vain desire so tortured them,
The poor grey lips, and now the hem
Of his sleeve brushed them.

                 With a start
Up Godmar rose, thrust them apart;
From Robert's throat he loosed the bands
Of silk and mail; with empty hands
Held out, she stood and gazed, and saw
The long bright blade without a flaw
Glide out from Godmar's sheath, his hand
In Robert's hair; she saw him bend
Back Robert's head; she saw him send

The thin steel down; the blow told well,
Right backward the knight Robert fell,
And moaned as dogs do, being half dead,
Unwitting, as I deem; so then
Godmar turned grinning to his men,
Who ran, some five or six, and beat
His head to pieces at their feet.

Then Godmar turned again, and said:
'So, Jehane, the first fitte is read!
Take note, my lady, that your way
Lies backward to the Châtelet!'
She shook her head and gazed awhile,
At her cold hands with a rueful smile,
As though this thing had made her mad.

This was the parting that they had
Beside the haystack in the floods.

In Time of Pestilence

Adieu, farewell earth's bliss!
This world uncertain is:
Fond are life's lustful joys,
Death proves them all but toys.
None from his darts can fly;
I am sick, I must die –
        Lord, have mercy on us!

Rich men, trust not in wealth,
Gold cannot buy you health;
Physic himself must fade;
All things to end are made;
The plague full swift goes by;
I am sick, I must die –
        Lord, have mercy on us!

Beauty is but a flower
Which wrinkles will devour;
Brightness falls from the air;
Queens have died young and fair;
Dust hath clos'd Helen's eye;
I am sick, I must die –
    Lord, have mercy on us!

Strength stoops unto the grave,
Worms feed on Hector brave;
Swords may not fight with fate;
Earth still holds ope her gate;
Come, come! the bells do cry;
I am sick, I must die –
    Lord, have mercy on us!

Wit with his wantonness
Tasteth death's bitterness;
Hell's executioner
Hath no ears for to hear
What vain art can reply;
I am sick, I must die –
    Lord, have mercy on us!

SIR HENRY NEWBOLT
1862–1938

A Letter from the Front

I was out early today, spying about
From the top of a haystack – such a lovely morning –
And when I mounted again to canter back
I saw across a field in the broad sunlight
A young Gunner Subaltern, stalking along
With a rook-rifle held at the ready, and – would you
                                        believe it? –
A domestic cat, soberly marching beside him.

So I laughed, and felt quite well disposed to the youngster,
And shouted out 'the top of the morning' to him,
And wished him 'Good sport!' – and then I remembered
My rank, and his, and what I ought to be doing:
And I rode nearer, and added, 'I can only suppose
You have not seen the Commander-in-Chief's order
Forbidding English officers to annoy their Allies
By hunting and shooting.'
                        But he stood and saluted
And said earnestly, 'I beg your pardon, Sir,
I was only going out to shoot a sparrow
To feed my cat with.'
                        So there was the whole picture,
The lovely early morning, the occasional shell
Screeching and scattering past us, the empty landscape –
Empty, except for the young Gunner saluting,
And the cat, anxiously watching his every movement.

I may be wrong, and I may have told it badly,
But it struck me as being extremely ludicrous.

MARGARET CAVENDISH, DUCHESS OF NEWCASTLE
1623–1673

Of Many Worlds in This World

Just like unto a nest of boxes round,
Degrees of sizes within each box are found,
So in this world may many worlds more be,
Thinner, and less, and less still by degree;
Although they are not subject to our sense,
A world may be no bigger than twopence.
Nature is curious, and such work may make
That our dull sense can never find, but scape.
For creatures small as atoms may be there,
If every atom a creature's figure bear.
If four atoms a world can make, then see
What several worlds might in an earring be.
For millions of these atoms may be in
The head of one small, little, single pin.
And if thus small, then ladies well may wear
A world of worlds as pendants in each ear.

JOHN HENRY NEWMAN
1801–1890

Praise to the Holiest in the Height

Praise to the Holiest in the height,
   And in the depth be praise:
In all His words most wonderful;
   Most sure in all His ways!

O loving wisdom of our God!
   When all was sin and shame,
A second Adam to the fight
   And to the rescue came.

O wisest love! that flesh and blood
   Which did in Adam fail,
Should strive afresh against their foe,
   Should strive and should prevail;

And that a higher gift than grace
   Should flesh and blood refine,
God's Presence and His very Self,
   And Essence all-divine.

O generous love! that He who smote
   In man for man the foe,
The double agony in man
   For man should undergo;

And in the garden secretly,
   And on the cross on high,
Should teach His brethren and inspire
   To suffer and to die.

ALFRED NOYES
1880–1959

The Highwayman

1

The wind was a torrent of darkness among the gusty trees.
The moon was a ghostly galleon tossed upon cloudy seas.
The road was a ribbon of moonlight over the purple moor,
And the highwayman came riding –
        Riding – riding –
The highwayman came riding, up to the old inn-door.

He'd a French cocked-hat on his forehead, a bunch of lace at
                                                his chin,
A coat of the claret velvet, and breeches of brown doe-skin.
They fitted with never a wrinkle. His boots were up to the thigh.
And he rode with a jewelled twinkle,
        His pistol butts a-twinkle,
His rapier hilt a-twinkle, under the jewelled sky.

Over the cobbles he clattered and clashed in the dark inn-yard.
He tapped with his whip on the shutters, but all was locked
                                                and barred.
He whistled a tune to the window, and who should be waiting
                                                there
But the landlord's black-eyed daughter,
        Bess, the landlord's daughter,
Plaiting a dark red love-knot into her long black hair.

And dark in the dark old inn-yard a stable-wicket creaked
Where Tim the ostler listened. His face was white and peaked.
His eyes were hollows of madness, his hair like mouldy hay,
But he loved the landlord's daughter,
        The landlord's red-lipped daughter.
Dumb as a dog he listened, and he heard the robber say –

'One kiss, my bonny sweetheart, I'm after a prize tonight,
But I shall be back with the yellow gold before the morning
                            light;
Yet, if they press me sharply, and harry me through the day,
Then look for me by moonlight;
        Watch for me by moonlight;
I'll come to thee by moonlight, though hell should bar the way!'

He rose upright in the stirrups. He scarce could reach her hand,
But she loosened her hair in the casement. His face burnt like
                            a brand
As the black cascade of perfume came tumbling over his breast;
And he kissed its waves in the moonlight,
        (O, sweet black waves in the moonlight!)
Then he tugged at his rein in the moonlight, and galloped away
                            to the west.

2

He did not come in the dawning. He did not come at noon;
And out of the tawny sunset, before the rise of the moon,
When the road was a gypsy's ribbon, looping the purple moor,
A red-coat troop came marching –
        Marching – marching –
King George's men came marching, up to the old inn-door.

They said no word to the landlord. They drank his ale instead.
But they gagged his daughter, and bound her to the foot of her
                          narrow bed
Two of them knelt at her casement, with muskets at their side!
There was death at every window;
        And hell at one dark window;
For Bess could see, through her casement, the road that *he*
                          would ride.

They had tied her up to attention, with many a sniggering jest.
They had bound a musket beside her, with the muzzle beneath
                          her breast!
'Now keep good watch!' and they kissed her. She heard the
                      doomed man say –

Look for me by moonlight;
        Watch for me by moonlight;
I'll come to thee by moonlight, though hell should bar the way!

She twisted her hands behind her; but all the knots held good!
She writhed her hands till her fingers were wet with sweat or
                                                    blood!
They stretched and strained in the darkness, and the hours
                                            crawled by like years,
Till, now on the stroke of midnight,
        Cold, on the stroke of midnight,
The tip of one finger touched it! The trigger at least was hers!

The tip of one finger touched it. She strove no more for the rest.
Up she stood up to attention, with the muzzle beneath her
                                                    breast.
She would not risk their hearing; she would not strive again;
For the road lay bare in the moonlight;
        Blank and bare in the moonlight;
And the blood of her veins, in the moonlight, throbbed to her
                                                love's refrain.

Tlot-tlot; tlot-tlot! Had they heard it? The horsehoofs ringing
                                                    clear;
Tlot-tlot, tlot-tlot, in the distance? Were they deaf that they did
                                                not hear?
Down the ribbon of moonlight, over the brow of the hill,
The highwayman came riding –
        Riding – riding –
The red-coats looked to their priming! She stood up, straight and
                                                    still.

Tlot-tlot, in the frosty silence! *Tlot-tlot,* in the echoing night!
Nearer he came and nearer. Her face was like a light.
Her eyes grew wide for a moment; she drew one last deep
                                                    breath,
Then her finger moved in the moonlight,
        Her musket shattered the moonlight,
Shattered her breast in the moonlight and warned him – with
                                                her death.

He turned. He spurred to the west; he did not know who stood
Bowed, with her head o'er the musket, drenched with her own
                                                    blood!
Not till the dawn he heard it, and his face grew grey to hear
How Bess, the landlord's daughter,
                    The landlord's black-eyed daughter,
Had watched for her love in the moonlight, and died in the
                                            darkness there.

Back, he spurred like a madman, shouting a curse to the sky,
With the white road smoking behind him and his rapier
    brandished high.
Blood-red were his spurs in the golden noon; wine-red was his
    velvet coat;
When they shot him down on the highway,
                    Down like a dog on the highway,
And he lay in his blood on the highway, with a bunch of lace at
                                            his throat.

                            *

And still of a winter's night, they say, when the wind is in the trees,
When the moon is a ghostly galleon tossed upon cloudy seas,
When the road is a ribbon of moonlight over the purple moor,
A highwayman comes riding —
            Riding — riding —
A highwayman comes riding, up to the old inn-door.
Over the cobbles he clatters and clangs in the dark inn-yard
He taps with his whip on the shutters, but all is locked and barred.
He whistles a tune to the window, and who should be waiting there
But the landlord's black-eyed daughter,
            Bess, the landlord's daughter,
Plaiting a dark red love-knot into her long black hair.

ARTHUR WILLIAM EDGAR O'SHAUGHNESSY
1844–1881

Ode

We are the music-makers,
  And we are the dreamers of dreams,
Wandering by lone sea-breakers,
  And sitting by desolate streams;
World-losers and world-forsakers,
  On whom the pale moon gleams:
Yet we are the movers and shakers
  Of the world for ever, it seems.

With wonderful deathless ditties
We build up the world's great cities,
  And out of a fabulous story
  We fashion an empire's glory:
One man with a dream, at pleasure,
  Shall go forth and conquer a crown;
And three with a new song's measure
  Can trample an empire down.

We, in the ages lying
  In the buried past of the earth,
Built Nineveh with our sighing,
  And Babel itself with our mirth;
And o'erthrew them with prophesying
  To the old of the new world's worth;
For each age is a dream that is dying,
  Or one that is coming to birth.

WILFRED OWEN
1893–1918

Dulce et Decorum Est

Bent double, like old beggars under sacks,
Knock-kneed, coughing like hags, we cursed through
          sludge,
Till on the haunting flares we turned our backs,
And towards our distant rest began to trudge.
Men marched asleep. Many had lost their boots,
But limped on, blood-shod. All went lame, all blind;
Drunk with fatigue; deaf even to the hoots
Of gas-shells dropping softly behind.

Gas! Gas! Quick, boys! – An ecstasy of fumbling,
Fitting the clumsy helmets just in time,
But someone still was yelling out and stumbling
And floundering like a man in fire or lime –
Dim through the misty panes and thick green light,
As under a green sea, I saw him drowning.

In all my dreams before my helpless sight
He plunges at me, guttering, choking, drowning.

If in some smothering dreams, you too could pace
Behind the wagon that we flung him in,
And watch the white eyes writhing in his face,
His hanging face, like a devil's sick of sin;
If you could hear, at every jolt, the blood
Come gargling from the froth-corrupted lungs,
Bitter as the cud
Of vile, incurable sores on innocent tongues –
My friend, you would not tell with such high zest,
To children ardent for some desperate glory,
The old lie: *Dulce et decorum est
Pro patria mori*.

Anthem for Doomed Youth

What passing-bells for these who die as cattle?
  Only the monstrous anger of the guns.
  Only the stuttering rifles' rapid rattle
Can patter out their hasty orisons.
No mockeries for them from prayers or bells,
  Nor any voice of mourning save the choirs,
The shrill, demented choirs of wailing shells;
  And bugles calling for them from sad shires.

What candles may be held to speed them all?
  Not in the hands of boys, but in their eyes
Shall shine the holy glimmers of goodbyes.
  The pallor of girls' brows shall be their pall;
Their flowers the tenderness of silent minds,
And each slow dusk a drawing-down of blinds.

Futility

Move him into the sun –
Gently its touch awoke him once,
At home, whispering of fields unsown.
Always it woke him, even in France,
Until this morning and this snow.
If anything might rouse him now
The kind old sun will know.

Think how it wakes the seeds –
Woke, once, the clays of a cold star.
Are limbs, so dear-achieved, are sides,
Full-nerved – still warm – too hard to stir?
Was it for this the clay grew tall?
O what made fatuous sunbeams toil
To break earth's sleep at all?

Strange Meeting

It seemed that out of battle I escaped
Down some profound dull tunnel, long since scooped
Through granites which titanic wars had groined.
Yet also there encumbered sleepers groaned,
Too fast in thought or death to be bestirred.
Then, as I probed them, one sprang up, and stared
With piteous recognition in fixed eyes,
Lifting distressful hands as if to bless.
And by his smile, I knew that sullen hall,
By his dead smile I knew we stood in Hell.
With a thousand pains that vision's face was grained;
Yet no blood reached there from the upper ground,
And no guns thumped, or down the flues made moan.
'Strange friend,' I said, 'here is no cause to mourn.'
'None,' said the other, 'save the undone years,
The hopelessness. Whatever hope is yours,
Was my life also; I went hunting wild
After the wildest beauty in the world,
Which lies not calm in eyes, or braided hair,
But mocks the steady running of the hour,
And if it grieves, grieves richlier than here.
For by my glee might many men have laughed,
And of my weeping something had been left,
Which must die now. I mean the truth untold,
The pity of war, the pity war distilled.
Now men will go content with what we spoiled.
Or, discontent, boil bloody, and be spilled.
They will be swift with swiftness of the tigress,
None will break ranks, though nations trek from progress.
Courage was mine, and I had mystery,
Wisdom was mine, and I had mastery;
To miss the march of this retreating world
Into vain citadels that are not walled.
Then, when much blood had clogged their chariot-wheels
I would go up and wash them from sweet wells,
Even with truths that lie too deep for taint.
I would have poured my spirit without stint

But not through wounds; not on the cess of war.
Foreheads of men have bled where no wounds were.
I am the enemy you killed, my friend.
I knew you in this dark; for so you frowned
Yesterday through me as you jabbed and killed.
I parried; but my hands were loath and cold.
Let us sleep now . . . '

GEORGE PEELE
1556–1596

A Sonnet

His golden locks time hath to silver turned;
    O time too swift, O swiftness never ceasing!
His youth 'gainst time and age hath ever spurned,
    But spurned in vain; youth waneth by increasing:
Beauty, strength, youth, are flowers but fading seen;
Duty, faith, love, are roots, and ever green.

His helmet now shall make a hive for bees;
    And, lovers' sonnets turned to holy psalms,
A man-at-arms must now serve on his knees,
    And feed on prayers, which are age's alms:
But though from court to cottage he depart,
His saint is sure of his unspotted heart.

And when he saddest sits in homely cell,
    He'll teach his swains this carol for a song:
'Blest be the hearts that wish my sovereign well,
    Curst be the souls that think her any wrong.'
Goddess, allow this agèd man his right,
To be your beadsman now, that was your knight.

Bethsabe's Song

Hot sun, cool fire, tempered with sweet air,
Black shade, fair nurse, shadow my white hair:
Shine, sun; burn, fire; breathe, air, and ease me;

Black shade, fair nurse, shroud me and please me:
Shadow, my sweet nurse, keep me from burning,
Make not my glad cause cause of mourning.
  Let not my beauty's fire
  Inflame unstaid desire,
  Nor pierce any bright eye
  That wandereth lightly.

AMBROSE PHILIPS
1674–1749

A Winter-Piece

To the Earl of Dorset
Copenhagen, 9 March 1709

From frozen climes, and endless tracts of snow,
From streams that northern winds forbid to flow,
What present shall the Muse to Dorset bring,
Or how, so near the Pole, attempt to sing?
The hoary winter here conceals from sight
All pleasing objects that to verse invite.
The hills and dales, and the delightful woods,
The flowery plains and silver-streaming floods,
By snow disguised, in bright confusion lie,
And with one dazzling waste fatigue the eye.
 No gentle-breathing breeze prepares the spring,
No birds within the desert region sing;
The ships unmoved the boisterous winds defy,
While rattling chariots o'er the ocean fly.
The vast leviathan wants room to play,

And spout his waters in the face of day;
The starving wolves along the main sea prowl,
And to the moon in icy valleys howl.
For many a shining league the level main
Here spreads itself into a glassy plain;
There solid billows of enormous size,
Alps of green ice, in wild disorder rise.
    And yet but lately have I seen, e'en here,
The winter in a lovely dress appear.
Ere yet the clouds let fall the treasured snow,
Or winds begun through hazy skies to blow,
At evening a keen eastern breeze arose,
And the descending rain unsullied froze.
Soon as the silent shades of night withdrew,
The ruddy morn disclosed at once to view
The face of nature in a rich disguise,
And brightened every object to my eyes.
For every shrub, and every blade of grass,
And every pointed thorn, seemed wrought in glass;
In pearls and rubies rich the hawthorns show,
While through the ice the crimson berries glow.
The thick-sprung reeds the watery marshes yield
Seem polished lances in a hostile field.
The stag in limpid currents, with surprise,
Sees crystal branches on his forehead rise.
The spreading oak, the beech and towering pine,
Glazed over, in the freezing ether shine:
The frighted birds the rattling branches shun,
That wave and glitter in the distant sun.
    When if a sudden gust of wind arise,
The brittle forest into atoms flies;
The crackling wood beneath the tempest bends,
And in a spangled shower the prospect ends;
Or, if a southern gale the region warm,
And by degrees unbind the wintry charm,
The traveller a miry country sees,
And journeys sad beneath the dropping trees.
    Like some deluded peasant Merlin leads
Through fragrant bowers and through delicious meads;
While here enchanted gardens to him rise,

And airy fabrics there attract his eyes,
His wandering feet the magic paths pursue;
And, while he thinks the fair illusion true,
The trackless scenes disperse in fluid air,
And woods and wilds and thorny ways appear:
A tedious road the weary wretch returns,
And, as he goes, the transient vision mourns.

EDGAR ALLAN POE
1809–1849

To Helen

Helen, thy beauty is to me
    Like those Nicéan barks of yore
That gently, o'er a perfumed sea,
    The weary, way-worn wanderer bore
    To his own native shore.

On desperate seas long wont to roam,
    Thy hyacinth hair, thy classic face,
Thy Naiad airs have brought me home
    To the glory that was Greece,
    And the grandeur that was Rome.

Lo! in yon brilliant window niche,
    How statue-like I see thee stand,
    The agate lamp within thy hand –
Ah! Psyche, from the regions which
    Are Holy Land!

The Bells

1

Hear the sledges with the bells –
Silver bells!
What a world of merriment their melody foretells!
How they tinkle, tinkle, tinkle,
In the icy air of night!
While the stars that oversprinkle
All the heavens, seem to twinkle
With a crystalline delight;
Keeping time, time, time,
In a sort of Runic rhyme,
To the tintinnabulation that so musically wells
From the bells, bells, bells, bells,
Bells, bells, bells –
From the jingling and the tinkling of the bells.

2

Hear the mellow wedding bells –
Golden bells!
What a world of happiness their harmony foretells!
Through the balmy air of night
How they ring out their delight! –
From the molten-golden notes,
And all in tune,
What a liquid ditty floats
To the turtle-dove that listens, while she gloats
On the moon!
Oh, from out the sounding cells,
What a gush of euphony voluminously wells!
How it swells!
How it dwells
On the Future! – how it tells
Of the rapture that impels
To the swinging and the ringing
Of the bells, bells, bells –
Of the bells, bells, bells, bells,
Bells, bells bells –
To the rhyming and the chiming of the bells!

3

Hear the loud alarum bells –
Brazen bells!
What a tale of terror, now, their turbulency tells!
In the startled ear of night
How they scream out their affright!
Too much horrified to speak,
They can only shriek, shriek,
Out of tune,
In a clamorous appealing to the mercy of the fire,
In a mad expostulation with the deaf and frantic fire,
Leaping higher, higher, higher,
With a desperate desire,
And a resolute endeavour
Now – now to sit, or never,
By the side of the pale-faced moon.
Oh, the bells, bells, bells!
What a tale their terror tells
Of Despair!
How they clang, and clash, and roar!
What a horror they outpour
On the bosom of the palpitating air!
Yet the ear, it fully knows,
By the twanging
And the clanging,
How the danger ebbs and flows;
Yet the ear distinctly tells,
In the jangling
And the wrangling,
How the danger sinks and swells,
By the sinking or the swelling in the anger of the bells –
Of the bells –
Of the bells, bells, bells, bells,
Bells, bells, bells –
In the clamour and the clangour of the bells!

4

Hear the tolling of the bells –
Iron bells!
What a world of solemn thought their monody compels!

In the silence of the night,
How we shiver with affright
At the melancholy menace of their tone!
For every sound that floats
From the rust within their throats
Is a groan.
And the people – ah, the people –
They that dwell up in the steeple,
All alone,
And who tolling, tolling, tolling,
In that muffled monotone,
Feel a glory in so rolling
On the human heart a stone –
They are neither man nor woman –
They are neither brute nor human –
They are Ghouls –
And their king it is who tolls –
And he rolls, rolls, rolls,
Rolls
A paean from the bells!
And his merry bosom swells
With the paean of the bells!
And he dances, and he yells;
Keeping lime, time, time,
In a sort of Runic rhyme,
To the paean of the bells –
Of the bells –
Keeping time, time, time,
In a sort of Runic rhyme,
To the throbbing of the bells –
Of the bells, bells, bells –
To the sobbing of the bells;
Keeping time, time, time,
As he knells, knells, knells,
In a happy Runic rhyme,
To the rolling of the bells –
Of the bells, bells, bells –
To the tolling of the bells –
Of the bells, bells, bells, bells,
Bells, bells, bells –
To the moaning and the groaning of the bells.

ALEXANDER POPE
1688–1744

Epistle to Miss Blount
on her Leaving the Town
after the Coronation

As some fond virgin, whom her mother's care
Drags from the town to wholesome country air,
Just when she learns to roll a melting eye,
And hear a spark, yet think no danger nigh;
From the dear man unwilling she must sever,
Yet takes one kiss before she parts for ever:
Thus from the world fair Zephalinda flew,
Saw others happy, and with sighs withdrew;
Not that their pleasures caused her discontent,
She sighed not that they stayed, but that she went.

   She went to plain-work, and to purling brooks,
Old-fashioned halls, dull aunts, and croaking rooks;
She went from op'ra, park, assembly, play,
To morning walks, and prayers three hours a day;
To pass her time 'twixt reading and bohea,
To muse, and spill her solitary tea,
Or o'er cold coffee trifle with the spoon,
Count the slow clock, and dine exact at noon;
Divert her eyes with pictures in the fire,
Hum half a tune, tell stories to the squire;
Up to her godly garret after seven,
There starve and pray, for that's the way to heaven.

   Some squire, perhaps, you take delight to rack,
Whose game is whisk, whose treat a toast in sack,
Who visits with a gun, presents you birds,
Then gives a smacking buss and cries – No words!
Or with his hound comes hollowing from the stable.
Makes love with nods, and knees beneath a table;
Whose laughs are hearty, though his jests are coarse,
And loves you best of all things – but his horse.

   In some fair evening, on your elbow laid,

You dream of triumphs in the rural shade;
In pensive thought recall the fancied scene,
See coronations rise on every green;
Before you pass th' imaginary sights
Of lords, and earls, and dukes, and gartered knights,
While the spread fan o'ershades your closing eyes;
Then give one flirt, and all the vision flies.
Thus vanish sceptres, coronets, and balls,
And leave you in lone woods, or empty walls.
    So when your slave, at some dear, idle time
(Not plagued with headaches, or the want of rhyme),
Stands in the streets, abstracted from the crew,
And while he seems to study, thinks of you
Just when his fancy points your sprightly eyes,
Or sees the blush of soft Parthenia rise,
Gay pats my shoulder, and you vanish quite;
Streets, chairs, and coxcombs rush upon my sight;
Vexed to be still in town, I knit my brow,
Look sour, and hum a tune – as you may now.

Elegy to the Memory
of an Unfortunate Lady

What beck'ning ghost, along the moonlight shade
Invites my steps, and points to yonder glade?
'Tis she! – but why that bleeding bosom gored,
Why dimly gleams the visionary sword?
Oh, ever beauteous, ever friendly! tell,
Is it, in heaven, a crime to love too well?
To bear too tender or too firm a heart,
To act a lover's or a Roman's part?
Is there no bright reversion in the sky
For those who greatly think, or bravely die?
    Why bade ye else, ye powers! her soul aspire
Above the vulgar flight of low desire?
Ambition first sprung from your blest abodes,
The glorious fault of angels and of gods:
Thence to their images on earth it flows,

And in the breasts of kings and heroes glows!
Most souls, 'tis true, but peep out once an age,
Dull, sullen prisoners in the body's cage:
Dim lights of life that burn a length of years,
Useless, unseen, as lamps in sepulchres;
Like Eastern kings a lazy state they keep,
And close confined to their own palace sleep.

From these perhaps (ere nature bade her die)
Fate snatched her early to the pitying sky.
As into air the purer spirits flow,
And sep'rate from their kindred dregs below;
So flew the soul to its congenial place,
Nor left one virtue to redeem her race.

But thou, false guardian of a charge too good,
Thou, mean deserter of thy brother's blood!
See on these ruby lips the trembling breath,
These cheeks now fading at the blast of death:
Cold is that breast which warmed the world before,
And those love-darting eyes must roll no more.
Thus, if eternal justice rules the ball,
Thus shall your wives, and thus your children fall:
On all the line a sudden vengeance waits,
And frequent hearses shall besiege your gates.
There passengers shall stand, and pointing say
(While the long fun'rals blacken all the way),
'Lo! these were they, whose souls the Furies steeled,
And cursed with hearts unknowing how to yield.'
Thus unlamented pass the proud away,
The gaze of fools, and pageant of a day!
So perish all, whose breast ne'er learned to glow
For others' good, or melt at others' woe.

What can atone (oh ever-injured shade!)
Thy fate unpitied, and thy rites unpaid?
No friend's complaint, no kind domestic tear
Pleased thy pale ghost, or graced thy mournful bier.
By foreign hands thy dying eyes were closed,
By foreign hands thy decent limbs composed,
By foreign hands thy humble grave adorned,
By strangers honoured, and by strangers mourned!
What though no friends in sable weeds appear,

Grieve for an hour, perhaps, then mourn a year,
And bear about the mockery of woe
To midnight dances, and the public show?
What though no weeping loves thy ashes grace,
Nor polished marble emulate thy face?
What though no sacred earth allow thee room,
Nor hallowed dirge be muttered o'er thy tomb?
Yet shall thy grave with rising flowers be dressed
And the green turf lie lightly on thy breast:
There shall the morn her earliest tears bestow,
There the first roses of the year shall blow;
While angels with their silver wings o'ershade
The ground now sacred by thy relics made.

So peaceful rests, without a stone, a name,
What once had beauty, titles, wealth, and fame.
How loved, how honoured once, avails thee not,
To whom related, or by whom begot;
A heap of dust alone remains of thee;
'Tis all thou art, and all the proud shall be!

Poets themselves must fall, like those they sung;
Deaf the praised ear, and mute the tuneful tongue.
Even he, whose soul now melts in mournful lays,
Shall shortly want the generous tear he pays;
Then from his closing eyes thy form shall part,
And the last pang shall tear thee from his heart,
Life's idle business at one gasp be o'er,
The Muse forgot, and thou beloved no more!

On a Certain Lady at Court

I know the thing that's most uncommon
   (Envy be silent and attend!);
I know a reasonable woman,
   Handsome and witty, yet a friend.

Not warped by passion, awed by rumour,
   Not grave through pride, or gay through folly;
An equal mixture of good humour
   And sensible soft melancholy.

'Has she no faults, then,' Envy says, 'sir?'
   Yes, she has one, I must aver:
When all the world conspires to praise her,
   The woman's deaf, and does not hear.

Epigram Engraved on the Collar of a Dog which I Gave to His Royal Highness

I am His Highness' dog at Kew;
Pray tell me, sir, whose dog are you?

Epistle to a Lady: Of the Characters of Women

Nothing so true as what you once let fall:
'Most women have no characters at all.'
Matter too soft a lasting mark to bear,
And best distinguished by black, brown, or fair.
   How many pictures of one nymph we view,
All how unlike each other, all how true!
Arcadia's Countess, here in ermined pride,
Is there, Pastora by a fountain side.
Here Fannia, leering on her own good man,
And there, a naked Leda with a swan.
Let then the fair one beautifully cry
In Magdalen's loose hair and lifted eye,
Or dress'd in smiles of sweet Cecilia shine,

With simpering angels, palms, and harps divine;
Whether the charmer sinner it, or saint it,
If folly grow romantic, I must paint it.
    Come, then, the colours and the ground prepare!
Dip in the rainbow, trick her off in air;
Choose a firm cloud before it fall, and in it
Catch, ere she change, the Cynthia of this minute.
    Rufa, whose eye quick glancing o'er the park
Attracts each light gay meteor of a spark,
Agrees as ill with Rufa studying Locke,
As Sappho's diamonds with her dirty smock;
Or Sappho at her toilet's greasy task,
With Sappho fragrant at an evening mask:
So morning insects, that in muck begun,
Shine, buzz, and fly-blow in the setting sun.
    How soft is Silia! fearful to offend;
The frail one's advocate, the weak one's friend.
To her, Calista proved her conduct nice;
And good Simplicius asks of her advice.
Sudden, she storms! she raves! You tip the wink,
But spare your censure – Silia does not drink.
All eyes may see from what the change arose,
All eyes may see – a pimple on her nose.
    Papillia, wedded to her doting spark,
Sighs for the shades – 'How charming is a park!'
A park is purchased, but the fair he sees
All bathed in tears – 'Oh odious, odious trees!'
    Ladies, like variegated tulips, show,
'Tis to their changes half their charms we owe;
Their happy spots the nice admirer take,
Fine by defect, and delicately weak.
'Twas thus Calypso once each heart alarmed,
Awed without virtue, without beauty charmed;
Her tongue bewitch'd as oddly as her eyes,
Less wit than mimic, more a wit than wise;
Strange graces still, and stranger flights she had,
Was just not ugly, and was just not mad;
Yet ne'er so sure our passion to create,
As when she touch'd the brink of all we hate.
    Narcissa's nature, tolerably mild,

To make a wash would hardly stew a child;
Has e'en been proved to grant a lover's prayer,
And paid a tradesman once, to make him stare;
Gave alms at Easter, in a Christian trim,
And made a widow happy for a whim.
Why then declare good-nature is her scorn,
When 'tis by that alone she can be borne?
Why pique all mortals, yet affect a name?
A fool to pleasure, yet a slave to fame:
Now deep in Taylor and the *Book of Martyrs*,
Now drinking citron with his Grace and Chartres:
Now conscience chills her, and now passion burns;
And atheism and religion take their turns;
A very heathen in the carnal part,
Yet still a sad, good Christian at her heart.
　See Sin in state, majestically drunk;
Proud as a peeress, prouder as a punk;
Chaste to her husband, frank to all beside,
A teeming mistress, but a barren bride.
What then? let blood and body bear the fault,
Her head's untouch'd, that noble seat of thought:
Such this day's doctrine – in another fit
She sins with poets through pure love of wit.
What has not fired her bosom or her brain?
Caesar and Tall-boy, Charles and Charlemagne.
As Helluo, late dictator of the feast,
The nose of *haut-goût* and the tip of taste,
Critiqued your wine, and analysed your meat,
Yet on plain pudding deigned at home to eat:
So Philomedé, lecturing all mankind
On the soft passion, and the taste refined,
The address, the delicacy – stoops at once,
And makes her hearty meal upon a dunce.
　Flavia's a wit, has too much sense to pray;
To toast our wants and wishes is her way;
Nor asks of God, but of her stars, to give
The mighty blessing, 'While we live, to live.'
Then all for death, that opiate of the soul!
Lucretia's dagger, Rosamonda's bowl.
Say, what can cause such impotence of mind?

A spark too fickle, or a spouse too kind.
Wise wretch! with pleasures too refined to please;
With too much spirit to be e'er at ease;
With too much quickness ever to be taught;
With too much thinking to have common thought;
You purchase pain with all that joy can give,
And die of nothing but a rage to live.
    Turn then from wits; and look on Simo's mate,
No ass so meek, no ass so obstinate.
Or her that owns her faults, but never mends,
Because she's honest, and the best of friends,
Or her whose life the church and scandal share,
Forever in a passion or a prayer.
Or her who laughs at hell, but (like her Grace)
Cries, 'Ah! how charming if there's no such place!'
Or who in sweet vicissitude appears
Of mirth and opium, ratafie and tears,
The daily anodyne, and nightly draught,
To kill those foes to fair ones, time and thought.
Woman and fool are two hard things to hit,
For true no-meaning puzzles more than wit.
    But what are these to great Atossa's mind?
Scarce once herself, by turns all womankind!
Who, with herself, or others, from her birth
Finds all her life one warfare upon earth:
Shines in exposing knaves and painting fools,
Yet is whate'er she hates and ridicules.
No thought advances, but her eddy brain
Whisks it about, and down it goes again.
Full sixty years the world has been her trade,
The wisest fool much time has ever made.
From loveless youth to unrespected age,
No passion gratified, except her rage,
So much the fury still outran the wit,
The pleasure missed her, and the scandal hit.
Who breaks with her, provokes revenge from hell,
But he's a bolder man who dares be well.
Her every turn with violence pursued,
No more a storm her hate than gratitude:
To that each passion turns, or soon or late;

Love, if it makes her yield, must make her hate.
Superiors? death! and equals? what a curse!
But an inferior not dependant? worse!
Offend her, and she knows not to forgive;
Oblige her, and she'll hate you while you live:
But die, and she'll adore you – then the bust
And temple rise – then fall again to dust.
Last night, her lord was all that's good and great;
A knave this morning, and his will a cheat.
Strange! by the means defeated of the ends,
By spirit robbed of power, by warmth of friends,
By wealth of followers! without one distress,
Sick of herself, through very selfishness!
Atossa, cursed with every granted prayer,
Childless with all her children, wants an heir.
To heirs unknown descends the unguarded store,
Or wanders, heaven-directed, to the poor.

Pictures like these, dear Madam, to design,
Ask no firm hand, and no unerring line;
Some wandering touches, some reflected light,
Some flying stroke alone can hit them right:
For how should equal colours do the knack?
Chameleons who can paint in white and black?

'Yet Cloe sure was formed without a spot.' –
Nature in her then erred not, but forgot.
'With every pleasing, every prudent part,
Say, what can Cloe want?' – She wants a heart.
She speaks, behaves, and acts, just as she ought,
But never, never reached one generous thought.
Virtue she finds too painful an endeavour,
Content to dwell in decencies for ever.
So very reasonable, so unmoved,
As never yet to love, or to be loved.
She, while her lover pants upon her breast,
Can mark the figures on an Indian chest;
And when she sees her friend in deep despair,
Observes how much a chintz exceeds mohair!
Forbid it, Heaven, a favour or a debt
She e'er should cancel – but she may forget.
Safe is your secret still in Cloe's ear;

But none of Cloe's shall you ever hear.
Of all her dears she never slandered one,
But cares not if a thousand are undone.
Would Cloe know if you're alive or dead?
She bids her footman put it in her head.
Cloe is prudent – would you too be wise?
Then never break your heart when Cloe dies.
    One certain portrait may (I grant) be seen,
Which Heaven has varnished out, and made a queen:
The same for ever! and described by all
With truth and goodness, as with crown and ball.
Poets heap virtues, painters gems, at will,
And show their zeal, and hide their want of skill.
'Tis well – but artists! who can paint or write,
To draw the naked is your true delight.
That robe of quality so struts and swells,
None see what parts of nature it conceals:
The exactest traits of body or of mind,
We owe to models of an humble kind.
If Queensberry to strip there's no compelling,
'Tis from a handmaid we must take a Helen.
From peer or bishop 'tis no easy thing
To draw the man who loves his God or king:
Alas! I copy (or my draught would fail)
From honest Mahomet, or plain Parson Hale.
 But grant, in public men sometimes are shown,
A woman's seen in private life alone:
Our bolder talents in full light displayed;
Your virtues open fairest in the shade.
Bred to disguise, in public 'tis you hide;
There, none distinguish 'twixt your shame or pride,
Weakness or delicacy; all so nice,
That each may seem a virtue or a vice.
    In men we various ruling passions find;
In women, two almost divide the kind:
Those, only fix'd, they first or last obey,
The love of pleasure, and the love of sway.
    That, Nature gives; and where the lesson taught
Is but to please, can pleasure seem a fault?
Experience, this; by man's oppression cursed,

They seek the second not to lose the first.
   Men, some to business, some to pleasure take;
But every woman is at heart a rake:
Men, some to quiet, some to public strife;
But every lady would be queen for life.
   Yet mark the fate of a whole sex of queens!
Power all their end, but beauty all the means.
In youth they conquer with so wild a rage,
As leaves them scarce a subject in their age:
For foreign glory, foreign joy, they roam;
No thought of peace or happiness at home.
But wisdom's triumph is well-timed retreat,
As hard a science to the fair as great!
Beauties, like tyrants, old and friendless grown,
Yet hate repose, and dread to be alone.
Worn out in public, weary every eye,
Nor leave one sigh behind them when they die.
   Pleasures the sex, as children birds, pursue,
Still out of reach, yet never out of view;
Sure, if they catch, to spoil the toy at most,
To covet flying, and regret when lost:
At last, to follies youth could scarce defend,
'Tis half their age's prudence to pretend;
Ashamed to own they gave delight before,
Reduced to feign it, when they give no more:
As hags hold sabbaths, less for joy than spite,
So these their merry, miserable night;
Still round and round the ghosts of beauty glide,
And haunt the places where their honour died.
   See how the world its veterans rewards!
A youth of frolics, an old age of cards;
Fair to no purpose, artful to no end,
Young without lovers, old without a friend;
A fop their passion, but their prize a sot,
Alive, ridiculous, and dead, forgot!
   Ah, friend! to dazzle let the vain design;
To raise the thought and touch the heart be thine!
That charm shall grow, while what fatigues the ring,
Flaunts and goes down, an unregarded thing:
So when the sun's broad beam has tired the sight,

All mild ascends the moon's more sober light,
Serene in virgin modesty she shines,
And unobserved the glaring orb declines.
　　Oh! blessed with temper, whose unclouded ray
Can make tomorrow cheerful as today;
She who can love a sister's charms, or hear
Sighs for a daughter with unwounded ear;
She who ne'er answers till a husband cools,
Or, if she rules him, never shows she rules;
Charms by accepting, by submitting sways,
Yet has her humour most when she obeys;
Lets fops or fortune fly which way they will,
Disdains all loss of tickets, or codille;
Spleen, vapours, or smallpox, above them all,
And mistress of herself, though China fall.
　　And yet, believe me, good as well as ill,
Woman's at best a contradiction still.
Heaven, when it strives to polish all it can
Its last best work, but forms a softer man;
Picks from each sex, to make the favourite blest,
Your love of pleasure, our desire of rest:
Blends, in exception to all general rules,
Your taste of follies, with our scorn of fools:
Reserve with frankness, art with truth allied,
Courage with softness, modesty with pride;
Fix'd principles, with fancy ever new;
Shakes all together, and produces – you!
　　Be this a woman's fame; with this unblest,
Toasts live a scorn, and queens may die a jest.
This Phoebus promised (I forget the year)
When those blue eyes first opened on the sphere;
Ascendant Phoebus watched that hour with care,
Averted half your parents' simple prayer,
And gave you beauty, but denied the pelf
That buys your sex a tyrant o'er itself.
The generous god, who wit and gold refines,
And ripens spirits as he ripens mines,
Kept dross for duchesses, the world shall know it,
To you gave sense, good humour, and a poet.

MATTHEW PRIOR
1664–1721

A True Maid

'No, no; for my virginity,
    When I lose that,' says Rose, 'I'll die.'
'Behind the elms last night,' cried Dick,
    'Rose, were you not extremely sick?'

The Lady Who Offers Her Looking-Glass to Venus

Venus, take my votive glass;
    Since I am not what I was.
What from this day I shall be,
    Venus, let me never see.

FRANCIS QUARLES
1592–1644

Hos Ego Versiculos

Like to the damask rose you see,
Or like the blossom on the tree,
Or like the dainty flower of May,
Or like the morning to the day,
Or like the sun, or like the shade,
Or like the gourd which Jonas had:
    Even such is man whose thread is spun,
    Drawn out and cut, and so is done.

The rose withers, the blossom blasteth,
The flower fades, the morning hasteth,
The sun sets, the shadow flies,

The gourd consumes, and man he dies.
Like to the blaze of fond delight;
Or like a morning clear and bright;
Or like a frost, or like a shower;
Or like the pride of Babel's tower;
Or like the hour that guides the time;
Or like to beauty in her prime:
    Even such is man, whose glory lends
    His life a blaze or two, and ends.

Delights vanish; the morn o'ercasteth,
The frost breaks, the shower hasteth;
The tower falls, the hour spends;
The beauty fades, and man's life ends.

SIR WALTER RALEIGH
1552–1618

As You Came from the Holy Land

As you came from the holy land
    Of Walsinghame,
Met you not with my true love
    By the way as you came?

How shall I know your true love,
    That have met many one
As I went to the holy land,
    That have come, that have gone?

She is neither white nor brown,
    But as the heavens fair,
There is none hath a form so divine
    In the earth or the air.

Such an one did I meet, good sir,
   Such an angel-like face,
Who like a queen, like a nymph, did appear
   By her gait, by her grace.

She hath left me here all alone,
   All alone as unknown,
Who sometimes did me lead with herself,
   And me loved as her own.

What's the cause that she leaves you alone
   And a new way doth take;
Who loved you once as her own
   And her joy did you make?

I have loved her all my youth,
   But now am old, as you see;
Love likes not the falling fruit
   From the withered tree.

Know that Love is a careless child,
   And forgets promise past;
He is blind, he is deaf when he list
   And in faith never fast.

His desire is a dureless content
   And a trustless joy;
He is won with a world of despair
   And lost with a toy.

Of womenkind such indeed is the love,
   Or the word love abused,
Under which many childish desires
   And conceits are excused.

But true love is a durable fire
   In the mind ever burning;
Never sick, never old, never dead,
   From itself never turning.

If All the World and Love were Young

If all the world and love were young,
And truth in every shepherd's tongue,
These pretty pleasures might me move
To live with thee and be thy love.

Time drives the flocks from field to fold,
When rivers rage and rocks grow cold,
And Philomel becometh dumb;
The rest complain of cares to come.

The flowers do fade, and wanton fields
To wayward Winter reckoning yields;
A honey tongue, a heart of gall,
Is fancy's spring, but sorrow's fall.

Thy gowns, thy shoes, thy beds of roses,
Thy cap, thy kirtle and thy posies
Soon break, soon wither, soon forgotten,
In folly ripe, in reason rotten.

Thy belt of straw and ivy buds,
Thy coral clasps and amber studs –
All those in me no means can move
To come to thee and be thy love.

But could youth last, and love still breed;
Had joys no date, nor age no need;
Then those delights my mind might move
To live with thee and be thy love.

What is Our life?

What is our life? A play of passion,
Our mirth the music of division.
Our mother's wombs the tiring-houses be,
Where we are dressed for this short comedy.
Heaven the judicious sharp spectator is,
Who sits and marks still who doth act amiss.
Our graves that hide us from the searching sun
Are like drawn curtains when the play is done.
Thus march we, playing, to our latest rest,
Only we die in earnest, that's no jest.

Verses Made the Night Before He Died

Even such is Time, which takes in trust
Our youth, our joys, and all we have,
And pays us but with age and dust;
Who, in the dark and silent grave,
When we have wandered all our ways,
Shuts up the story of our days:
And from which earth, and grave, and dust,
The Lord shall raise me up, I trust.

JOHN WILMOT, EARL OF ROCHESTER
1648–1680

A Song of a Young Lady:
To Her Ancient Lover

Ancient person, for whom I
All the flattering youth defy,
Long be it ere thou grow old,
Aching, shaking, crazy cold;
But still continue as thou art,
Ancient person of my heart.

On thy withered lips and dry,
Which like barren furrows lie,
Brooding kisses I will pour,
Shall thy youthful heat restore.
Such kind showers in autumn fall,
And a second spring recall;
Nor from thee will ever part,
Ancient person of my heart.

Thy nobler part, which but to name
In our sex would be counted shame,
By age's frozen grasp possessed,
From his ice shall be released,
And, soothed by my reviving hand,
In former warmth and vigour stand.
All a lover's wish can reach,
For thy joy my love shall teach;

And for thy pleasure shall improve
All that art can add to love.
Yet still I love thee without art,
Ancient person of my heart.

On Charles II

Here lies Our Sovereign Lord the King,
 Whose word no man relies on,
Who never said a foolish thing
 Nor ever did a wise one.

Upon Nothing

Nothing! thou elder brother even to Shade,
Thou hadst a being ere the world was made,
And (well fixt) art alone of ending not afraid.

Ere time and place were, time and place were not,
When primitive Nothing something straight begot,
Then all proceeded from the great united – What?

Something, the general attribute of all,
Severed from thee, its sole original,
Into thy boundless self must undistinguished fall.

Yet something did thy mighty power command,
And from thy fruitful emptiness's hand,
Snatch'd men, beasts, birds, fire, air and land.

Matter, the wicked'st offspring of thy race,
By Form assisted, flew from thy embrace,
And rebel Light obscur'd thy reverend dusky face.

With Form, and Matter, Time and Place did join,
Body, thy foe, with these did leagues combine,
To spoil thy peaceful realm, and ruin all thy line.

But turncoat Time assists the foe in vain,
And, bribed by thee, assists thy short-lived reign,
And to thy hungry womb drives back thy slaves again.

Though mysteries are barred from laick eyes,
And the Divine alone, with warrant, pries
Into thy bosom, where the truth in private lies,

Yet this of thee the wise may freely say,
Thou from the virtuous nothing tak'st away,
And to be part with thee the wicked wisely pray.

Great Negative, how vainly would the wise
Enquire, define, distinguish, teach, devise?
Didst thou not stand to point their dull philosophies?

Is, or *is not*, the two great ends of fate,
And, true or false, the subject of debate,
That perfect, or destroy, the vast designs of fate,

When they have racked the politician's breast.
Within thy bosom must securely rest,
And, when reduced to thee, are least unsafe and best.

But, Nothing, why does Something still permit,
That sacred monarchs should at council sit,
With persons highly thought, at best, for nothing fit?

Whilst weighty Something modestly abstains,
From princes' coffers, and from statesmen's brains,
And Nothing there like stately Nothing reigns.

Nothing, who dwell'st with fools in grave disguise,
For whom they reverend shapes and forms devise.
Lawn sleeves, and furs, and gowns, when they like thee
    look wise.

French truth, Dutch prowess, British polity,
Hibernian learning, Scotch civility,
Spaniards' dispatch, Danes' wit are mainly seen in thee.

The great man's gratitude to his best friend,
Kings' promises, whores' vows, towards thee they bend,
Flow swiftly into thee, and in thee ever end.

ISSAC ROSENBERG
1890–1918

Marching
As Seen from the Left File

My eyes catch ruddy necks
Sturdily pressed back –
All a red-brick moving glint.
Like flaming pendulums, hands
Swing across the khaki –
Mustard-coloured khaki
To the automatic feet.

We husband the ancient glory
In these bared necks and hands.
Not broke is the forge of Mars;
But a subtler brain beats iron
To shoe the hoofs of death
(Who paws dynamic air now).
Blind fingers loose an iron cloud
To rain immortal darkness
On strong eyes.

Break of Day in the Trenches

The darkness crumbles away –
It is the same old druid Time as ever.
Only a live thing leaps my hand –
A queer sardonic rat –
As I pull the parapet's poppy
To stick behind my ear.
Droll rat, they would shoot you if they knew
Your cosmopolitan sympathies.
Now you have touched this English hand

You will do the same to a German –
Soon, no doubt, if it be your pleasure
To cross the sleeping green between.
It seems you inwardly grin as you pass
Strong eyes, fine limbs, haughty athletes
Less chanced than you for life,
Bonds to the whims of murder,
Sprawled in the bowels of the earth,
The torn fields of France.
What do you see in our eyes
At the shrieking iron and flame
Hurled through still heavens?
What quaver – what heart aghast?
Poppies whose roots are in man's veins
Drop, and are ever dropping;
But mine in my ear is safe,
Just a little white with the dust.

CHRISTINA G. ROSSETTI
1830–1894

A Dirge

Why were you born when the snow was falling?
You should have come to the cuckoo's calling,
Or when grapes are green in the cluster,
Or, at least, when lithe swallows muster
    For their far off flying
    From summer dying.

Why did you die when the lambs were cropping?
You should have died at the apples' dropping,
When the grasshopper comes to trouble,
And the wheatfields are sodden stubble,
    And all winds go sighing
    For sweet things dying.

Song

When I am dead, my dearest,
   Sing no sad songs for me;
Plant thou no roses at my head,
   Nor shady cypress tree:
Be the green grass above me
   With showers and dewdrops wet;
And if thou wilt, remember,
   And if thou wilt, forget.

I shall not see the shadows,
   I shall not feel the rain;
I shall not hear the nightingale
   Sing on, as if in pain:
And dreaming trough the twilight
   That doth not rise nor set,
Haply I may remember,
   And haply may forget.

A Birthday

My heart is like a singing bird
   Whose nest is in a watered shoot;
My heart is like an apple tree
   Whose boughs are bent with thickset fruit;
My heart is like a rainbow shell
   That paddles in a halcyon sea;
My heart is gladder than all these
   Because my love is come to me.

Raise me a dais of silk and down;
   Hang it with vair and purple dyes;
Carve it in doves and pomegranates,
   And peacocks with a hundred eyes;
Work it in gold and silver grapes,
   In leaves and silver fleurs-de-lys;
Because the birthday of my life
   Is come, my love is come to me.

A Christmas Carol

In the bleak midwinter
  Frosty wind made moan,
Earth stood hard as iron,
  Water like a stone;
Snow had fallen, snow on snow,
  Snow on snow,
In the bleak midwinter
  Long ago.

Our God, Heaven cannot hold Him
  Nor earth sustain;
Heaven and earth shall flee away
  When He comes to reign:
In the bleak midwinter
  A stable-place sufficed
The Lord God Almighty
  Jesus Christ.

Enough for Him whom cherubim
  Worship night and day,
A breastful of milk
  And a mangerful of hay;
Enough for Him whom angels
  Fall down before,
The ox and ass and camel
  Which adore.

Angels and archangels
  May have gathered there,
Cherubim and seraphim
  Throng'd the air,
    But only His mother
      In her maiden bliss
    Worshipped the Beloved
      With a kiss.

What can I give Him,
  Poor as I am?
If I were a shepherd
  I would bring a lamb,
If I were a wise man
  I would do my part –
Yet what I can I give Him,
  Give my heart.

DANTE GABRIEL ROSSETTI
1828–1882

The Woodspurge

The wind flapped loose, the wind was still,
Shaken out dead from tree and hill:
I had walked on at the wind's will –
I sat now, for the wind was still.

Between my knees my forehead was –
My lips drawn in, said not Alas!
My hair was over in the grass,
My naked ears heard the day pass.

My eyes, wide open, had the run
Of some ten weeds to fix upon;
Among those few, out of the sun,
The woodspurge flowered, three cups in one.

From perfect grief there need not be
Wisdom or even memory:
One thing then learnt remains to me –
The woodspurge has a cup of three.

Sudden Light

I have been here before,
    But when or how I cannot tell:
I know the grass beyond the door,
    The sweet, keen smell,
The sighing sound, the lights around the shore.

You have been mine before –
    How long ago I may not know:
But just when at that swallow's soar
    Your neck turned so,
Some veil did fall – I knew it all of yore.

Has this been thus before?
    And shall not thus time's eddying flight
Still with our lives our love restore
    In death's despite,
And day and night yield one delight once more?

SAKI (H. H. MUNRO)
1870–1916

Carol

While shepherds watched their flocks by night
    All seated on the ground,
A high-explosive shell came down
    And mutton rained around.

CARL SANDBURG
1878–1967

Cool Tombs

When Abraham Lincoln was shovelled into the tombs he forgot the copperheads and the assassin . . . in the dust, in the cool tombs.

   And Ulysses Grant lost all thought of con men and Wall Street, cash and collateral turned ashes . . . in the dust, in the cool tombs.

   Pocahontas' body, lovely as a poplar, sweet as a red haw in November or a paw-paw in May, did she wonder, does she remember? . . . in the dust, in the cool tombs?

   Take any streetful of people buying clothes and groceries, cheering a hero or throwing confetti and blowing tin horns . . . tell me if the lovers are losers . . . tell me if any get more than lovers . . . in the dust . . . in the cool tombs.

SIEGFRIED SASSOON
1886–1967

The General

'Good-morning; good-morning!' the General said,
When we met him last week on our way to the Line.
Now the soldiers he smiled at are most of 'em dead,
And we're cursing his staff for incompetent swine.
'He's a cheery old card,' grunted Harry to Jack,
As they slogged up to Arras with rifle and pack.

*

But he did for them both by his plan of attack.

Glory of Women

You love us when we're heroes, home on leave,
Or wounded in a mentionable place.
You worship decorations; you believe
That chivalry redeems the war's disgrace.
You make us shells. You listen with delight,
By tales of dirt and danger fondly thrilled.
You crown our distant ardours while we fight,
And mourn our laurelled memories when we're killed.
You can't believe that British troops 'retire'
When hell's last horror breaks them, and they run,
Trampling the terrible corpses – blind with blood.
    O German mother dreaming by the fire,
      While you are knitting socks to send your son,
      His face is trodden deeper in the mud.

SIR WALTER SCOTT
1771–1832

Proud Maisie

Proud Maisie is in the wood,
   Walking so early;
Sweet Robin sits on the bush,
   Singing so rarely.

'Tell me, thou bonny bird,
   When shall I marry me?'
– 'When six braw gentlemen
   Kirkward shall carry ye.'

'Who makes the bridal bed,
   Birdie, say truly?'
– 'The grey-headed sexton
   That delves the grave duly.

'The glow-worm o'er grave and stone
   Shall light thee steady;
The owl from the steeple sing
   Welcome, proud lady!'

Lochinvar

O young Lochinvar is come out of the west,
Through all the wide Border his steed was the best;
And save his good broadsword he weapons had none,
He rode all unarmed, and he rode all alone.
So faithful in love, and so dauntless in war,
There never was knight like the young Lochinvar.

He staid not for brake, and he stopped not for stone,
He swam the Eske river where ford there was none;
But ere he alighted at Netherby gate,
The bride had consented, the gallant came late:
For a laggard in love, and a dastard in war,
Was to wed the fair Ellen of brave Lochinvar.

So boldly he entered the Netherby Hall,
Among bride's-men, and kinsmen, and brothers, and all;
Then spoke the bride's father, his hand on his sword
(For the poor craven bridegroom said never a word),
'O come ye in peace here, or come ye in war,
Or to dance at our bridal, young Lord Lochinvar?'

'I long wooed your daughter, my suit you denied;
Love swells like the Solway, but ebbs like its tide –
And now am I come, with this lost love of mine
To lead but one measure, drink one cup of wine.
There are maidens in Scotland more lovely by far,
That would gladly be bride to the young Lochinvar.'

The bride kissed the goblet: the knight took it up,
He quaffed off the wine, and he threw down the cup.
She looked down to blush, and she looked up to sigh,
With a smile on her lips, and a tear in her eye.
He took her soft hand, ere her mother could bar –
'Now tread we a measure!' said young Lochinvar.

So stately his form, and so lovely her face,
That never a hall such a galliard did grace;
While her mother did fret, and her father did fume,
And the bridegroom stood dangling his bonnet and plume;
And the bride-maidens whispered, 'Twere better by far
To have matched our fair cousin with young Lochinvar.'

One touch to her hand, and one word in her ear,
When they reached the hall-door, and the charger stood near;
So light to the croupe the fair lady he swung,
So light to the saddle before her he sprung!
'She is won! we are gone, over bank, bush, and scaur;
They'll have fleet steeds that follow,' quoth young Lochinvar.

There was mounting 'mong Graemes of the Netherby clan;
Forsters, Fenwicks, and Musgraves, they rode and they ran:
There was racing and chasing on Cannobie Lee,
But the lost bride of Netherby ne'er did they see.
So daring in love, and so dauntless in war,
Have ye e'er heard of gallant like young Lochinvar?

Answer

Sound, sound the clarion, fill the fife!
    To all the sensual world proclaim,
One crowded hour of glorious life
    Is worth an age without a name.

ANNA SEWARD
1749–1809

An Old Cat's Dying Soliloquy

Years saw me still Acasto's mansion grace,
The gentlest, fondest of the tabby race;
Before him frisking through the garden glade,
Or at his feet in quiet slumber laid;
Praised for my glossy back of zebra streak,
And wreaths of jet encircling round my neck;
Soft paws that ne'er extend the clawing nail,
The snowy whisker and the sinuous tail;
Now feeble age each glazing eyeball dims,
And pain has stiffened these once supple limbs;
Fate of eight lives the forfeit gasp obtains,
And e'en the ninth creeps languid through my veins.
   Much sure of good the future has in store,
When on my master's hearth I bask no more,
In those blest climes, where fishes oft forsake
The winding river and the glassy lake;
There, as our silent-footed race behold
The crimson spots and fins of lucid gold,
Venturing without the shielding waves to play,
They gasp on shelving banks, our easy prey:
While birds unwinged hop careless o'er the ground,
And the plump mouse incessant trots around,
Near wells of cream that mortals never skim,
Warm marum creeping round their shallow brim;
Where green valerian tufts, luxuriant spread,
Cleanse the sleek hide and form the fragrant bed.
   Yet, stern dispenser of the final blow,
Before thou lay'st an aged grimalkin low,
Bend to her last request a gracious ear,
Some days, some few short days, to linger here;
So to the guardian of his tabby's weal
Shall softest purrs these tender truths reveal:
   'Ne'er shall thy now expiring puss forget

To thy kind care her long-enduring debt,
Nor shall the joys that painless realms decree
Efface the comforts once bestowed by thee;
To countless mice thy chicken-bones preferred,
Thy toast to golden fish and wingless bird;
O'er marum borders and valerian bed
Thy Selima shall bend her moping head,
Sigh that no more she climbs, with grateful glee,
Thy downy sofa and thy cradling knee;
Nay, e'en at founts of cream shall sullen swear,
Since thou, her more loved master, art not there.'

WILLIAM SHAKESPEARE
1564–1616

Songs from The Plays

Who is Silvia? what is she,
    That all our swains commend her?
Holy, fair, and wise is she;
    The heaven such grace did lend her,
That she might admired be.

Is she kind as she is fair?
    For beauty lives with kindness.
Love doth to her eyes repair,
    To help him of his blindness;
And, being helped, inhabits there.

Then to Silvia let us sing,
    That Silvia is excelling;
She excels each mortal thing
    Upon the dull earth dwelling;
To her let us garlands bring.

The Two Gentlemen of Verona

When daisies pied and violets blue
   And lady-smocks all silver-white
And cuckoo-buds of yellow hue
   Do paint the meadows with delight,
The cuckoo then, on every tree,
Mocks married men; for thus sings he,
       'Cuckoo,
Cuckoo, cuckoo' – O, word of fear,
Unpleasing to a married ear!

When shepherds pipe on oaten straws,
   And merry larks are ploughmen's clocks,
When turtles tread, and rooks and daws,
   And maidens bleach their summer smocks,
The cuckoo then, on every tree,
Mocks married men; for thus sings he,
       'Cuckoo,
Cuckoo, cuckoo' – O, word of fear,
Unpleasing to a married ear!

*

When icicles hang by the wall,
   And Dick the shepherd blows his nail,
And Tom bears logs into the hall,
   And milk comes frozen home in pail;
When blood is nipped, and ways be foul,
Then nightly sings the staring owl,
'Tu-whit, tu-who!' – a merry note,
While greasy Joan doth keel the pot.

When all aloud the wind doth blow,
   And coughing drowns the parson's saw,
And birds sit brooding in the snow,
   And Marian's nose looks red and raw,
When roasted crabs hiss in the bowl,
Then nightly sings the staring owl,
'Tu-whit, tu-who!' – a merry note,
While greasy Joan doth keel the pot.

Love's Labour's Lost

You spotted snakes with double tongue,
  Thorny hedgehogs, be not seen;
Newts and blind-worms, do no wrong;
  Come not near our fairy queen.

  Philomel, with melody,
  Sing in our sweet lullaby;
Lulla, lulla, lullaby; lulla, lulla, lullaby.
    Never harm,
    Nor spell, nor charm,
  Come our lovely lady nigh.
  So, good night, with lullaby.

Weaving spiders, come not here;
    Hence, you long-legged spinners, hence!
Beetles black, approach not near;
    Worm nor snail, do no offence.

  Philomel, with melody,
  Sing in our sweet lullaby;
Lulla, lulla, lullaby; lulla, lulla, lullaby.
    Never harm,
    Nor spell, nor charm,
  Come our lovely lady nigh.
  So, good night, with lullaby.

A Midsummer Night's Dream

Blow, blow, thou winter wind,
  Thou art not so unkind
    As man's ingratitude;
  Thy tooth is not so keen,
  Because thou art not seen,
    Although thy breath be rude.
Heigh-ho, sing heigh-ho, unto the green holly:
Most friendship is feigning, most loving mere folly.
    Then heigh-ho, the holly,
    This life is most jolly.

Freeze, freeze, thou bitter sky,
That dost not bite so nigh
    As benefits forgot:
Though thou the waters warp,
Thy sting is not so sharp
    As friend remembered not.
Heigh-ho, sing heigh-ho, unto the green holly:
Most friendship is feigning, most loving mere folly.
        Then heigh-ho, the holly,
        This life is most jolly.

*

It was a lover and his lass,
    With a hey, and a ho, and a hey nonino,
That o'er the green cornfield did pass,
    In springtime, the only pretty ring time,
When birds do sing, hey ding a ding, ding;
Sweet lovers love the spring.

Between the acres of the rye,
    With a hey, and a ho, and a hey nonino,
These pretty country folks would lie,
    In springtime, the only pretty ring time,
When birds do sing, hey ding a ding, ding;
Sweet lovers love the spring.

This carol they began that hour,
    With a hey, and a ho, and a hey nonino,
How that a life was but a flower
    In springtime, the only pretty ring time,
When birds do sing, hey ding a ding, ding;
Sweet lovers love the spring.

And therefore take the present time,
    With a hey, and a ho, and a hey nonino;
For love is crowned with the prime
    In springtime, the only pretty ring time,
When birds do sing, hey ding a ding, ding;
Sweet lovers love the spring.

As You Like It

O mistress mine, where are you roaming?
O, stay and hear; your true love's coming,
  That can sing both high and low.
Trip no further, pretty sweeting;
Journeys end in lovers meeting,
  Every wise man's son doth know.

What is love? 'Tis not hereafter;
Present mirth hath present laughter;
  What's to come is still unsure.
In delay there lies no plenty;
Then come kiss me, sweet and twenty;
  Youth's a stuff will not endure.

*

Come away, come away, death,
  And in sad cypress let me be laid.
Fly away, fly away, breath;
  I am slain by a fair cruel maid.
My shroud of white, stuck all with yew,
      O, prepare it!
My part of death, no one so true
      Did share it.

Not a flower, not a flower sweet,
  On my black coffin let there be strown;
Not a friend, not a friend greet
  My poor corpse, where my bones shall be
                          thrown.
A thousand thousand sighs to save,
      Lay me, O, where
Sad true lover never find my grave,
      To weep there.

*

When that I was and a little tiny boy,
  With hey, ho, the wind and the rain;
A foolish thing was but a toy,
  For the rain it raineth every day.

But when I came to man's estate,
   With hey, ho, the wind and the rain;
'Gainst knaves and thieves men shut their gate,
   For the rain it raineth every day.

But when I came, alas, to wive,
   With hey, ho, the wind and the rain;
By swaggering could I never thrive,
   For the rain it raineth every day.

But when I came unto my beds,
   With hey, ho, the wind and the rain;
With toss-pots still had drunken heads,
   For the rain it raineth every day.

A great while ago the world begun,
   With hey, ho, the wind and the rain;
But that's all one, our play is done,
   And we'll strive to please you every day.

Twelfth Night

Take, O take those lips away,
   That so sweetly were forsworn,
And those eyes, the break of day,
   Lights that do mislead the morn;
But my kisses bring again, bring again,
Seals of love, but sealed in vain, sealed in vain.

Measure for Measure

Hark, hark, the lark at heaven's gate sings,
   And Phoebus gins arise,
His steeds to water at those springs
   On chaliced flowers that lies;
And winking Mary-buds begin to ope their golden eyes;
With every thing that pretty is, my lady sweet, arise:
   Arise, arise!

*

Fear no more the heat of the sun,
   Nor the furious winter's rages,
Thou thy worldly task hast done,
   Home art gone, and ta'en thy wages.
Golden lads and girls all must,
As chimney-sweepers, come to dust.

Fear no more the frown of the great,
   Thou art past the tyrant's stroke;
Care no more to clothe and eat,
   To thee the reed is as the oak.
The sceptre, learning, physic, must
All follow this, and come to dust.

Fear no more the lightning-flash,
   Nor the all-dreaded thunder-stone.
Fear not slander, censure rash.
   Thou hast finished joy and moan.
All lovers young, all lovers must
Consign to thee, and come to dust.

No exorciser harm thee.
Nor no witchcraft charm thee.
Ghost unlaid forbear thee.
Nothing ill come near thee.
Quiet consummation have,
And renowned be thy grave.

Cymbeline

Come unto these yellow sands,
    And then take hands:
Curtsied when you have, and kissed,
    The wild waves whist:
Foot it featly here and there,
And, sweet sprites, the burden bear.
Hark, hark!
                    Bow-wow.
The watch-dogs bark!
                    Bow-wow.
Hark, hark, I hear
The strain of strutting Chanticleer:
                    Cock-a-diddle-dow.

*

Full fathom five thy father lies;
    Of his bones are coral made:
Those are pearls that were his eyes:
    Nothing of him that doth fade,
But doth suffer a sea-change
Into something rich and strange.
Sea-nymphs hourly ring his knell:
                    Ding-dong.
Hark now I hear them – ding-dong bell.

*

Where the bee sucks, there suck I,
In a cowslip's bell I lie;
There I couch when owls do cry.
On the bat's back I do fly
After summer merrily.
    Merrily, merrily shall I live now
    Under the blossom that hangs on the bough.

The Tempest

Sonnets

15

When I consider everything that grows
   Holds in perfection but a little moment,
That this huge stage presenteth naught but shows
   Whereon the stars in secret influence comment;
When I perceive that men as plants increase,
   Cheered and checked even by the self-same sky,
Vaunt in their youthful sap, at height decrease,
   And wear their brave state out of memory;
Then the conceit of this inconstant stay
   Sets you most rich in youth before my sight,
Where wasteful Time debateth with Decay,
   To change your day of youth to sullied night;
  And, all in war with Time, for love of you,
  As he takes from you, I engraft you new.

18

Shall I compare thee to a summer's day?
   Thou art more lovely and more temperate:
Rough winds do shake the darling buds of May,
   And summer's lease hath all too short a date:
Sometime too hot the eye of heaven shines,
   And often is his gold complexion dimmed;
And every fair from fair sometime declines,
   By chance, or nature's changing course, untrimmed;
But thy eternal summer shall not fade,
   Nor lose possession of that fair thou owest;
Nor shall Death brag thou wander'st in his shade,
   When in eternal lines to time thou growest:
  So long as men can breathe, or eyes can see,
  So long lives this, and this gives life to thee.

20

A woman's face, with Nature's own hand painted,
　　Hast thou, the master-mistress of my passion;
A woman's gentle heart, but not acquainted
　　With shifting change, as is false women's fashion;
An eye more bright than theirs, less false in rolling,
　　Gilding the object whereupon it gazeth;
A man in hew all *Hews* in his controlling,
　　Which steals men's eyes, and women's souls amazeth.
And for a woman wert thou first created;
　　Till Nature, as she wrought thee, fell a-doting,
And by addition me of thee defeated,
　　By adding one thing to my purpose nothing.
　　But since she pricked thee out for women's pleasure,
　　Mine be thy love, and thy love's use their treasure.

23

As an unperfect actor on the stage,
　　Who, with his fear is put besides his part,
Or some fierce thing replete with too much rage,
　　Whose strength's abundance weakens his own heart;
So I, for fear of trust, forget to say
　　The perfect ceremony of love's rite,
And in mine own love's strength seem to decay,
　　O'ercharged with burden of mine own love's might.
O, let my books be, then, the eloquence
　　And dumb presagers of my speaking breast;
Who plead for love, and look for recompense,
　　More than that tongue that more hath more expressed.
　　O, learn to read what silent love hath writ:
　　To hear with eyes belongs to love's fine wit.

29

When, in disgrace with fortune and men's eyes,
   I all alone beweep my outcast state,
And trouble deaf heaven with my bootless cries,
   And look upon myself, and curse my fate,
Wishing me like to one more rich in hope,
   Featured like him, like him with friends possessed,
Desiring this man's art, and that man's scope,
   With what I most enjoy contented least;
Yet in these thoughts myself almost despising,
   Haply I think on thee – and then my state,
Like to the lark at break of day arising
   From sullen earth, sings hymns at heaven's gate;
  For thy sweet love remembered such wealth brings,
  That then I scorn to change my state with kings.

30

When to the sessions of sweet silent thought
   I summon up remembrance of things past,
I sigh the lack of many a thing I sought,
   And with old woes new wail my dear time's waste:
Then can I drown an eye, unused to flow,
   For precious friends hid in death's dateless night,
And weep afresh love's long-since-cancelled woe,
   And moan the expense of many a vanished sight:
Then can I grieve at grievances foregone,
   And heavily from woe to woe tell o'er
The sad account of fore-bemoaned moan,
   Which I new pay as if not paid before.
  But if the while I think on thee, dear friend,
  All losses are restored, and sorrows end.

33

Full many a glorious morning have I seen
   Flatter the mountain-tops with sovereign eye,
Kissing with golden face the meadows green,
   Gilding pale streams with heavenly alchemy;
Anon permit the basest clouds to ride
   With ugly rack on his celestial face,
And from the forlorn world his visage hide,
   Stealing unseen to west with this disgrace:
Even so my sun one early morn did shine
   With all-triumphant splendour on my brow;
But, out, alack! he was but one hour mine,
   The region cloud hath masked him from me now.
   Yet him for this my love no whit disdaineth;
   Suns of the world may stain when heaven's sun staineth.

55

Not marble, nor the gilded monuments
   Of princes, shall outlive this powerful rhyme;
But you shall shine more bright in these contents
   Than unswept stone, besmeared with sluttish time.
When wasteful war shall statues overturn,
   And broils root out the work of masonry,
Nor Mars his sword nor war's quick fire shall burn
   The living record of your memory.
'Gainst death and all-oblivious enmity
   Shall you pace forth; your praise shall still find room
Even in the eyes of all posterity
   That wears this world out to the ending doom.
   So, till the judgement that yourself arise,
   You live in this, and dwell in lovers' eyes.

60

Like as the waves make towards the pebbled shore,
    So do our minutes hasten to their end;
Each changing place with that which goes before,
    In sequent toil all forwards do contend.
Nativity, once in the main of light,
    Crawls to maturity, wherewith being crowned,
Crooked eclipses 'gainst his glory fight,
    And Time that gave doth now his gift confound.
Time doth transfix the flourish set on youth,
    And delves the parallels in beauty's brow;
Feeds on the rarities of nature's truth,
    And nothing stands but for his scythe to mow:
  And yet, to times in hope my verse shall stand,
  Praising thy worth, despite his cruel hand.

64

When I have seen by Time's fell hand defaced
    The rich proud cost of outworn buried age;
When sometime lofty towers I see down-razed,
    And brass eternal slave to mortal rage;
When I have seen the hungry ocean gain
    Advantage on the kingdom of the shore,
And the firm soil win of the watery main,
    Increasing store with loss, and loss with store;
When I have seen such interchange of state,
    Or state itself confounded to decay;
Ruin hath taught me thus to ruminate –
    That Time will come and take my love away.
  This thought is as a death, which cannot choose
  But weep to have that which it fears to lose.

66

Tired with all these, for restful death I cry –
   As, to behold Desert a beggar born,
And needy Nothing trimmed in jollity,
   And purest Faith unhappily forsworn,
And gilded Honour shamefully misplaced,
   And maiden Virtue rudely strumpeted,
And right Perfection wrongfully disgraced',
   And Strength by limping Sway disabled,
And Art made tongue-tied by Authority,
   And Folly, doctor-like, controlling Skill,
And simple Truth miscalled Simplicity,
   And captive Good attending captain Ill:
  Tired with all these, from these would I be gone,
  Save that, to die, I leave my love alone.

71

No longer mourn for me when I am dead
   Than you shall hear the surly sullen bell
Give warning to the world that I am fled
   From this vile world, with vilest worms to dwell:
Nay, if you read this line, remember not
   The hand that writ it; for I love you so,
That I in your sweet thoughts would be forgot,
   If thinking on me then should make you woe.
O, if, I say, you look upon this verse
   When I perhaps compounded am with clay,
Do not so much as my poor name rehearse;
   But let your love even with my life decay;
  Lest the wise world should look into your moan,
  And mock you with me after I am gone.

73

That time of year thou mayst in me behold
    When yellow leaves, or none, or few, do hang
Upon those boughs which shake against the cold,
    Bare ruined choirs, where late the sweet birds sang.
In me thou see'st the twilight of such day
    As after sunset fadeth in the west;
Which by and by black night doth take away,
    Death's second self, that seals up all in rest.
In me thou see'st the glowing of such fire,
    That on the ashes of his youth doth lie,
As the death-bed whereon it must expire,
    Consumed with that which it was nourished by.
  This thou perceiv'st, which makes thy love more strong,
  To love that well which thou must leave ere long.

86

Was it the proud full sail of his great verse,
    Bound for the prize of all-too-precious you,
That did my ripe thoughts in my brain inhearse,
    Making their tomb the womb wherein they grew?
Was it his spirit, by spirits taught to write
    Above a mortal pitch, that struck me dead?
No, neither he, nor his compeers by night
    Giving him aid, my verse astonished.
He, nor that affable familiar ghost
    Which nightly gulls him with intelligence,
As victors, of my silence cannot boast;
    I was not sick of any fear from thence:
  But when your countenance filled up his line,
  Then lacked I matter; that enfeebled mine.

87

Farewell! thou art too dear for my possessing,
 And like enough thou know'st thy estimate:
The charter of thy worth gives thee releasing;
 My bonds in thee are all determinate.
For how do I hold thee but by thy granting?
 And for that riches where is my deserving?
The cause of this fair gift in me is wanting,
 And so my patent back again is swerving.
Thyself thou gav'st, thy own worth then not knowing,
 Or me, to whom thou gav'st it, else mistaking;
So thy great gift, upon misprision growing,
 Comes home again, on better judgement making.
 Thus have I had thee, as a dream doth flatter,
 In sleep a king, but waking no such matter.

94

They that have power to hurt and will do none,
 That do not do the thing they most do show,
Who, moving others, are themselves as stone,
 Unmoved, cold, and to temptation slow;
They rightly do inherit heaven's graces,
 And husband nature's riches from expense;
They are the lords and owners of their faces,
 Others but stewards of their excellence.
The summer's flower is to the summer sweet,
 Though to itself it only live and die;
But if that flower with base infection meet,
 The basest weed outbraves his dignity:
 For sweetest things turn sourest by their deeds;
 Lilies that fester smell far worse than weeds.

97

How like a winter hath my absence been
  From thee, the pleasure of the fleeting year!
What freezings have I felt, what dark days seen!
  What old December's bareness everywhere!
And yet this time removed was summer's time;
  The teeming autumn, big with rich increase,
Bearing the wanton burden of the prime,
  Like widowed wombs after their lords' decease:
Yet this abundant issue seemed to me
  But hope of orphans and unfathered fruit;
For summer and his pleasures wait on thee,
  And, thou away, the very birds are mute;
  Or, if they sing, 'tis with so dull a cheer,
  That leaves look pale, dreading the winter's near.

116

Let me not to the marriage of true minds
  Admit impediments. Love is not love
Which alters when it alteration finds,
  Or bends with the remover to remove:
O, no! it is an ever-fixèd mark,
  That looks on tempests, and is never shaken;
It is the star to every wandering bark,
  Whose worth's unknown, although his height be taken.
Love's not Time's fool, though rosy lips and cheeks
  Within his bending sickle's compass come;
Love alters not with his brief hours and weeks,
  But bears it out even to the edge of doom.
  If this be error, and upon me proved,
  I never writ, nor no man ever loved.

129

The expense of spirit in a waste of shame
   Is lust in action; and till action, lust
Is perjured, murderous, bloody, full of blame,
   Savage, extreme, rude, cruel, not to trust;
Enjoyed no sooner but despised straight;
   Past reason hunted; and no sooner had,
Past reason hated, as a swallowed bait,
   On purpose laid to make the taker mad:
Mad in pursuit, and in possession so;
   Had, having, and in quest to have, extreme;
A bliss in proof, and proved, a very woe;
   Before, a joy proposed; behind, a dream.
  All this the world well knows; yet none knows well
  To shun the heaven that leads men to this hell.

130

My mistress' eyes are nothing like the sun;
   Coral is far more red than her lips red;
If snow be white, why then her breasts are dun;
   If hairs be wires, black wires grow on her head.
I have seen roses damasked, red and white,
   But no such roses see I in her cheeks;
And in some perfumes is there more delight
   Than in the breath that from my mistress reeks.
I love to hear her speak, yet well I know
   That music hath a far more pleasing sound.
I grant I never saw a goddess go;
   My mistress, when she walks, treads on the ground.
 And yet, by heaven, I think my love as rare
  As any she belied with false compare.

138

When my love swears that she is made of truth,
  I do believe her, though I know she lies,
That she might think me some untutored youth,
  Unlearned in the world's false subtleties.
Thus vainly thinking that she thinks me young,
  Although she knows my days are past the best,
Simply I credit her false-speaking tongue:
  On both sides thus is simple truth suppressed.
But wherefore says she not she is unjust?
  And wherefore say not I that I am old?
O, love's best habit is in seeming trust,
  And age in love loves not to have years told:
  Therefore I lie with her and she with me,
  And in our faults by lies we flattered be.

144

Two loves I have of comfort and despair,
  Which like two spirits do suggest me still:
The better angel is a man right fair,
  The worser spirit a woman colour'd ill.
To win me soon to hell, my female evil
  Tempteth my better angel from my side,
And would corrupt my saint to be a devil,
  Wooing his purity with her foul pride.
And whether that my angel be turn'd fiend
  Suspect I may, yet not directly tell;
But being both from me, both to each friend,
  I guess one angel in another's hell:
  Yet this shall I ne'er know, but live in doubt,
  Till my bad angel fire my good one out.

146

Poor soul, the centre of my sinful earth –
　　My sinful earth these rebel powers array –
Why dost thou pine within and suffer dearth,
　　Painting thy outward walls so costly gay?
Why so large cost, having so short a lease,
　　Dost thou upon thy fading mansion spend?
Shall worms, inheritors of this excess,
　　Eat up thy charge? Is this thy body's end?
Then, soul, live thou upon thy servant's loss,
　　And let that pine to aggravate thy store;
Buy terms divine in selling hours of dross;
　　Within be fed, without be rich no more:
　So shalt thou feed on Death, that feeds on men,
　And Death once dead, there's no more dying then.

PERCY BYSSHE SHELLEY
1792–1822

Ozymandias

I met a traveller from an antique land
Who said: Two vast and trunkless legs of stone
Stand in the desert . . . Near them, on the sand,
Half sunk, a shattered visage lies, whose frown,
And wrinkled lip, and sneer of cold command,
Tell that its sculptor well those passions read
Which yet survive, stamped on these lifeless things,
The hand that mocked them, and the heart that fed:
And on the pedestal these words appear:
'My name is Ozymandias, King of Kings:
Look on my works, ye Mighty, and despair!'
Nothing beside remains. Round the decay
Of that colossal wreck, boundless and bare
The lone and level sands stretch far away.

Love's Philosophy

1

The fountains mingle with the river
   And the rivers with the Ocean,
The winds of Heaven mix for ever
   With a sweet emotion;
Nothing in the world is single;
   All things by a law divine
In one spirit meet and mingle.
   Why not I with thine?

2

See the mountains kiss high Heaven
   And the waves clasp one another;
No sister-flower would be forgiven
   If it disdained its brother;

And the sunlight clasps the earth
And the moonbeams kiss the sea:
What is all this sweet work worth
If thou kiss not me?

Ode to the West Wind

1

O wild West Wind, thou breath of Autumn's being,
Thou from whose unseen presence the leaves dead
Are driven, like ghosts from an enchanter fleeing,

Yellow and black and pale and hectic red,
Pestilence stricken multitudes: O thou,
Who chariotest to their dark wintry bed

The wingèd seeds, where they lie cold and low,
Each like a corpse within its grave, until
Thine azure sister of the Spring shall blow

Her chariot o'er the dreaming earth, and fill
(Driving sweet buds like flocks to feed in air)
With living hues and odours plain and hill;

Wild spirit which art moving everywhere,
Destroyer and preserver; hear, oh, hear!

2

Thou on whose stream, mid the steep sky's commotion,
Loose clouds like earth's decaying leaves are shed,
Shook from the tangled boughs of Heaven and Ocean,

Angels of rain and lightning: there are spread
On the blue surface of thine aëry surge,
Like the bright hair uplifted from the head

Of some bright Maenad, even from the dim verge
Of the horizon to the zenith's height:
The locks of the approaching storm. Thou dirge

Of the dying year, to which this closing night
Will be the dome of a vast sepulchre,
Vaulted with all thy congregated might

Of vapours, from whose solid atmosphere
Black rain, and fire, and hail will burst: oh, hear!

3

Thou who didst waken from his summer dreams
The blue Mediterranean, where he lay,
Lulled by the coil of his crystalline streams,

Beside a pumice isle in Baiae's bay,
And saw in sleep old palaces and towers
Quivering within the wave's intenser day,

All overgrown with azure moss, and flowers
So sweet, the sense faints picturing them! Thou
For whose path the Atlantic's level powers

Cleave themselves into chasms, while far below
The sea-blooms and the oozy woods which wear
The sapless foliage of the ocean, know

Thy voice and suddenly grow grey with fear,
And tremble, and despoil themselves: oh, hear!

4

If I were a dead leaf thou mightest bear;
If I were a swift cloud to fly with thee;
A wave to pant beneath thy power, and share

The impulse of thy strength, only less free
Than thou, O uncontrollable! If even
I were as in my boyhood, and could be

The comrade of thy wanderings over Heaven,
As then, when to outstrip thy skiey speed
Scarce seemed a vision; I would ne'er have striven

As thus with thee in prayer in my sore need.
Oh, lift me as a wave, a leaf, a cloud!
I fall upon the thorns of life! I bleed!

A heavy weight of hours has chained and bowed
One too like thee, tameless and swift and proud.

5

Make me thy lyre, even as the forest is:
What if my leaves are falling like its own?
The tumult of thy mighty harmonies

Will take from both a deep, autumnal tone,
Sweet though in sadness. Be thou, Spirit fierce,
My spirit! Be thou me, impetuous one!

Drive my dead thoughts over the universe
Like withered leaves to quicken a new birth!
And, by the incantation of this verse,

Scatter, as from an unextinguished hearth,
Ashes and sparks, my words among mankind!
Be through my lips to unawakened earth

The trumpet of a prophecy! O Wind,
If Winter comes, can Spring be far behind?

The Indian Serenade

1

I arise from dreams of thee
In the first sweet sleep of night.
When the winds are breathing low,
And the stars are shining bright:
I arise from dreams of thee,
And a spirit in my feet
Hath led me – who knows how? –
To thy chamber window, Sweet!

2

The wandering airs they faint
On the dark, the silent stream –
The Champak odours fail
Like sweet thoughts in a dream;
The nightingale's complaint,
It dies upon her heart –
As I must on thine,
Oh, belovèd as thou art!

3

Oh lift me from the grass!
I die! I faint! I fail!
Let thy love in kisses rain
On my lips and eyelids pale.
My cheek is cold and white, alas!
My heart beats loud and fast –
Oh! press it to thine own again,
Where it will break at last.

Song

A widow bird sat mourning for her love
    Upon a wintry bough;
The frozen wind crept on above,
    The freezing stream below.

There was no leaf upon the forest bare,
    No flower upon the ground,
And little motion in the air
    Except the mill-wheel's sound.

Sonnet: England in 1819

An old, mad, blind, despised, and dying king –
Princes, the dregs of their dull race, who flow
Through public scorn – mud from a muddy spring –
Rulers who neither see, nor feel, nor know,
But leech-like to their fainting country cling,
Till they drop, blind in blood, without a blow –
A people starved and stabbed in the untilled field –
An army, which liberticide and prey
Makes as a two-edged sword to all who wield –
Golden and sanguine laws which tempt and slay;
Religion Christless, Godless – a book sealed;
A Senate – Time's worst statute unrepealed –
Are graves, from which a glorious Phantom may
Burst, to illumine our tempestuous day.

To a Skylark

Hail to thee, blithe Spirit!
    Bird thou never wert,
That from Heaven, or near it,
    Pourest thy full heart
In profuse strains of unpremeditated art.

Higher still and higher
    From the earth thou springest
Like a cloud of fire;
    The blue deep thou wingest,
And singing still dost soar, and soaring ever singest.

In the golden lightning
    Of the sunken sun,
O'er which clouds are brightening,
    Thou dost float and run;
Like an unbodied joy whose race is just begun.

The pale purple even
   Melts around thy flight;
Like a star of Heaven,
   In the broad daylight
Thou art unseen, but yet I hear thy shrill delight,

Keen as are the arrows
   Of that silver sphere,
Whose intense lamp narrows
   In the white dawn clear
Until we hardly see – we feel that it is there.

All the earth and air
   With thy voice is loud,
As, when night is bare,
   From one lonely cloud
The moon rains out her beams, and Heaven is
   overflowed.

What thou art we know not;
   What is most like thee?
From rainbow clouds there flow not
   Drops so bright to see
As from thy presence showers a rain of melody.

Like a poet hidden
   In the light of thought,
Singing hymns unbidden,
   Till the world is wrought
To sympathy with hopes and fears it heeded not:

Like a high-born maiden
   In a palace-tower,
Soothing her love-laden
   Soul in secret hour
With music sweet as love, which overflows her bower:

Like a glow-worm golden
   In a dell of dew,
Scattering unbeholden
   Its aëreal hue
Among the flowers and grass, which screen it from
   the view!

Like a rose embowered
    In its own green leaves,
  By warm winds deflowered,
    Till the scent it gives
Makes faint with too much sweet those heavy-winged
    thieves:

Sound of vernal showers
    On the twinkling grass,
  Rain-awakened flowers,
    All that ever was
Joyous, and clear, and fresh, thy music doth surpass:

Teach us, Sprite or Bird,
    What sweet thoughts are thine:
I have never heard
    Praise of love or wine
That panted forth a flood of rapture so divine.

Chorus Hymeneal,
    Or triumphal chant,
Matched with thine would be all
    But an empty vaunt,
A thing wherein we feel there is some hidden want.

What objects are the fountains
    Of thy happy strain?
What fields, or waves, or mountains?
    What shapes of sky or plain?
What love of thine own kind? what ignorance of pain?

Will thy clear keen joyance
    Languor cannot be:
Shadow of annoyance
    Never came near thee:
Thou lovest – but ne'er knew love's sad satiety.

Waking or asleep,
    Thou of death must deem
Things more true and deep
    Than we mortals dream,
Or how could thy notes flow in such a crystal stream?

We look before and after,
    And pine for what is not:
  Our sincerest laughter
    With some pain is fraught;
Our sweetest songs are those that tell of saddest thought.

Yet if we could scorn
    Hate, and pride, and fear;
If we were things born
    Not to shed a tear,
I know not how thy joy we ever should come near.

Better than all measures
    Of delightful sound,
Better than all treasures
    That in books are found,
Thy skill to poet were, thou scorner of the ground!

Teach me half the gladness
    That thy brain must know,
Such harmonious madness
    From my lips would flow
The world should listen then – as I am listening now.

Adonais

1

I weep for Adonais – he is dead!
O, weep for Adonais! though our tears
Thaw not the frost which binds so dear a head!
And thou, sad Hour, selected from all years
To mourn our loss, rouse thy obscure compeers,
And teach them thine own sorrow, say: 'With me
Died Adonais; till the Future dares
Forget the Past, his fate and fame shall be
An echo and a light unto eternity!'

2

Where wert thou, mighty Mother, when he lay,
When thy Son lay, pierced by the shaft which flies
In darkness? where was lorn Urania
When Adonais died? With veilèd eyes,
'Mid listening Echoes, in her Paradise
She sat, while one, with soft enamoured breath,
Rekindled all the fading melodies,
With which, like flowers that mock the corse beneath,
He had adorned and hid the coming bulk of Death.

3

Oh, weep for Adonais – he is dead!
Wake, melancholy Mother, wake and weep!
Yet wherefore? Quench within their burning bed
Thy fiery tears, and let thy loud heart keep
Like his, a mute and uncomplaining sleep;
For he is gone, where all things wise and fair
Descend – oh, dream not that the amorous Deep
Will yet restore him to the vital air;
Death feeds on his mute voice, and laughs at our despair.

4

Most musical of mourners, weep again!
Lament anew, Urania! – He died,
Who was the Sire of an immortal strain,
Blind, old, and lonely, when his country's pride,
The priest, the slave, and the liberticide,
Trampled and mocked with many a loathèd rite
Of lust and blood; he went, unterrified,
Into the gulf of death; but his clear Sprite
Yet reigns over earth; the third among the sons of light.

5

Most musical of mourners, weep anew!
Not all to that bright station dared to climb;
And happier they their happiness who knew,
Whose tapers yet burn through that night of time
In which suns perished; others more sublime,

Struck by the envious wrath of man or god,
Have sunk, extinct in their refulgent prime;
And some yet live, treading the thorny road,
Which leads, through toil and hate, to Fame's serene abode.

6

But now, thy youngest, dearest one, has perished –
The nursling of thy widowhood, who grew,
Like a pale flower by some sad maiden cherished,
And fed with true-love tears, instead of dew;
Most musical of mourners, weep anew!
Thy extreme hope, the loveliest and the last,
The bloom, whose petals nipped before they blew
Died on the promise of the fruit, is waste;
The broken lily lies – the storm is overpast.

7

To that high Capital, where kingly Death
Keeps his pale court in beauty and decay,
He came; and bought, with price of purest breath,
A grave among the eternal. – Come away!
Haste, while the vault of blue Italian day
Is yet his fitting charnel-roof! while still
He lies, as if in dewy sleep he lay;
Awake him not! surely he takes his fill
Of deep and liquid rest, forgetful of all ill.

8

He will awake no more, oh, never more!
Within the twilight chamber spreads apace
The shadow of white Death, and at the door
Invisible Corruption waits to trace
His extreme way to her dim dwelling-place;
The eternal Hunger sits, but pity and awe
Soothe her pale rage, nor dares she to deface
So fair a prey, till darkness, and the law
Of change, shall o'er his sleep the mortal curtain draw.

9

Oh, weep for Adonais! – The quick Dreams,
The passion-wingèd Ministers of thought,
Who were his flocks, whom near the living streams
Of his young spirit he fed, and whom he taught
The love which was its music, wander not –
Wander no more, from kindling brain to brain,
But droop there, whence they sprung; and mourn
                            their lot
Round the cold heart, where, after their sweet pain,
They ne'er will gather strength, or find a home again.

10

And one with trembling hands clasps his cold head,
And fans him with her moonlight wings, and cries:
'Our love, our hope, our sorrow, is not dead;
See, on the silken fringe of his faint eyes,
Like dew upon a sleeping flower, there lies
A tear some Dream has loosened from his brain.'
Lost Angel of a ruined Paradise!
She knew not 'twas her own; as with no stain
She faded, like a cloud which had outwept its rain.

11

One from a lucid urn of starry dew
Washed his light limbs as if embalming them;
Another clipped her profuse locks, and threw
The wreath upon him, like an anadem,
Which frozen tears instead of pearls begem;
Another in her wilful grief would break
Her bow and wingèd reeds, as if to stem
A greater loss with one which was more weak;
And dull the barbèd fire against his frozen cheek.

12

Another Splendour on his mouth alit,
That mouth, whence it was wont to draw the breath
Which gave it strength to pierce the guarded wit,
And pass into the panting heart beneath
With lightning and with music: the damp death

Quenched its caress upon his icy lips;
And, as a dying meteor stains a wreath
Of moonlight vapour, which the cold night clips,
It flushed through his pale limbs, and passed to its eclipse.

13

And others came . . . Desires and Adorations,
Wingèd Persuasions and veiled Destinies,
Splendours, and Glooms, and glimmering Incarnations
Of hopes and fears, and twilight Phantasies;
And Sorrow, with her family of Sighs,
And Pleasure, blind with tears, led by the gleam
Of her own dying smile instead of eyes,
Came in slow pomp – the moving pomp might seem
Like pageantry of mist on an autumnal stream.

14

All he had loved, and moulded into thought,
From shape, and hue, and odour, and sweet sound,
Lamented Adonais. Morning sought
Her eastern watch-tower, and her hair unbound,
Wet with the tears which should adorn the ground,
Dimmed the aëreal eyes that kindle day;
Afar the melancholy thunder moaned,
Pale Ocean in unquiet slumber lay,
And the wild Winds flew round, sobbing in their dismay.

15

Lost Echo sits amid the voiceless mountains,
And feeds her grief with his remembered lay,
And will no more reply to winds or fountains,
Or amorous birds perched on the young green spray,
Or herdsman's horn, or bell at closing day;
Since she can mimic not his lips, more dear
Than those for whose disdain she pined away
Into a shadow of all sounds – a drear
Murmur, between their songs, is all the woodmen hear.

16

Grief made the young Spring wild, and she threw down
Her kindling buds, as if she Autumn were,
Or they dead leaves; since her delight is flown,
For whom should she have waked the sullen year?
To Phoebus was not Hyacinth so dear
Nor to himself Narcissus, as to both
Thou, Adonais: wan they stand and sere
Amid the faint companions of their youth,
With dew all turned to tears; odour, to sighing ruth.

17

Thy spirit's sister, the lorn nightingale,
Mourns not her mate with such melodious pain;
Not so the eagle, who like thee could scale
Heaven, and could nourish in the sun's domain
Her mighty youth with morning, doth complain,
Soaring and screaming round her empty nest,
As Albion wails for thee: the curse of Cain
Light on his head who pierced thy innocent breast,
And scared the angel soul that was its earthly guest!

18

Ah, woe is me! Winter is come and gone,
But grief returns with the revolving year;
The airs and streams renew their joyous tone;
The ants, the bees, the swallows reappear;
Fresh leaves and flowers deck the dead Season's bier;
The amorous birds now pair in every brake,
And build their mossy homes in field and brere;
And the green lizard, and the golden snake,
Like unimprisoned flames, out of their trance awake.

19

Through wood and stream and field and hill and Ocean
A quickening life from the Earth's heart has burst
As it has ever done, with change and motion,
From the great morning of the world when first
God dawned on Chaos; in its stream immersed,

The lamps of Heaven flash with a softer light;
All baser things pant with life's sacred thirst:
Diffuse themselves; and spend in love's delight,
The beauty and the joy of their renewèd might.

20

The leprous corpse, touched by this spirit tender,
Exhales itself in flowers of gentle breath;
Like incarnations of the stars, when splendour
Is changed to fragrance, they illumine death
And mock the merry worm that wakes beneath;
Nought we know, dies. Shall that alone which knows
Be as a sword consumed before the sheath
By sightless lightning? – the intense atom glows
A moment, then is quenched in a most cold repose.

21

Alas! that all we loved of him should be,
But for our grief, as if it had not been,
And grief itself be mortal! Woe is me!
Whence are we, and why are we? of what scene
The actors or spectators? Great and mean
Meet massed in death, who lends what life must
                                        borrow.
As long as skies are blue, and fields are green,
Evening must usher night, night urge the morrow,
Month follow month with woe, and year wake year to
                                        sorrow.

22

He will awake no more, oh, never more!
'Wake thou,' cried Misery, 'childless Mother, rise
Out of thy sleep, and slake, in thy heart's core,
A wound more fierce than his, with tears and sighs.'
And all the Dreams that watched Urania's eyes,
And all the Echoes whom their sister's song
Had held in holy silence, cried: 'Arise!'
Swift as a Thought by the snake Memory stung,
From her ambrosial rest the fading Splendour sprung.

23

She rose like an autumnal Night, that springs
Out of the East, and follows wild and drear
The golden Day, which, on eternal wings,
Even as a ghost abandoning a bier,
Had left the Earth a corpse. Sorrow and fear
So struck, so roused, so rapt Urania;
So saddened round her like an atmosphere
Of stormy mist; so swept her on her way
Even to the mournful place where Adonais lay.

24

Out of her secret Paradise she sped,
Through camps and cities rough with stone, and steel,
And human hearts, which to her aëry tread
Yielding not, wounded the invisible
Palms of her tender feet where'er they fell:
And barbèd tongues, and thoughts more sharp than
they,
Rent the soft Form they never could repel,
Whose scared blood, like the young tears of May,
Paved with eternal flowers that undeserving way.

25

In the death-chamber for a moment Death,
Shamed by the presence of that living Might.
Blushed to annihilation, and the breath
Revisited those lips, and Life's pale light
Flashed through those limbs, so late her dear delight.
'Leave me not wild and drear and comfortless,
As silent lightning leaves the starless night!
Leave me not!' cried Urania: her distress
Roused Death: Death rose and smiled, and met her vain
caress.

26

'Stay yet awhile! speak to me once again;
Kiss me, so long but as a kiss may live;
And in my heartless breast and burning brain
That word, that kiss, shall all thoughts else survive,

With food of saddest memory kept alive,
Now thou art dead, as if it were a part
Of thee, my Adonais! I would give
All that I am to be as thou now art!
But I am chained to Time, and cannot thence depart!

27

'O gentle child, beautiful as thou wert,
Why didst thou leave the trodden paths of men
Too soon, and with weak hands though mighty heart
Dare the unpastured dragon in his den?
Defenceless as thou wert, oh, where was then
Wisdom the mirrored shield, or scorn the spear?
Or hadst thou waited the full cycle, when
Thy spirit should have filled its crescent sphere,
The monsters of life's waste had fled from thee like deer.

28

'The herded wolves, bold only to pursue;
The obscene ravens, clamorous o'er the dead;
The vultures to the conqueror's banner true
Who feed where Desolation first has fed,
And whose wings rain contagion – how they fled,
When, like Apollo, from his golden bow
The Pythian of the age one arrow sped
And smiled! – The spoilers tempt no second blow,
They fawn on the proud feet that spurn them lying low.

29

'The sun comes forth, and many reptiles spawn;
He sets, and each ephemeral insect then
Is gathered into death without a dawn,
And the immortal stars awake again;
So is it in the world of living men:
A godlike mind soars forth, in its delight
Making earth bare and veiling heaven, and when
It sinks, the swarms that dimmed or shared its light
Leave to its kindred lamps the spirit's awful night.'

30

Thus ceased she: and the mountain shepherds came,
Their garlands sere, their magic mantles rent;
The Pilgrim of Eternity, whose fame
Over his living head like Heaven is bent,
An early but enduring monument,
Came, veiling all the lightnings of his song
In sorrow; from her wilds Ierne sent
The sweetest lyrist of her saddest wrong,
And Love taught Grief to fall like music from his tongue.

31

Midst others of less note, came one frail Form,
A phantom among men; companionless
As the last cloud of an expiring storm
Whose thunder is its knell; he, as I guess,
Had gazed on Nature's naked loveliness,
Actaeon-like, and now he fled astray
With feeble steps o'er the world's wilderness,
And his own thoughts, along that rugged way,
Pursued, like raging hounds, their father and their prey.

32

A pardlike Spirit beautiful and swift –
A Love in desolation masked; – a Power
Girt round with weakness – it can scarce uplift
The weight of the superincumbent hour;
It is a dying lamp, a falling shower,
A breaking billow – even whilst we speak
Is it not broken? On the withering flower
The killing sun smiles brightly: on a cheek
The life can burn in blood, even while the heart may break.

33

His head was bound with pansies overblown,
And faded violets, white, and pied, and blue;
And a light spear topped with a cypress cone,
Round whose rude shaft dark ivy-tresses grew

Yet dripping with the forest's noonday dew,
Vibrated, as the ever-beating heart
Shook the weak hand that grasped it; of that crew
He came the last, neglected and apart;
A herd-abandoned deer struck by the hunter's dart.

34

All stood aloof, and at his partial moan
Smiled through their tears; well knew that gentle band
Who in another's fate now wept his own,
As in the accents of an unknown land
He sung new sorrow; sad Urania scanned
The Stranger's mien, and murmured: 'Who art thou?'
He answered not, but with a sudden hand
Made bare his branded and ensanguined brow,
Which was like Cain's or Christ's – oh! that it should be so!

35

What softer voice is hushed over the dead?
Athwart what brow is that dark mantle thrown?
What form leans sadly o'er the white death-bed,
In mockery of monumental stone,
The heavy heart heaving without a moan?
If it be He, who, gentlest of the wise,
Taught, soothed, loved, honoured the departed one,
Let me not vex, with inharmonious sighs,
The silence of that heart's accepted sacrifice.

36

Our Adonais has drunk poison – oh!
What deaf and viperous murderer could crown
Life's early cup with such a draught of woe?
The nameless worm would now itself disown:
It felt, yet could escape, the magic tone
Whose prelude held all envy, hate, and wrong,
But what was howling in one breast alone,
Silent with expectation of the song,
Whose master's hand is cold, whose silver lyre unstrung.

37

Live thou, whose infamy is not thy fame!
Live! fear no heavier chastisement from me,
Thou noteless blot on a remembered name!
But be thyself, and know thyself to be!
And ever at thy season be thou free
To spill the venom when thy fangs o'erflow;
Remorse and Self-contempt shall cling to thee;
Hot Shame shall burn upon thy secret brow,
And like a beaten hound tremble thou shalt – as now.

38

Nor let us weep that our delight is fled
Far from these carrion kites that scream below;
He wakes or sleeps with the enduring dead;
Thou canst not soar where he is sitting now.
Dust to the dust! but the pure spirit shall flow
Back to the burning fountain whence it came,
A portion of the Eternal, which must glow
Through time and change, unquenchably the same,
Whilst thy cold ember's choke the sordid hearth of shame.

39

Peace, peace! he is not dead, he doth not sleep –
He hath awakened from the dream of life –
'Tis we, who lost in stormy visions, keep
With phantoms an unprofitable strife,
And in mad trance, strike with our spirit's knife
Invulnerable nothings. – We decay
Like corpses in a charnel; fear and grief
Convulse us and consume us day by day,
And cold hopes swarm like worms within our living clay.

40

He has outsoared the shadow of our night;
Envy and calumny and hate and pain,
And that unrest which men miscall delight,
(Can touch him not and torture not again;
From the contagion of the world's slow stain

He is secure, and now can never mourn
A heart grown cold, a head grown grey in vain;
Nor, when the spirit's self has ceased to burn,
With sparkless ashes load an unlamented urn.

41

He lives, he wakes – 'tis Death is dead, not he;
Mourn not for Adonais – thou young Dawn,
Turn all thy dew to splendour, for from thee
The spirit thou lamentest is not gone;
Ye caverns and ye forests, cease to moan!
Cease, ye faint flowers and fountains, and thou Air,
Which like a mourning veil thy scarf hadst thrown
O'er the abandoned Earth, now leave it bare
Even to the joyous stars which smile on its despair!

42

He is made one with Nature: there is heard
His voice in all her music, from the moan
Of thunder, to the song of night's sweet bird;
He is a presence to be felt and known
In darkness and in light, from herb and stone,
Spreading itself where'er that Power may move
Which has withdrawn his being to its own;
Which wields the world with never-wearied love,
Sustains it from beneath, and kindles it above.

43

He is a portion of the loveliness
Which once he made more lovely: he doth bear
His part, while the one Spirit's plastic stress
Sweeps through the dull dense world, compelling there,
All new successions to the forms they wear;
Torturing the unwilling dross that checks its flight
To its own likeness, as each mass may bear;
And bursting in its beauty and its might
From trees and beasts and men into the Heaven's light.

44

The splendours of the firmament of time
May be eclipsed, but are extinguished not,
Like stars to their appointed height they climb,
And death is a low mist which cannot blot
The brightness it may veil. When lofty thought
Lifts a young heart above its mortal lair,
And love and life contend in it, for what
Shall be its earthly doom, the dead live there
And move like winds of light on dark and stormy air.

45

The inheritors of unfulfilled renown
Rose from their thrones, built beyond mortal thought,
Far in the Unapparent. Chatterton
Rose pale – his solemn agony had not
Yet faded from him; Sidney, as he fought
And as he fell and as he lived and loved,
Sublimely mild, a Spirit without spot,
Arose; and Lucan, by his death approved:
Oblivion as they rose shrank like a thing reproved.

46

And many more, whose names on Earth are dark,
But whose transmitted effluence cannot die
So long as fire outlives the parent spark,
Rose, robed in dazzling immortality.
'Thou art become as one of us,' they cry,
'It was for thee yon kingless sphere has long
Swung blind in unascended majesty,
Silent alone amid an Heaven of Song.
Assume thy wingèd throne, thou Vesper of our throng!'

47

Who mourns for Adonais? Oh, come forth,
Fond wretch! and know thyself and him aright.
Clasp with thy panting soul the pendulous Earth;
As from a centre, dart thy spirit's light
Beyond all worlds, until its spacious might

Satiate the void circumference: then shrink
Even to a point within our day and night;
And keep thy heart light lest it make thee sink
When hope has kindled hope, and lured thee to the
brink.

48

Or go to Rome, which is the sepulchre,
Oh, not of him, but of our joy: 'tis nought
That ages, empires, and religions there
Lie buried in the ravage they have wrought;
For such as he can lend – they borrow not
Glory from those who made the world their prey;
And he is gathered to the kings of thought
Who waged contention with their time's decay,
And of the past are all that cannot pass away.

49

Go thou to Rome – at once the Paradise,
The grave, the city, and the wilderness;
And where its wrecks like shattered mountains rise,
And flowering weeds, and fragrant copses dress
The bones of Desolation's nakedness
Pass, till the spirit of the spot shall lead
Thy footsteps to a slope of green access
Where, like an infant's smile, over the dead
A light of laughing flowers along the grass is spread;

50

And grey walls moulder round, on which dull Time
Feeds, like slow fire upon a hoary brand;
And one keen pyramid with wedge sublime,
Pavilioning the dust of him who planned
This refuge for his memory, doth stand
Like flame transformed to marble; and beneath,
A field is spread, on which a newer band
Have pitched in Heaven's smile their camp of death,
Welcoming him we lose with scarce extinguished breath.

51

Here pause: these graves are all too young as yet
To have outgrown the sorrow which consigned
Its charge to each; and if the seal is set,
Here, on one fountain of a mourning mind,
Break it not thou! too surely shalt thou find
Thine own well full, if thou returnest home,
Of tears and gall. From the world's bitter wind
Seek shelter in the shadow of the tomb.
What Adonais is, why fear we to become?

52

The One remains, the many change and pass;
Heaven's light forever shines, Earth's shadows fly;
Life, like a dome of many-coloured glass,
Stains the white radiance of Eternity,
Until Death tramples it to fragments. – Die,
If thou wouldst be with that   which thou dost seek!
Follow where all is fled! Rome's azure sky,
Flowers, ruins, statues, music, words, are weak
The glory they transfuse with fitting truth to speak.

53

Why linger, why turn back, why shrink, my Heart?
Thy hopes are gone before: from all things here
They have departed; thou shouldst now depart!
A light is passed from the revolving year,
And man, and woman; and what still is dear
Attracts to crush, repels to make thee wither.
The soft sky smiles – the low wind whispers near:
'Tis Adonais calls! oh, hasten thither,
No more let Life divide what Death can join together.

54

That Light whose smile kindles the Universe,
That Beauty in which all things work and move,
That Benediction which the eclipsing Curse
Of birth can quench not, that sustaining Love
Which through the web of being blindly wove
By man and beast and earth and air and sea,

Burns bright or dim, as each are mirrors of
  The fire for which all thirst; now beams on me,
Consuming the last clouds of cold mortality.

55

The breath whose might I have invoked in song
  Descends on me; my spirit's bark is driven,
Far from the shore, far from the trembling throng
  Whose sails were never to the tempest given;
  The massy earth and spherèd skies are riven!
I am borne darkly, fearfully, afar;
  Whilst, burning through the inmost veil of Heaven,
  The soul of Adonais, like a star,
Beacons from the abode where the Eternal are.

To —

Music, when soft voices die,
Vibrates in the memory –
Odours, when sweet violets sicken,
Live within the sense they quicken.

Rose leaves, when the rose is dead,
Are heaped for the belovèd's bed;
And so thy thoughts, when thou art gone,
Love itself shall slumber on.

SIR EDWARD SHERBURNE
1618–1702

And She Washed His Feet with Her Tears, and Wiped Them with the Hairs of Her Head

The proud Egyptian queen, her Roman guest
(To express her love in height of state, and pleasure)
  With pearl dissolved in gold, did feast:
    Both food, and treasure.

And now, dear Lord, thy lover, on the fair
 And silver tables of thy feet, behold!
  Pearl in her tears, and in her hair,
    Offers thee gold.

RICHARD BRINSLEY SHERIDAN
1751–1816

Song

Here's to the maiden of bashful fifteen;
  Here's to the widow of fifty;
Here's to the flaunting, extravagant queen,
  And here's to the housewife that's thrifty.
    Let the toast pass –
    Drink to the lass,
I'll warrant she'll prove an excuse for the glass.

Here's to the charmer whose dimples we prize;
  Now to the maid who has none, sir;
Here's to the girl with a pair of blue eyes,
  And here's to the nymph with but *one*, sir.
    Let the toast pass, &c.

Here's to the maid with a bosom of snow,
　　Now to her that's as brown as a berry:
Here's to the wife with a face full of woe,
　　And now for the damsel that's merry.
　　　Let the toast pass, &c.

For let 'em be clumsy, or let 'em be slim,
　　Young or ancient, I care not a feather;
So fill a pint-bumper quite up to the brim,
　　And let us e'en toast 'em together.
　　　Let the toast pass, &c.

JAMES SHIRLEY
1596–1666

Goodnight

Bid me no more goodnight; because
　　'Tis dark, must I away?
Love doth acknowledge no such laws,
　　And love 'tis I obey;
Which blind, doth all your light despise,
　　And hath no need of eyes
　　　When day is fled.
　　Besides, the sun, which you
　　Complain is gone, 'tis true,
　　　Is gone to bed:
　　Oh, let us do so too.

Of Death

The glories of our blood and state
   Are shadows, not substantial things;
There is no armour against fate;
   Death lays his icy hand on kings:
         Sceptre and crown
         Must tumble down,
And in the dust be equal made
With the poor crooked scythe and spade.

Some men with swords may reap the field,
   And plant fresh laurels where they kill;
But their strong nerves at last must yield;
   They tame but one another still:
         Early or late,
         They stoop to fate,
And must give up their murmuring breath,
When they, pale captives, creep to death.

The garlands wither on your brow,
   Then boast no more your mighty deeds;
Upon Death's purple altar now,
   See where the victor-victim bleeds:
         Your heads must come
         To the cold tomb;
Only the actions of the just
Smell sweet and blossom in their dust.

SIR PHILIP SIDNEY
1554–1586

O Sweet Woods

O sweet woods, the delight of solitariness,
O how much I do like your solitariness!
Where man's mind hath a freed consideration
Of goodness to receive lovely direction;
Where senses do behold the order of heavenly host,
And wise thoughts do behold what the creator is.
Contemplation here holdeth his only seat,
Bounded with no limits, borne with a wing of hope,
Climbs even unto the stars; Nature is under it.
Nought disturbs thy quiet; all to thy service yield;
Each sight draws on a thought, thought mother of science;
Sweet birds kindly do grant harmony unto thee;
Fair trees' shade is enough fortification,
Nor danger to thyself if be not in thyself.

O sweet woods, the delight of solitariness,
O how much I do like your solitariness!
Here no treason is hid, veiled in innocence,
Nor envy's snaky eye finds any harbour here,
Nor flatterers' venomous insinuations,
Nor cunning humorists' puddled opinions,
Nor courteous ruin of proffered usury,
Nor time prattled away, cradle of ignorance,
Nor causeless duty, nor cumber of arrogance;
Nor trifling title of vanity dazzleth us,
Nor golden manacles stand for a paradise.
Here wrong's name is unheard; slander a monster is.
Keep thy sprite from abuse, here no abuse doth haunt.
What man grafts in a tree dissimulation?

O sweet woods, the delight of solitariness,
O how well I do like your solitariness!
Yet dear soil, if a soul closed in a mansion

As sweet as violets, fair as a lily is,
Straight as a cedar, a voice stains the canary birds,
Whose shade safety doth hold, danger avoideth her;
Such wisdom, that in her lives speculation;
Such goodness, that in her simplicity triumphs;
Where envy's snaky eye winketh or else dieth;
Slander wants a pretext, flattery gone beyond;
O, if such a one have bent to a lonely life
Her steps, glad we receive, glad we receive her eyes,
And think not she doth hurt our solitariness:
For such company decks such solitariness.

My True Love Hath My Heart

My true love hath my heart, and I have his,
By just exchange one for the other given.
I hold his dear, and mine he cannot miss:
There never was a better bargain driven.
His heart in me keeps me and him in one;
My heart in him his thoughts and senses guides;
He loves my heart, for once it was his own;
I cherish his, because in me it bides.
His heart his wound received from my sight;
My heart was wounded with his wounded heart;
For as from me on him his hurt did light;
So still, methought, in me his hurt did smart;
    Both equal hurt, in this change sought our bliss:
    My true love hath my heart, and I have his.

Come Sleep, O Sleep

Come sleep, O sleep, the certain knot of peace,
The baiting place of wit, the balm of woe,
The poor man's wealth, the prisoner's release,
The indifferent judge between the high and low;
With shield of proof shield me from out the prease
Of those fierce darts despair at me doth throw:
O make in me those civil wars to cease;
I will good tribute pay, if thou do so.
Take thou of me sweet pillows, sweetest bed,
A chamber deaf to noise, and blind to light;
A rosy garland, and a weary head;
And if these things, as being thine by right,
   Move not thy heavy grace, thou shalt in me,
   Livelier than elsewhere, Stella's image see.

With How Sad Steps

With how sad steps, O moon, thou climb'st the skies;
How silently, and with how wan a face.
What, may it be that even in heavenly place
That busy archer his sharp arrows tries?
Sure, if that long with love acquainted eyes
Can judge of love, thou feel'st a lover's case;
I read it in thy looks; thy languished grace
To me, that feel the like, thy state descries.
Then even of fellowship, O moon, tell me,
Is constant love deemed there but want of wit?
Are beauties there as proud as here they be?
Do they above love to be loved, and yet
   Those lovers scorn whom that love doth possess?
   Do they call virtue there ungratefulness?

JOHN SKELTON
*c.*1460–1529

To Mistress Isabel Pennell

By saint Mary, my lady,
Your mammy and your daddy
Brought forth a goodly baby!

My maiden Isabel,
Reflaring rosabel,
The flagrant camomel;

The ruddy rosary,
The sovereign rosemary,
The pretty strawberry;

The columbine, the nept,
The jelofer well set,
The proper violet;

Ennewed your colour
Is like the daisy flower
After the April shower.

Star of the morning grey,
The blossom on the spray,
The freshest flower of May,

Maidenly demure,
Of womanhood the lure;
Wherefore I make you sure,

It were an heavenly health,
It were an endless wealth,
A life for God himself,

To hear this nightingale
Among the birdes smale,
Warbling in the vale,

'Dug, dug,
Jug, jug!
Good year and good luck!'
With 'Chuck, chuck, chuck, chuck!'

To Mistress Margaret Hussey

Merry Margaret
As midsummer flower,
Gentle as falcon
Or hawk of the tower;

With solace and gladness,
Much mirth and no madness,
All good and no badness;
So joyously,
So maidenly,
So womanly
Her demeaning,
In everything
Far far passing
That I can endite
Or suffice to write
Of merry Margaret
As midsummer flower,
Gentle as falcon
Or hawk of the tower.

As patient and as still,
And as full of good will
As fair Isyphill;
Coliander,
Sweet pomander,
Good Cassander;

Steadfast of thought,
Well made, well wrought.
Far may be sought
Erst that ye can find
So courteous, so kind
As merry Margaret,
This midsummer flower,
Gentle as falcon
Or hawk of the tower.

CHRISTOPHER SMART
1722–1771

My Cat Jeoffrey

from Jubilate Agno

For I will consider my Cat Jeoffrey.

For he is the servant of the Living God, duly and daily serving him.

For at the first glance of the glory of God in the East he worships in his way.

For is this done by wreathing his body seven times round with elegant quickness.

For then he leaps up to catch the musk, which is the blessing of God upon this prayer.

For he rolls upon prank to work it in.

For having done duty and received blessing he begins to consider himself.

For this he performs in ten degrees.

For first he looks upon his fore-paws to see if they are clean.

For secondly he kicks up behind to clear away there.

For thirdly he works it upon stretch with the fore-paws extended.

For fourthly he sharpens his paws by wood.

For fifthly he washes himself.

For sixthly he rolls upon wash.

For seventhly he fleas himself, that he may not be interrupted upon the beat.

For eighthly he rubs himself against a post.

For ninthly he looks up for his instructions.

For tenthly he goes in quest of food.

For having consider'd God and himself he will consider his neighbour.

For if he meets another cat he will kiss her in kindness.

For when he takes his prey he plays with it to give it a chance.

For one mouse in seven escapes by his dallying.

For when his day's work is done his business more properly begins.

For he keeps the Lord's watch in the night against the adversary.

For he counteracts the powers of darkness by his electrical skin and glaring eyes.

For he counteracts the Devil, who is death, by brisking about the life.

For in his morning orisons he loves the sun and the sun loves him.

For he is of the tribe of Tiger.

For the Cherub Cat is a term of the Angel Tiger.

For he has the subtlety and hissing of a serpent, which in goodness he suppresses.

For he will not do destruction if he is well fed, neither will he spit without provocation.

For he purrs in thankfulness, when God tells him he's a good Cat.

For he is an instrument for the children to learn benevolence upon.

For every house is incomplete without him and a blessing is lacking in the spirit.

For the Lord commanded Moses concerning the cats at the departure of the Children of Israel from Egypt.

For every family had one cat at least in the bag.

For the English Cats are the best in Europe.

For he is the cleanest in the use of his fore-paws of any quadrupede.

For the dexterity of his defence is an instance of the love of God to him exceedingly.

For he is the quickest to his mark of any creature.

For he is tenacious of his point.

For he is a mixture of gravity and waggery.

For he knows that God is his Saviour.

For there is nothing sweeter than his peace when at rest.

For there is nothing brisker than his life when in motion.

For he is of the Lord's poor and so indeed is he called by
 benevolence perpetually – Poor Jeoffrey! poor Jeoffrey! the rat
 has bit thy throat.

For I bless the name of the Lord Jesus that Jeoffrey is better.

For the divine spirit comes about his body to sustain it in
 complete cat.

For his tongue is exceeding pure so that it has in purity what it
 wants in music.

For he is docile and can learn certain things.

For he can set up with gravity which is patience upon
 approbation.

For he can fetch and carry, which is patience in employment.

For he can jump over a stick which is patience upon proof
 positive.

For he can spraggle upon waggle at the word of command.

For he can jump from an eminence into his master's bosom.

For he can catch the cork and toss it again.

For he is hated by the hypocrite and miser.

For the former is afraid of detection.

For the latter refuses the charge.

For he camels his back to bear the first notion of business.

For he is good to think on, if a man would express himself
 neatly.

For he made a great figure in Egypt for his signal services.

For he killed the Ichneumon-rat very pernicious by land.

For his ears are so acute that they sting again.

For from this proceeds the passing quickness of his attention.

For by stroking of him I have found out electricity.

For I perceived God's light upon him both wax and fire.

For the electrical fire is the spiritual substance which God sends
 from heaven to sustain the bodies both of man and beast.

For God has blessed him in the variety of his movements.

For, though he cannot fly, he is an excellent clamberer.

For his motions upon the face of the earth are more than any
 other quadrupede.

For he can tread to all the measures upon the music.

For he can swim for life.

For he can creep.

SYDNEY SMITH
1771–1845

Salad Dressing

To make this condiment your poet begs
The pounded yellow of two hard-boiled eggs;
Two boiled potatoes, passed through kitchen sieve,
Smoothness and softness to the salad give.
Let onion atoms lurk within the bowl,
And, half-suspected, animate the whole.
Of mordant mustard add a single spoon,
Distrust the condiment that bites so soon;
But deem it not, thou man of herbs, a fault
To add a double quantity of salt;
Four times the spoon with oil of Lucca crown,
And twice with vinegar procured from town;
And lastly o'er the flavoured compound toss
A magic soupçon of anchovy sauce.
Oh, green and glorious! Oh, herbaceous treat!
'Twould tempt the dying anchorite to eat;
Back to the world he'd turn his fleeting soul,
And plunge his fingers in the salad-bowl!
Serenely full, the epicure would say,
'Fate cannot harm me, I have dined today.'

CHARLES HAMILTON SORLEY
1895–1915

When you see millions of the mouthless dead
Across your dreams in pale battalions go.
Say not soft things as other men have said
That you'll remember. For you need not so.
Give them not praise. For, deaf, how should they know
It is not curses heaped on each gashed head?
Nor tears. Their blind eyes see not your tears flow.
Nor honour. It is easy to be dead.
Say only this, 'They are dead.' Then add thereto.
'Yet many a better one has died before.'
Then, scanning all the o'ercrowded mass, should you
Perceive one face that you loved heretofore,
It is a spook. None wears the face you knew.
Great death has made all his for evermore.

ROBERT SOUTHWELL
*c.*1561–1595

The Burning Babe

As I in hoary winter's night stood shivering in the snow,
Surprised I was with sudden heat which made my heart to glow;
And lifting up a fearful eye to view what fire was near,
A pretty Babe all burning bright did in the air appear;
Who, scorched with excessive heat, such floods of tears did
shed,
As though his floods should quench his flames which with his
tears were fed.
'Alas!' quoth he, 'but newly born in fiery heats I fry,
Yet none approach to warm their hearts or feel my fire but I.
My faultless breast the furnace is, the fuel wounding thorns;
Love is the fire, and sighs the smoke, the ashes shame and
scorns;
The fuel justice layeth on, and mercy blows the coals;
The metal in this furnace wrought are men's defiled souls:
For which, as now on fire I am to work them to their good,
So will I melt into a bath to wash them in my blood.'
With this he vanished out of sight and swiftly shrunk away,
And straight I called unto mind that it was Christmas day.

EDMUND SPENSER
c 1552–1599

Easter

Most glorious Lord of life, that on this day
   Didst make thy triumph over death and sin;
   And, having harrowed hell, didst bring away
   Captivity thence captive, us to win:
This joyous day, dear Lord, with joy begin;
   And grant that we, for whom thou diddest die,
   Being with thy dear blood clean washed from sin,
   May live for ever in felicity.
And that thy love we weighing worthily,
   May likewise love thee for the same again;
   And for thy sake, that all like dear didst buy,
   With love may one another entertain.
So let us love, dear love, like as we ought:
Love is the lesson which the Lord us taught.

One Day I Wrote Her Name upon the Strand

One day I wrote her name upon the strand,
But came the waves, and washèd it away.
Again I wrote it with a second hand,
But came the tide, and made my pains his prey.
'Vain man,' said she, 'that dost in vain essay
A mortal thing so to immortalise;
For I myself shall like to this decay,
And eke my name be wipèd out likewise.'
'Not so,' quoth I; 'let baser things devise
To die in dust, but you shall live by fame:
My verse your virtues rare shall eternise,
And in the heavens write your glorious name:
Where, whenas Death shall all the world subdue,
Our love shall live, and later life renew.'

Prothalamion

Calm was the day, and through the trembling air
Sweet breathing Zephyrus did softly play,
A gentle spirit, that lightly did delay
Hot Titan's beams, which then did glister fair;
When I whose sullen care,
Through discontent of my long fruitless stay
In prince's court, and expectation vain
Of idle hopes, which still do fly away
Like empty shadows, did afflict my brain,
Walked forth to ease my pain
Along the shore of silver streaming Thames,
Whose rutty bank, the which his river hems,
Was painted all with variable flowers,
And all the meads adorned with dainty gems,
Fit to deck maidens' bowers,
And crown their paramours,
Against the bridal day, which is not long:
    Sweet Thames, run softly, till I end my song.

There, in a meadow, by the river's side,
A flock of nymphs I chanced to espy,
All lovely daughters of the flood thereby,
With goodly greenish locks all loose untied,
As each had been a bride;
And each one had a little wicker basket,
Made of fine twigs entrailed curiously,
In which they gathered flowers to fill their flasket,
And with fine fingers cropped full featously
The tender stalks on high.
Of every sort, which in that meadow grew,
They gathered some: the violet pallid blue,
The little daisy, that at evening closes,
The virgin lily, and the primrose true,
With store of vermeil roses,
To deck their bridegrooms' posies,
Against the bridal day, which was not long:
    Sweet Thames, run softly, till I end my song.

With that, I saw two swans of goodly hue
Come softly swimming down along the Lee;
Two fairer birds I yet did never see.
The snow, which doth the top of Pindus strew,
Did never whiter show,
Nor Jove himself, when he a swan would be
For love of Leda, whiter did appear:
Yet Leda was they say as white as he,
Yet not so white as these, nor nothing near.
So purely white they were,
That even the gentle stream, the which them bare,
Seemed foul to them, and bade his billows spare
To wet their silken feathers, lest they might
Soil their fair plumes with water not so fair,
And mar their beauties bright,
That shone as heaven's light,
Against their bridal day, which was not long:
    Sweet Thames, run softly, till I end my song.

Eftsoons the nymphs, which now had flowers their fill,
Ran all in haste, to see that silver brood,
As they came floating on the crystal flood.
Whom when they saw, they stood amazed still,
Their wondering eyes to fill.
Them seemed they never saw a sight so fair,
Of fowls so lovely, that they sure did deem
Them heavenly born, or to be that same pair
Which through the sky draw Venus' silver team;
For sure they did not seem
To be begot of any earthly seed,
But rather angels or of angels' breed:
Yet were they bred of Somers-heat they say,
In sweetest season, when each flower and weed
The earth did fresh array,
So fresh they seemed as day,
Even as their bridal day, which was not long:
    Sweet Thames, run softly, till I end my song.

Then forth they all out of their baskets drew
Great store of flowers, the honour of the field,
That to the sense did fragrant odours yield,
All which upon those goodly birds they threw,
And all the waves did strew,
That like old Peneus' waters they did seem,
When down along by pleasant Tempe's shore,
Scattered with flowers, through Thessaly they stream,
That they appear through lilies' plenteous store,
Like a bride's chamber floor.
Two of those nymphs meanwhile, two garlands bound,
Of freshest flowers which in that mead they found,
The which presenting all in trim array,
Their snowy foreheads therewithal they crowned,
Whilst one did sing this lay,
Prepared against that day,
Against their bridal day, which was not long:
   Sweet Thames, run softly, till I end my song.

'Ye gentle birds, the world's fair ornament,
And heaven's glory, whom this happy hour
Doth lead unto your lovers' blissful bower,
Joy may you have and gentle heart's content
Of your love's couplement:
And let fair Venus, that is queen of love,
With her heart-quelling son upon you smile,
Whose smile, they say, hath virtue to remove
All love's dislike, and friendship's faulty guile
For ever to assoil.
Let endless peace your steadfast hearts accord,
And blessed plenty wait upon your board,
And let your bed with pleasures chaste abound,
That fruitful issue may to you afford,
Which may your foes confound,
And make your joys redound,
Upon your bridal day, which is not long:
   Sweet Thames, run softly, till I end my song.'

So ended she; and all the rest around
To her redoubled that her undersong,

Which said, their bridal day should not be long.
And gentle echo from the neighbour ground
Their accents did resound.
So forth those joyous birds did pass along,
Adown the Lee, that to them murmured low,
As he would speak, but that he lacked a tongue,
Yet did by signs his glad affection show,
Making his stream run slow.
And all the fowl which in his flood did dwell
Gan flock about these twain, that did excel
The rest so far as Cynthia doth shend
The lesser stars. So they, enranged well,
Did on those two attend,
And their best service lend,
Against their wedding day, which was not long:
　Sweet Thames, run softly till I end my song.

At length they all to merry London came,
To merry London, my most kindly nurse,
That to me gave this life's first native source;
Though from another place I take my name,
An house of ancient fame.
There when they came, whereas those bricky towers,
The which on Thames' broad aged back do ride,
Where now the studious lawyers have their bowers
There whilom wont the Templar Knights to bide,
Till they decayed through pride:
Next whereunto there stands a stately place,
Where oft I gained gifts and goodly grace
Of that great lord, which therein wont to dwell,
Whose want too well now feels my friendless case.
But ah, here fits not well
Old woes but joys to tell
Against the bridal day, which is not long:
　Sweet Thames, run softly, till I end my song

Yet therein now doth lodge a noble peer,
Great England's glory and the world's wide wonder,
Whose dreadful name late through all Spain did thunder,
And Hercules' two pillars standing near

Did make to quake and fear.
Fair branch of honour, flower of chivalry,
That fillest England with thy triumph's fame,
Joy have thou of thy noble victory,
And endless happiness of thine own name
That promiseth the same:
That through thy prowess and victorious arms,
Thy country may be freed from foreign harms;
And great Elisa's glorious name may ring
Through all the world, filled with thy wide alarms,
Which some brave Muse may sing
To ages following,
Upon the bridal day, which is not long:
   Sweet Thames, run softly, till I end my song.

From those high towers this noble lord issuing,
Like radiant Hesper when his golden hair
In the Ocean billows he hath bathed fair,
Descended to the river's open viewing,
With a great train ensuing.
Above the rest were goodly to be seen
Two gentle knights of lovely face and feature
Beseeming well the bower of any Queen,
With gifts of wit and ornaments of nature,
Fit for so goodly stature;
That like the twins of Jove they seemed in sight,
Which deck the baldric of the heavens bright.
They two forth pacing to the river's side,
Received those two fair birds, their love's delight,
Which at the appointed tide
Each one did make his bride,
Against their bridal day, which is not long:
   Sweet Thames, run softly, till I end my song.

ROBERT LOUIS STEVENSON
1850–1894

As with heaped bees at hiving time
The boughs are clotted, as (ere prime)
Heaven swarms with stars, or the city street
Pullulates with faring feet;
So swarmed my senses once; that now
Repose behind my tranquil brow,
Unsealed, asleep, quiescent, clear;
Now only the vast shapes I hear,
Hear – and my hearing slowly fills –
Rivers and winds among the twisting hills,
And hearken – and my face is lit –
Life facing; death pursuing it.

Requiem

Under the wide and starry sky,
Dig the grave and let me lie.
Glad did I live and gladly die,
   And I laid me down with a will.

This be the verse you grave for me:
Here he lies where he longed to be;
Home is the sailor, home from sea,
   And the hunter home from the hill.

Farewell to Love

Well, shadowed landskip, fare ye well:
How I have loved you, none can tell,
   At least, so well
  As he that now hates more
Than e'er he loved before.

But, my dear nothings, take your leave:
No longer must you me deceive,
    Since I perceive
  All the deceit, and know
  Whence the mistake did grow.

As he, whose quicker eye doth trace
A false star shot to a mark'd place,
    Does run apace,
  And, thinking it to catch,
  A jelly up does snatch.

So our dull souls, tasting delight
Far of, by sense and appetite,
    Think that is right
  And real good; when yet
  'Tis but the counterfeit.

O, how I glory now, that I
Have made this new discovery!
    Each wanton eye
  Inflam'd before: no more
  Will I increase that score.

If I gaze now, 'tis but to see
What manner of death's-head 'twill be,
    When it is free
  From that fresh upper skin,
  The gazer's joy and sin.

The gum and glistening, which, with art
And studied method in each part,
    Hangs down the hair, 't
  Looks just as if that day
  Snails there had crawl'd the hay.

The locks, that curled o'er each ear be,
Hang like two master-worms to me,
    That (as we see)
  Have tasted to the rest
Two holes, where they like 't best.

A quick corse, methinks, I spy
In every woman; and mine eye,
    At passing by,
    Checks, and is troubled, just
    As if it rose from dust.

They mortify, not heighten me;
These of my sins the glasses be:
    And here I see
    How I have loved before;
    And so I love no more.

The Garden of Proserpine

Here, where the world is quiet;
Here, where all trouble seems
Dead winds' and spent waves' riot
In doubtful dreams of dreams;
I watch the green field growing
For reaping folk and sowing,
For harvest-time and mowing,
A sleepy world of streams.

I am tired of tears and laughter,
And men that laugh and weep;
Of what may come hereafter
For men that sow to reap:
I am weary of days and hours,
Blown buds of barren flowers,
Desires and dreams and powers
And everything but sleep.

Here life has death for neighbour,
And far from eye or ear
Wan waves and wet winds labour,
Weak ships and spirits steer;
They drive adrift, and whither
They wot not who make thither;
But no such winds blow hither,
And no such things grow here.

No growth of moor or coppice,
No heather-flower or vine,
But bloomless buds of poppies,
Green grapes of Proserpine,
Pale beds of blowing rushes
Where no leaf blooms or blushes
Save this whereout she crushes
For dead men deadly wine.

Pale, without name or number,
In fruitless fields of corn,
They bow themselves and slumber
All night till light is born;
And like a soul belated,
In hell and heaven unmated,
By cloud and mist abated
Comes out of darkness morn.

Though one were strong as seven,
He too with death shall dwell,
Nor wake with wings in heaven,
Nor weep for pains in hell;
Though one were fair as roses,
His beauty clouds and closes;
And well though love reposes,
In the end it is not well.

Pale, beyond porch and portal,
Crowned with calm leaves, she stands
Who gathers all things mortal
With cold immortal hands;
Her languid lips are sweeter
Than love's who fears to greet her
To men that mix and meet her
From many times and lands.

She waits for each and other,
She waits for all men born;
Forgets the earth her mother,
The life of fruits and corn;

And spring and seed and swallow
Take wing for her and follow
Where summer song rings hollow
And flowers are put to scorn.

There go the loves that wither,
The old loves with wearier wings;
And all dead years draw thither,
And all disastrous things;
Dead dreams of days forsaken,
Blind buds that snows have shaken
Wild leaves that winds have taken,
Red strays of ruined springs.

We are not sure of sorrow,
And joy was never sure;
Today will die tomorrow;
Time stoops to no man's lure;
And love, grown faint and fretful,
With lips but half regretful
Sighs, and with eyes forgetful
Weeps that no loves endure.

From too much love of living
From hope and fear set free,
We thank with brief thanksgiving
Whatever gods may be
That no life lives for ever,
That dead men rise up never;
That even the weariest river
Winds somewhere safe to sea.

Then star nor sun shall waken,
Nor any change of light:
Nor sound of waters shaken,
Nor any sound or sight:
Nor wintry leaves nor vernal,
Nor days nor things diurnal;
Only the sleep eternal
In an eternal night.

Chorus from Atlanta

When the hounds of spring are on winter's traces,
    The mother of months in meadow or plain,
Fills the shadows and windy places
    With lisp of leaves and ripple of rain;
And the brown bright nightingale amorous
Is half assuaged for Itylus,
For the Thracian ships and the foreign faces,
    The tongueless vigil, and all the pain.

Come with bows bent and with emptying of quivers,
    Maiden most perfect, lady of light,
With a noise of winds and many rivers,
    With a clamour of waters, and with might;
Bind on thy sandals, O thou most fleet,
Over the splendour and speed of thy feet;
For the faint east quickens, the wan west shivers,
    Round the feet of the day and the feet of the night.

Where shall we find her, how shall we sing to her,
    Fold our hands round her knees, and cling?
O that man's heart were as fire and could spring to her,
    Fire, or the strength of the streams that spring!
For the stars and the winds are unto her
As raiment, as songs of the harp-player;
For the risen stars and the fallen cling to her,
    And the southwest-wind and the west-wind sing.

For winter's rains and ruins are over,
    And all the season of snows and sins;
The days dividing lover and lover,
    The light that loses, the night that wins;
And time remembered is grief forgotten,
And frosts are slain and flowers begotten,
And in green underwood and cover
    Blossom by blossom the spring begins.

The full streams feed on flower of rushes,
   Ripe grasses trammel a travelling foot,
The faint fresh flame of the young year flushes
   From leaf to flower and flower to fruit;
And fruit and leaf are as gold and fire,
And the oat is heard above the lyre,
And the hoofèd heel of a satyr crushes
   The chestnut-husk at the chestnut-root.

And Pan by noon and Bacchus by night,
   Fleeter of foot than the fleet-foot kid,
Follows with dancing and fills with delight
   The Maenad and the Bassarid;
And soft as lips that laugh and hide
The laughing leaves of the trees divide,
And screen from seeing and leave in sight
   The god pursuing, the maiden hid.

The ivy falls with the Bacchanal's hair
   Over her eyebrows hiding her eyes;
The wild vine slipping down leaves bare
   Her bright breast shortening into sighs;
The wild vine slips with the weight of its leaves,
But the berried ivy catches and cleaves
To the limbs that glitter, the feet that scare
   The wolf that follows, the fawn that flies.

JONATHAN SWIFT
1667–1745

A Description of the Morning

Now hardly here and there a hackney-coach
Appearing, showed the ruddy morn's approach.
Now Betty from her master's bed had flown,
And softly stole to discompose her own.
The slipshod 'prentice from his master's door
Had pared the dirt, and sprinkled round the floor.
Now Moll had whirled her mop with dexterous airs,
Prepared to scrub the entry and the stairs.
The youth with broomy stumps began to trace
The kennel-edge, where wheels had worn the place.
The small-coal man was heard with cadence deep,
Till drowned in shriller notes of chimney-sweep.
Duns at his lordship's gate began to meet,
And Brickdust Moll had screamed through half the street.
The turnkey now his flock returning sees,
Duly let out a-nights to steal for fees.
The watchful bailiffs take their silent stands,
And schoolboys lag with satchels in their hands.

NAHUM TATE
1652–1715

Hymn

While shepherds watched their flocks by night,
   All seated on the ground,
The angel of the Lord came down,
   And glory shone around.

'Fear not,' said he, for mighty dread
   Had seized their troubled mind;
'Glad tidings of great joy I bring
   To you and all mankind.

'To you, in David's town, this day
   Is born of David's line
The saviour, who is Christ the Lord,
   And this shall be the sign:

'The heavenly babe you there shall find
   To human view displayed,
All meanly wrapped in swathing bands,
   And in a manger laid.'

Thus spake the seraph; and forthwith
   Appeared a shining throng
Of angels, praising God, who thus
   Addressed their joyful song:

'All glory be to God on high,
   And to the Earth be peace;
Goodwill henceforth from heaven to men
   Begin and never cease.'

HENRY TAYLOR
1711–1785

The County Curate

In t'other hundred, o'er yon swarthy moor,
    Deep in the mire with tawny rush beset,
Where bleak sea-breezes echo from the shore
    And foggy damps infect the noontide heat,
    There lies a country curate's dismal seat:
View well those barren heaths with sober eye,
And wonder how a man can live so wretchedly.

See, to the farmer's yard where close allied
    A ragged church the adjacent dykes commands;
One bell the steeple fills (the tinker's pride!),
    The beams are wreathed about with hempen bands,
    Wove, as the roof decayed, by pious hands.
Drops from the thatch still keep the whitewash wet:
God bless the holy man that dares to preach in it!

The house stands near, this church's foster-brother,
    On crutches, both advanced in hoary eld;
A double rail runs from the one to t'other,
    And saves the curate from the dirty field,
    Where muck of various kind and hue is melled:
O'er this each Sunday to the church he climbs
And, to preserve his ancient cassock, risks his limbs.

Him liveth near, in dirty neighbourhood,
    His clerk, a blacksmith, he of sallow hue,
Whose empty cellar long hath open stood,
    A certain sign of penury or rue;
    Him would the curate fain persuade to brew.
Still happy man, if I should leave untold
The shrew, who of his life shrill government doth hold.

The well-known power of an English wife
  Nor day nor night she ceases to explain;
Her wit unreined promotes eternal strife,
  Her beauty makes her arrogant and vain,
  And both conspire to sharpen her disdain,
While rank ill-nature poisons all his joys,
Confused in endless squabble and unceasing noise.

Eight years hath heaven plagued 'em with a boy,
  Who hates a sister younger by a year;
Whose hungry, meagre looks, sans life or joy,
  They view, and frown upon the wrangling pair
  (Who like two ravenous locusts do appear
On one small flower), repent that e'er they sped,
Since Cupid's golden shafts they find are tipped with lead.

Each sun arises in a noisome fog;
  Tired of their beds, they rise as soon as light.
With like disgust their summers on they drag,
  And o'er a few stray chips the winter night:
  Such is the married Essex-curate's plight!
Though seasons change, no sense of change they know,
But look with discontent on all things here below.

When meagre Lent her famished look uprears,
  Her eyes indent with penury and pine,
Forth go the hungry family to prayers
  And pious sermon, while the farmers dine.
  In vain the children for their meals repine:
The blooming fields administer no cheer,
Joyless they view the purple promise of the year.

Summer attends them with fresh troubles plied,
  His breeches hung aloft for winter's wear,
He spies the flocks fly the returning tide,
  And every tenth he wishes to his share:
  Now to the hayfield trudge the hapless pair,
And, if they kindly treat the country folk,
They compliment his rector with the biggest cock.

Now autumn fruitful fills the teeming mead,
   And plenty frees the farmer's heart from care;
Meantime the thought of surplice-fees delayed,
   And the hollow gulping of the filtered beer,
   Unpaid for yet! distract his mind with fear:
No hopes another vessel to procure,
Unless with learned scraps he funs the admiring brewer.

When icy bands the stiffened waves enfold,
   At grudging neighbour's is he often seen,
Chafing with borrowed heat the outward cold;
   But oh! no beer to thaw the cold within;
   And then his wife pursues with hideous din:
Thence in the barn he muses what to say
To mend, yet not offend, her on next Sabbath-day.

Still worse and worse her lashing tongue he feels,
   The spurns of fortune and the weight of years.
The post-horse thus, an ancient racer, reels:
   No longer now a steady course he steers:
   His weak knees tremble and he hangs his ears;
He sweats, he totters, covered o'er with gore,
And falls, alas! unpitied, as he lived before.

ALFRED, LORD TENNYSON
1809–1892

The Eagle

He clasps the crag with crooked hands;
Close to the sun in lonely lands,
Ringed with the azure world, he stands.
The wrinkled sea beneath him crawls;
He watches from his mountain walls,
And like a thunderbolt he falls.

Mariana

'Mariana in the moated grange'
MEASURE FOR MEASURE

With blackest moss the flower-plots
   Were thickly crusted, one and all:
The rusted nails fell from the knots
   That held the pear to the garden-wall.
The broken sheds looked sad and strange:
   Unlifted was the clinking latch;
   Weeded and worn the ancient thatch
Upon the lonely moated grange.
      She only said, 'My life is dreary,
        He cometh not,' she said;
      She said, 'I am aweary, aweary,
        I would that I were dead!'

Her tears fell with the dews at even;
   Her tears fell ere the dews were dried;
She could not look on the sweet heaven,
   Either at morn or eventide.
After the flitting of the bats,
   When thickest dark did trance the sky,
   She drew her casement-curtain by,
And glanced athwart the glooming flats.
      She only said, 'The night is dreary,
        He cometh not,' she said;
      She said, 'I am aweary, aweary,
        I would that I were dead!'

Upon the middle of the night,
   Waking she heard the night-fowl crow:
The cock sung out an hour ere light:
   From the dark fen the oxen's low
Came to her: without hope of change,
   In sleep she seem'd to walk forlorn,
   Till cold winds woke the grey-eyed morn
About the lonely moated grange.
      She only said, 'The day is dreary,
        He cometh not,' she said;

She said, 'I am aweary, aweary,
   I would that I were dead! '

About a stone-cast from the wall
   A sluice with blackened waters slept,
And o'er it many, round and small,
   The clustered marish-mosses crept.
Hard by a poplar shook alway,
   All silver-green with gnarlèd bark:
   For leagues no other tree did mark
The level waste, the rounding grey.
     She only said, 'My life is dreary,
       He cometh not,' she said;
     She said, 'I am aweary, aweary,
       I would that I were dead!'

And ever when the moon was low,
   And the shrill winds were up and away,
In the white curtain, to and fro,
   She saw the gusty shadow sway.
But when the moon was very low,
   And wild winds bound within their cell,
   The shadow of the poplar fell
Upon her bed, across her brow.
     She only said, 'The night is dreary,
       He cometh not,' she said;
     She said, 'I am aweary, aweary,
       I would that I were dead!'

All day within the dreamy house,
   The doors upon their hinges creaked;
The blue fly sung in the pane; the mouse
   Behind the mouldering wainscot shrieked,
Or from the crevice peered about.
   Old faces glimmered thro' the doors,
   Old footsteps trod the upper floors,
Old voices called her from without.
     She only said, 'My life is dreary,
       He cometh not,' she said;
   She said, 'I am aweary, aweary,
     I would that I were dead!'

The sparrow's chirrup on the roof,
    The slow clock ticking, and the sound
Which to the wooing wind aloof
    The poplar made, did all confound
Her sense; but most she loathed the hour
    When the thick-moted sunbeam lay
    Athwart the chambers, and the day
Was sloping toward his western bower.
        Then, said she, 'I am very dreary,
        He will not come,' she said;
        She wept, 'I am aweary, aweary,
            Oh God, that I were dead!'

The Kraken

Below the thunders of the upper deep;
Far far beneath in the abysmal sea,
His ancient, dreamless, uninvaded sleep
The Kraken sleepeth: faintest sunlights flee
About his shadowy sides: above him swell
Huge sponges of millennial growth and height;
And far away into the sickly light,
From many a wondrous grot and secret cell
Unnumbered and enormous polypi
Winnow with giant fins the slumbering green.
There hath he lain for ages and will lie,
Battening upon huge seaworms in his sleep,
Until the latter fire shall heat the deep;
Then once by men and angels to be seen,
In roaring he shall rise and on the surface die.

The Lady of Shalott

PART 1

On either side the river lie
Long fields of barley and of rye,
That clothe the wold and meet the sky;
And through the field the road runs by
     To many-towered Camelot;
And up and down the people go,
Gazing where the lilies blow
Round an island there below,
     The island of Shalott.

Willows whiten, aspens quiver,
Little breezes dusk and shiver
Through the wave that runs for ever
By the island in the river
     Flowing down to Camelot.
Four grey walls, and four grey towers,
Overlook a space of flowers,
And the silent isle imbowers
     The Lady of Shalott.

By the margin, willow-veiled,
Slide the heavy barges trailed
By slow horses; and unhailed
The shallop flitteth silken-sailed
     Skimming down to Camelot:
But who hath seen her wave her hand?
Or at the casement seen her stand?
Or is she known in all the land,
     The Lady of Shalott?

Only reapers, reaping early
In among the bearded barley,
Hear a song that echoes cheerly
From the river winding clearly,
     Down to towered Camelot:
And by the moon the reaper weary,

Piling sheaves in uplands airy,
Listening, whispers,' 'Tis the fairy
    Lady of Shalott.'

PART 2

There she weaves by night and day
A magic web with colours gay.
She has heard a whisper say,
A curse is on her if she stay
    To look down to Camelot.
She knows not what the curse may be,
And so she weaveth steadily,
And little other care hath she,
    The Lady of Shalott.

And moving through a mirror clear
That hangs before her all the year,
Shadows of the world appear.
There she sees the highway near
    Winding down to Camelot:
There the river eddy whirls,
And there the surly village-churls,
And the red cloaks of market girls,
    Pass onward from Shalott.

Sometimes a troop of damsels glad,
An abbot on an ambling pad,
Sometimes a curly shepherd-lad,
Or long-hair'd page in crimson clad,
    Goes by to towered Camelot;
And sometimes through the mirror blue
The knights come riding two and two:
She hath no loyal knight and true,
    The Lady of Shalott.

But in her web she still delights
To weave the mirror's magic sights,
For often through the silent nights
A funeral, with plumes and lights
    And music, went to Camelot:

Or when the moon was overhead,
Came two young lovers lately wed;
'I am half sick of shadows,' said
    The Lady of Shalott.

PART 3

A bow-shot from her bower-eaves,
He rode between the barley-sheaves,
The sun came dazzling through the leaves,
And flamed upon the brazen greaves
    Of bold Sir Lancelot.
A red-cross knight forever kneeled
To a lady in his shield,
That sparkled on the yellow field,
    Beside remote Shalott.

The gemmy bridle glittered free,
Like to some branch of stars we see
Hung in the golden Galaxy.
The bridle bells rang merrily
    As he rode down to Camelot:
And from his blazoned baldric slung
A mighty silver bugle hung,
And as he rode his armour rung,
    Beside remote Shalott.

All in the blue unclouded weather
Thick-jewelled shone the saddle-leather,
The helmet and the helmet-feather
Burned like one burning flame together,
    As he rode down to Camelot.
As often through the purple night,
Below the starry clusters bright,
Some bearded meteor, trailing light,
    Moves over still Shalott.

His broad clear brow in sunlight glowed;
On burnished hooves his war-horse trod;
From underneath his helmet flowed
His coal-black curls as on he rode,

As he rode down to Camelot.
From the bank and from the river
He flashed into the crystal mirror,
'Tirra lirra,' by the river
    Sang Sir Lancelot.

She left the web, she left the loom,
She made three paces through the room,
She saw the water-lily bloom,
She saw the helmet and the plume,
    She looked down to Camelot.
Out flew the web and floated wide;
The mirror cracked from side to side;
'The curse is come upon me,' cried
    The Lady of Shalott.

PART 4

In the stormy east-wind straining,
The pale yellow woods were waning,
The broad stream in his banks complaining,
Heavily the low sky raining
    Over towered Camelot;
Down she came and found a boat
Beneath a willow left afloat,
And round about the prow she wrote,
    The Lady of Shalott.

And down the river's dim expanse –
Like some bold seër in a trance,
Seeing all his own mischance –
With a glassy countenance
    Did she look to Camelot.
And at the closing of the day
She loosed the chain, and down she lay;
The broad stream bore her far away,
    The Lady of Shalott.

Lying, robed in snowy white
That loosely flew to left and right –

The leaves upon her falling light –
Through the noises of the night
    She floated down to Camelot:
And as the boat-head wound along
The willowy hills and fields among,
They heard her singing her last song,
    The Lady of Shalott.

Heard a carol, mournful, holy
Chanted loudly, chanted lowly,
Till her blood was frozen slowly,
And her eyes were darkened wholly,
    Turned to towered Camelot.
For ere she reached upon the tide
The first house by the waterside,
Singing in her song she died,
    The Lady of Shalott.

Under tower and balcony,
By garden-wall and gallery,
A gleaming shape she floated by,
Dead-pale between the houses high,
    Silent into Camelot.
Out upon the wharfs they came,
Knight and burgher, lord and dame,
And round the prow they read her name,
    The Lady of Shalott.

Who is this? and what is here?
And in the lighted palace near
Died the sound of royal cheer;
And they cross'd themselves for fear,
    All the knights at Camelot:
But Lancelot mused a little space;
He said, 'She has a lovely face;
God in his mercy lend her grace,
    The Lady of Shalott.'

Ulysses

It little profits that an idle king,
By this still hearth, among these barren crags,
Matched with an aged wife, I mete and dole
Unequal laws unto a savage race,
That hoard, and sleep, and feed, and know not me.
I cannot rest from travel: I will drink
Life to the lees: all times I have enjoyed
Greatly, have suffered greatly, both with those
That loved me, and alone; on shore, and when
Through scudding drifts the rainy Hyades
Vext the dim sea; I am become a name:
For always roaming with a hungry heart
Much have I seen and known: cities of men
And manners, climates, councils, governments,
Myself not least, but honoured of them all;
And drunk delight of battle with my peers,
Far on the ringing plains of windy Troy.
I am a part of all that I have met;
Yet all experience is an arch wherethrough
Gleams that untravelled world whose margin fades
For ever and for ever when I move.
How dull it is to pause, to make an end,
To rust unburnished, not to shine in use!
As tho' to breathe were life. Life piled on life
Were all too little, and of one to me
Little remains: but every hour is saved
From that eternal silence, something more,
A bringer of new things; and vile it were
For some three suns to store and hoard myself,
And this grey spirit yearning in desire
To follow knowledge, like a sinking star,
Beyond the utmost bound of human thought.
This is my son, mine own Telemachus,
To whom I leave the sceptre and the isle –
Well loved of me, discerning to fulfil
This labour, by slow prudence to make mild
A rugged people, and through soft degrees

Subdue them to the useful and the good.
Most blameless is he, centred in the sphere
Of common duties, decent not to fail
In offices of tenderness, and pay
Meet adoration to my household gods,
When I am gone. He works his work, I mine.
There lies the port: the vessel puffs her sail:
There gloom the dark broad seas. My mariners,
Souls that have toiled, and wrought, and thought with me –
That ever with a frolic welcome took
The thunder and the sunshine, and opposed
Free hearts, free foreheads – you and I are old;
Old age hath yet his honour and his toil;
Death closes all: but something ere the end,
Some work of noble note, may yet be done,
Not unbecoming men that strove with Gods.
The lights begin to twinkle from the rocks;
The long day wanes; the slow moon climbs; the deep
Moans round with many voices. Come, my friends,
'Tis not too late to seek a newer world.
Push off, and sitting well in order smite
The sounding furrows; for my purpose holds
To sail beyond the sunset, and the baths
Of all the western stars, until I die.
It may be that the gulfs will wash us down:
It may be we shall touch the Happy Isles,
And see the great Achilles, whom we knew.
Though much is taken, much abides; and though
We are not now that strength which in old days
Moved earth and heaven; that which we are, we are;
One equal temper of heroic hearts,
Made weak by time and fate, but strong in will
To strive, to seek, to find, and not to yield.

The Splendour Falls on Castle Walls

The splendour falls on castle walls
    And snowy summits old in story:
The long light shakes across the lakes,
    And the wild cataract leaps in glory.
Blow, bugle, blow, set the wild echoes flying,
Blow, bugle; answer, echoes, dying, dying, dying.

O hark, O hear! how thin and clear,
    And thinner, clearer, farther going!
O sweet and far from cliff and scar
    The horns of Elfland faintly blowing!
Blow, let us hear the purple glens replying:
Blow, bugle; answer, echoes, dying, dying, dying.

O love, they die in yon rich sky,
    They faint on hill or field or river:
Our echoes roll from soul to soul,
    And grow for ever and for ever.
Blow, bugle, blow, set the wild echoes flying,
And answer, echoes, answer, dying, dying, dying.

Come Down, O Maid

Come down, O maid, from yonder mountain height:
What pleasure lives in height (the shepherd sang),
In height and cold, the splendour of the hills?
But cease to move so near the Heavens, and cease
To glide a sunbeam by the blasted Pine,
To sit a star upon the sparkling spire;
And come, for Love is of the valley, come,
For Love is of the valley, come thou down
And find him; by the happy threshold, he,
Or hand in hand with Plenty in the maize,
Or red with spirted purple of the vats,
Or foxlike in the vine; nor cares to walk
With Death and Morning on the silver horns,

Nor wilt thou snare him in the white ravine,
Nor find him dropt upon the firths of ice,
That huddling slant in furrow-cloven falls
To roll the torrent out of dusky doors:
But follow; let the torrent dance thee down
To find him in the valley; let the wild
Lean-headed Eagles yelp alone, and leave
The monstrous ledges there to slope, and spill
Their thousand wreaths of dangling water-smoke,
That like a broken purpose waste in air:
So waste not thou; but come; for all the vales
Await thee; azure pillars of the hearth
Arise to thee; the children call, and I
Thy shepherd pipe, and sweet is every sound,
Sweeter thy voice, but every sound is sweet;
Myriads of rivulets hurrying through the lawn,
The moan of doves in immemorial elms,
And murmuring of innumerable bees.

Now Sleeps the Crimson Petal

Now sleeps the crimson petal, now the white;
Nor waves the cypress in the palace walk;
Nor winks the gold fin in the porphyry font:
The firefly wakens: waken thou with me.

Now droops the milkwhite peacock like a ghost,
And like a ghost she glimmers on to me.

Now lies the Earth all Danaë to the stars,
And all thy heart lies open unto me.

Now slides the silent meteor on, and leaves
A shining furrow, as thy thoughts in me.

Now folds the lily all her sweetness up,
And slips into the bosom of the lake:
So fold thyself, my dearest, thou, and slip
Into my bosom and be lost in me.

Crossing the Bar

Sunset and evening star,
   And one clear call for me!
And may there be no moaning of the bar,
   When I put out to sea,

But such a tide as moving seems asleep,
   Too full for sound and foam,
When that which drew from out the boundless deep
   Turns again home.

Twilight and evening bell,
   And after that the dark!
And may there be no sadness of farewell,
   When I embark;

For though from out our bourne of Time and Place
   The flood may bear me far,
I hope to see my Pilot face to face
   When I have crost the bar.

Adlestrop

Yes. I remember Adlestrop –
The name, because one afternoon
Of heat the express-train drew up there
Unwontedly. It was late June.

The steam hissed. Someone cleared his throat.
No one left and no one came
On the bare platform. What I saw
Was Adlestrop – only the name –

And willows, willow-herb, and grass,
And meadowsweet, and haycocks dry,
No whit less still and lonely fair
Than the high cloudlets in the sky.

And for that minute a blackbird sang
Close by, and round him, mistier,
Farther and farther, all the birds
Of Oxfordshire and Gloucestershire.

EDWARD THOMAS
1878–1917

As the Team's Head-Brass

As the team's head-brass flashed out on the turn
The lovers disappeared into the wood.
I sat among the boughs of the fallen elm
That strewed an angle of the fallow, and
Watched the plough narrowing a yellow square
Of charlock. Every time the horses turned
Instead of treading me down, the ploughman leaned
Upon the handles to say or ask a word,
About the weather, next about the war.
Scraping the share he faced towards the wood,
And screwed along the furrow till the brass flashed
Once more.
              The blizzard felled the elm whose crest
I sat in, by a woodpecker's round hole,
The ploughman said, 'When will they take it away?'
'When the war's over.' So the talk began –
One minute and an interval of ten,
A minute more and the same interval.
'Have you been out?' 'No.' 'And don't want to, perhaps?'
'If I could only come back again, I should.
I could spare an arm. I shouldn't want to lose
A leg. If I should lose my head, why, so,
I should want nothing more . . . Have many gone
From here?' 'Yes.' 'Many lost?' 'Yes, good few.
Only two teams work on the farm this year.
One of my mates is dead. The second day
In France they killed him. It was back in March,
The very night of the blizzard, too. Now if
He had stayed here we should have moved the tree.'
'And I should not have sat here. Everything
Would have been different. For it would have been
Another world.' 'Ay, and a better, though
It we could see all all might seem good.' Then

The lovers came out of the wood again:
The horses started and for the last time
I watched the clods crumble and topple over
After the ploughshare and the stumbling team.

FRANCIS THOMPSON
1859–1907

The Kingdom of God
In No Strange Land

O World invisible, we view thee,
O World intangible, we touch thee,
O World unknowable, we know thee,
Inapprehensible, we clutch thee!

Does the fish soar to find the ocean,
The eagle plunge to find the air –
That we ask of the stars in motion
If they have rumour of thee there?

Not where the wheeling systems darken,
And our benumbed conceiving soars!
The drift of pinions, would we hearken,
Beats at our own clay-shuttered doors.

The angels keep their ancient places –
Turn but a stone, and start a wing!
'Tis ye, 'tis your estrangèd faces,
That miss the many-splendoured thing.

But (when so sad thou canst not sadder)
Cry – and upon thy so sore loss
Shall shine the traffic of Jacob's ladder
Pitched betwixt Heaven and Charing Cross.

Yea, in the night, my Soul, my daughter,
Cry – clinging Heaven by the hems;
And lo, Christ walking on the water,
Not of Gennesareth, but Thames!

JAMES THOMSON
1700–1748

Rule, Britannia

When Britain first, at heaven's command,
　　Arose from out the azure main,
This was the charter of the land,
　　And guardian angels sung this strain –
　　　　'Rule, Britannia, rule the waves;
　　　　Britons never will be slaves.'

The nations not so blest as thee
　　Must in their turns to tyrants fall;
While thou shalt flourish, great and free,
　　The dread and envy of them all.
　　　　'Rule,' &c.

Still more majestic shalt thou rise,
　　More dreadful from each foreign stroke;
As the loud blast that tears the skies
　　Serves but to root thy native oak.
　　　　'Rule,' &c.

Thee haughty tyrants ne'er shall tame;
　　All their attempts to bend thee down
Will but arouse thy generous flame,
　　But work their woe and thy renown.
　　　　'Rule,' &c.

To thee belongs the rural reign;
　　Thy cities shall with commerce shine;
All thine shall be the subject main,
　　And every shore it circles thine.
　　　　'Rule,' &c.

The Muses, still with freedom found,
　　Shall to thy happy coast repair:
Blest isle! with matchless beauty crowned,
　　And manly hearts to guard the fair.
　　　　'Rule, Britannia, rule the waves:
　　　　Britons never will be slaves.'

CHIDIOCK TICHBORNE
d.1586

Tichborne's Elegy
*Written with his own hand in the Tower
before his execution.*

My prime of youth is but a frost of cares,
  My feast of joy is but a dish of pain,
MY crop of corn is but a field of tares,
  And all my good is but vain hope of gain.
    The day is past, and yet I saw no sun,
    And now I live, and now my life is done.

My tale was heard and yet it was not told,
  My fruit is fallen and yet my leaves are green;
My youth is spent and yet I am not old,
  I saw the world and yet I was not seen.
    My thread is cut and yet it is not spun,
    And now I live, and now my life is done.

I sought my death and found it in my womb,
  I looked for life and saw it was a shade;
I trod the earth and knew it was my tomb,
  And now I die, and now I was but made.
    My glass is full, and now my glass is run,
    And now I live, and now my life is done.

AUGUSTUS MONTAGU TOPLADY
1740–1778

A Living and Dying Prayer
for the Holiest Believer in the World

Rock of ages, cleft for me,
Let me hide myself in thee!
Let the water and the blood,
From thy riven side which flowed,
Be of sin the double cure;
Cleanse me from its guilt and power.

Not the labours of my hands
Can fulfil thy law's demands:
Could my zeal no respite know,
Could my tears for ever flow,
All for sin could not atone:
Thou must save, and thou alone!

Nothing in my hand I bring;
Simply to thy Cross I cling;
Naked, come to thee for dress;
Helpless, look to thee for grace;
Foul, I to the fountain fly:
Wash me, Saviour, or I die!

While I draw this fleeting breath –
When my eye-strings break in death –
When I soar through tracts unknown –
See thee on thy judgement-throne –
Rock of ages, cleft for me,
Let me hide myself in thee.

THOMAS TRAHERNE
c.1636–1674

Wonder

1

How like an Angel came I down!
How bright are all things here!
When first among His works I did appear
O how their Glory me did crown!
The world resembled His Eternity,
In which my soul did walk;
And everything that I did see
Did with me talk.

2

The skies in their magnificence,
The lively, lovely air;
Oh how divine, how soft, how sweet, how fair!
The stars did entertain my sense,
And all the works of God, so bright and pure,
So rich and great did seem,
As if they ever must endure
In my esteem,

3

A native health and innocence
Within my bones did grow,
And while my God did all his Glories show,
I felt a vigour in my sense
That was all Spirit. I within did flow
With seas of life, like wine;
I nothing in the world did know
But 'twas divine.

4

Harsh ragged objects were concealed,
    Oppressions, tears and cries,
Sins, griefs, complaints, dissensions, weeping eyes
    Were hid, and only things revealed
Which heavenly Spirits and the Angels prize.
        The state of Innocence
    And bliss, not trades and poverties,
        Did fill my sense.

5

The streets were paved with golden stones,
    The boys and girls were mine,
Oh how did all their lovely faces shine!
    The sons of men were holy ones,
In joy and beauty they appeared to me,
        And everything which here I found,
    While like an angel I did see,
        Adorned the ground.

6

Rich diamond and pearl and gold
    In every place was seen;
Rare splendours, yellow, blue, red, white and green,
    Mine eyes did everywhere behold.
Great Wonders clothed with glory did appear,
        Amazement was my bliss,
    That and my wealth was everywhere;
        No joy to this!

7

Cursed and devised proprieties,
    With envy, avarice
And fraud, those fiends that spoil even Paradise,
    Flew from the splendour of mine eyes,
And so did hedges, ditches, limits, bounds,
        I dreamed not aught of those,
    But wandered over all men's grounds,
        And found repose.

8

Proprieties themselves were mine
  And hedges ornaments,
Walls, boxes, coffers, and their rich contents
  Did not divide my joys, but all combine.
Clothes, ribbons, jewels, laces, I esteemed
  My joys by others worn:
For me they all to wear them seemed
  When I was born.

HENRY VAUGHAN
1621–1693

Peace

My Soul, there is a country
  Far beyond the stars,
Where stands a wingèd sentry
  All skilful in the wars;
There, above noise and danger,
  Sweet Peace sits crowned with smiles,
And One born in a manger
  Commands the beauteous files,
He is thy gracious friend,
  And (O my Soul awake!)
Did in pure love descend
  To die here for thy sake;
If thou canst get but thither,
  There grows the flower of Peace,
The Rose that cannot wither,
  Thy fortress, and thy ease.
Leave then thy foolish ranges,
  For none can thee secure,
But One, who never changes,
  Thy God, thy life, thy cure.

The Morning Watch

O joys! Infinite sweetness! With what flowers,
And shoots of glory, my soul breaks, and buds!
      All the long hours
      Of night, and rest
      Through the still shrouds
      Of sleep, and clouds,
    This dew fell on my breast;
      O how it *bloods*,
And *spirits* all my earth! Hark! In what rings,
And *hymning circulations* the quick world
      Awakes, and sings;
      The rising winds,
      And falling springs,
      Birds, beasts, all things
    Adore Him in their kinds.
      Thus all is hurled
In sacred *Hymns*, and *Order*, the great *Chime*
And *Symphony* of Nature. Prayer is
      The world in tune,
      A spirit-voice
      And vocal joys
    Whose *Echo* is Heaven's bliss.
      O let me climb
When I lie down! The pious soul by night
Is like a clouded star, whose beams though said
      To shed their light
      Under some cloud
      Yet are above,
      And shine, and move
    Beyond that misty shroud.
      So in my bed,
That curtained grave, though sleep, like ashes, hide
My lamp, and life, both shall in Thee abide.

The Retreat

Happy those early days! When I
Shined in my angel-infancy.
Before I understood this place
Appointed for my second race,
Or taught my soul to fancy aught
But a white, celestial thought;
When yet I had not walked above
A mile, or two, from my first love,
And looking back (at that short space)
Could see a glimpse of his bright face;
When on some *gilded cloud*, or *flower*,
My gazing soul would dwell an hour,
And in those weaker glories spy
Some shadows of eternity;
Before I taught my tongue to wound
My conscience with a sinful sound,
Or had the black art to dispense
A several sin to every sense,
But felt through all this fleshly dress
Blight *shoots* of everlastingness.
    O how I long to travel back
And tread again that ancient track!
That I might once more reach that plain,
Where first I left my glorious train,
From whence the enlightened spirit sees
That shady City of palm trees;
But (ah!) my soul with too much stay
Is drunk, and staggers in the way.
Some men a forward motion love,
But I by backward steps would move,
And when this dust falls to the urn,
In that state I came, return.

The Night

Through that pure Virgin-shrine,
That sacred veil drawn o'er thy glorious noon
That men might look and live as glow-worms shine,
    And face the moon:
    Wise Nicodemus saw such light
    As made him know his God by night.

Most blest believer he!
Who in that land of darkness and blind eyes
Thy long expected healing wings could see,
    When thou didst rise,
    And what can never more be done,
    Did at midnight speak with the Sun!

O who will tell me where
He found thee at that dead and silent hour!
What hallowed solitary ground did bear
    So rare a flower,
    Within whose sacred leaves did lie
    The fullness of the Deity.

No mercy-seat of gold,
No dead and dusty cherub, nor carved stone,
But his own living works did my Lord hold
    And lodge alone;
    Where trees and herbs did watch and peep
    And wonder, while the Jews did sleep.

Dear night! this world's defeat;
The stop to busy fools; cares check and curb;
The day of spirits; my soul's calm retreat
    Which none disturb!
    Christ's progress, and his prayer time;
    The hours to which high Heaven doth chime.

God's silent, searching flight:
When my Lord's head is filled with dew, and all
His locks are wet with the clear drops of night;
His still, soft call;
His knocking time; the soul's dumb watch,
When spirits their fair kindred catch.

Were all my loud, evil days
Calm and unhaunted as is thy dark tent,
Whose peace but by some angel's wing or voice
Is seldom rent;
Then I in Heaven all the long year
Would keep, and never wander here.

But living where the sun
Doth all things wake, and where all mix and tire
Themselves and others, I consent and run
To every mire,
And by this world's ill-guiding light,
Err more then I can do by night.

There is in God (some say)
A deep, but dazzling darkness; as men here
Say it is late and dusky, because they
See not all clear;
O for that night! where I in him
Might live invisible and dim.

They are All Gone into the World of Light

They are all gone into the world of light!
And I alone sit lingering here;
Their very memory is fair and bright,
And my sad thoughts doth clear.

It glows and glitters in my cloudy breast
　　Like stars upon some gloomy grove,
Or those faint beams in which this hill is dressed,
　　After the sun's remove.

I see them walking in an air of glory,
　　Whose light doth trample on my days:
My days, which are at best but dull and hoary,
　　Mere glimmering and decays.

O holy hope! And high humility,
　　High as the Heavens above!
These are your walks, and you have showed them me
　　To kindle my cold love.

Dear, beauteous Death! The jewel of the just,
　　Shilling nowhere, but in the dark;
What mysteries do lie beyond thy dust,
　　Could man outlook that mark!

He that hath found some fledged bird's nest may know,
　　At first sight, if the bird be flown;
But what fair well or grove he sings in now,
　　That is to him unknown.

And yet, as angels in some brighter dreams
　　Call to the soul, when man doth sleep;
So some strange thoughts transcend our wonted themes,
　　And into glory peep.

If a star were confined into a tomb,
　　Her captive flames must needs burn there;
But when the hand that locked her up gives room,
　　She'll shine through all the sphere.

O Father of eternal life, and all
　　Created glories under Thee!
Resume Thy spirit from this world of thrall
　　Into true liberty.

Either disperse these mists, which blot and fill
　　My perspective (still) as they pass,
Or else remove me hence unto that hill,
　　Where I shall need no glass.

The World

I saw Eternity the other night
Like a great Ring of pure and endless light,
    All calm, as it was bright,
And round beneath it, Time in hours, days, years,
      Driven by the spheres,
Like a vast shadow moved, in which the world
    And all her train were hurled;
The doting lover in his quaintest strain
      Did there complain,
Near him his lute, his fancy, and his flights,
      Wit's sour delights,
With gloves, and knots, the silly snares of pleasure,
      Yet his dear treasure
All scattered lay, while he his eyes did pour
      Upon a flower.

The darksome statesman hung with weights and woe
Like a thick midnight-fog moved there so slow
    He did nor stay, nor go;
Condemning thoughts (like sad eclipses) scowl
      Upon his soul,
And clouds of crying witnesses without
    Pursued him with one shout.
Yet digged the mole and, lest his ways be found,
      Worked underground,
Where he did clutch his prey; but One did see
      That policy.
Churches and altars fed him, perjuries
      Were gnats and flies,
It rained about him blood and tears, but he
      Drank them as free.

The fearful miser on a heap of rust
Sat pining all his life there, did scarce trust
    His own hands with the dust,
Yet would not place one piece above, but lives
      In fear of thieves.

Thousands there were as frantic as himself
    And hugged each one his pelf.
The downright Epicure placed Heaven in sense
      And scorned pretence;
While others, slipped into a wide excess,
    Said little less;
The weaker sort, slight trivial wares enslave,
    Who think them brave;
And poor, despisèd Truth sat counting by
    Their victory.

Yet some, who all this while did weep and sing,
And sing and weep, soared up into the Ring,
    But most would use no wing.
O fools (said I) thus to prefer dark night
    Before true light,
To live in grots, and caves, and hate the day
    Because it shows the way,
The way which from this dead and dark abode
    Leads up to God,
A way where you might tread the sun, and be
    More bright than he.
But as I did their madness so discuss
    One whispered thus:
This Ring the Bridegroom did for none provide
    But for His bride.

EDMUND WALLER
1606–1687

Song

   Go, lovely rose!
Tell her that wastes her time and me
   That now she knows,
When I resemble her to thee,
How sweet and fair she seems to be.

   Tell her that's young,
And shuns to have her graces spied,
   That, hadst thou sprung
In deserts where no men abide,
Thou must have uncommended died.

   Small is the worth
Of beauty from the light retired;
   Bid her come forth,
Suffer herself to be desired,
And not blush so to be admired.

   Then die; that she
The common fate of all things rare
   May read in thee:
How small a part of time they share
That are so wondrous sweet and fair!

To a Fair Lady Playing with a Snake

Strange! that such horror and such grace
Should dwell together in one place:
A Fury's arm, an angel's face!

'Tis innocence and youth which makes
In Cloris' fancy such mistakes,
To start at love, and play with snakes.

By this and by her coldness barred,
Her servants have a task too hard:
The tyrant has a double guard.

Thrice happy snake, that in her sleeve
May boldly creep; we dare not give
Our thoughts so unconfined a leave.

Contented in that nest of snow
He lies, as he his bliss did know,
And to the wood no more would go.

Take heed, fair Eve, you do not make
Another tempter of this snake:
A marble one, so warmed, would speak.

ISSAC WATTS
1674–1748

The Day of Judgement

When the fierce North-wind with his airy forces
Rears up the Baltic to a foaming fury;
And the red lightning with a storm of hail comes
                              Rushing amain down;

How the poor sailors stand amazed and tremble,
While the hoarse thunder, like a bloody trumpet,
Roars a loud onset to the gaping waters,
                              Quick to devour them.

Such shall the noise be, and the wild disorder
(If things eternal may be like these earthly),
Such the dire terror when the great Archangel
                              Shakes the creation;

Tears the strong pillars of the vault of Heaven,
Breaks up old marble, the repose of princes;
See the graves open, and the bones arising,
                              Flames all around 'em.

Hark the shrill outcries of the guilty wretches!
Lively bright horror and amazing anguish
Stare through their eyelids, while the living worm lies
                        Gnawing within them.

Thoughts like old vultures prey upon their heart-strings,
And the smart twinges, when their eye beholds the
Lofty judge frowning, and a flood of vengeance
                        Rolling afore him.

Hopeless immortals! how they scream and shiver,
While devils push them to the pit wide-yawning,
Hideous and gloomy, to receive them headlong
                        Down to the centre!

Stop here my fancy (all away, ye horrid
Doleful ideas): come arise to Jesus,
How He sits God-like! and the saints around Him
                        Throned, yet adoring!

O may I sit there when he comes triumphant,
Dooming the nations: then ascend to glory,
While our Hosannas all along the passage
                        Shout the Redeemer!

Hymn

Our God, our help in ages past,
  Our hope for years to come,
Our shelter from the stormy blast,
  And our eternal home.

Beneath the shadow of thy throne
  Thy Saints have dwelt secure;
Sufficient is thine arm alone,
  And our defence is sure.

Before the hills in order stood,
  Or Earth received her frame.
From everlasting thou art God,
  To endless years the same.

Thy Word commands our flesh to dust,
  Return, ye sons of men:
All nations rose from Earth at first,
  And turn to Earth again.

A thousand ages in thy sight
  Are like an evening gone;
Short as the watch that ends the night
  Before the rising sun.

The busy tribes of flesh and blood
  With all their lives and cares
Are carried downwards by thy flood,
  And lost in following years.

Time like an ever-rolling stream
  Bears all its sons away;
They fly forgotten as a dream
  Dies at the opening day.

Like flowery fields the nations stand
  Pleased with the morning-light;
The flowers beneath the mower's hand
  Lie withering ere 'tis night.

Our God, our help in ages past,
  Our hope for years to come,
Be thou our guard while troubles last,
  And our eternal home.

CHARLES WESLEY
1707–1788

Hymn

Jesu, lover of my soul,
    Let me to thy bosom fly,
While the nearer waters roll,
    While the tempest still is high.
Hide me, O my Saviour, hide,
    Till the storm of life is past:
Safe into the haven guide;
    O receive my soul at last.

Other refuge have I none,
    Hangs my helpless soul on thee.
Leave, ah leave me not alone,
    Still support and comfort me.
All my trust on thee is stayed,
    All my help from thee I bring;
Cover my defenceless head
    With the shadow of thy wing.

Wilt thou not regard my call?
    Wilt thou not accept my prayer?
Lo, I sink, I faint, I fall!
    Lo, on thee I cast my care.
Reach me out thy gracious hand!
    While I of thy strength receive,
Hoping against hope I stand,
    Dying, and behold I live!

Thou, O Christ, art all I want;
    More than all in thee I find.
Raise the fallen, cheer the faint,
    Heal the sick, and lead the blind.
Just and holy is thy name;
    I am all unrighteousness:
False and full of sin I am,
    Thou art full of truth and grace.

Plenteous grace with thee is found,
　　Grace to cover all my sin:
Let the healing streams abound
　　Make and keep me pure within.
Thou of life the fountain art:
　　Freely let me take of thee,
Spring thou up within my heart,
　　Rise to all eternity!

PHILLIS WHEATLEY
c.1753–1784

On Being Brought from Africa to America

'Twas mercy brought me from my pagan land,
Taught my benighted soul to understand
That there's a God, that there's a Saviour too:
Once I redemption neither sought nor knew.
Some view our sable race with scornful eye:
'Their colour is a diabolic dye.'
Remember, Christians, negroes black as Cain
May be refined and join the angelic train.

GILBERT WHITE
1720–1793

The Naturalist's Summer-Evening Walk
To Thomas Pennant, Esq.

When day declining sheds a milder gleam,
What time the mayfly haunts the pool or stream;
When the still owl skims round the grassy mead,
What time the timorous hare limps forth to feed;
Then be the time to steal adown the vale,

And listen to the vagrant cuckoo's tale;
To hear the clamorous curlew call his mate,
Or the soft quail his tender pain relate;
To see the swallow sweep the darkening plain
Belated, to support her infant train;
To mark the swift in rapid giddy ring
Dash round the steeple, unsubdued of wing:
Amusive birds! – say where your hid retreat
When the frost rages and the tempests beat;
Whence your return, by such nice instinct led,
When spring, soft season, lifts her bloomy head?
Such baffled searches mock man's prying pride,
The God of Nature is your secret guide!

While deepening shades obscure the face of day,
To yonder bench leaf-sheltered let us stray,
Till blended objects fail the swimming sight,
And all the fading landscape sinks in night;
To hear the drowsy dor come brushing by
With buzzing wing, or the shrill cricket cry;
To see the feeding bat glance through the wood;
To catch the distant falling of the flood;
While o'er the cliff the awakened churn-owl hung
Through the still gloom protracts his chattering song;
While high in air, and poised upon his wings,
Unseen, the soft, enamoured woodlark sings:
These, Nature's works, the curious mind employ,
Inspire a soothing melancholy joy:
As fancy warms, a pleasing kind of pain
Steals o'er the cheek, and thrills the creeping vein!

Each rural sight, each sound, each smell, combine;
The tinkling sheep-bell, or the breath of kine;
The new-mown hay that scents the swelling breeze,
Or cottage-chimney smoking through the trees

The chilling night-dews fall – away, retire;
For see, the glow-worm lights her amorous fire!
Thus, ere night's veil had half obscured the sky,
The impatient damsel hung her lamp on high:
True to the signal, by love's meteor led,
Leander hastened to his Hero's bed.

WALT WHITMAN
1819–1892

O Captain! My Captain!

To Abraham Lincoln

O Captain! my Captain! our fearful trip is done:
The ship has weathered every rack, the prize we sought is won,
The port is near, the bells I hear, the people all exulting,
While follow eyes the steady keel, the vessel grim and daring.
  But O heart! heart! heart!
    O the bleeding drops of red!
      Where on the deck my Captain lies,
        Fallen cold and dead.

O Captain! my Captain! rise up and hear the bells;
Rise up – for you the flag is flung – for you the bugle trills,
For you bouquets and ribboned wreaths – for you the shores
                            a-crowding –
For you they call, the swaying mass, their eager faces turning.
  Here, Captain! dear father!
    This arm beneath your head!
      It is some dream that on the deck
        You've fallen cold and dead . . .

My Captain does not answer, his lips are pale and still,
My father does not feel my arm! he has no pulse nor will;
The ship is anchored safe and sound, its voyage closed and
                            done.
From fearful trip the victor ship comes in with object won.
  Exult, O shores! and ring, O bells!
    But I, with mournful tread,
      Walk the deck my Captain lies,
        Fallen cold and dead.

OSCAR WILDE
1854–1900

Symphony in Yellow

An omnibus across the bridge
   Crawls like a yellow butterfly,
   And, here and there, a passer-by
Shows like a little restless midge.

Big barges full of yellow hay
   Are moved against the shadowy wharf,
   And, like a yellow silken scarf,
The thick fog hangs along the quay.

The yellow leaves begin to fade
   And flutter from the Temple elms,
   And at my feet the pale green Thames
Lies like a rod of rippled jade.

GERRARD WINSTANLEY
c.1609–1676

The Diggers' Song

You noble Diggers all, stand up now, stand up now;
   You noble Diggers all, stand up now,
The waste land to maintain, seeing Cavaliers by name
Your digging does disdain, and persons all defame.
     Stand up now, stand up now.

Your houses they pull down; stand up now, stand up now;
   Your houses they pull down; stand up now.
Your houses they pull down to fright poor men in town
But the gentry must come down, and the poor shall wear the
                        crown.
     Stand up now, Diggers all.

With spades and hoes and ploughs, stand up now, stand up now;
  With spades and hoes and ploughs, stand up now,
Your freedom to uphold, seeing Cavaliers are bold
To kill you if they could, and rights from you to hold.
      Stand up now, Diggers all.

Their self-will is their law; stand up now, stand up now;
  Their self-will is their law; stand up now.
Since tyranny came in, they count it now no sin
To make a gaol a gin, to starve poor men therein.
      Stand up now, stand up now.

The gentry are all round; stand up now, stand up now;
  The gentry are all round; stand up now.
The gentry are all round; on each side they are found,
This wisdom's so profound, to cheat us of our ground.
      Stand up now, stand up now.

The lawyers they conjoin; stand up now, stand up now;
  The lawyers they conjoin; stand up now.
To arrest you they advise, such fury they devise,
The devil in them lies and hath blinded both their eyes.
      Stand up now, stand up now.

The clergy they come in; stand up now, stand up now;
  The clergy they come in; stand up now.
The clergy they come in, and say it is a sin
That we should now begin our freedom for to win.
      Stand tip now, Diggers all.

The tithes they yet will have; stand up now, stand up now;
  The tithes they yet will have; stand up now.
The tithes they yet will have, the lawyers their fees crave,
And this they say is brave, to make the poor their slave.
      Stand up now, Diggers all.

'Gainst lawyers and 'gainst priests, stand up now, stand up now;
  'Gainst lawyers and 'gainst priests, stand up now.
For tyrants they are both, even flat against their oath,
To grant us they are loath, free meat and drink and cloth.
      Stand up now, Diggers all.

The club is all their law; stand up now, stand up now;
   The club is all their law; stand up now.
The club is all their law, to keep men in awe,
But they no vision saw, to maintain such a law.
     Stand up now, Diggers all.

The Cavaliers are foes; stand up now, stand up now;
   The Cavaliers are foes; stand up now.
The Cavaliers are foes; themselves they do disclose
By verses not in prose, to please the singing boys.
     Stand up now, Diggers all.

To conquer them by love, come in now, come in now;
   To conquer them by love, come in now;
To conquer them by love, as it does you behove;
For He is king above: no power is like to love.
     Glory here, Diggers all.

HUMBERT WOLFE
1885–1940

The British Journalist

You cannot hope
   To bribe or twist
(Thank God!) the British
   Journalist;
But, seeing what
   The man will do
Unbribed, there's no
   Occasion to.

Iliad

False dreams, all false,
mad heart, were yours.
The word, and nought else,
in time endures.
Not you long after,
perished and mute,
will last, but the defter
viol and lute.
Sweetly they'll trouble
the listeners
with the cold dropped pebble
of painless verse.
Not you will be offered,
but the poet's false pain.
Mad heart, you have suffered,
and loved in vain.
What joy doth Helen
or Paris have
where these lie still in
a nameless grave?
Her beauty's a wraith,
and the boy Paris
muffles in death
His mouth's cold cherries.
Aye! these are less,
that were love's summer,
than one gold phrase
of old blind Homer!
Not Helen's wonder
nor Paris stirs,
But the bright untender
hexameters.
And thus, all passion
is nothing made,
but a star to flash in
an *Iliad*.
Mad heart you were wrong!
No love of yours,
but only what is sung,
when love's over, endures.

WILLIAM WORDSWORTH
1770–1850

Lines Written in Early Spring

I heard a thousand blended notes,
While in a grove I sat reclined,
In that sweet mood when pleasant thoughts
Bring sad thoughts to the mind.

To her fair works did nature link
The human soul that through me ran;
And much it grieved my heart to think
What man has made of man.

Through primrose-tufts, in that sweet bower,
The periwinkle trailed its wreathes;
And 'tis my faith that every flower
Enjoys the air it breathes.

The birds around me hopped and played:
Their thoughts I cannot measure,
But the least motion which they made,
It seemed a thrill of pleasure.

The budding twigs spread out their fan,
To catch the breezy air;
And I must think, do all I can,
That there was pleasure there.

If I these thoughts may not prevent,
If such be of my creed the plan,
Have I not reason to lament
What man has made of man?

Lines Written a Few Miles above Tintern Abbey
On revisiting the banks of the Wye during a tour, 13 July 1798

Five years have passed; five summers, with the length
Of five long winters! and again I hear
These waters, rolling from their mountain-springs
With a sweet inland murmur. – Once again
Do I behold these steep and lofty cliffs,
Which on a wild secluded scene impress
Thoughts of more deep seclusion; and connect
The landscape with the quiet of the sky.
The day is come when I again repose
Here, under this dark sycamore, and view
These plots of cottage-ground, these orchard-tufts,
Which, at this season, with their unripe fruit,
Among the woods and copses lose themselves,
Nor, with their green and simple hue, disturb
The wild green landscape. Once again I see
These hedgerows, hardly hedgerows, little lines
Of sportive wood run wild; these pastoral farms,
Green to the very door; and wreathes of smoke
Sent up, in silence, from among the trees,
With some uncertain notice, as might seem,
Of vagrant dwellers in the houseless woods,
Or of some hermit's cave, where by his fire
The hermit sits alone.

              Though absent long,
These forms of beauty have not been to me,
As is a landscape to a blind man's eye:
But oft, in lonely rooms, and 'mid the din
Of towns and cities, I have owed to them,
In hours of weariness, sensations sweet,
Felt in the blood, and felt along the heart,
And passing even into my purer mind
With tranquil restoration – feelings too
Of unremembered pleasure; such perhaps,
As may have had no trivial influence
On that best portion of a good man's life;

His little, nameless, unremembered acts
Of kindness and of love. Nor less, I trust,
To them I may have owed another gift,
Of aspect more sublime; that blessed mood,
In which the burthen of the mystery,
In which the heavy and the weary weight
Of all this unintelligible world
Is lightened – that serene and blessed mood,
In which the affections gently lead us on,
Until, the breath of this corporeal frame,
And even the motion of our human blood
Almost suspended, we are laid asleep
In body, and become a living soul:
While with an eye made quiet by the power
Of harmony, and the deep power of joy,
We see into the life of things.

                           If this
Be but a vain belief, yet, oh! how oft,
In darkness, and amid the many shapes
Of joyless daylight; when the fretful stir
Unprofitable, and the fever of the world,
Have hung upon the beatings of my heart,
How oft, in spirit, have I turned to thee
O sylvan Wye! Thou wanderer through the woods,
How often has my spirit turned to thee!
 And now, with gleams of half-extinguished thought,
With many recognitions dim and faint,
And somewhat of a sad perplexity,
The picture of the mind revives again:
While here I stand, not only with the sense
Of present pleasure, but with pleasing thoughts
That in this moment there is life and food
For future years. And so I dare to hope
Though changed, no doubt, from what I was, when first
I came among these hills; when like a roe
I bounded o'er the mountains, by the sides
Of the deep rivers, and the lonely streams,
Wherever nature led; more like a man
Flying from something that he dreads, than one

Who sought the thing he loved. For nature then
(The courser pleasure of my boyish days
And their glad animal movements all gone by)
To me was all in all. – I cannot paint
What then I was. The sounding cataract
Haunted me like a passion: the tall rock,
The mountain and the deep and gloomy wood,
Their colours and their forms, were then to me
An appetite: a feeling and a love,
That had no need of a remoter charm,
By thought supplied, or any interest
Unborrowed from the eye. – That time is past,
And all its aching joys are now no more,
And all its dizzy raptures. Not for this
Faint I, nor mourn nor murmur: other gifts
Have followed, for such loss, I would believe,
Abundant recompense. For I have learned
To look on nature, not as in the hour
Of thoughtless youth, but hearing oftentimes
The still, sad music of humanity,
Nor harsh nor grating, though of ample power
To chasten and subdue. And I have felt
A presence that disturbs me with the joy
Of elevated thoughts; a sense sublime
Of something far more deeply interfused,
Whose dwelling is the light of setting suns,
And the round ocean, and the living air,
And the blue sky, and in the mind of man,
A motion and a spirit, that impels
All thinking things, all objects of all thought,
And rolls through all things. Therefore am I still
A lover of the meadows and the woods
And mountains; and of all that we behold
From this green earth; of all the mighty world
Of eye and ear, both what they half-create,
And what perceive; well pleased to recognise
In nature and the language of the sense,
The anchor of my purest thoughts, the nurse,
The guide, the guardian of my heart, and soul
Of all my moral being.

Nor, perchance,
If I were not thus taught, should I the more
Suffer my genial spirits to decay:
For thou art with me, here, upon the banks
Of this fair river; thou, my dearest Friend,
My dear, dear Friend, and in thy voice I catch
The language of my former heart, and read
My former pleasures in the shooting lights
Of thy wild eyes. Oh! yet a little while
May I behold in thee what I was once,
My dear, dear Sister! And this prayer I make,
Knowing that Nature never did betray
The heart that loved her; 'tis her privilege,
Through all the year of this our life, to lead
 From joy to joy: for she can so inform
The mind that is within us, so impress
With quietness and beauty, and so feed
With lofty thoughts, that neither evil tongues,
Rash judgements, nor the sneers of selfish men,
Nor greetings where no kindness is, nor all
The dreary intercourse of daily life,
Shall e'er prevail against us, or disturb
Our cheerful faith that all which we behold
Is full of blessings. Therefore let the moon
Shine on thee in thy solitary walk;
And let the misty mountain winds be free
To blow against thee: and in after years,
When these wild ecstasies shall be matured
Into a sober pleasure, when thy mind
Shall be a mansion for all lovely forms,
Thy memory be as a dwelling-place
For all sweet sounds and harmonies; oh! then,
If solitude, or fear, or pain, or grief,
Should be thy portion, with what healing thoughts
Of tender joy wilt thou remember me,
And these my exhortations! Nor, perchance,
If I should be, where I no more can hear
Thy voice, nor catch from thy wild eyes these gleams
Of past existence, wilt thou then forget
That on the banks of this delightful stream

We stood together; and that I, so long
A worshipper of Nature, hither came,
Unwearied in that service: rather say
With warmer love, oh! with far deeper zeal
Of holier love. Nor wilt thou then forget,
That after many wanderings, many years
Of absence, these steep woods and lofty cliffs,
And this green pastoral landscape, were to me
More dear, both for themselves, and for thy sake.

A Slumber Did My Spirit Seal

A slumber did my spirit seal;
    I had no human fears:
She seemed a thing that could not feel
    The touch of earthly years.

No motion has she now, no force;
    She neither hears nor sees,
Rolled round in earth's diurnal course
    With rocks and stones and trees.

My Heart Leaps Up When I Behold

My heart leaps up when I behold
    A rainbow in the sky:
So was it when my life began;
So is it now I am a man;
So be it when I shall grow old,
    Or let me die!
The child is father of the man;
And I could wish my days to be
Bound each to each by natural piety.

To Toussaint L'Ouverture

Toussaint, the most unhappy man of men!
Whether the rural milkmaid by her cow
Sing in thy hearing, or thou liest now
Alone in some deep dungeon's earless den,
O miserable chieftain! where and when
Wilt thou find patience? Yet die not; do thou
Wear rather in thy bonds a cheerful brow:
Though fallen thyself, never to rise again,
Live, and take comfort. Thou hast left behind
Powers that will work for thee; air, earth, and skies;
There's not a breathing of the common wind
That will forget thee; thou hast great allies;
Thy friends are exultations, agonies,
And love, and man's unconquerable mind.

Composed upon Westminster Bridge
2 September 1802

Earth has not anything to show more fair:
Dull would he be of soul who could pass by
A sight so touching in its majesty:
This city now doth like a garment wear
The beauty of the morning; silent, bare,
Ships, towers, domes, theatres, and temples lie
Open unto the fields, and to the sky;
All bright and glittering in the smokeless air.
Never did sun more beautifully steep
In his first splendour valley, rock, or hill;
Ne'er saw I, never felt, a calm so deep!
The river glideth at his own sweet will:
Dear God! the very houses seem asleep;
And all that mighty heart is lying still!

Ode

Intimations of Immortality from
Recollections of Early Childhood

There was a time when meadow, grove, and stream,
    The earth, and every common sight,
        To me did seem
    Apparelled in celestial light,
The glory and the freshness of a dream.
It is not now as it has been of yore –
      Turn wheresoe'er I may,
        By night or day,
The things which I have seen I now can see no more.

    The rainbow comes and goes,
    And lovely is the rose,
    The moon doth with delight
Look round her when the heavens are bare;
    Waters on a starry night
    Are beautiful and fair;
    The sunshine is a glorious birth;
    But yet I know, where'er I go,
That there hath passed away a glory from the earth.

Now, while the birds thus sing a joyous song,
    And while the young lambs bound
      As to the tabor's sound,
To me alone there came a thought of grief:
A timely utterance gave that thought relief,
      And I again am strong.
The cataracts blow their trumpets from the steep,
No more shall grief of mine the season wrong;
I hear the echoes through the mountains throng,
The winds come to me from the fields of sleep,
      And all the earth is gay,
        Land and sea
    Give themselves up to jollity,
      And with the heart of May
    Doth every beast keep holiday;
      Thou Child of Joy,

Shout round me, let me hear thy shouts, thou happy
    Shepherd Boy!

Ye blessed creatures, I have heard the call
      Ye to each other make; I see
The heavens laugh with you in your jubilee;
      My heart is at your festival,
        My head hath its coronal,
The fullness of your bliss, I feel – feel it all.
      Oh evil day! if I were sullen
      While the Earth herself is adorning,
        This sweet May-morning,
      And the children are culling,
        On every side,
      In a thousand valleys far and wide,
      Fresh flowers; while the sun shines warm,
And the Babe leaps up on his mother's arm –
      I hear, I hear, with joy I hear!
      – But there's a tree, of many one,
A single field which I have looked upon,
Both of them speak of something that is gone;
      The pansy at my feet
      Doth the same tale repeat;
Whither is fled the visionary gleam?
Where is it now, the glory and the dream?

Our birth is but a sleep and a forgetting:
The Soul that rises with us, our life's Star,
      Hath had elsewhere its setting,
        And cometh from afar:
      Not in entire forgetfulness,
      And not in utter nakedness,
But trailing clouds of glory do we come
        From God who is our home;
Heaven lies about us in our infancy!
Shades of the prison-house begin to close
        Upon the growing Boy,
But he beholds the light, and whence it flows,
      He sees it in his joy;
The Youth, who daily farther from the east
      Must travel, still is Nature's priest,

And by the vision splendid
Is on his way attended;
At length the Man perceives it die away,
And fade into the light of common day.

Earth fills her lap with pleasures of her own;
Yearnings she hath in her own natural kind,
And, even with something of a mother's mind,
And no unworthy aim,
The homely nurse doth all she can
To make her foster child, her inmate Man,
Forget the glories he hath known,
And that imperial palace whence he came.

Behold the Child among his new-born blisses,
A four year's darling of a pigmy size!
See, where 'mid work of his own hand he lies
Fretted by sallies of his mother's kisses,
With light upon him from his father's eyes!
See, at his feet, some little plan or chart,
Some fragment from his dream of human life,
Shaped by himself with newly-learnèd art;
A wedding or a festival,
A mourning or a funeral
And this hath now his heart,
And unto this he frames his song:
Then will he fit his tongue
To dialogues of business, love, or strife;
But it will not be long
Ere this be thrown aside,
And with new joy and pride
The little actor cons another part,
Filling from time to time his 'humorous stage'
With all the persons, down to palsied Age,
That Life brings with her in her equipage;
As if his whole vocation
Were endless imitation.

Thou, whose exterior semblance doth belie
Thy soul's immensity,
Thou best philosopher, who yet dost keep

Thy heritage, thou eye among the blind,
That, deaf and silent, read'st the eternal deep,
Haunted for ever by the eternal mind –
        Mighty prophet! Seer blest!
        On whom those truths do rest,
Which we are toiling all our lives to find;
Thou, over whom thy Immortality
Broods like the day, a master o'er a slave,
A presence which is not to be put by;
        To whom the grave
Is but a lonely bed without the sense or sight
        Of day or the warm light,
A place of thought where we in waiting lie;
Thou little Child, yet glorious in the might
Of untamed pleasures, on thy being's height,
Why with such earnest pains dost thou provoke
The Years to bring the inevitable yoke,
Thus blindly with thy blessedness at strife?
Full soon thy soul shall have her earthly freight,
And custom lie upon thee with a weight,
Heavy as frost, and deep almost as life!

        O joy! that in our embers
        Is something that doth live,
        That nature yet remembers
        What was so fugitive!
The thought of our past years in me doth breed
Perpetual benedictions: not indeed
For that which is most worthy to be blest;
Delight and liberty, the simple creed
Of childhood, whether fluttering or at rest,
With new-born hope for ever in his breast –
        Not for these I raise
        The song of thanks and praise;
    But for those obstinate questionings
    Of sense and outward things,
    Fallings from us, vanishings;
    Blank misgivings of a creature
Moving about in worlds not realised,
High instincts before which our mortal nature

Did tremble like a guilty thing surprised:
  But for those first affections,
  Those shadowy recollections,
   Which, be they what they may,
Are yet the fountain light of all our day,
Are yet a master light of all our seeing;
   Uphold us, cherish us, and make
Our noisy years seem moments in the being
Of the eternal Silence: truths that wake,
   To perish never;
Which neither listlessness, nor mad endeavour,
   Nor Man nor Boy,
Nor all that is at enmity with joy,
Can utterly abolish or destroy!
  Hence, in a season of calm weather,
   Though inland far we be,
Our souls have sight of that immortal sea
   Which brought us hither,
  Can in a moment travel thither,
And see the children sport upon the shore,
And hear the mighty waters rolling evermore.

Then, sing ye birds, sing, sing a joyous song!
   And let the young lambs bound
   As to the tabor's sound!
  We in thought will join your throng,
   Ye that pipe and ye that play,
   Ye that through your hearts today
   Feel the gladness of the May!
What though the radiance which was once so bright
Be now for ever taken from my sight,
  Though nothing can bring back the hour
Of splendour in the grass, of glory in the flower;
   We will grieve not, rather find
   Strength in what remains behind,
   In the primal sympathy
   Which having been must ever be,
   In the soothing thoughts that spring
   Out of human suffering,
   In the faith that looks through death,

In years that bring the philosophic mind.

And oh ye fountains, meadows, hills, and groves,
Think not of any severing of our loves!
Yet in my heart of hearts I feel your might;
I only have relinquished one delight
To live beneath your more habitual sway.
I love the brooks which down their channels fret,
Even more than when I tripped lightly as they;
The innocent brightness of a newborn Day
        Is lovely yet;
The clouds that gather round the setting sun
Do take a sober colouring from an eye
That hath kept watch o'er man's mortality;
Another race hath been, and other palms are won.
Thanks to the human heart by which we live,
Thanks to its tenderness, its joys, and fears,
To me the meanest flower that blows can give
Thoughts that do often lie too deep for tears.

I Wandered Lonely as a Cloud

I wandered lonely as a cloud
    That floats on high o'er vales and hills,
When all at once I saw a crowd,
    A host, of golden daffodils:
Beside the lake, beneath the trees,
Fluttering and dancing in the breeze.

Continuous as the stars that shine
    And twinkle on the Milky Way,
They stretched in never-ending line
    Along the margin of a bay:
Ten thousand saw I at a glance,
Tossing their heads in sprightly dance.

The waves beside them danced, but they
    Outdid the sparkling waves in glee:
A poet could not but be gay,
    In such a jocund company:

I gazed – and gazed – but little thought
What wealth the show to me had brought:

For oft, when on my couch I lie
  In vacant or in pensive mood,
They flash upon that inward eye
  Which is the bliss of solitude;
And then my heart with pleasure fills,
And dances with the daffodils.

The Solitary Reaper

Behold her, single in the field,
Yon solitary highland lass!
Reaping and singing by herself;
Stop here, or gently pass!
Alone she cuts, and binds the grain,
And sings a melancholy strain;
O listen! for the vale profound
Is overflowing with the sound.

No nightingale did ever chaunt
So sweetly to reposing bands
Of travellers in some shady haunt,
Among Arabian sands;
No sweeter voice was ever heard
In springtime from the cuckoo-bird,
Breaking the silence of the seas
Among the farthest Hebrides.

Will no one tell me what she sings?
Perhaps the plaintive numbers flow
For old, unhappy, far-off things,
And battles long ago;
Or is it some more humble lay,
Familiar matter of today?
Some natural sorrow, loss, or pain,
That has been, and may be again?

Whate'er the theme, the maiden sang
As if her song could have no ending;
I saw her singing at her work,
And o'er the sickle bending;
I listened till I had my fill:
And, as I mounted up the hill,
The music in my heart I bore,
Long after it was heard no more.

Surprised by Joy – Impatient as the Wind

Surprised by joy – impatient as the wind,
I wished to share the transport – Oh! with whom
But thee, long buried in the silent tomb,
That spot which no vicissitude can find?
Love, faithful love, recalled thee to my mind –
But how could I forget thee! Through what power,
Even for the least division of an hour,
Have I been so beguiled as to be blind
To my most grievous loss? – That thought's return
Was the worst pang that sorrow ever bore,
Save one, one only, when I stood forlorn,
Knowing my heart's best treasure was no more;
That neither present time, nor years unborn,
Could to my sight that heavenly face restore.

On the Extinction of the Venetian Republic, 1802

Once did she hold the gorgeous east in fee;
And was the safeguard of the west; the worth
Of Venice did not fall below her birth,
Venice, the eldest child of Liberty.
She was a maiden city, bright and free;
No guile seduced, no force could violate;
And, when she took unto herself a mate,
She must espouse the everlasting sea.

And what if she had seen those glories fade,
Those titles vanish, and that strength decay;
Yet shall some tribute of regret be paid
When her long life hath reached its final day:
Men are we, and must grieve when even the shade
Of that which once was great is passed away.

SIR HENRY WOTTON
1568–1639

On His Mistress, the Queen of Bohemia

You meaner beauties of the night,
    That poorly satisfy our eyes
More by your number than your light:
    You common people of the skies,
    What are you when the sun shall rise?

You curious chanters of the wood,
    That warble forth Dame Nature's lays,
Thinking your voices understood
    By your weak accents: what's your praise
    When Philomel her voice shall raise?

You violets that first appear,
    By your pure purple mantles known,
Like the proud virgins of the year,
    As if the spring were all your own:
    What are you when the rose is blown?

So when my mistress shall be seen
    In form and beauty of her mind,
By virtue first, then choice, a queen,
    Tell me, if she were not designed
    The eclipse and glory of her kind?

SIR THOMAS WYATT
1503–1542

They Flee from Me

They flee from me that sometime did me seek
With naked foot, stalking in my chamber.
I have seen them gentle, tame, and meek,
That now are wild, and do not remember
That sometime they put themselves in danger
To take bread at my hand; and now they range
Busily seeking with a continual change.

Thanked be fortune, it hath been otherwise
Twenty times better; but once in special,
In thin array after a pleasant guise,
When her loose gown from her shoulders did fall
And she me caught in her arms long and small,
Therewithal sweetly did me kiss
And softly said, 'Dear heart, how like you this?'

It was no dream: I lay broad waking.
But all is turned, through my gentleness,
Into a strange fashion of forsaking.
And I have leave to go of her goodness,
And she also to use newfangleness.
But since that I so kindly am served
I would fain know what she hath deserved.

Forget Not Yet

Forget not yet the tried intent
Of such a truth as I have meant,
My great travail so gladly spent.
    Forget not yet.

Forget not yet when first began
The weary life ye know, since when
The suit, the service none tell can.
　　Forget not yet.

Forget not yet the great assays,
The cruel wrong, the scornful ways,
The painful patience in denays.
　　Forget not yet.

Forget not yet, forget not this:
How long ago hath been, and is,
The mind that never meant amiss.
　　Forget not yet.

Forget not then thine own approved,
The which so long hath thee so loved,
Whose steadfast faith yet never moved.
　　Forget not yet.

Whoso List to Hunt

Whoso list to hunt, I know where is an hind,
　　But as for me, helas, I may no more.
　　The vain travail hath wearied me so sore,
I am of them that farthest cometh behind.
Yet may I by no means my wearied mind
　　Draw from the deer, but as she fleeth afore,
　　Fainting I follow. I leave off therefore,
Sithens in a net I seek to hold the wind.
Who list her hunt, I put him out of doubt,
　　As well as I may spend his time in vain.
　　And graven with diamonds in letters plain
There is written her fair neck round about:
　　'*Noli me tangere,* for Caesar's I am,
　　And wild for to hold though I seem tame.'

W. B. YEATS
1865–1939

Down by the Salley Gardens

Down by the salley gardens my love and I did meet;
She passed the salley gardens with little snow-white feet.
She bid me take love easy, as the leaves grow on the tree;
But I, being young and foolish, with her would not agree.

In a field by the river my love and I did stand,
And on my leaning shoulder she laid her snow-white hand.
She bid me take life easy, as the grass grows on the weirs;
But I was young and foolish, and now am full of tears.

The Lake Isle of Innisfree

I will arise and go now, and go to Innisfree,
And a small cabin build there, of clay and wattles made:
Nine bean-rows will I have there, a hive for the honey-bee,
And live alone in the bee-loud glade.

And I shall have some peace there, for peace comes
                                    dropping slow,
Dropping from the veils of the morning to where the cricket
                                    sings;
There midnight's all a glimmer, and noon a purple glow,
And evening full of the linnet's wings.

I will arise and go now, for always night and day
I hear lake water lapping with low sounds by the shore;
While I stand on the roadway, or on the pavements grey,
I hear it in the deep heart's core.

When You are Old

When you are old and grey and full of sleep,
And nodding by the fire, take down this book,
And slowly read, and dream of the soft look
Your eyes had once, and of their shadows deep;

How many loved your moments of glad grace,
And loved your beauty with love false or true,
But one man loved the pilgrim soul in you,
And loved the sorrows of your changing face;

And bending down beside the glowing bars,
Murmur, a little sadly, how Love fled
And paced upon the mountains overhead
And hid his face amid a crowd of stars.

The Song of Wandering Aengus

I went out to the hazel wood,
Because a fire was in my head,
And cut and peeled a hazel wand,
And hooked a berry to a thread;
And when white moths were on the wing,
And moth-like stars were flickering out,
I dropped the berry in a stream
And caught a little silver trout.

When I had laid it on the floor
I went to blow the fire aflame,
But something rustled on the floor,
And someone called me by my name:
It had become a glimmering girl
With apple blossom in her hair
Who called me by my name and ran
And faded through the brightening air.

Though I am old with wandering
Through hollow lands and hilly lands,
I will find out where she has gone,
And kiss her lips and take her hands;
And walk among long dappled grass,
And pluck till time and times are done
The silver apples of the moon,
The golden apples of the sun.

The Wild Swans at Coole

The trees are in their autumn beauty,
The woodland paths are dry,
Under the October twilight the water
Mirrors a still sky;
Upon the brimming water among the stones
Are nine-and-fifty swans.

The nineteenth autumn has come upon me
Since I first made my count;
I saw, before I had well finished,
All suddenly mount
And scatter wheeling in great broken rings
Upon their clamorous wings.

I have looked upon those brilliant creatures,
And now my heart is sore.
All's changed since I, hearing at twilight,
The first time on this shore,
The bell-beat of their wings above my head,
Trod with a lighter tread.

Unwearied still, lover by lover,
They paddle in the cold
Companionable streams or climb the air;
Their hearts have not grown old;
Passion or conquest, wander where they will,
Attend upon them still.

But now they drift on the still water,
Mysterious, beautiful;
Among what rushes will they build,
By what lake's edge or pool
Delight men's eyes when I awake someday
To find they have flown away?

He Wishes for the Cloths of Heaven

Had I the heavens' embroidered cloths,
Enwrought with golden and silver light,
The blue and the dim and the dark cloths
Of night and light and the half-light,
I would spread the cloths under your feet:
But I, being poor, have only my dreams;
I have spread my dreams under your feet;
Tread softly because you tread on my dreams.

On Those That Hated
The Playboy of the Western World, 1907

Once, when midnight smote the air,
Eunuchs ran through Hell and met
On every crowded street to stare
Upon great Juan riding by:
Even like these to rail and sweat,
Staring upon his sinewy thigh.

The Magi

Now as at all times I can see in the mind's eye,
In their stiff, painted clothes, the pale unsatisfied ones
Appear and disappear in the blue depth of the sky,
With all their ancient faces like rain-beaten stones,
And all their helms of silver hovering side by side,
And all their eyes still fixed, hoping to find once more,
Being by Calvary's turbulence unsatisfied,
The uncontrollable mystery on the bestial floor.

An Irish Airman Foresees his Death

I know that I shall meet my fate
Somewhere among the clouds above;
Those that I fight I do not hate,
Those that I guard I do not love;
My country is Kiltartan Cross,
My countrymen Kiltartan's poor,
No likely end could bring them loss
Or leave them happier than before.
Nor law, nor duty bade me fight,
Nor public men, nor cheering crowds,
A lonely impulse of delight
Drove to this tumult in the clouds;
I balanced all, brought all to mind,
The years to come seemed waste of breath,
A waste of breath the years behind
In balance with this life, this death.

Easter, 1916

I have met them at close of day
Coming with vivid faces
From counter or desk among grey
Eighteenth-century houses.
I have passed with a nod of the head
Or polite meaningless words,
Or have lingered awhile and said
Polite meaningless words,
And thought before I had done
Of a mocking tale or a gibe
To please a companion
Around the fire at the club,
Being certain that they and I
But lived where motley is worn:
All changed, changed utterly:
A terrible beauty is born.

That woman's days were spent
In ignorant good-will,
Her nights in argument
Until her voice grew shrill.
What voice more sweet than hers
When, young and beautiful,
She rode to harriers?
This man had kept a school
And rode our wingèd horse;
This other his helper and friend
Was coming into his force;
He might have won fame in the end,
So sensitive his nature seemed,
So daring and sweet his thought.
This other man I had dreamed
A drunken, vainglorious lout.
He had done most bitter wrong
To some who are near my heart,
Yet I number him in the song;
He, too, has resigned his part
In the casual comedy;
He, too, has been changed in his turn,
Transformed utterly:
A terrible beauty is born.

Hearts with one purpose alone
Through summer and winter seem
Enchanted to a stone
To trouble the living stream.
The horse that comes from the road,
The rider, the birds that range
From cloud to tumbling cloud,
Minute by minute they change;
A shadow of cloud on the stream
Changes minute by minute;
A horse-hoof slides on the brim,
And a horse plashes within it;
The long-legged moorhens dive,
And hens to moorcocks call;
Minute by minute they live:
The stone's in the midst of all.

Too long a sacrifice
Can make a stone of the heart.
O when may it suffice?
That is Heaven's part, our part
To murmur name upon name,
As a mother names her child
When sleep at last has come
On limbs that had run wild.
What is it but nightfall?
No, no, not night but death;
Was it needless death after all?
For England may keep faith
For all that is done and said.
We know their dream; enough
To know they dreamed and are dead;
And what if excess of love
Bewildered them till they died?
I write it out in a verse –
MacDonagh and MacBride
And Connolly and Pearse
Now and in time to be,
Wherever green is worn,
Are changed, changed utterly:
A terrible beauty is born.

The Second Coming

Turning and turning in the widening gyre
The falcon cannot hear the falconer;
Things fall apart; the centre cannot hold;
Mere anarchy is loosed upon the world,
The blood-dimmed tide is loosed, and everywhere
The ceremony of innocence is drowned;
The best lack all conviction, while the worst
Are full of passionate intensity.

Surely some revelation is at hand;
Surely the Second Coming is at hand.

The Second Coming! Hardly are those words out
When a vast image out of *Spiritus Mundi*
Troubles my sight: somewhere in sands of the desert
A shape with lion body and the head of a man,
A gaze blank and pitiless as the sun,
Is moving its slow thighs, while all about it
Reel shadows of the indignant desert birds.
The darkness drops again; but now I know
That twenty centuries of stony sleep
Were vexed to nightmare by a rocking cradle,
And what rough beast, its hour come round at last,
Slouches towards Bethlehem to be born?

Sailing to Byzantium

1

That is no country for old men. The young
In one another's arms, birds in the trees,
 – Those dying generations – at their song,
The salmon-falls, the mackerel-crowded seas,
Fish, flesh, or fowl, commend all summer long
Whatever is begotten, born, and dies.
Caught in that sensual music all neglect
Monuments of unageing intellect.

2

An agèd man is but a paltry thing,
A tattered coat upon a stick, unless
Soul clap its hands and sing, and louder sing
For every tatter in its mortal dress,
Nor is there singing school but studying
Monuments of its own magnificence;
And therefore I have sailed the seas and come
To the holy city of Byzantium.

3

O sages standing in God's holy fire
As in the gold mosaic of a wall,
Come from the holy fire, perne in a gyre,
And be the singing-masters of my soul.
Consume my heart away; sick with desire
And fastened to a dying animal
It knows not what it is; and gather me
Into the artifice of eternity.

4

Once out of nature I shall never take
My bodily form from any natural thing,
But such a form as Grecian goldsmiths make
Of hammered gold and gold enamelling
To keep a drowsy Emperor awake;
Or set upon a golden bough to sing
To lords and ladies of Byzantium
Of what is past, or passing, or to come.

Leda and the Swan

A sudden blow: the great wings beating still
Above the staggering girl, her thighs caressed
By the dark webs, her nape caught in his bill,
He holds her helpless breast upon his breast.

How can those terrified vague fingers push
The feathered glory from her loosening thighs?
And how can body, laid in that white rush,
But feel the strange heart beating where it lies?

A shudder in the loins engenders there
The broken wall, the burning roof and tower
And Agamemnon dead.

                    Being so caught up,
So mastered by the brute blood of the air,
Did she put on his knowledge with his power
Before the indifferent beak could let her drop?

Among Schoolchildren

1

I walk through the long schoolroom questioning;
A kind old nun in a white hood replies;
The children learn to cipher and to sing,
To study reading-books and histories,
To cut and sew, be neat in everything
In the best modern way – the children's eyes
In momentary wonder stare upon
A sixty-year-old smiling public man.

2

I dream of a Ledaean body, bent
Above a sinking fire, a tale that she
Told of a harsh reproof, or trivial event
That changed some childish day to tragedy –
Told, and it seemed that our two natures blent
Into a sphere from youthful sympathy,
Or else, to alter Plato's parable,
Into the yolk and white of the one shell.

3

And thinking of that fit of grief or rage
I look upon one child or t'other there
And wonder if she stood so at that age –
For even daughters of the swan can share
Something of every paddler's heritage –
And had that colour upon cheek or hair,
And thereupon my heart is driven wild:
She stands before me as a living child.

4

Her present image floats into the mind –
Did Quattrocento finger fashion it
Hollow of cheek as though it drank the wind
And took a mess of shadows for its meat?
And I though never of Ledaean kind
Had pretty plumage once – enough of that,
Better to smile on all that smile, and show
There is a comfortable kind of old scarecrow.

5

What youthful mother, a shape upon her lap
Honey of generation had betrayed,
And that must sleep, shriek, struggle to escape
As recollection or the drug decide,
Would think her son, did she but see that shape
With sixty or more winters on its head,
A compensation for the pang of his birth,
Or the uncertainty of his setting forth?

6

Plato thought nature but a spume that plays
Upon a ghostly paradigm of things;
Solider Aristotle played the taws
Upon the bottom of a king of kings;
World-famous golden-thighed Pythagoras
Fingered upon a fiddle-stick or strings
What a star sang and careless Muses heard:
Old clothes upon old sticks to scare a bird.

7

Both nuns and mothers worship images,
But those the candles light are not as those
That animate a mother's reveries,
But keep a marble or a bronze repose.
And yet they too break hearts – O Presences
That passion, piety or affection knows,
And that all heavenly glory symbolise –
O self-born mockers of man's enterprise;

8

Labour is blossoming or dancing where
The body is not bruised to pleasure soul,
Nor beauty born out of its own despair,
Nor blear-eyed wisdom out of midnight oil.
O chestnut tree, great rooted blossomer,
Are you the leaf, the blossom or the bole?
O body swayed to music, O brightening glance,
How can we know the dancer from the dance?

Three Movements

Shakespearean fish swam the sea, far away from land;
Romantic fish swam in nets coming to the hand;
What are all those fish that lie gasping on the strand?

Byzantium

The unpurged images of day recede;
The Emperor's drunken soldiery are abed;
Night resonance recedes, night-walkers' song
After great cathedral gong;
A starlit or a moonlit dome disdains
All that man is,
All mere complexities,
The fury and the mire of human veins.

Before me floats an image, man or shade,
Shade more than man, more image than a shade;
For Hades' bobbin bound in mummy-cloth
May unwind the winding path;
A mouth that has no moisture and no breath
Breathless mouths may summon;
I hail the superhuman;
I call it death-in-life and life-in-death.

Miracle, bird or golden handiwork,
More miracle than bird or handiwork,
Planted on the starlit golden bough,
Can like the cocks of Hades crow,
Or, by the moon embittered, scorn aloud
In glory of changeless metal
Common bird or petal
And all complexities of mire or blood.

At midnight on the Emperor's pavement flit
Flames that no faggot feeds, nor steel has lit,
Nor storm disturbs, flames begotten of flame,
Where blood-begotten spirits come

And all complexities of fury leave,
Dying into a dance,
An agony of trance,
An agony of flame that cannot singe a sleeve.

Astraddle on the dolphin's mire and blood,
Spirit after spirit! The smithies break the flood,
The golden smithies of the Emperor!
Marbles of the dancing floor
Break bitter furies of complexity,
Those images that yet
Fresh images beget,
That dolphin-torn, that gong-tormented sea.

INDEX OF FIRST LINES

INDEX OF POEM TITLES

The Wordsworth Poetry Library

Works of

Matthew Arnold

William Blake

The Brontë Sisters

Rupert Brooke

Robert Browning

Elizabeth Barrett Browning

Robert Burns

Lord Byron

Geoffrey Chaucer

G. K. Chesterton

John Clare

Samuel Taylor Coleridge

Emily Dickinson

John Donne

John Dryden

Thomas Hardy

George Herbert

Gerard Manley Hopkins

A. E. Housman

James Joyce

John Keats

Rudyard Kipling

D. H. Lawrence

Henry Wadsworth Longfellow

Macaulay

Andrew Marvell

John Milton

Wilfred Owen

'Banjo' Paterson

Edgar Allen Poe

Alexander Pope

John Wilmot, Earl of Rochester

Christina Rossetti

Sir Walter Scott

William Shakespeare

P. B. Shelley

Edmund Spenser

Algernon Swinburne

Alfred Lord Tennyson

Edward Thomas

Walt Whitman

Oscar Wilde

William Wordsworth

W. B. Yeats

Anthologies & Collections

Restoration and Eighteenth-Century Verse

Nineteenth-Century Verse

First World War Poetry

The Metaphysical Poets

Love Poetry

Sonnets